Hard-Science Liı

Hard-Science Linguistics

Edited by

Victor H. Yngve
and
Zdzisław Wąsik

continuum

Continuum

The Tower Building,	80 Maiden Lane,
11 York Road,	Suite 704
London, SE1 7NX	New York, NY 10038

First published 2004 by Continuum
Paperback edition 2006

British Library Cataloguing-in-Publication Data
A catalogue record for this book is available from the British Library

ISBN 0-8264-6114-X (hardback)
ISBN 0-8264-9239-8 (paperback)

Library of Congress Cataloguing-in-Publication Data
Hard-science linguistics/edited by Victor H. Yngve and Zdzisław Wąsik.
   p. cm.
  Includes bibliographical references and index.
  ISBN 0-9264-6114-X
  1. Linguistics–Methodology. I. Yngve, Victor H., 1920–   II. Wąsik, Zdzisław.

  P126.H295 2004
  410´.1-dc22   2003062657

Typeset by Bookend Ltd, Royston, Herts
Printed on acid-free paper in Great Britain by Biddles Ltd., King's Lynn, Norfolk

Contents

PART VII: DISCIPLINARY CONSIDERATIONS

Dedication

We dedicate this book to the memory of Carl Mills (May 5, 1942–August 23, 2003), loyal friend, valued core supporter and early pioneer in hard-science linguistics, and author of Chapter 15. He intended to re-awaken his research on Uralic languages, saying "I am confident I can carry out areal linguistics in a human linguistics context. In fact, I don't see how one could use the linguistics of languages to gain much insight into area phenomena. Human linguistics, on the other hand, should provide a natural, possibly the only natural way to approach such matters."

Epigraph

If what we are discussing were a point of law or of the humanities, in which neither true nor false exists, one might trust in subtlety of mind and readiness of tongue and in the greater experience of the writers, and expect him who excelled in those things to make his reasoning most plausible, and one might judge it to be the best. But in the natural sciences, whose conclusions are true and necessary and have nothing to do with human will, one must take care not to place oneself in the defense of error; for here a thousand Demostheneses and a thousand Aristotles would be left in the lurch by every mediocre wit who happened to hit upon the truth for himself. Therefore, Simplicio, give up this idea and this hope of yours that there may be men so much more learned, erudite, and well-read than the rest of us as to be able to make that which is false become true in defiance of nature.

Galileo, *Dialogue Concerning the Two Chief World Systems*

Preface

How do people communicate? We do it every day but it remains an unsolved mystery. How does it work? How is it that when I open my mouth and some sound comes out that you can, most of the time, understand what I mean? Sometimes even before I open my mouth! The mystery extends beyond just you and me. It extends to how we communicate in groups of all sizes and to how groups and communities and nations communicate with each other. It extends to how these abilities develop in each new generation, and to how they change historically. To find answers to these questions is of the greatest important for knowing ourselves. To find answers that meet standard scientific criteria is our greatest challenge.

Since the availability in 1996 of a textbook on the new foundations for general linguistics, a growing number of pioneers have risen to that challenge and are moving linguistics into standard science. They envision linguistics as taking its proper place as a natural (hard) science along with physics, chemistry, and biology. In this first multi-author collection on hard-science linguistics, 15 of these intrepid adventurers present accounts of their travels and discoveries in a wide range of interrelated disciplines.

A move of linguistics into science moves it away from the ancient grammatical tradition. Yet school grammar remains quite useful in certain didactic and editorial tasks where the conceptual structure assumed is bound to follow, not lead, the best that linguistic theory can offer. This presents an obstacle to science where one must avoid improper influence from familiar conceptual structures that may not be scientifically justified. Thus you will find the authors, as a matter of course and necessity, questioning the received wisdom of the ubiquitous semiotic-grammatical tradition. You will find them exploring how best to build a proper hard science that honors only the standard criteria and assumptions of modern science. These authors are true pioneers. They are laying out the roads and founding the first thriving settlements in a new world for linguistics, the world of standard science.

The idea for preparing such a collection came from my esteemed coeditor Prof. dr hab. Zdzisław Wąsik at the annual meeting of Societas Linguistica Europaea (SLE) in Ljubljana, Slovenia, in July, 1999. He suggested that we organize a workshop on hard-science linguistics at the next SLE meeting to be held in Poznań, Poland. We would invite contributions to the workshop and to a volume that we would coedit.

Prof. Wąsik co-organized that workshop. He also supervised two master's theses in this new area in the Adam Mickiewicz University at Poznań and stimulated four papers which are included here. He is also the coauthor of two more chapters and of the Introduction. I wish to thank him for his encouragement and willingness to help as coeditor. His timely offer made it possible for me to seriously contemplate a project of this magnitude that I certainly would not have been willing to undertake alone. I owe him a debt of gratitude for all he has done to bring our plans to fruition. I hope you as readers will find the results valuable.

Victor H. Yngve

Introduction

Victor H. Yngve and Zdzisław Wąsik

This book is an intellectual adventure story. It is a story about exploring an entirely new scientific field. You will read here about the exploits of some of the early pioneers who have been concerned with moving linguistics from the ancient semiotic-grammatical tradition into the world of modern science and with building a new hard-science linguistics there, a natural science cognate with the other natural sciences of physics, chemistry, and biology.

Some might initially think that this is nothing new, that linguistics is already a science and has been for about two centuries. They might point out that its textbooks define it as the scientific study of language. True. But many linguists today understand correctly that current linguistics is a soft science, not a hard science like physics, chemistry, and biology. The pioneers in this new world propose that linguistics actually accept modern standard science and build a proper hard-science linguistic discipline. It will be a natural science, a human science focused on real-world people and their relevant real-world surroundings instead of on traditional concepts of language and signs. The difference is important as will become clear to readers of this volume.

Some might initially think that this is a work in the philosophy of language or the philosophy of science. Nothing could be further from the truth. It is a work in standard science, pure and simple. Although the scientific status of the soft sciences has always been at issue, the scientific status of the natural sciences is not in question.

Some might initially think that a book on hard-science linguistics, like hundreds of other books on linguistics, would offer a new form of grammar. This would also be a false preconception. Hard-science linguistics is not a new brand of grammar, of which there have been too many already. Instead it proposes to move linguistics out of grammar entirely and into science. It shows how linguistics can leave the domain of grammar and sentences and meanings and signs altogether and completely accept modern standard science. This book simply argues for standard science, on which the authors and editors have no patent. The contributions reported here show some of the many exciting advantages that can accrue from choosing this course, advantages including improved approaches to such long-standing problems in linguistics as those associated with context and variation and phonology and pragmatics. A review of some of the many advantages in adopting a hard-science approach to linguistic phenomena will be found in Chapter 20.

This book is primarily addressed to professionals in the many disciplines in the humanities and the biological and social sciences centered around language, linguistics, and communication. This would include applied linguistics and language teaching as well.

The material should also be easily accessible to anyone with a good general education who likes adventure and has a healthy curiosity about language and about how people communicate and who might even relish a chance to contemplate making a contribution in this largely unexplored area. This would certainly include beginning graduate students and bright undergraduates who will favor a literal rather than a metaphorical interpretation of what they read.

For these the material may actually be easier than for professionals who may have to set aside interfering preconceptions and habits of mind developed in any of the many current or traditional theoretical approaches to language or grammar or signs and who should therefore resist the temptation to skim lest they see in the book their own hopes and expectations rather than what is clearly laid out in the text. Such readers may find some help in Chapter 21.

The chapters have been arranged to be read in the order in which they appear in the book. They are laid out logically with introductory material appearing in the first few chapters and with material necessary for understanding some of the later chapters covered in the chapters that precede them.

The development of new hard-science foundations for linguistics owes much to the vision of those many individuals who have a breathtakingly broad conception of the phenomena that need to be accommodated and unified by appropriate theory. These farsighted individuals are found scattered throughout disciplines as seemingly diverse as linguistics, semiotics, pragmatics, discourse analysis, text linguistics, interactional studies, cognitive studies, sociolinguistics, sociology, psycholinguistics, psychology, anthropological linguistics, translation studies, and others. The development of human (hard-science) linguistics owes much to the inspiration they have supplied.

To single out the contributions of any particular individuals would be to slight the many others who have influenced this development over more than four decades.

The new foundations for general linguistics that have been laid try to meet the obvious and sometimes eloquently expressed need for sounder and more appropriate theoretical foundations in this whole area. It may thus be possible for readers who become interested to retain their present disciplinary ties centered around some chosen area of phenomena while moving their work onto scientifically sound foundations. They may see the way to abandon old theoretical positions that are hard to justify and have proved overly constraining or unaccommodating of the desired breadth of coverage and deficient in providing insight and understanding. In making this move they may gain the sense of freedom that some have remarked on moving their work onto the new hard-science foundations.

With this we are delighted to welcome interested readers to the exciting program of moving linguistics out of the logical domain into the physical domain and reconstructing it there as a true natural science. As new explorers you will find many people among the pioneers willing to lend you a helping hand.

PART I

ORIENTATION TO HARD-SCIENCE LINGUISTICS

Chapter 1

The Depth Hypothesis and the New Hard-Science Linguistics

Victor H. Yngve

This summer of 1999 marks the 40th anniversary of the discoveries leading to the depth hypothesis, which related language structure to a limited human temporary memory (Yngve 1960). Many of the predictions of the depth hypothesis have been borne out by synchronic, diachronic, and psycholinguistic evidence. But despite its many successes, it cannot be scientifically tested. Therefore it is my obligation to withdraw it.

Present-day linguistics reveals itself as a soft science cognate with the social and psychological sciences. It cannot support any scientifically testable hypotheses at all. Linguistics needs to be reconstituted as a hard science cognate with physics, chemistry, and biology. It needs to become a natural science.

The major difference between the hard sciences and philosophy is that the hard sciences offer theories of the real world and test them against the real world whereas philosophy offers theories of theories. The major difference between the hard sciences and the soft sciences is that the hard sciences confine themselves to studying the real natural world whereas the soft sciences study also nonphysical entities such as signs, conventions, language, customs, opinions, ideas, and the like. These are not objects of the real world and theories of them cannot be tested against the real world. Current linguistics is a prototypical soft science, as many linguists would agree. A hard-science linguistics would study real people and other relevant parts of the real world.

A decades-long search for an improved linguistic model has led to new foundations for general linguistics that *can* support scientifically testable hypotheses and that do make it possible for linguistics to be reconstituted as a true hard science.

The depth hypothesis (Yngve 1960) came out of research on the machine translation of languages at MIT over four decades ago. The output routine of the translation scheme would produce sentences one at a time to order as needed. So to produce the sentence *the man hit the ball*, the machine would execute the following steps in temporal sequence (see Figure 1.1)[1]:

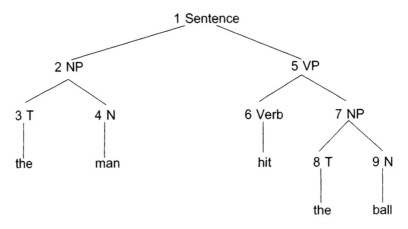

Figure 1.1

First an initial node *sentence* (1) would be expanded into *NP* and *VP* with the *VP* stored in a temporary memory of the push-down type (last in first out).

Then the *NP* (2) would be expanded into *T* and *N* with the *N* also stored in the temporary memory.

The *T* (3) would then be expanded into the word *the* and written out.

The mechanism would then retrieve the *N* (4) from the temporary memory, expand it into the word *man*, and write it out.

Then it would retrieve and expand the *VP* (5).

So we see that to produce this sentence, the temporary memory needs to store a maximum of two nodes, *VP* and *N*. The question arose as to how much computer memory space would be needed for storing unexpanded nodes for any arbitrary sentence. This would be the maximum number of unexpanded nodes in simultaneously open constructions while the sentence is being produced. This maximum number of unexpanded nodes is defined as the *depth of regression* of the sentence. The depth of regression of this sentence is thus two.

An investigation showed that most sentences would require only a few nodes to be stored and it was difficult to construct sentences with a depth of more than about six or eight. This brought to mind the span of immediate memory of 7 ± 2 proposed by the psychologist George Miller. Further investigation led to proposing the depth hypothesis (Yngve 1960). Briefly, grammars are structured so as to:

(1) limit the depth of sentences actually used to the span of immediate memory, about 7 ± 2;
(2) provide alternatives of lesser depth to maintain the power of expression of the language; and
(3) allow unlimited progressive (right) branching for very long sentences.

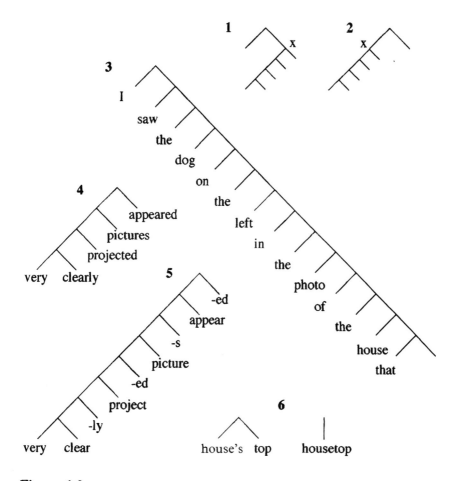

Figure 1.2

All of these features are abundantly found in the grammar of English. Note in (1) in Figure 1.2 that a regressive structure X attached to a right node starts at a depth of one less than the same structure attached to a left node as in (2). This provides an explanation for Behaghel's law, attested in all language families of the world, that longer and heavier constituents are preferred on the right while shorter and lighter ones are preferred on the left. (3) shows a typical progressive structure of English that can be continued virtually indefinitely with a depth of only one. This contrasts with the regressive structure at (4), which is limited grammatically by the part-of-speech hierarchy of English that counts out a limited number of regressive steps, here four. However, this is made possible by suffixes, which conserve depth at the expense of increasing the vocabulary. If the suffixes were separate words, the depth would be a prohibitive eight, as in diagram (5). English allows additional depth to be saved by compounding as shown in (6). There are no such depth-conserving devices in the progressive direction (3) and none is needed. Nor is affixation needed: separate words (prepositions) can be used instead. Thus the depth hypothesis explains the curious preference for suffixing and agglutination in head final languages.

How could these otherwise unmotivated complexities arise in a grammar? A causal mechanism for language change was proposed (Yngve 1960):

(1) Speakers who exceed the depth limit might become trapped and have to stop and start over. To test this we tried to cause speakers to exceed their memory limit by introducing a sudden short competing task that would make additional demands on the temporary memory (Yngve 1973). Speakers then did in fact sometimes stop with a glottal closure, process the competing task, and try to start over. And then they often forgot what they were going to say! Frequent competing memory demands may account for the observation that most sentences have depths much less than 7 ± 2.

(2) Speakers would be aware of becoming trapped. In fact they did report the familiar feeling of having forgotten what they were about to say.

(3) Speakers would try to avoid the troublesome constructions by marking them as awkward in the grammar. Exactly the predicted structures are the ones that are seen as awkward or do not even occur at all.

(4) If speakers avoid troublesome constructions, children will not learn them.

(5) This would result in language change. Precisely the language changes predicted are attested in the history of the English genitive as is shown in the historical data of Charles Carpenter Fries (Fries 1938, 1940). These data are compared in detail with the predictions of the depth hypothesis in Yngve (1975).

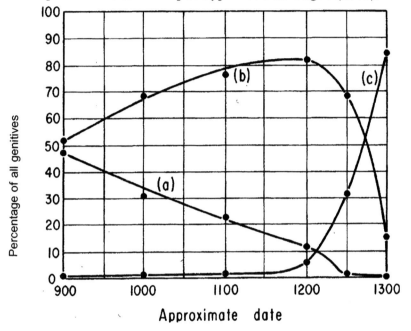

Figure 1.3

The attested historical changes in the English genitive under depth pressures can easily be seen in Figure 1.3, which displays some of the Fries data.

Old English marked the direction of modification in modifier-noun constructions by inflections. The modifier could either precede or follow the noun, but for depth reasons short modifiers generally preceded and long modifiers followed.

Then when inflections were lost, the word order of short modifier before the noun became fixed and came to signal modification. The inflected genitives followed the same pattern, as *king's daughter* rather than *daughter king's*.

Then as longer inflected genitive modifiers moved before the noun ((b) in Figure 1.3), they developed awkwardness as in the current English *the man who visited us at school yesterday's sister*.

Then, by about 1150, after the depth pressure on these awkward preposed inflected genitive modifiers (b) became severe, an alternative (c) was found in the postposed prepositional genitive modifier with *of*, which had existed earlier in Old English but was rare. So in modern English we have the alternative *the sister of the man who visited us at school yesterday.*

The prepositional genitive with *of* (c) then rapidly replaced most of the awkward preposed inflected genitive modifiers (b) and all the remaining postposed inflected genitive modifiers (a) as well.

Note that the depth hypothesis explains why the genitive marker when preposed is a separate word (*of*), and when postposed it is an affix (*-s*).

All the genitives participated in these changes, regardless of type: possessive, subjective, objective, and so on. This rules out semantic and other explanations. However note these stunning figures from Fries: whereas 94.8 per cent of the inflected *noun* genitives were replaced by the genitive with *of*, 97 per cent of the inflected *pronouns* stayed behind and were *not* replaced by the genitive with *of*! The reason is that they are depth safe and there was no depth pressure on them as there was on the preposed inflected noun genitives. Many preposed inflected noun genitives were replaced by uninflected adjunct nouns, as for example *the table leg* for *the table's leg*. And this feeds into compounding such as *rooftop*. Both are mechanisms for conserving depth. Most of the remaining preposed inflected genitives are short depth-safe proper names and human nouns. The inflected genitive has been so decimated by these changes that it causes little problem for speakers of current English. Why has the preposed inflected genitive survived at all in English? It is useful when there is more than one modifier of the same noun, as in *the staff's summary of the evidence.* Repeated genitives such as *John's father's father's father*, which were at one time thought to be counterexamples to the depth hypothesis, still actually show the awkwardness that has been driving these changes. And alternatives of lesser depth are available. Observed awkwardness is marked in the grammar and represents current pressures on speakers for linguistic change. When changes go to completion we are left with constructions that are either grammatical or they do not occur at all.

There is abundant evidence supporting the depth hypothesis. It explains much of the synchronic complexity of grammar. It explains a potent force for linguistic change. And it is supported by relevant textual and psycholinguistic studies. One might think that it should be accepted. So why did I start out by saying that it is my obligation to withdraw the depth hypothesis as not being scientifically testable? In the first place, it is a hypothesis about syntactic tree structures, but linguists cannot agree on how to draw syntactic trees. In the second place it is a hypothesis about features of grammar, but linguists cannot agree on grammatical theory. There is no scientific way to resolve these questions. Unfortunately, linguistics has no scientifically justified body of grammatical theory on which a testable scientific hypothesis could be based. Lacking such a body of theory the depth hypothesis cannot be tested scientifically and as a scientist I am obliged to withdraw it as a hypothesis about language structure. Where can we turn for adequate theory?

It became clear that what is right about the hypothesis is the degree to which it is stated in terms of people, their memory properties, and what they actually do when they speak. And what is wrong with it is the degree to which it rests on the abstractions of grammatical theory. It is untestable because, as a hypothesis about *language* structure, it rests on a number of unsupported assumptions about language and grammar. It is a hypothesis in a soft-science linguistics that cannot support *any* scientifically testable hypotheses at all. It needs to be reformulated as a hypothesis not about language structure but about *people* in a proper hard-science linguistics. But up to now no hard-science linguistics has existed. The lack of proper hard-science foundations has been holding back the scientific development of linguistics now for nearly two centuries.

A hard-science linguistics would accept only the four standard assumptions of science:

(1) There is a real world out there to be investigated; it's not just a figment of our imagination.
(2) The real world is coherent so we have a chance of finding out something about it. It's not completely chaotic.
(3) We can reason from true premises to true conclusions and calculate predictions from our theories for comparison with the evidence.
(4) From observed effects we can infer real-world causes. We can test our theories against the real world by observation and experiment.

The soft sciences, on the other hand, accept a number of special assumptions not scientifically supportable. Current linguistics rests on familiar assumptions of language, signs, meanings, and the like, many of which date back to Aristotle and the Stoics. If people are studied at all, they are studied indirectly through language and grammar. Such assumptions cannot be scientifically justified and must be rejected by a hard-science linguistics.

The hard sciences honor the standard criteria of science for deciding what to believe about the world:

(1) The criterion for accepting theories when doubts arise is the comparison of their predictions against the real world.
(2) The criterion for accepting observational and experimental evidence is its reproducibility when questioned.

The soft sciences, on the other hand, appeal to a variety of criteria on which there is little agreement and which often stand in conflict. There are appeals to tradition, authority, intuition, explication, simplicity, symmetry, conventional wisdom, and claims of superior insight. Such appeals must be rejected by a hard-science linguistics.

A hard-science linguistics would study only people and their physical surroundings rather than language and grammar, at least in part. It would propose scientific theories of people and other real-world objects rather than developing grammars as theories of language. It would test its theories of people against observations of people rather than seeing people in terms of language and grammar and testing grammars against intuition and other soft criteria. It would require reproducibility of observations and would reject theories and observations resting in part on unjustified assumptions of signs and language.

Decades of frustration trying to find a proper linguistic model that could support the depth hypothesis have led to new foundations for a hard-science linguistics on which we can build (Yngve 1996). Please note that I have no patent on standard science, which belongs to us all and should need no defending among scientists. I am simply accepting standard science as it has developed over the last four centuries in the hard sciences of physics, chemistry, and biology, and showing how linguistics, too, can become a true hard science.

Linguistic phenomena are both individual and social. People don't just talk to themselves, they participate in groups and communities. Thus the new foundations offer two orders of theory, individual and social, instead of just one, grammar.

We set up systems as theoretical constructs to model the parts of the real world we are studying. Systems modeling individual persons are called *communicating individuals*. Systems modeling groups or assemblages of people and the relevant parts of their physical surroundings are called *linkages*. Linkages are made up of *participants* modeling group members, *channels* modeling the communicative energy flow and means of energy flow, *props* modeling communicatively relevant physical objects, and *settings* modeling other relevant parts of the surroundings.

These systems are defined in terms of *properties*. Properties are constructs in the theories of the persons and assemblages being studied. The properties of communicating individuals are set up on the basis of observed similarities and differences of different persons and the same person at different times; the properties of linkages are set up on the basis of observed similarities and differences of different assemblages and the same assemblage at different times. Properties are organized in terms of dynamic plex structures. Plex structures do not amount to internal grammars or to grammars of a community since that would introduce scientifically unjustified assumptions. Plex structures may, however, include task hierarchies, which are related in a way to phrase structure and may make possible a scientifically justified reformulation of the depth hypothesis. And much more.

With the new hard-science foundations for general linguistics the way is now open to give up our reliance on questionable soft-science concepts and methods that have been standing in the way of progress. We can push aside the political and other irrelevant criteria characteristic of much of current linguistics. The way is now open to give standard science a chance.

In giving standard science a chance, we accept an obligation to question our own assumptions and test our own hypotheses and theories so as to avoid publishing nonsense. I can attest from personal experience that it is difficult to question one's own basic assumptions, even to discover what they are. And then if they prove unfounded, it's hard to give them up.

In turning to hard-science methods and criteria, we can achieve results that rise above the level of simple plausibility and will be widely accepted on their merits. We can start with the simpler and easier things first. Pioneering psycholinguistics research on the new foundations is needed to further investigate the memory and forgetting phenomena mentioned above. We need to find out more about the plex structures in the individual and their dynamic operation. Pioneering sociolinguistic research is needed to investigate the plex structures of small groups and their dynamic operation. In text linguistics and related areas, including literary studies, we need to find out how to reconstitute the so-called textual worlds as plex-structure properties of individuals and linkages. In pragmatics we need to reconstitute essentially philosophical insights into testable hard-science plex structures and their dynamic operation. In the areas of variation and historical change we need to remember what the Neogrammarians already knew in the nineteenth century, but could not treat, that it is not language that changes, but the people, individually and collectively. Pioneering work is needed in many other areas of general linguistics where pockets of excellence are to be found. You will have to seek out what is potentially most valuable and easiest for you.

All these efforts will benefit from the interdependence and mutual support of disparate studies of the same real objects and the consequent unification of results characteristic of the hard sciences. There is the possibility that if we build wisely and carefully, what we build will remain as a permanent part of science.

For over a century and a half the goal of linguistics to become a science has been frustrated by concepts, assumptions, and methods inherited from the ancient semiotic-grammatical tradition. We can now write an end to that era. We can reconstitute linguistics as a true hard science. It needs to be done. The foundations are there. It *can* be done. We now only need to do it.

Notes

This is a revised version of a paper presented at the 32nd annual meeting of Societas Linguistica Europaea (SLE), Ljubljana, Slovenia, 8–11 July, 1999 and published in the proceedings: Irena Kovačič, Milena Milojević-Sheppard, Silvana Orel-Kos, and Janez Orešnik (2000), *Linguistics and Language Studies: Exploring Language from Different Perspectives.* Ljubljana: Filozofska fakultete Univerze v Ljubljani, pp.191–202.

1. Note that producing sentences to order one at a time as needed and from left to right in analogy to a person actually speaking them is quite different from generating them mathematically 'from the top down and all at once' as it were, in the sense of a generative grammar following Chomsky, where there is no conception of a temporal sequence of steps at all.

References

Fries, Charles C. (1938), 'Some notes on the inflected genitive in present-day English'. *Language,* 14, 121–133.
Fries, Charles C. (1940), 'On the development of the structural use of word-order in modern English'. *Language,* 16, 199–208.
Yngve, Victor H. (1960), 'A model and an hypothesis for language

structure'. *Proceedings of the American Philosophical Society*, 104, 444–466.

Yngve, Victor H. (1973), 'I forget what I was going to say', in Claudia Corum, *et al.*, *Papers from the Ninth Regional Meeting, Chicago Linguistic Society*. Chicago: Chicago Linguistic Society, pp. 688–699.

Yngve, Victor H. (1975), 'Depth and the historical change of the English genitive'. *Journal of English Linguistics*, 9, 47–57.

Yngve, Victor H. (1996), *From Grammar to Science: New Foundations for General Linguistics*. Amsterdam/Philadelphia: John Benjamins.

Chapter 2

Issues in Hard-Science Linguistics

Victor H. Yngve

What is human or hard-science linguistics?

I take linguistics in the usual sense as a discipline with a research community, a cohesive literature, faculties and students in academic departments, and organized professional societies. This is meant to be indicative, not exclusionary. I would not exclude from this discipline people of whatever age with whatever training and from whatever walk of life who have a sincere interest in helping to find out how people communicate, which is, after all, one of the most important things about our humanness. The term *linguistics* does not rule out an interest in systems of communicating used by the deaf or by monks who have taken a vow of silence, or interest in facial expressions and body motion. Linguistics in this broad sense embraces a freely expandable scope of interrelated phenomena that have long been recognized as being both individual and social in nature.

Essentially all leading linguists for the past two centuries have agreed that linguistics either is or aspires to be a science. No particular body of theory, however, grammatical or other, has emerged as acceptable to all. Indeed, linguistic theory has suffered frequent changes as one school after another has achieved a measure of dominance. And the proper shape of linguistic theory has throughout history been the subject of heated but inconclusive debate.

1. Linguistics and science

So what then is hard-science linguistics?

It is called hard-science linguistics to distinguish it from most current brands of linguistics which are properly characterized as soft science. There are a number of crucial differences that can be a source of confusion if they are not kept well in mind:

(1) Hard-science linguistics is a natural science, like physics, chemistry, and biology. This is its major difference from current approaches, which are philosophically based.

(2) Hard-science linguistics takes science seriously. As a natural science it studies parts of the real physical world. Current linguistics, on the other hand, studies nonphysical constructs.

(3) Thus hard-science linguistics focuses primarily on people from the point of view of how they communicate, and on the sound waves of speech, the light waves of gestures, and other physical means of communicative energy flow. It also includes consideration of other relevant parts of the real physical world. Soft-science linguistics, on the other hand, focuses on the nonphysical constructs of language and signs.

(4) In the hard sciences it is standard practice to test the predictions of theory against the real world through careful observation and experiment. But in the soft sciences theories are not testable against the real world.

(5) In the hard sciences theories are testable because the hard sciences study observable real-world objects, whereas the soft sciences study unobservable nonphysical objects, for which there is no objective evidence.

(6) The hard sciences have developed standard objective criteria for deciding what to believe about the natural world.

   (a) The criterion for assessing theories is that they must be testable against the real world and that their predictions must agree with the results of tests through real-world observations and experiments.

   (b) The criterion for assessing observational and experimental results is their reproducibility.

   These criteria cannot be applied in the soft sciences, which do not study the real world. They are forced to fall back on various *a priori* philosophical criteria such as simplicity, symmetry, 'naturalness', etc. or on sheer intuition about what is plausible. Investigators can and do differ on these matters, which are subjective and arbitrary. The result is that the discipline then drifts from one fashionable body of theory to another and from the dictates of one charismatic linguist to another.

(7) The hard sciences have paid careful attention to what assump-

tions they are willing to accept. They have pared them down to only four standard assumptions. The soft sciences, on the other hand, freely admit as many untestable assumptions as they wish. The four standard assumptions of the hard sciences are:

(a) that there is a real world out there to be studied;
(b) that it is coherent so we have a chance of finding out something about it;
(c) that we can reach valid conclusions by reasoning from valid premises; and
(d) that observed effects flow from immediate real-world causes.

All other assumptions have been converted into hypotheses to be tested. Those that do not pass tests against real-world evidence or that are untestable have been eliminated. Soft-science linguistics, however, typically accepts a number of scientifically unjustified special assumptions that take it outside of the natural sciences. There are assumptions about utterances, language, meanings, signs, and typically dozens of others, either explicit or implicit and hidden.

2. Two incompatible goals and a dilemma

It has not been generally realized that the current difficulties in linguistics stem in large part from the incompatibility of the modern goal of making linguistics a science and the traditional goal of studying language.

Accepting language as an object of study leads to accepting the scientifically unjustified special assumptions involved in continuing a philosophically-based program of grammatical and semiotic research that can be traced back to the ancients. In hard-science linguistics we must continually be on guard against traditional soft-science assumptions that threaten to lead us astray. It's a question of priority of goals. If we give priority to studying language, we cannot have a true science. If we give priority to science, we must give up the goal of studying language.

Giving up language in favor of science would be a victory for linguistics, not a defeat. If we study the people who speak and understand rather than studying language, we can actually build a genuine hard-science linguistics that can stand among the other natural sciences and take the place of the present autonomous soft-science linguistics.

The other natural sciences are built on hard-science foundations and each has a conceptual structure that is specific to its subject matter. Physics studies selected parts of the real world from the physical point of view and has concepts of mass, energy, momentum, force, and so on. Chemistry studies parts of the real world from a chemical point of view and has concepts of atoms, molecules, valence, reaction rate, and so on. Hard-science linguistics also rests on hard-science foundations rather than on the traditional semiotic-grammatical foundations. It studies selected parts of the real world, people, from the point of view of how they communicate. To support such studies a new subject-matter-specific conceptual structure on which to build a new hard-science linguistics is now available (Yngve 1996). This replaces the conceptual structure of grammar.

But if we start over and build a new linguistics on hard-science foundations and the new conceptual structure, we are faced with a dilemma. There is a vast literature accumulated over centuries containing a wealth of linguistic knowledge, almost all from a soft-science point of view. Thus it is based on or incorporates many scientifically unjustified assumptions. The dilemma is whether to try to make use of this vast treasure and possibly be misled by it, or to ignore it and risk losing the many valid insights it may contain.

For two centuries we have been trying to make linguistics a science, not by moving it onto proper hard-science foundations but by continuing to give priority to the study of language rather than to science. In this we have been encouraged by those philosophers trying to redefine science and legitimize the soft sciences. The result has been a soft-science linguistics dedicated to studying an object, language, introduced only by scientifically unjustified and untestable assumptions. After two centuries it is now clear that this course has led only to confusion and chaos in the discipline.

What we must do instead to resolve the dilemma is to make use of what is already known where possible, but leave the old world of the soft sciences once and for all and become pioneers in the new world of the hard sciences. We must mount a program of research to *reconstitute* linguistics on hard-science foundations and the new conceptual structure that is now available.

3. Reconstituting linguistics on hard-science foundations

Let us see how one might begin.

Suppose two people are in conversation. There are three distinct physical things here, person A, person B, and the sound waves that pass between them (shown in the bottom line of Figure 2.1).

Physical Domain — Hard Science			Soft
Linkage:		[the couple]	
		2	
Role parts:	[the husband]	[the wife]	
Participants:	[the man]	[the woman]	L? — SH
		1	
Communicating individuals	[person A]	[person B]	utterance?
Real-world objects:	person A sound waves person B		sound

Figure 2.1

In the natural sciences a distinction is always honored between the real world and our theories of the real world. In hard-science linguistics, our linguistic theories of real-world persons are called *communicating individuals*, which are systems in the normal natural-science sense. Thus 'person A' in the bottom line of Figure 2.1 refers to a real person whereas in the line above, our linguistic theory of person A is a communicating individual, which for convenience we have decided to call [person A]. All names of systems will be placed in square brackets to avoid confusion with the ordinary names of the real-world objects. Thus [person A] names the system that offers a linguistic theory of the real-world object person A. The communicating individuals, participants, role parts, and the linkage of Figure 2.1 are all systems in this sense and objects of theory.

When person A and person B communicate with each other, all the linguistic structure lies in these two people and in the pair of them communicating by sound waves and other energy flow. This linguistic structure is represented in the theory in terms of the properties of the systems, where 'property' is again taken in its normal sense in the natural sciences. The sound waves are seen simply for what they physically are, pure energy flow: they carry no linguistic structure at all.

I have chosen a husband and wife as an example for clarity because we happen to have a name for the two of them, a couple. A couple is part of the real physical world. You could invite them to dinner. The couple, together with the sound waves and other relevant parts of the real world, are referred to as an *assemblage*. An assemblage is represented in the theory as a system called a *linkage*, which is characterized by properties in the same way as the other systems. So we introduce as an object of theory a linkage which we call, for convenience, [the couple]. (See Figure 2.1.)

How can we understand linkage properties? If the couple discusses a question and comes to agree on the matter, the agreeing is a property of the two of them. No one can agree alone. It takes at least two people to agree. Where is the agreeing? We might be tempted to say that agreeing is a real property of the real-world couple and then ask how it can be understood in real-world terms. However, it must be realized that it is the scientist that attributes a property of agreeing to the couple. Because it is attributed by the scientist, it exists only in the scientist's theory. In this sense the agreeing is an object of theory. The scientist would want the object of theory to accurately represent the real world. How could the scientist find out whether one can truly attribute agreeing to the real-world couple? The best way to find out is to test it, to conduct careful observations and experiments with the real-world people. The testing of theories against the real world is a standard procedure of science. So we see that in science, properties are of necessity objects of theory that represent the real-world objects the scientist is studying. So in hard-science linguistics we say that the linkage system [the couple] is characterized by a property of agreeing on the question discussed. Doubtless there are many other things involving the two of them relevant for understanding how they communicate with each other. These also would all be represented in theory as properties of the linkage system [the couple].

When person A and person B communicate with each other, we represent them as systems called *participants* in the linkage [the couple]. So we set up two participants in the linkage [the couple] and for convenience call them [the man] and [the woman]. Since the properties of the communicating individuals [person A] and [person B] undoubtedly include many properties not relevant to the linkage [the couple], perhaps properties relevant to a work or employment situation involving other special ways of communicating, we see that the properties of the participants [the man] and [the woman] actually constitute only small subsets of the total sets of the properties of the communicating individuals [person A] and [person B].

There are various kinds of couples: married, engaged, divorced, dating, dance partners, and others. If this is a married couple, the man plays the role of husband and the woman plays the role of wife, which fact is reflected in some of the ways they communicate. To recognize this in linguistic theory, we set up two systems called *role parts* and for convenience call them [the husband] and [the wife]. Besides couples there are a variety of other assemblages of multiple persons and objects that can likewise be analyzed as linkages. Some other examples of two-person assemblages would be mother and child, tutor and student, older sibling and younger sibling, hostess and guest, and salesperson and customer. The role parts for each of these linkages would be different in important respects from the role parts of the others. There are also larger and more complex assemblages that can be analyzed in more complex ways, for which theory is available. Examples would include a family with children, a classroom with students and a teacher, a club with dozens of members, and a political party. Still more complex assemblages would include two teams playing football with each other, and a football league with a number of teams. For analyzing the more complex structures we may find in the assemblages we are interested in studying, we can set up linkages that participate in other higher-level linkages. By setting up hierarchies of individuals and linkages in this way we can represent the linguistic structure of the many systems in a complex community or society.

In the tradition, on the other hand, the sound waves are seen as somehow supporting assumed 'utterances' that are analyzed in terms of some theory of language, L (on the right in Figure 2.1), and that in some mysterious ways carry a 'meaning' or 'message' or 'information' from one person to the other, who are then seen as 'using' language. Note that the linguistic structure postulated for utterances is not at all inherent in the physical sound waves. It cannot be recorded by instruments. The similarities and differences, on which phonemes were postulated, for example, require a person to perceive them, and different persons perceive them differently. Traditional theory does not take any persons into account. A proper scientific linguistics must be a linguistics focused not on language but on people, for that's where the linguistic structure really lies.

4. Two new domains of theory

So we see that hard-science linguistics provides two domains of theory (Figure 2.1): domain 1 (individual) at the individual and participant levels, and domain 2 (social) at the role part and linkage levels, to match the fact that communicating is both individual and social. These two domains of theory differ in the real-world evidence, individual or social, on which the properties of the systems are postulated. Properties of individuals and properties of participants in domain 1 (individual) are set up on the basis of observed similarities and differences of individual persons. Properties of role parts and properties of linkages in domain 2 (social) are set up on the basis of observed similarities and differences of assemblages of people and objects at the social level.

The tradition, on the other hand, provides only one domain of theory, language, and it has never been clear whether it is individual or social or some abstraction which is neither. Note that Chomsky's ideal speaker-hearer, SH in Figure 2.1, does not answer to any real-world evidence from real persons. There is nobody underlying it that you could invite to dinner. Incredibly, it is defined entirely in terms of language, which does not exist in the real world, and is completely subservient to the assumptions and definitions of a particular linguist. In fact, even the structured utterances here, or the text in other theories, has to be introduced by a special subject-matter-specific assumption, as Bloomfield already pointed out.

5. Properties of systems

We observe that everyone is different communicatively from everyone else. The uniqueness of the individual is expressed in terms of postulated properties of the systems that model them. Properties are set up on the basis of observed real-world communicative similarities and differences of persons and assemblages. They may be taken as binary variables without loss of generality. These properties can be represented here as:

A B C̲ D E F G̲ H I J K L M N̲ O P Q̲ R S T U ...

where the underlined properties will figure in the discussion below concerning how properties change.

Hard-science linguistics is often called human linguistics to distinguish it from the traditional linguistics of language. The name human linguistics is particularly apt since its theory is founded on the very uniqueness of individuals and groups celebrated in the humanities rather than on the normative basis of grammar which would make everyone the same.

Properties change dynamically as people learn and speak and understand. Some properties change quite rapidly, others may stay fixed for longer periods of time. The knowledge of how to communicate is represented in terms of properties.

We also observe that communicative behavior is heavily context-dependent. Properties reflect both inputs to the system and its current state, which represents the current context in which the ongoing communicative behavior is understood.

It has been shown that the structures of properties in the various systems such as individuals, participants, role parts, and linkages can all be organized according to the same conceptual structure and formal theory.

6. Procedures

Properties are structured in part in terms of procedures. Procedures are dynamic causal laws of communicative behavior postulated on the basis of observational and experimental evidence from the real-world objects modeled. A procedure specifies how some property changes value in dependence on the current values of other properties, some of which may represent the situation or context, others the results of inputs.

Procedures are triggered when specific properties (inputs and context) take the values specified in the logic expression on the left. They then change the value of a property as specified on the right after a specified time delay Δt, as for example:

$$C x - G v N :: Q, \Delta t$$

where x is 'and', − is 'not', v is 'or', and :: is read as 'sets' (the indicated property on the right to the indicated value).

Thus communicative behavior results in change, not accretion, so hard-science linguistics is basically pragmatic in its foundations, in contrast to the tradition, which treats pragmatics as an afterthought, if at all.

The current situation or context that affects ongoing communicative behavior is represented in the properties. Those properties that affect current communicative behavior are referred to as the domain of control. The execution of procedures in dependence on the dynamically changing properties in the domain of control answers to what would be spoken of colloquially as a person following a conversation or being 'with it'. This accords with the observation that what a person says or understands in any given situation depends on the situation, which is dynamically changing. Thus the proper handling of context is a central feature of the theory, and a major difference from grammar. Rules of grammar do not involve the situation or context in this ongoing sense. They are generally set up on the basis of examples taken out of context.

The term human linguistics is thus apt for another reason. Since it focuses on what individual persons do and say and understand in particular circumstances, it accommodates the uniqueness of situations of the humanities. It can do this in a true science because it generalizes in terms of individual properties rather than in terms of a whole language.

The linguistics of language provides little more than a grammatical straitjacket, a stance not far removed from the prescriptive tradition.

Procedures are often organized in terms of a hierarchy of communicative tasks and subtasks. There can also be parallel tasks to accommodate the possibility that a person or a group may do several things at the same time. Communicative tasks are often subtasks of nonlinguistic tasks representing what it is that the communicative behavior is coordinating. Thus hard-science linguistics is closely connected with other social and social-psychological disciplines and interfaces naturally with practical affairs. It does not exist in the splendid isolation of language and autonomous grammar.

The organization of properties, procedures, task hierarchies, etc. of a system is called the plex structure of that system. So in hard-science linguistics we observe and experiment on how people communicate so as to postulate and test plex structures for them. This is quite different from taking people as informants or witnesses for the study of language.

If we keep well in mind the kinds of differences highlighted here so as not to be confused or misled by them, it should be a fairly straightforward though lengthy task to reconstitute all of linguistics piece by piece on hard-science foundations.

7. Evidence

Let us now look at some more examples with a particular focus on evidence. Evidence is always relative to the theory that it is interpreted in terms of – the theory it is designed to support or contradict. Thus it is also relative to any hidden assumptions underlying that theory. Hidden false assumptions can lead to false interpretations. The depth hypothesis proved untestable because of hidden false assumptions underlying the phrase-structure theory it was interpreted in terms of.

In hard-science linguistics we seek evidence for properties of systems modeling real-world people from the point of view of how they communicate, not evidence for properties of immaterial objects like words and sentences. We seek evidence for similarities and differences between different persons and the same person at different times, and between different groups and the same group at different times.

Let us take the example of two women bargaining over the price for an antique offered for sale. See Figure 2.2.

First, there are properties postulated and tested against evidence from individual persons. Here at the *individual* level there are general properties representing the person's knowledge, abilities, aspirations, values, etc. At the *participant* level there are properties concerned with how much the collector would be willing to give for the antique during this bargaining session and properties concerned with how little the dealer would be willing to accept.

Second, there are properties postulated and tested against evidence from assemblages of persons and other associated real-world objects. Here at the *role-part* level there are properties concerned with customer offering, salesperson refusing and making a counter offer, customer making a show of walking out, etc. At the *linkage* level, there are properties representing the current changing state of negotiation of the sales group, the antique, the money, and other relevant real objects.

As another example, consider two strangers getting acquainted, as videotaped and described in earlier publications.

Here at the *individual* level we find properties representing the personal backgrounds of the two persons (that they later discuss). At the *participant* level there are properties representing the original request of the researcher separately to each, what little he told them about each other, and the task he gave them of getting acquainted.

Regarding social properties: at the *role-part* level are properties

Linkage:		[sales linkage]	
Role parts, Prop part:	[customer]	salesperson	[merchandise]
Participants:	[the collector]	[the dealer]	[the antique]
Communicating individuals:	[person A]	[person B]	e.g. vase
Real-world objects:	person A	person B	real object

Figure 2.2

representing each person's moves and responses in dialog, and such things as checking with each other on the extent of their actual commonality in knowing what the task is. Thus we find the woman saying, 'and, I don't know how much you know about me – at all', and he says, 'I know nothing about you at all. It's all a big secret'. To which she replies, 'All right – should I start, then?'. And he says, 'You start (single nod)'. In this way the information about their common task is moved up from the individual participant level to the social role-part level. They both now know what activity 'start' refers to. Then at the *linkage* level are properties of the changing current state of their dialog and their growing acquaintanceship.

There are also ongoing investigations of historical change, linguistic variation, multilingualism, translation, etc. The specific nature of evidence in each case is different and relative to the area under investigation.

In spite of what some philosophers of science may say, scientific research is not focused single-mindedly on so-called falsification. We're in the physical domain, not the logical domain of theorems and proofs. In seeking the truth about nature, we emphasize real-world exploration. Research in the physical domain is more like a detective trying to solve a crime. There's no single simple route to a guaranteed solution. A number of techniques are available to us including field observations, videotapes, and interviews.

In hard-science linguistics, we are all studying the same physical reality, people, from the point of view of how they communicate, and the relevant physical surroundings. Thus evidence and theory from one area of linguistics is often relevant to the study of questions in other areas and even in neighboring disciplines that study people from other points of view. Linguistics thus moves from its isolation in autonomous grammar into the real world of the natural sciences. We can say goodbye to the era of grammatical fads and fashions and enter a new era for linguistics where our theories will have the solidity, permanence, and real-world relevance already familiar in the other natural sciences.

Note

This chapter is an improved version of a paper presented at the 28th LACUS Forum, July 31–August 4, 2001 in Montreal, Canada, and at the 34th Annual Meeting of Societas Linguistica Europaea (SLE) August 28–September 1, 2001 in Leuven, Belgium.

References

Yngve, Victor H. (1996), *From Grammar to Science: New Foundations for General Linguistics*. Amsterdam/Philadelphia: John Benjamins.

Chapter 3

An Introduction to Hard-Science Linguistics

Victor H. Yngve

1. What is hard-science linguistics?

Although the roots of modern science reach deep into antiquity, the flowering of science in the seventeenth century in the work of Galileo and his contemporaries was marked by self-conscious doubt and the questioning of ancient beliefs. Traditional assumptions about the natural world dating to Aristotle and other revered writers were increasingly replaced by explicit theories of the real world that were subject to rigorous tests against careful real-world observations and experiments. The startling advances of modern science in the last four centuries were the result.

The roots of linguistics also reach back to ancient times, but for nearly two centuries linguists have desired to make their discipline a science. In 1830, for example, Rasmus Rask invoked the names of Linnaeus and Newton. He took language to be an organism of nature and its study to be a natural science. The conception grew that the study of language was coordinate with the study of rocks, plants, and animals. Essentially every major linguist down to the present has taken the position that linguistics is or ought to be a science. But this has proved difficult to carry out in practice.

Hard-science linguistics follows the lead of the rest of science. It starts by questioning ancient beliefs and assumptions dating primarily to Aristotle and the Stoics. They do not stand up to probing doubt. It becomes clear that since signs and language are introduced by assumption, and thus are not part of the real physical world, that theories of them cannot be tested against the real world. Under the traditional conception of language and the standard conception of science, language cannot be studied scientifically and we cannot have a coherent scientific study of language. As Saussure noted, the other sciences study objects of the real world that are given in advance and that can then be studied from different points of view, but not linguistics.

But the people who speak and understand and communicate in other ways actually are parts of the real physical world given in advance like the objects studied in the other sciences. They, too, can be studied from different points of view. People can be studied in physics from the point of view of their physical properties and in chemistry from the point of view of their chemical properties. They can be studied from the point of view of their biochemical properties, their molecular genetic properties, and their neurological properties. People can also be studied scientifically from a linguistic point of view in terms of their linguistic properties.

That is what we do in hard-science linguistics. We study people from the point of view of their linguistic properties. We have no need for concepts of language and the objects of language. Linguistics then becomes the scientific study of how people communicate rather than the scientific study of language, which is impossible. It becomes a human linguistics rather than a linguistics of language. It becomes a hard science cognate with biology, chemistry, and physics.

2. How do we decide what to believe?

Hard-science linguistics does not tell anyone what to believe or what not to believe in linguistics. Every person is free to decide for himself or herself what to believe. This is a tradition in modern science. But in hard-science linguistics we insist on basing our work on the same standard criteria and assumptions worked out in modern science and honored today in physics, chemistry, and biology.

(1) The standard criterion for accepting theories is the ability of their predictions to pass tests against the real world through careful observation and experiment.
(2) The standard criterion for accepting observational and experimental results is their reproducibility.

We honor no other criteria for deciding what to believe in hard-science linguistics, especially not any of the many other criteria familiar from philosophy and grammar.

Modern science has reduced its assumptions to the absolute minimum. They are four in number. Other proposed assumptions are regularly turned into hypotheses to be tested. If they fail the tests or if they cannot even be tested, they are rejected. The standard assumptions of science are:

(1) We assume that there is a real world out there to be studied; it's not just an illusion.
(2) We assume that the real world is coherent so we have a chance of finding out something about it.
(3) We assume that we can reach valid conclusions by reasoning from valid premises.
(4) We assume that observed effects flow from immediate real-world causes.

We accept these standard criteria and assumptions of science and aim to abide by them. If some other linguists also accept these standard criteria and assumptions, there is the possibility of our coming to agreement on linguistic matters in ways well-known in the hard sciences.

3. What do we study?

Hard-science linguistics is a human linguistics. It studies how people communicate. We ask: How does it work? How does it happen that when I open my mouth and some sound comes out that you can, most of the time, understand what I am saying? How does it happen that when I hesitate, you can often volunteer exactly what I was going to say? How is it that a brief exchange between good friends will often suffice where an extensive dialog would be needed between strangers? How is it that a glance or slight gesture is sometimes sufficient? How can we understand that even simple silence may sometimes be truly eloquent? How can mere sound waves serve to inquire, to inform, to comfort, to convince, to inspire, even to incite? Whence this power over us of sound waves, light, and other forms of physical energy flow?

People form social groups of all sizes, from friendships and families to whole communities, through communicating with each other, and it is through communicating that culture is transmitted from one generation to the next. But how in detail does it work? How can we understand the relation of the individual to the community and the community to the individuals that make it up?

Hard-science linguistics studies these matters. It also studies how children learn to talk and how people keep on learning new communicative skills throughout their lifetimes. It studies how different people communicate differently in different parts of the world and even in different situations. It studies variation within the individual and variation within the community. It studies historical change. It inquires about the possible prehistoric origins of the distinctly human method of communicating colloquially called 'language'.

Consequently, hard-science linguistics studies people, individually and collectively, and the communicative energy flow such as sound and light. It also studies relevant parts of the physical surroundings including written materials and communicatively relevant objects. These are all parts of the real physical world. They exist in nature prior to our investigating and theorizing about them. A science of them can be a hard science.

4. How do we set up theory and how do we test it?

Science distinguishes everywhere between the real world and our theories of the real world. Real objects are modeled in theory by systems having convenient arbitrary boundaries and characterized by postulated properties testable against the real world by observation and experiment.

Hard-science linguistics distinguishes between *persons* in the real world and systems we set up called *communicating individuals* to represent them in theory. People show communicatively relevant similarities and differences from which we postulate *properties* of the communicating individuals. These postulated properties are then testable against real persons by observation and experiment.

The sound waves of speech and other communicatively relevant *energy flow* and the physical means of energy flow are modeled as systems called *channels* with properties reflecting the physical reality.

Since communicative energy is produced and received by people, the theory recognizes inputs and outputs across the system boundaries of the communicating individuals.

The production and reception of communicative energy is modeled in the execution of *procedures* in the properties of the communicating individuals. The associated changes in people are modeled as changes in the properties of the communicating individuals. Properties are changed by procedures which execute depending on the current values of certain properties.

Procedures are actually *dynamic causal laws* of communicative behavior.

People do not generally communicate alone but in groups of two or more. *Assemblages* of people together with the communicatively relevant parts of their surroundings are modeled as systems called *linkages*. Linkage boundaries can be set arbitrarily so as to simplify the theory and model various communicatively relevant groups and communities and their possible interactions and overlappings.

Linkage properties are postulated from observed similarities and differences of groups of people and the related real-world objects.

The *relevant objects* and the physical *surroundings* are modeled as systems called *props* and *settings*. Writing is accommodated through props or channels.

Thus, there are two separate but interrelated orders of theory in hard-science linguistics, one focused on persons and one focused on groups, instead of just one focused on language. Since the unit of generalization is the property, not language, both variation in the individual and variation in the group are accommodated right in the foundations. We do not assume uniformity in the community.

5. How are persons related to groups?

If John and a salesman, Bill, agree on a price, we note that it takes both of them to agree. One cannot agree on a price by oneself. The agreement is a property of the linkage representing the group of John and the salesman. Linkage properties are not the same as individual properties.

In relating persons to groups, the theory relates communicating individuals to linkages through three steps:

(1) When a communicating individual participates in a linkage, only a subset of his properties are involved. The many other properties specialized to other linkages are irrelevant. John's properties in his family linkages may be irrelevant, as also Bill's properties in his club. So we set up systems called *participants*. A participant in a linkage is a system characterized by just the subset of properties of the communicating individual that are involved in that linkage. The relation of communicating individual to participant is thus a relation of *set to subset* of properties.

(2) In this linkage, John is functioning in the role of customer and Bill in the role of salesman. We set up two systems called *role parts* as functional parts of the linkage. The relation of the participant John to his customer role part, and the relation of the participant Bill to his salesman role part, is a relation of *form to function*. Misunderstandings reflect form-function discrepancies between participants and role parts.

(3) This sales linkage has two functional parts, a customer and a salesman role part. The relation of these functional parts of the sales linkage to the sales linkage itself is a relation of *part to whole*. Linkage properties also include properties of the *arrangement* of the functional parts with respect to each other.

There is extreme flexibility in defining linkages so as to do justice to the evidence from complex social interactions. There can be *prop parts*, *channel parts*, and *setting parts*. There can be linkages *directly coupled* through *overlapping participants* in the same individual. There can be subordinate linkages and superordinate linkages in a *hierarchy of linkages* reaching from the smallest groups all the way up to the largest communities.

When children learn to communicate, their participant properties change so as to play appropriate role parts in the linkages constituting their linguistic environment.

Historical change is understood as changes at the linkage level originating in changes at the individual level.

6. How are properties structured?

The properties of systems in hard-science linguistics are organized in terms of *plex structures* of dynamic causal laws of communicative behavior. Although the details of plex structure vary from system to system, underlying plex-structure theory proves to be the same for all systems from communicating individuals, participants, and role parts to linkages, and includes all the systems associated with channels, props, and settings. This provides a great simplification in theory. One way in which plex structures are organized is in terms of *task hierarchies*. Another way is in terms of simultaneously executing tasks.

The current communicatively relevant properties in the plex constitute what is called the *domain of control*. Properties in the domain of control model the changing context of situation in all its currently relevant details. It includes the slowly or rapidly changing properties involved in communicative interactions and perceptions of the physical surroundings. This allows the unified handling of contextual effects such as the resolution of reference, the effect of the social situation, the effects of simultaneously executing tasks, the effect of stereotypes and other presuppositions, and the understanding of metaphoric and other figurative exchanges.

Thus hard-science linguistics handles context in its very foundations and at every level of analysis. We can work down through task hierarchies from the hard-science equivalent of pragmatics all the way down to physiology and physics and always have the appropriate context available. The ability to take the context of situation explicitly into account often eliminates what would be severe problems in any version of grammatical theory. Results building on the new foundations are clearer and do better justice to the phenomena.

However, hard-science linguistics is sufficiently different from the linguistics of language that one cannot simply translate into it from grammar in the way that one can often translate from an older grammatical scheme to a newer one. This is because results in the linguistics of language are inevitably stated in terms that intimately embody scientifically unjustified assumptions from the semiotic-grammatical tradition or some currently popular version of it. Nevertheless there are enough similarities that results expressed in existing theory can often provide valuable clues.

The challenge is to extricate real results from mere artefacts of one grammatical theory or another and to *reconstitute linguistics on hard-science foundations*.

7. How is hard-science linguistics related to the rest of science?

Hard-science linguistics studies real people and their communicatively relevant surroundings from the point of view of how they communicate. Thus hard-science linguistics is not only cognate with the other sciences in its criteria and assumptions, it joins the family of sciences in studying aspects of the real physical world.

As is well known, science is organized in terms of a hierarchy of levels from physics up through chemistry to the biological sciences. There are relations between the levels. Linus Pauling showed how the chemical bond can be understood at the lower level of molecular physics and Watson and Crick showed how the genetic properties of people can be understood in terms of the lower level of biochemistry.

Hard-science linguistics shows how properties of groups of people at the social level are related to properties of persons at the lower individual level. It also has in its foundations the conceptual structure for studying how the linguistic properties of persons can be understood in terms of lower-level biological properties. Thus a hard-science linguistics builds at its own level in the hierarchy of the sciences and can rest solidly on the levels of science lower down in the hierarchy.

The properties of systems in hard-science linguistics represent real properties of real people related to how they communicate. They do not rest on any arbitrary assumptions beyond the standard assumptions of all science. They represent aspects of a reality existing in nature prior to our investigations. They represent aspects of the real physical world that can be biologically inherited, selected for, and subject to the normal processes of biological evolution.

Language and grammar, on the other hand, are theories of theories in the logical domain representing imaginary objects introduced by assumption. Being fictions, they are not the sorts of things that could be innate. To argue otherwise is to confuse fiction with reality, to confuse the logical domain and the physical, to confuse philosophy with science. One cannot have a science that invents its own objects of study and introduces them by assumption.

For too long modern linguistics has been dominated by the concerns of philosophy and grammar, received in a long tradition of inspired speculation from ancient times but walling it off from science. The methods of philosophy and grammar are not appropriate for modern scientific investigations in linguistics or anywhere else. Linguistics needs to be reconstituted as a hard science.

Note

This paper was presented August 31, 2000 at the 33rd Annual Meeting of Societas Linguistica Europaea (SLE) in Poznań, Poland and on September 4, 2000 at the special session 'Alternatives to Chomsky: A New Paradigm for Language Studies for a New Millennium', preceding the 16th Annual Meeting of the Language Origins Society, Rutgers University, New Brunswick, New Jersey.

References

Yngve, Victor H. (1986), *Linguistics as a Science*. Bloomington and Indianapolis: Indiana University Press.

Yngve, Victor H. (1996), *From Grammar to Science: New Foundations for General Linguistics*. Amsterdam/Philadelphia: John Benjamins.

Chapter 4

Rules of Order

Victor H. Yngve

In this paper are presented some example analyzes built on the new foundations for general linguistics (Yngve 1996). The material analyzed is previously published data on the regulation of debate in deliberative assemblies.

1. The criteria of science

Science starts with doubt. But in science there are external objective criteria for resolving scientific doubt. The standard criteria of science for deciding what to believe have been developed over the last four centuries. They are employed everywhere in the natural sciences and can be used by anyone in deciding what to believe about the world. As a scientist confronted by a new linguistic theory or piece of linguistic analysis, my question always is, 'Why should I believe this?'. In most cases no good scientific reason is provided, so I don't believe it.

Professional skepticism must of course extend to the scientist's own work. Here, intellectual honesty requires a scientist to bring to bear these same external criteria to keep from publishing nonsense.

But, unfortunately, linguists trying to build a scientific linguistics have not been able to apply these criteria in judging their theories and analyzes. Although it is real physical people who speak and understand, language has, from ancient times, been conceived as in the logical domain, not the physical. Theories of language and grammar are not theories of the real world and are incapable of making predictions about the real world. Thus they cannot be tested against the real world and the standard criteria of science cannot properly be applied. They are not scientific theories at all.

Although this distressing state of affairs was suspected by Saussure and well understood by Bloomfield, we have tended to ignore it pending possible developments in the distant future. That future is now upon us. We need no longer struggle with the impossible task of trying to build a true science on a foundation of ancient grammatical lore and promulgating scientific nonsense. It is now actually possible to strive for scientific integrity in linguistics all the way from top to bottom. The new foundations for general linguistics focus on the real physical world where the standard criteria of science can be applied. The standard criteria of science, now available to all linguists for deciding what to believe in their discipline, are as follows:

The standard criterion of acceptance of hypotheses when doubts arise is the ability of their predictions to pass tests against the real world by means of careful observation and experiment.

The standard criterion of acceptance of observational and experimental results is their reproducibility when questioned.

2. The new foundations

For several decades I have been working to lay proper scientifically sound foundations for linguistics and have presented progress reports over the years and in Yngve (1986). The final results are now available (Yngve 1996). These new foundations move linguistics into the physical domain of people and sound waves. They allow linguists to abide by the standard criteria of acceptance of science and to admit no assumptions other than the four standard assumptions of all science as known particularly in the physical and biological sciences. These are:

(1) that there is a real world out there,
(2) that it is coherent so we can find out something about it,
(3) that we can reason from true premises to true conclusions,
(4) that from observed effects we can infer real-world causes.

At the 1997 LACUS meeting and in an internet posting I laid out 17 advantages of the new scientifically sound foundations over the ancient semiotic-grammatical foundations we have inherited (Yngve 1998). Some linguists have asked for more. They have wanted to see some examples. The purpose of this paper is to respond to the felt need with a tutorial giving example analyzes. For convenient reference, the discussion below has been keyed to the relevant sections in Yngve (1996).

3. The source of data

There is an advantage in using already published data so we can concentrate on analytic issues. Since the new foundations are pragmatic from top to bottom, we chose our examples from obviously pragmatic phenomena.

A convenient source of data is the regulation of debate in deliberative assemblies, otherwise known in the United States as Robert's Rules of Order. We will follow the descriptions in Robert (1990), which goes back 120 years, and the newer Sturgis (1988).

Although these manuals are designed for the general public and can be seen as prescriptive, they actually represent fairly accurately an oral and written tradition going back through the US Senate manual of Thomas Jefferson (Howell 1988; Johnson 1997) to practice in the English parliament at least as early as 1565 (Smith 1583). Smith explains that he is not inventing these rules but merely compiling and setting down what he has observed as accepted practice.

We can take these manuals as compendia of type descriptions. They can be understood as giving information about linkage types and role types. (See §15.4 in Yngve 1996.) In this paper we will select for analysis some of the linkages and role parts that are tokens of the types these manuals give us descriptions of.

4. A meeting of an assembly

The assembly of an organization usually has a membership list and some sort of bylaws that specify when meetings should be held. There will be a call to a meeting and on the appointed day and time some of the members will assemble, meet, and then disperse. We will discuss example analyzes at the linkage level, the role-part level, and the participant level.

4.1. Analysis at the linkage level

Considering the members of the assembly of the organization as constituents in a linkage (§10.6), there will be a linkage property describing the changing arrangement of the members as some of them assemble for a meeting at the appointed time and place and take their seats. This changeable property of the assembly linkage can be described in terms of an arrangement (§14.2). Other properties of the linkage described in terms of an arrangement would be concerned with the opinions of the members and any factions or subgroups of the members. There would be a linkage property of common agreement on the purpose of the organization (Sturgis 1988:2) and common agreement to abide by the rules of order and the rules of the organization (Sturgis 1988: 210–215).

There is some flexibility in defining linkages so as to simplify analysis. It will simplify matters if we define a linkage as including just the members that have assembled for a meeting and call it [meeting] (we use square brackets to enclose the names of systems of all kinds). Robert (1990:24) has this to say about opening a meeting:

(1) When the time of a meeting has arrived, the presiding officer opens it, after he has determined that a quorum is present, by *calling the meeting to order*. He takes the chair (that is, occupies the presiding officer's station in the hall), waits or signals for quiet, and while standing, announces in a clear voice, "The meeting will come to order" or "The meeting will be in order."

Sturgis (1988:109) has:

(2) The presiding officer calls the meeting to order promptly at the scheduled time by rapping with a gavel and announcing: "The meeting will please come to order," or "The Eighty-third Annual Meeting of the House of Delegates of the American Dental Association is now convened."

In view of the above type descriptions we will make a first cut at an analysis of calling a meeting to order. Here we will make use of setting procedures (§13.2):

(3) time x quorum x –quiet x rap :: quiet
　　　　　　　　　? v ? v ? :: –quiet
(4) –open x quiet x call to order :: open
　　　　open x declare adjourned :: –open

Note that *quiet* and *open* here are properties of the [meeting] linkage as a whole. For clarity we write them as < quiet > and < open > (we use angle brackets to enclose the names of properties of systems). Their values at any time can be determined by observing the behavior of the assembled members: whether they are quiet or not and whether communicative behavior associated with the conduct of business is observed to take place or not.

The possibility of an analysis in terms of setting procedures is scientifically justified on the basis of three general laws of communicative behavior: the law of componential partitioning (§11.2), the law of small changes (§12.4), and the law of restricted causation (§12.6). Particular setting procedures are postulated as specific dynamic causal laws of communicative behavior. They are set up on the basis of observational evidence, or, as here, on the basis of type descriptions in the manuals. They are ultimately testable against observational evidence of actual deliberative assemblies.

The analysis in (3) and (4) in terms of setting procedures is incomplete and raises several questions. It could be corrected and elaborated appropriately but there is a better way: the new foundations offer an improved notation for analysis in terms of task procedures, task hierarchies, and other convenient constructs given in Chapters 19 and 20 of Yngve (1996). These can all be represented entirely in terms of setting procedures and are therefore also completely scientifically justified. They allow a clearer graphical representation to which we turn for a second cut at analysis of a deliberative assembly linkage. For this we will draw on additional data from Robert and Sturgis but in the interest of brevity will not cite it explicitly.

The task hierarchy (Figure 4.1) of the [meeting] linkage shows that the <convene> task has three sequential subtasks: <assemble>,

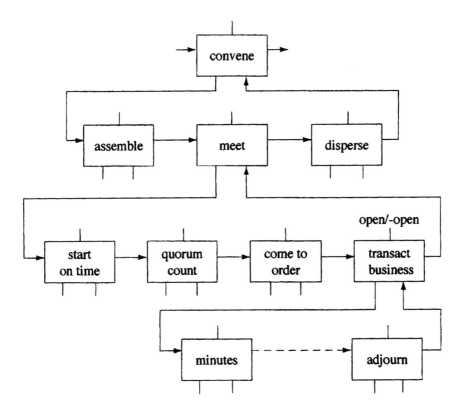

Figure 4.1

<meet>, and <disperse>. The <meet> subtask has further subsubtasks as indicated, and so on. Although a graphical representation of a task hierarchy has the advantage of clarity, we can write it more compactly in a linear notation under development as: <convene> = <assemble> -> <meet> -> <disperse>. This can be read as 'The task <convene> consists of the subtask <assemble> followed by the subtask <meet> followed by the subtask <disperse>'. And we can further write: <meet> = <start on time> -> <quorum count> -> <come to order> -> <transact business> ? <open/-open>. This can be read as 'The task <meet> consists of the subtask <start on time> followed by the subtask <quorum count> followed by the subtask <come to order> followed by the subtask <transact business>, which if executing sets the <open/-open> category to the value <open>'. Note that the <start on time> subtask operates in conjunction with the clock on the wall, a prop, which is a constituent of the meeting assemblage that functions as a prop part in the [meeting] linkage. Note also that the task-active output of the <transact business> task is the <open/-open> category that provides an indication of whether the meeting is <open> or <-open>. As with the other task-active outputs, it can serve as a contextual condition for other procedures.

This box notation and its linear representation is not strictly analogous to phrase structure as it may appear to be here, so be careful. There are additional sorts of boxes given in Chapters 19 and 20 of Yngve 1996 that can be used; it is possible to represent parallel simultaneous tasks that may or may not interact with each other and to represent connectivity that is not hierarchical. The notation represents dynamic structure in a theory of real physical objects rather than static abstractions postulated in the domain of language; and the notation takes into account the dynamically changing properties of real objects, the properties that constitute the changeable context within which communicative behavior takes place and is understood.

But most important, this notation is not postulated *a priori* as all grammatical notations have been. Although it is in general intuitively correct, it is not justified on that basis: all of the features of the notation have been carefully scientifically justified down to bedrock. If desired it can easily be represented in the original linear form without diagrams in terms of setting procedures and control procedures (§19.3) and it can easily be programd on a computer for testing and research purposes (§13.6).

Remember that in the task hierarchy of Figure 4.1 we are analyzing the group and its assemblage as a whole. All the task procedures and properties are parts of the plex structure of the [meeting] linkage. They can all be understood at a lower level, however, as carried out by the presiding officer and other members in terms of the functioning of the constituents of the [meeting] linkage. That requires analysis at the role-part level.

4.2. The presiding officer role part

We now turn to an example partial analysis at the role-part level (§15.2, §15.3). The manuals give evidence of several different role parts. There is the presiding officer, the secretary, possibly other officers, and the other members. Each role part is analyzed separately on the basis of the same evidence used to analyze the [meeting] linkage itself.

We look first at the [presiding officer] role part in connection with the <meet> subtask of <convene> in Figure 4.1.

For the names of role-part tasks we can sometimes use the same names as the corresponding linkage tasks as long as we keep in mind that they are properties of different systems. Thus there can be a role-part task of <transact business> for the [presiding officer] role part as well as a <transact business> task for the [meeting] linkage. It describes the part that the presiding officer plays in the linkage task.

From the above descriptions in the manuals we can analyze the presiding officer <preside> task as in Figure 4.2.

Of note here in the <wait for quiet> subtask is the use of scalar categories (§19.2) <V> for the volume of sound in the hall and the threshold value <L> of loud sound as the presiding officer waits and possibly raps for quiet, and a *V less-than L* control procedure, <VltL> (§19.4), as the presiding officer judges the degree of quiet. We assume here, as do the manuals, knowledge on the part of the presiding officer of the threshold value of loud sound L. This could be determined by experiment.

The <time> and <quorum> tasks would be analyzed similarly in terms of time <T> and member count <N> variables and *greater-than* control procedures (§19.4) that compare them with the time <M> of the meeting and the number of members <Q> constituting a quorum. We assume the [presiding officer] knows these. They would be given in the bylaws of the organization and in the membership roll and available for analysis through the analysis of writing (§17.8).

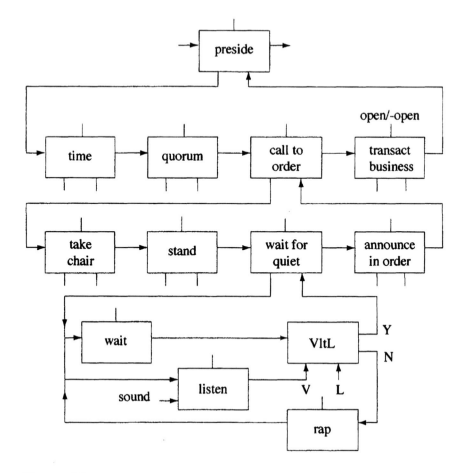

Figure 4.2

4.3. A member role part

We next turn to an example analysis of a member role part. Again, the task hierarchy of the role part parallels in large degree the linkage task hierarchy because it is the working together of the role parts that constitutes the work of the linkage. A partial task hierarchy of a [member] role part is given in Figure 4.3.

Note here that the < time > subtask of the < attend > task is similar to the < time > subtask of the presiding officer < preside > task except that the member will try to be seated a few minutes before the scheduled time of the meeting.

Also note the use of the expectation procedures < expect stand >, < expect rap >, and < expect quiet > (§20.4) for the member

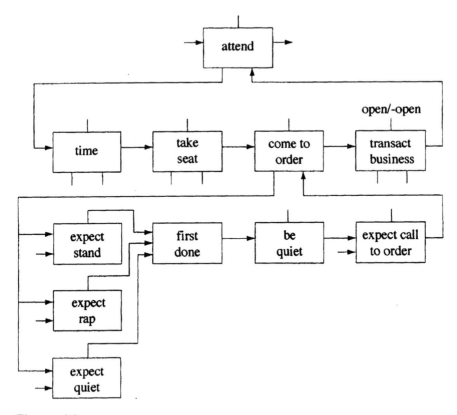

Figure 4.3

expecting the presiding officer to stand or to rap for quiet or for growing quiet in the hall. They execute simultaneously as parallel tasks that trigger the < be quiet > task when the first one is satisfied (§20.11). A tentative linear notation for this is: < come to order > = < expect stand >, < expect rap >, < expect quiet > -> < first done > -> < be quiet > -> < expect call to order >. Here it is noteworthy how expectation procedures provide the context within which something is understood. The presiding officer standing at the podium on some other occasion when not expected in connection with a < come to order > task would not be understood as a signal for quiet and might not even be noticed. Understanding in context is central to analyzes built on the new foundations.

4.4. Analysis at the participant level

We are now ready to note that the quotations (1) and (2) from the manuals provide several alternative wordings for the presiding officer in opening a meeting. We have:

(5) "The meeting will come to order."
(6) "The meeting will be in order."
(7) "The meeting will please come to order."
(8) "The Eighty-third Annual Meeting of the House of Delegates of the American Dental Association is now convened."

The implication is that there may also be other acceptable wordings. Presumably the authors of the manuals had observed a number of meetings and consulted various authorities and are reporting here something of the variation observed in tokens of the linkage types and role types described. We can freely choose one in describing a typical deliberative assembly, but note that a member role part must be prepared to cope with the expected variation.

In each of these wordings it appears that the presiding officer first refers to the meeting and then pronounces it open or convened. But for such an analysis we need to go well beyond the data available just from deliberative assemblies. We need to enter into the realm of general communicative behavior. The way to do this is to move our analysis down to the level of the participants (§10.4).

Participants are the forms that fill the role-part functions (§15.2). The methods of analysis are the same except that their properties are a subset of the properties of a communicating individual and answer to data on similarities and differences of a given person interacting in a number of different groups. We may then be able to accommodate data that would help us understand on the new foundations the anaphora (§7.2, §21.7) of the definite article in (5), (6), and (7), how it is different from that in (8) and why *is now convened* is found as the second subtask in (8) but would probably not be found as the second subtask of (5), (6), or (7). See §7.2, §21.3, §21.4, §21.6.

Note that the participant task hierarchy can be expected to go down through the linguistic levels until the nature of the evidence changes and we enter into biology and physics. In this way we can seamlessly connect through a consistent and scientifically justified body of linguistic theory the social realm of how people "unite in organizations for the achievement of common aims" (Sturgis 1988:2) to the underlying realm of the physical and biological sciences (§18.6).

5. Conclusion

There is now within reach, and it is well worth striving for, a linguistics that accepts only the minimum standard assumptions of all science and uses only the standard criteria of science in deciding what to believe. Such a linguistics fulfills its natural role of standing as a true science between the social sciences and the biological and physical sciences, connecting them reductively, and finally bringing to reality the unity of knowledge that has long been an unrealized dream.

There has been a lot of talk of late about 'consilience' between the social sciences and the lower-level natural sciences, but precious little in the way of details of how consilience can actually be realized. I hope I have convinced you that the key to consilience is to move everything into the physical domain, the domain of standard science, and that linguistics on the new foundations holds that key.

I hope I have shown that research on the new foundations is reasonably straightforward and that you could carry this analysis further to cover more of the copious data available in the manuals.

I hope I have shown that you could thereby help develop the techniques that will be useful in building a new linguistics that is completely scientifically justified, a human linguistics that is pragmatic all the way down from social phenomena to the level formerly covered by phonology and on to physiology. There is much that needs to be done.

Note

This is a revised and updated version of a paper presented at the LACUS Forum XXV at Claremont Graduate University, California, July 28–August 1, 1998, and subsequently available on the internet and as Memorandum 3 to people interested in the new foundations for general linguistics.

References

Howell, Wilbur Samuel (1988), *The Papers of Thomas Jefferson, Second Series: Jefferson's Parliamentary Writings: "Parliamentary Pocket-Book" and A Manual of Parliamentary Practice*. Princeton: Princeton University Press.

Johnson, Charles W. (1997), *Constitution, Jefferson's Manual, and Rules of the House of Representatives of the United States, One Hundred Fifth Congress*. Washington: US Government Printing Office. [House Document No. 104–272]

Robert, Henry M. (1990), *The Scott Foresman Robert's Rules of Order Newly Revised, a new and enl. ed.* by Sara Corbin Robert, *with the assistance of Henry M. Robert III, William J. Evans*. N.p.: Scott Foresman.

Smith (or Smyth), Thomas (1583), *De Republica Anglorum: The manner of Gouernement or policie of the Realme of England, compiled by the Honorable man Thomas Smyth, Doctor of the ciuil lawes, Knight, and principall Secretarie unto the two most worthie Princes, King Edward the sixt, and Queene Elizabeth.* London: Printed by Henrie Midleton for Gregorie Seton. [Facsimile reprint edition 1970, Menston, England: The Scholar Press Limited.]

Sturgis, Alice (1988), *The Standard Code of Parliamentary Procedure* (3rd edn, new and revised). New York: McGraw-Hill.

Yngve, Victor H. (1986), *Linguistics as a Science.* Bloomington and Indianapolis: Indiana University Press.

Yngve, Victor H. (1996), *From Grammar to Science: New Foundations for General Linguistics.* Amsterdam/Philadelphia: John Benjamins.

Yngve, Victor H. (1998), 'Two foundations for linguistics briefly compared', in Sheila Embleton, *LACUS Forum XXIV.* Chapel Hill, NC: The Linguistic Association of Canada and the United States, pp. 471–477.

PART II

RECONSTITUTING PHONETICS-PHONOLOGY

Chapter 5

Towards a Physical Definition of the Vowel Systems of Languages

Laura L. Koenig

My purpose in this chapter is to discuss a set of observations suggesting that what are sometimes superficially described as 'the same' vowels may differ when produced by speakers of different languages. The studies reviewed here straddle the traditional boundary between phonetics and phonology in that they investigate how specifics of production (phonetics) vary depending on the speaker's language, in particular the set of sound contrasts relevant in that language (phonology). Although I find some of the results of this work compelling, I believe that the conceptual framework underlying many of the research questions is misguided. Ultimately, I will argue that cross-linguistic speech research questions can only be formulated in physical terms, based on speakers' articulatory behavior and its acoustic consequences, and on the associated behavior of listeners. Phonological descriptions that assume sound categories as abstract entities selected by languages and utilized by speakers lend themselves to misunderstanding and inappropriate descriptions of human linguistic behavior. Yngve's (1996) framework, which begins with a physical description of actions or sounds, and from this proposes speaker and listener properties defined within the context of communicative interaction, offers a promising alternative perspective.

1. Physical description of vowels

The following is a brief tutorial on the typical ways in which vowels have been described in articulatory and acoustic terms to aid those without phonetic training in understanding the work outlined below.

As in any review, this description is simplified, and omits many details not critical for present purposes. More extensive discussions of vowel description can be found in introductory phonetics texts (e.g. Ladefoged 1993; MacKay 1987). The relationships between vowel articulation and acoustics have been explored by many researchers over the years, including Chiba and Kajiyama (1941), Fant (1960), Gay, Boé, and Perrier (1992), Lindblom and Sundberg (1971), and Stevens and House (1961).

Vowels can be defined simply as linguistic sounds produced with a relatively open vocal tract and little impedance to airflow. Three articulatory parameters that differentiate vowels in many languages of the world are (a) the degree of opening of the jaw-tongue complex; (b) the relative position of the tongue mass in the supralaryngeal vocal tract; and (c) the configuration of the lips. The first dimension is usually referred to as vowel height: high vowels have relatively high jaw-tongue positions, whereas low vowels are more open. Raising the tongue from the floor of the mouth also tends to draw the root of the tongue forward and expand the pharyngeal cavity, so some authors speak in terms of tongue root position or pharyngeal width (e.g. Lindau 1979). The second dimension has to do with whether the bulk of the tongue is shifted towards the alveopalatal region (front vowels) or the velar/uvular region (back vowels). Lip configurations usually include rounded or unrounded/spread.

Much of the variation in these three articulatory parameters is reflected acoustically in the first and second resonant (or formant) frequencies of the vocal tract (F1 and F2, respectively). Perceptual experiments have indicated that relative F1 and F2 differences in speakers' productions can account for a large portion of listeners' labeling behavior for vowels (see Hillenbrand and Gayvert 1993; Peterson and Barney 1952), although other acoustic cues, including durational information, formant change over time, and phonetic context may also play significant roles in vowel perception (see Lindblom and Studdert-Kennedy 1967; Nearey 1989; Strange, Jenkins, and Johnson 1983). The following summary gives the basic relationships between articulatory posture and formant frequencies.

High jaw-tongue positions and expanded pharyngeal cavities are associated with low F1's; low jaw-tongue positions and constricted pharyngeal cavities are associated with high F1's.

Front vowels, with anterior tongue constrictions, are associated with high F2's, whereas back vowels are associated with low F2's.

Lip rounding has the effect of lowering all formants, but its effects are often quite pronounced for F2, and there is some evidence to suggest that speakers can trade off lip rounding and tongue backing to achieve a lower F2 (Perkell, Svirsky, Matthies, and Jordan 1991). This is one example of a well-known indeterminacy in working back to articulation from an acoustic signal: a given acoustic pattern may be associated with different underlying articulations (cf. also Stevens and House 1955). Articulatory measurements, while more invasive and labor-intensive, thus provide a valuable complement to acoustic data.

Another complication in dealing with the acoustics of vowels (indeed, speech in general) is that the actual frequencies associated with an articulatory configuration (or set of vocal tract cavity sizes) will vary inversely with overall vocal tract size. In general, formant frequencies are lowest in men, intermediate in women, and highest in children, reflecting that vocal tract sizes are typically largest in men and smallest in children. Thus, formant frequency ranges, and hence vowel perception, are scaled as a function of vocal tract size, and determining whether a given formant frequency is high or low depends on the system in question, that is, the anatomy of the actual speaker.

Because acoustic signals can be obtained simply and non-invasively, most researchers undertaking quantitative study of vowels have relied on formant frequency measurements. To restrict formant frequency variation, many researchers have used exclusively adult male subjects. A more limited set of studies has included both male and female subjects, and a few have explored vowel articulation directly using imaging techniques or articulatory tracking.

2. History

The idea that languages differ in their 'phonetic substance' is nothing new. Perhaps the most fundamental example of this insight is the cardinal vowel system, which still forms the basis of vowel transcription using the International Phonetic Alphabet (IPA). Developed by Daniel Jones (see Jones 1956), the cardinal vowels were intended to define a language-independent set of articulatory reference points that phoneticians could use in describing the vowels of individual languages. Thus, one might use the [i] transcription for several languages, but the actual vowel productions represented by the transcription would be closer in some languages than others to the articulatory extreme represented by cardinal [i]. A phonetician trained in the cardinal vowel system should thus be well-equipped to apprehend and describe language-specific phonetic patterns.

Implicit in this enterprise is the realization that transcriptional labels represent a family of productions and acoustic characteristics whose precise details may not be identical across languages.

Pierre Delattre carried out pioneering cross-linguistic research using both acoustic and articulatory data. A multilingual speaker, foreign-language teacher, and perceptive impressionistic phonetician, Delattre was engaged in early studies using the sound spectrograph and pattern playback at Haskins Laboratories, and was thus uniquely equipped to carry out instrumental enquiries into the details of language-specific patterns. The work most relevant to the present discussion was an investigation of how vowels in four languages (English, French, German, and Spanish) vary depending on whether the vowel is stressed or not (Delattre 1969). The stress factor was manipulated by selecting pairs of related words in which the vowel of interest appeared in both stressed and unstressed contexts (e.g., the vowel in the second syllable of adápting vs. adaptátion). Five male speakers were recorded for each language, and all data were analyzed in terms of the F1-F2 values at the most open point in the vowel. X-ray images were also obtained from a subset of speakers.

In brief, Delattre observed that the effects of stress on a vowel varied depending on the language in question. For example, in English, unstressed vowel productions showed a range of F2 values 16 per cent smaller than the stressed vowels (hence, front-back differentiation of vowels was reduced). For the other three languages, F2 ranges were only reduced by 5–7 per cent. The X-ray data suggested that variation in vowels as a function of stress also had distinct articulatory underpinnings in the different languages. Whereas an English speaker showed considerable tongue centralization and reduction of lip rounding for unstressed [o u], a French speaker showed reduction of lip rounding but little change in tongue position. In short, the articulatory configurations and acoustic patterns associated with a vowel category, which can, in turn, be associated with a phonetic transcription, depended on the speaker's language history. A French [u] and an English [u], although they share some physical similarities, are not identical vowels, as a transcriptional representation would suggest.

In 1972, Liljencrants and Lindblom sought to explain certain universal patterns of vowel systems by appealing to a principle of perceptual contrast. The authors reasoned that, within a language community, listeners would tend to have more success differentiating between vowels that were more acoustically different rather than those that were less so. Speakers, to avoid being misunderstood, would accordingly adopt articulatory patterns that maximized acoustic contrast (i.e., dispersion within perceptual vowel space). Lindblom (1986) subsequently drew on data from the Stanford Project on Language Universals Archive to refine a model of perceptual contrast in vowels. Crothers (1978) had provided a phonological analysis of the Stanford data, representing each vowel in a language as the transcriptional value of the most common phonetic realization, and then comparing the vowel qualities (transcriptions) found in languages with various numbers of contrasts. Crothers found that, where three vowels were differentiated within a language, the most common inventory was [i ɑ u], the three vowels that form the extremes of F1-F2 space. As more distinctions were made, the additional vowel qualities tended to be predictable; in a five-vowel system, for example, mid front and back vowels such as [e] or [o] were usually found in addition to [i ɑ u]. Lindblom (1986) attempted to generate the Crothers data using an algorithm that began with the frequency spectrum of a vowel, adjusted for features of the human auditory system (differences in hearing threshold as a function of frequency, upward spread of masking, and transformation to the sone scale of loudness), and maximized the resulting perceptual dispersion. This effort was somewhat more successful than Lindblom and Liljencrants at predicting vowel qualities given a certain number of contrasts, but some systematic discrepancies remained (in particular, non-peripheral vowels were predicted more often than observed). Moreover, even for a given inventory size, the Crothers data indicated that the actual phonetic quality of the vowels could vary to some extent; thus, a five-vowel system might include the vowels [ɛ] and [ɔ] rather than [e] and [o]. Lindblom conceded that vowel differentiation in language may be driven by a principle of sufficient, rather than maximal, perceptual contrast. In other words, the number of vowel contrasts made in a language may explain some aspects of speakers' vowel productions for that language, but unexplained language-specific patterns remained.

The general idea that the acoustic characteristics of vowels can be predicted based on the system of vowel contrasts in a language has continued to drive cross-linguistic work. Keating and Huffman (1984), in a study of Japanese, focused on acoustic variability over repeated productions of a vowel. Speakers of Japanese differentiate among five vowel sounds, typically transcribed as [i e ɑ o ɯ]. Keating and Huffman predicted that [i] and [e] would show relatively little variation in F2, because they lie close together in acoustic space, whereas the back unrounded vowel [ɯ] and the low vowel [ɑ], which do not have close acoustic neighbors, would vary more. Seven speakers of Tokyo Japanese read passages and produced words in citation form. Results provided partial support in that F1 variation was considerable in [ɑ] productions, and F2 variation was extensive for [ɯ]. A principle of contrast did not entirely explain the data, however, because the acoustic spaces for contrastive vowels showed some overlap of formant values (suggesting that contrasts were not always maintained).

Perhaps the strongest evidence for cross-language differences in vowel production comes from studies that explicitly compare vowels produced by speakers of different languages under controlled conditions. A pilot study by Manuel and Krakow (1984) compared formant frequencies in two men, one speaker of Swahili and one of English. In Swahili, five vowels are contrasted, whereas in English 11–12 monophthongal vowels are typically differentiated, depending on dialect. (Some speakers of English, for example, do not differentiate between the words cot and caught, whereas for other speakers these words have distinct pronunciations, i.e., different vowels). Manuel and Krakow hypothesized that the English speaker, with more vowel distinctions to make, would show relatively less variability for a given vowel sound than the Swahili speaker. The specific type of variability under investigation was coarticulation, that is, variations in the pronunciation of a sound that arise as a function of neighboring sounds in the word or syllable. The speakers read nonsense two-syllable words constructed to yield all possible combinations of the vowels [i e ɑ o u] in the two syllables, and formant frequency measurements were carried out to determine whether the speaker of Swahili showed greater acoustic variation in his vowels as the neighboring vowel changed. Results indicated significant vowel context effects on both F1 and F2 in the Swahili speaker's productions, but only on F2 for the English speaker. The authors tentatively concluded that speakers of languages with fewer vowels may show more extensive coarticulatory effects, and that, in general, production details for speech sounds are constrained by the system of contrasts relevant for the language in question.

Manuel (1990) followed up on this idea with a more extensive study of three African languages: Shona and Ndebele, with five vowel contrasts, and Sotho, with seven vowels. Three men were recorded for each language. Analysis focused on how the mid-to-low unrounded vowels [ɑ e] varied depending on whether the following vowel was rounded ([u]) or not ([i]). A complex pattern of results emerged. For [ɑ], statistically significant F2 context effects were found at vowel midpoints and offsets for both Ndebele and Shona, but the formant frequency variation was more extreme in Ndebele. The Sotho speakers had significant F2 effects at vowel endpoints, but not midpoints, and the frequency differences (in Hertz) were smaller than in the other two languages. The results for F1 did not clearly differentiate languages, however. Further, no language showed much variation in [e] as a function of context, and there were no clear language differences. To a limited extent, then, Manuel's results did support the premise that the vowel inventory of a language may be related to the amount of coarticulatory influence speakers show during vowel production. At the same time, the differences between Ndebele and Shona were at odds with the strong hypothesis that vowel inventory size alone can predict coarticulatory extent as measured by formant frequencies.

The studies discussed thus far suggest that one way in which vowels may differ across languages is in the degree of variability, including coarticulatory variation induced by surrounding speech sounds or movements. Another body of work suggests, in contrast, that speakers across languages may differ in the overall range of articulatory configurations they use. For example, an English speaker, who needs to differentiate a large number of vowels, may utilize more extreme articulations for some vowels, and hence produce a wider range of formant frequencies, than a speaker of a language in which fewer vowel distinctions are required. Jongman, Fourakis, and Sereno (1989) measured formant frequencies of Greek (a five-vowel system) and German (a 14-vowel system). Four speakers of Greek and three speakers of German were recorded saying real words that included all the distinctive vowels of their language, with neighboring sounds kept similar to reduce coarticulatory effects. Results indicated that the Greek speakers produced a narrower range of formant frequency values in both F1 and F2 than the speakers of German. Bradlow (1995) similarly compared formant frequencies of vowels produced by speakers of English and Spanish (a five-vowel system). The Greek data from Jongman *et al.* were used as another example of a five-vowel language. Results showed that the overall formant frequency ranges, in Hertz, were 13 per cent larger for English speakers than Spanish, and 17 per cent larger than Greek. Formant frequency standard deviations of individual vowels did not differ between English and Spanish. Coefficients of variation (a relative measure, computed as the standard deviation divided by the mean value) did approach significance for F1, however, with more relative variability in Spanish than English. Bradlow also found that F2 values for English tended to be higher overall than in Spanish, suggesting that the English speakers were, in general, using more anterior tongue positions. The latter finding, that speakers of a language may adopt a characteristic vocal tract posture or setting, has been termed a language-specific setting or base of articulation (see Laver 1980).

Flege (1989) asked whether within-category variability or the overall size of vowel space would best account for language-related vowel differences in the speech of bilingual English-Spanish speakers. The subjects, Spanish-dominant immigrants to the USA, were recorded under normal speaking conditions and in a bite-block experiment, in which speakers' jaws were fixed in a slightly open position. Flege hypothesized that, if speaking English required greater constraint on the range of tongue postures (or formant frequencies) so as to maintain necessary sound distinctions, subjects might compensate more effectively for the bite block when speaking English than Spanish. The speech production measure was the distance between the tongue and the hard palate, with tongue position tracked by means of sensors on the tongue. Results indicated that the highest vowels, [i] and [u], were produced with smaller tongue-palate distances in English than in Spanish. Standard deviations of sensor positions did not differ between English and Spanish. Significant differences were not seen for the normal vs. the bite-block condition. Finally, average tongue position, calculated over all sensors, did not differ between the two languages, but Flege noted that the average tongue contour (obtained by fitting a polynomial to the four sensors) was somewhat more convex for English. Again, then, some language differences were found, but the pattern of results was more complex than what would have been predicted simply on the basis of phonetic inventory size.

Recently, a colleague and I have undertaken a comparison of formant frequencies in vowels produced by monolingual speakers of Greek and English. This work is in its early stages, and presently only one male and one female speaker of each language have been analyzed fully. Our pilot results (Okalidou and Koenig 1999), however, seem to support the findings of Jongman *et al.* (1989) and Bradlow (1995) in that the English speakers produced a wider range of formant frequencies than the Greek speakers, suggesting that more extreme articulatory postures may be used when speakers need to differentiate a larger number of vowel sounds in their native language.

The study of acoustic and articulatory differences among languages is in its infancy. The preliminary hypotheses of some authors have been partially supported, but much more data from more languages needs to be collected to refine these hypotheses. For those languages that have been investigated, only a handful of speakers have been recorded, and only a limited range of contextual variation has been explored. The available data do, however, appear to indicate that 'the same' vowel, produced by speakers of different languages, may differ in several respects, including the range of token-to-token variability, extent of contextual effects, extremity of articulatory postures or formant frequencies, and base of articulation. Some of these differences may be related to the number of vowel contrasts a speaker needs to maintain in order to be understood in his or her speech community, but other findings currently lack a general explanatory theory.

3. Critique

The basic logic of the studies reviewed above has been to start with the system of vowel contrasts in a language, and then to correlate acoustic or articulatory features of actual (phonetic) vowel productions with aspects of the phonological system. The data tend to support the very general hypothesis that vowel categories have language-specific acoustic and/or articulatory patterns. Thus, although we may use the IPA symbol [i] when transcribing English as well as Greek, it is not really accurate to say that English and Greek share 'the vowel [i]'.

This discussion begs the question, however, of what one means by the vowel [i] (or any other vowel). On what basis would one ever suggest that English and Greek share a vowel? Such a view is promoted by transcriptional representations of speech which provide a finite set of symbols for vocal tract configurations and sound patterns from which languages are assumed to select. At the same time, traditional phonemic analyzes of speech (e.g. Bloomfield 1933; Swadesh 1934) argued that a sound category (phoneme) can only be defined within a specific language, i.e., in the context of a specific set of sound contrasts maintained among a set of speakers and listeners involved in regular communicative exchange. According to this view, an IPA representation is a shorthand notation for a class of sounds that speakers of a language produce under certain circumstances, and to which listeners respond in a particular way. The data presented above suggest that one insight of traditional phonemic analysis was essentially correct: sound categorization within a language can really only be defined for a specific linguistic community, that is, a particular group of communicating individuals.

Explicitly formulating the issue this way, *viz.*, in terms of the communicative participants, offers straightforward explanations for phenomena in speech perception as well as production. For example, studies of infants' responses to speech have documented numerous instances of perceptual attunement to the sound system of the ambient language, including loss of response to sound differences that are irrelevant in the infant's speech community (e.g. Best 1992; Best, McRoberts, and Sithole 1988; Burnham 1986; Jusczyk 1993; Werker 1989). Refinement of the details of speech sound categorization may persist into childhood (see Bernstein 1983; Nittrouer 1992; Nittrouer and Studdert-Kennedy 1987; Ohde 1994; Ohde and Haley 1997; Zlatin and Koenigsknecht 1975). Although some aspects of speech perception abilities may well be innate (see, e.g., Grieser and Kuhl 1989), any discussion of perceptual attunement to the surrounding language must begin with a description of the physical signals the infant receives, and proceed to describe how the infant responds to those signals.

When category formation is conceived of as being an active process of establishing behavioral responses to physical signals, it follows that we should expect children brought up in different language communities to develop different response criteria for specific acoustic patterns. Language-specific patterns of speech discrimination and labeling behavior in adults also follow as a direct consequence. Decades of cross-linguistic work on speech perception have established that some details of listener response depend on his or her language background (e.g. Abramson and Lisker 1970; Flege and Eefting 1986; Lisker and Abramson 1970; Miyawaki, Strange, Verbrugge, Liberman, Jenkins, and Fujimura 1975; Polka 1991; Schmidt 1996; Sekiyama and Tohkura 1991; Terbeek 1977), for both vowel and consonant distinctions. If we recognize that Spanish speakers and English speakers have developed linguistic-phonetic properties appropriate to their language communities, it is immediately clear why a native English speaker differentiates easily between the words beet and bit, whereas a native Spanish speaker might protest that these words sound the same.

The experience of teaching introductory phonetics courses to a linguistically diverse student population has provided me with many examples of the conceptual quandries one encounters by adopting language-universal notions of sound categories as a starting point for discussion. One particularly memorable incident for me involved a Jamaican student who, when faced with the IPA representations for the vowels of 'Standard American English' (SAE) and a sample list of words in which such vowels typically occur, asked (quite appropriately) why her productions of those words seemed to involve a completely different set of sounds – indeed, hardly one item of our word list would have included the same transcriptional symbol for her speech as what I had presented for SAE. Answering such a question requires that the definition of 'a vowel of a language' be utterly reworded and reconceptualized as being a set of sounds that a certain set of speakers produces to yield a particular kind of response (or understanding) in their listeners. The focus of emphasis shifts, rightly, to the speakers and listeners involved in communicative exchange. With this kind of definition, there is little reason to expect that the physical production and acoustic structure of sounds be constant across dialects of English, or across languages, except as may occur because all humans share essentially the same sound-producing and sound-perceiving mechanisms. What is constant is simply that communication is possible and largely error-free within a single speech community; across communities, misunderstandings may occur. With this redefinition, we stop thinking about a set of 'universal' vowels (or rather, vowel symbols) and concentrate instead on the human beings who produce and interpret these sounds.

I do not give this example in order to argue that phonetic transcription is a useless tool. I do, however, find it illustrative of the kinds of difficulties encountered when one takes too seriously the notion that linguistic interchange involves a set of objects or entities that are defined independently of actual speakers and listeners. For purposes of an introductory course in which the students share a considerable amount of linguistic knowledge (or have shared linguistic-phonetic properties), there is probably some utility in presenting a set of examples and their simplified transcriptional representations for a dialect all or most students in the class may be expected to share. But any real understanding of phonetics as a linguistic pursuit must acknowledge that the reality is not a set of predetermined categories, as defined by the International Phonetic Association or anyone else, but rather classes of behaviors that occur in the context of human communication. The categorization of these classes of behaviors into vowel qualities that can be represented transcriptionally is quite secondary to the inquiry.

One could, of course, argue that this conceptual leap is properly the stuff of an introduction to phonetics, and that anyone working in the field of speech understands this. The work reviewed above suggests that this may not be as true as one might hope, however. The formulation of questions in the cross-language vowel research implies that a set of vowel categories is assumed for human language in general, and the burden of proof is on the researcher to establish that these categories are manifested in phonetically different ways across languages. I believe that this is a backwards way of thinking about the issue. Rather than assuming linguistic objects (represented by phonemic, transcriptional notation) *a priori* and determining their physical realizations, we should first be assessing the physical signals produced by speakers of a specific language, and observe how listeners in that language community respond to the physical variations in these productions. Despite considerable evidence for language-specific sound patterns, and some compelling arguments from speech researchers to build phonetic science up from speech signals (or movements) rather than assuming phonological categories (e.g. Liljencrants and Lindblom 1972), traditional notions of linguistic objects have generally persisted within phonology, and are borrowed into phonetic research when researchers attempt to deal with the issue of language-specific sound systems. At present, making the leap across the traditional phonetics-phonology divide typically involves a drastic change in the nature of the phenomena under investigation. It is certainly true that some phonologists over the years have attempted to incorporate aspects of physical speakers into their phonological descriptions. Theories of feature geometry (e.g. Broe 1992; Clements 1985; Sagey 1986) essentially acknowledge that speech is produced with a vocal tract that has a variety of coupled components, and articulatory phonology (Browman and Goldstein 1992) proposes that speakers' articulatory activities form the basis of phonological contrasts. Nevertheless, the field of phonology still remains largely a study of abstractly defined units, schematized as sound types which occur across languages. Only at low, peripheral levels are these types 'converted' into the physical signals that serve as the communicative channel between participants. In this kind of conceptualization, the details of language-specific sound patterns revealed by cross-language work are difficult to predict or explain.

I do not believe that the difficulty lies in simply explicating the details of such a conversion; speech researchers are quite accustomed to dealing with continuous scales upon which individual speaker-listeners impose some kind of categorization. Rather, I believe that there is a larger problem, *viz.*, having any notion of linguistic sounds as a set of abstract objects that can be selected by languages or speakers of a language. Instead of a process of selection, we ought to be able to say, simply (or not so simply), that human linguistic communication involves making interpretations of physical signals, and that those intepretations are made by listeners in accord with habits they have learned by growing up as speaker-listeners of their particular language. If we subsequently find that speakers' productions or listeners' interpretations and categorizations share some similarities across languages, that may tell us something interesting about limitations of the human vocal tract or auditory-perceptual system. Such an alternative conception, where we begin with physical signals and listeners' responses to them, and work back to linguistic theory from there, is essentially the perspective that Yngve's work embodies.

4. An alternative formulation

Let us outline briefly how this research enterprise might be reformulated. A phonetician interested in studying Greek and English might begin by noting that a Greek speaker utters a sound (or combination of sounds) to communicate something about a flat piece of bread. An IPA transcription [pitə] or even the Greek spelling πίττα might yield some information about the vocal tract activities the speaker uses and his/her categorization of those actions. Alternatively, the phonetician might simply observe that the speaker begins with a bilabial closure; initiates vocal-fold vibration on release of the closure; moves into a vocal tract configuration in which the jaw is fairly high, the tongue is bunched toward the hard palate, and the lips are spread; produces a tongue-tip closure; and then ends with a fairly open vocal tract position. The latter description has the advantage of making no assumptions that the specific vocal-tract activities and corresponding acoustic output of a Greek speaker are the same as those used by an English speaker requesting a similar piece of flat bread at a Middle Eastern restaurant. The phonetician might go on to have the speaker repeat how s/he would request such a piece of bread. A native Greek listener could then be recruited to listen to this set of productions and verify that s/he would respond by supplying the bread and not some other item, indicating that these vocal productions yielded a consistent effect in the listener. The phonetician could then go about making systematic measurements of the speaker's vocal tract activities and/or the corresponding acoustic record. The results of such an investigation would yield a range of activities and/or acoustic patterns that constitute a functionally equivalent class in Greek – what, in traditional terms, we would call the word pita and the Greek vowel /i/.

The researcher might then carry out a study asking an English speaker how s/he would communicate something about a kind of red root vegetable, and obtain a set of productions that traditionally we would call repetitions of the word beet. Comparison of the Greek and English speakers' productions might indicate certain articulatory or acoustic similarities. Such a comparison would make no assumptions that English and Greek both use a vowel [i]; it might, however, suggest that Greek and English speakers hear certain similarities in each others' languages. We might further suspect that the English speaker would use his set of beet vowels to speak about pita bread, regardless of whether he were speaking to an English or a Greek speaker. A Greek speaker, listening to the English speaker say pita, might note that the English speaker produced a similar set of movements/sounds to that of a Greek speaker, but further recognize that the English speaker's activities don't exactly match those of a native Greek speaker. In other words, the English speaker might speak Greek with an English accent. On the other hand, if an English listener, hearing a Greek speaker, thinks that some of the Greek words include vowels more similar to those in the word bit than the word beet, that tells us that the linguistic-phonetic properties of the English listener differ from those of the Greek listener.

At face value, the above formulation may appear to be little more than a rewording of the existing cross-language work. There is one very important difference, however: at no point do we assume – are we even led to assume – that there exists a generic linguistic object [i] which is used by speakers of English and Greek. Given that linguists have historically used the same symbol in transcriptions of English and Greek, we may expect to find certain physical similarities between an English speaker's production of beet and the Greek speaker's production of pita, but the extent and nature of those similarities remain empirical questions. To adopt predefined transcriptional categories is effectively to assume similarity (indeed, sameness) across languages rather than treating it as a fundamental question for research.

Although instrumental analyzes of speech have been carried out for many years, only during the past couple of decades has it been possible for an individual speech researcher to contemplate carrying out the analyzes necessary to determine the full acoustic space for the vowels of a language, taking into account contextual variations, for even a few speakers. As such data become more widely available, we will begin to define precisely how vowels differ across languages. I believe that these data will ultimately lead to definitions of individual vowels which are inherently specific to a given speech community. Taking as our starting place the speech signal and listeners' judgments, we have every reason to expect cross-linguistic differences in both speech production and speech perception. At the same time, after a considerable body of data have been amassed on many languages, we may well discover that some characteristics of speech sound categories or categorization occur frequently or universally across languages. These will form the basis of quantitative, empirically-testable human phonetic universals.

Note

This chapter is dedicated to the memory of Karen Landahl of the University of Chicago who first introduced me to the field of phonetics and has always been an inspiration to me.

References

Abramson, A. S. and Lisker, L. (1970), 'Discriminability along the voicing continuum: Cross-language tests', in B. Hála, M. Romportl, and P. Janota, *Proceedings of the 6th International Congress of Phonetic Sciences, Prague 1967*. Prague: Academia Publishing House, Czechoslovak Academy of Sciences, pp. 569–573.

Bernstein, L. E. (1983), 'Perceptual development for labeling words varying in voice onset time and fundamental frequency'. *Journal of Phonetics*, 11, 383–393.

Best, C. T. (1992), 'The emergence of language-specific phonemic influences in infant speech perception', in H. C. Nusbaum and J. Goodman, *The Transition from Speech Sounds to Spoken Words: The Development of Speech Perception*. Cambridge, MA: MIT Press.

Best, C. T., McRoberts, G. W., and Sithole, N. M. (1988), 'Examination of perceptual reorganization for nonnative speech contrasts: Zulu click discrimination by English-speaking adults and infants'. *Journal of Experimental Psychology: Human Perception and Performance*, 14, 345–360.

Bloomfield, L. (1933), *Language*. New York: Holt.

Bradlow, A. R. (1995), 'A comparative acoustic study of English and Spanish vowels'. *Journal of the Acoustical Society of America*, 97, 1916–1924.

Broe, M. (1992), 'An introduction to feature geometry', in G. J. Docherty and R. D. Ladd, *Papers in Laboratory Phonology II: Gesture, Segment, Prosody*. Cambridge: Cambridge University Press, pp. 149–165.

Browman, C. P. and Goldstein, L. M. (1992), 'Articulatory phonology: An overview'. *Phonetica*, 49, 155–180.

Burnham, D. K. (1986), 'Developmental loss of speech perception: Exposure to and experience with a first language'. *Applied Psycholinguistics*, 7, 207–240.

Chiba, T. and Kajiyama, M. (1941), *The Vowel: Its Nature and Structure*. Tokyo: Tokyo-Kaiseikan Publishing Company Ltd.

Clements, G. N. (1985), 'The geometry of phonological features'. *Phonology Yearbook*, 2, 225–252.

Crothers, J. (1978), 'Typology and universals of vowel systems', in J. H. Greenberg, C. A. Ferguson, and E. A. Moravcsik, *Universals of Human Language, Vol. 2: Phonology*. Stanford: Stanford University Press, pp. 93–152.

Delattre, P. C. (1969), 'An acoustic and articulatory study of vowel reduction in four languages'. *International Review of Applied Linguistics*, 7, 295–325.

Fant, G. (1960), *Acoustic Theory of Speech Production*. The Hague: Mouton.

Flege, J. E. (1989), 'Differences in inventory size affect the location but not the precision of tongue positioning of vowel production'. *Language and Speech*, 32, 123–147.

Flege, J. E. and Eefting, W. (1986), 'Linguistic and developmental effects on the production and perception of stop consonants'. *Phonetica*, 43, 155–171.

Gay, T., Boé, L.-J., and Perrier, P. (1992), 'Acoustic and perceptual effects of changes in vocal tract constrictions for vowels'. *Journal of the Acoustical Society of America*, 92, 1301–1309.

Grieser, D. and Kuhl, P. K. (1989), 'Categorization of speech by infants: Support for speech-sound prototypes'. *Developmental Psychology*, 25, 577–588.

Hillenbrand, J. and Gayvert, R. T. (1993), 'Identification of steady-state vowels synthesized from the Peterson and Barney measurements'. *Journal of the Acoustical Society of America*, 94, 668–675.

Jones, Daniel (1956), *An Outline of English Phonetics* (8th edn). Cambridge: W. Heffer & Sons Ltd.

Jongman, A., Fourakis, M., and Sereno, J. A. (1989), 'The acoustic vowel space of Modern Greek and German'. *Language and Speech*, 32, 221–248.

Jusczyk, P. W. (1993), 'From general to language-specific capacities: The WRAPSA model of how speech perception develops'. *Journal of Phonetics*, 21, 3–28.

Keating, P. A. and Huffman, M. K. (1984), 'Vowel variation in Japanese'. *Phonetica*, 41, 191–207.

Ladefoged, P. (1993), *A Course in Phonetics* (3rd edn). Orlando: Harcourt Brace College Publishers.

Laver, J. (1980), *The Phonetic Description of Voice Quality*. Cambridge: Cambridge University Press.

Liljencrants, J. L. and Lindblom, B. (1972), 'Numerical simulation of vowel quality systems: The role of perceptual contrast'. *Language*, 48, 839–862.

Lindau, M. (1979), 'The feature expanded'. *Journal of Phonetics*, 7, 163–176.

Lindblom, B. E. (1986), 'Phonetic universals in vowel systems', in J. J.

Ohala and J. Jaeger, *Experimental Phonology*. New York: Academic Press, pp. 13–44.

Lindblom, B. E. F. and Studdert-Kennedy, M. (1967), 'On the role of formant transitions in vowel recognition'. *Journal of the Acoustical Society of America*, 42, 830–843.

Lindblom, B. E. F. and Sundberg, J. E. F. (1971). 'Acoustical consequences of lip, tongue, jaw, and larynx movement'. *Journal of the Acoustical Society of America*, 50, 1166–1179.

Lisker, L. and Abramson, A. S. (1970), 'The voicing dimension: Some experiments in comparative phonetics', in B. Hála, M. Romportl, and P. Janota, *Proceedings of the 6th International Congress of Phonetic Sciences, Prague 1967*. Prague: Academia Publishing House, Czechoslovak Academy of Sciences, pp. 563–567.

MacKay, I. R. A. (1987), *Phonetics: The Science of Speech Production* (2nd edn). Boston: Allyn and Bacon.

Manuel, S. Y. (1990), 'The role of contrast in limiting vowel-to-vowel coarticulation in different languages'. *Journal of the Acoustical Society of America*, 88, 1286–1298.

Manuel, S. Y. and Krakow, R. A. (1984), 'Universal and language particular aspects of vowel-to-vowel coarticulation'. *Haskins Laboratories Status Reports on Speech Research*, 77/78, 69–78.

Miyawaki, K., Strange, W., Verbrugge, R., Liberman, A. M., Jenkins, J. J., and Fujimura, O. (1975), 'An effect of linguistic experience: The discrimination of [r] and [l] by native speakers of Japanese and English'. *Perception and Psychophysics*, 18, 331–340.

Nearey, T. M. (1989), 'Static, dynamic and relational properties in vowel perception'. *Journal of the Acoustical Society of America*, 85, 2088–2113.

Nittrouer, S. (1992), 'Age-related differences in perceptual effects of formant transitions within syllables and across syllable boundaries'. *Journal of Phonetics*, 20, 351–382.

Nittrouer, S. and Studdert-Kennedy, M. (1987), 'The role of coarticulatory effects in the perception of fricatives by children and adults'. *Journal of Speech and Hearing Research*, 30, 319–329.

Ohde, R. N. (1994), 'The development of the perception of cues to the [m]-[n] distinction in CV syllables'. *Journal of the Acoustical Society of America*, 96, 675–686.

Ohde, R. N. and Haley, K. L. (1997), 'Stop-consonant and vowel perception in 3- and 4-year-old children'. *Journal of the Acoustical Society of America*, 102, 3711–3722.

Okalidou, A. and Koenig, L. L. (1999), 'Patterns of vowel-to-vowel coarticulation in Greek and English', in *Collected Papers from the Joint Meeting "Berlin 99": 137th Regular Meeting of the Acoustical Society of America and 2nd Convention of the EAA: Forum Acusticum*. Oldenburg: Deutsche Gesellschaft für Akustik e.V.

Perkell, J. S., Svirsky, M. A., Matthies, M. L., and Jordan, M. I. (1991),

'Trading relations between tongue body raising and lip rounding in production of the vowel /u/', in O. Engstrand and C. Kylander, *Papers from the Symposium on Current Phonetic Research Paradigms: Implications for Speech Motor Control* [Volume 14 of PERILUS: Phonetic Experimental Research at the Institute of Linguistics, University of Stockholm].

Peterson, G. E. and Barney, H. L. (1952), 'Control methods used in a study of vowels'. *Journal of the Acoustical Society of America*, 24, 175–184.

Polka, L. (1991), 'Cross-language speech perception in adults: Phonemic, phonetic, and acoustic contributions'. *Journal of the Acoustical Society of America*, 89, 2961–2977.

Sagey, E. (1986), 'The representation of features and relations in non-linear phonology'. Doctoral dissertation, Massachusetts Institute of Technology.

Schmidt, A. M. (1996), 'Cross-language identification of consonants. Part 1. Korean perception of English'. *Journal of the Acoustical Society of America*, 99, 3201–3211.

Sekiyama, K. and Tohkura, Y. (1991). 'McGurk effect in non-English listeners: Few visual effects for Japanese subjects hearing Japanese syllables of high auditory intelligibility'. *Journal of the Acoustical Society of America*, 90, 1797–1805.

Stevens, K. N. and House, A. S. (1955), 'Development of a quantitative description of vowel articulation'. *Journal of the Acoustical Society of America*, 27, 484–493.

Stevens, K. N. and House, A. S. (1961), 'An acoustical theory of vowel production and some of its implications'. *Journal of Speech and Hearing Research*, 4, 75–92.

Strange, W., Jenkins, J. J., and Johnson, T. L. (1983), 'Dynamic specification of coarticulated vowels'. *Journal of the Acoustical Society of America*, 74, 695–705.

Swadesh, M. (1934), 'The phonemic principle'. *Language*, 10, 117–129. [Reprinted in Joos, M. (1957), *Readings in Linguistics I.* Chicago: University of Chicago Press.]

Terbeek, D. (1977), 'A cross-language multidimensional scaling study of vowel perception'. *UCLA Working Papers in Phonetics, 37.*

Werker, J. F. (1989), 'Becoming a native listener'. *American Scientist, 77,* 54–59.

Yngve, V. H. (1996), *From Grammar to Science: New Foundations for General Linguistics.* Amsterdam/Philadelphia: John Benjamins.

Zlatin, M. A. and Koenigsknecht, R. A. (1975), 'Development of the voicing contrast: Perception of stop consonants'. *Journal of Speech and Hearing Research*, 18, 541–553.

Chapter 6

Articulatory Events are Given in Advance

Douglas N. Honorof

1. Introduction

Since his early work on turn-taking (1970), Yngve has been asking how people communicate rather than how people 'use language' to communicate. Yngve redefines the problem in these terms because he is convinced that we have inherited a flawed rhetoric for talking about people as communicators – a rhetoric dependent upon ancient, but, ultimately, unworkable assumptions about linguistic objects. Yngve also questions the scientific adequacy of standard discovery procedures used in investigating people as communicators. Specifically, he discourages bottom-up approaches that begin with phonetics and end with pragmatics, challenging us, instead, to begin from careful observation of exchanges between people and work our way down only when a lower level of structure suggests itself. In discouraging bottom-up approaches, Yngve redirects our attention from 'linguistic communities' and the micro-level grammatical constructs their ideal speaker-hearers are widely held to share, toward actual individual people and their properties as communicators.

Yngve's shift of focus from language to people is perhaps best understood in historical context. Yngve (1996, Chapter 3) recounts how, during the early years of twentieth-century structuralist linguistics, real-world objects – the acoustics and physiology of acts of speech – came to be viewed as belonging, in Bloomfield's terms, to other sciences. Differences in speech behavior among individuals fared no better under Bloomfield's fundamental assumption: '... in every speech-community some utterances are alike in form and meaning' (Bloomfield 1933:78). In spite of much rhetoric about the 'scientific' advances linguistics was making, the structuralists robbed the field of its primary tie to the observable world by excluding the study of acts of speaking and individual variation from linguistics. More recent structuralist models stemming from Chomsky's early work in transformational-generative grammar have perpetuated the divorce of 'performance' from 'competence', the former being very nearly neglected in practice and held to lie outside the realm of linguistics proper. Thus language, a 'logical domain' construct based on the arbitrary and field-specific assumptions of the grammatical-semiotic and normative-grammatical traditions, has come to be mistaken for a legitimate object of scientific inquiry. As modern linguists, we have busied ourselves defining and redefining the objects of our study, but, in Yngve's view, failed to recognize that science does not study objects of its own creation. Rather, he insists, science studies objects given in advance. Within Yngve's Human Linguistics, unlike the syntactic constituents, words, phonemes, and other units of traditional grammar, people are the real-world objects that exist in advance of our observation of them, and therefore constitute more suitable objects for scientific investigation.

I agree with Yngve that, in adopting the methods of formal logic and creating grammars that do not attempt to model real-world communicative behavior (and that therefore cannot be tested against behavior), we introduce a noticeable level of circularity into linguistic theory. Our inability to test hypotheses empirically has led Yngve to recommend that we reject all *ad hoc* grammatical building blocks. In this connection, I am especially intrigued by Yngve's rejection of the segmentation of utterances. He very rightly points out that segmentation is 'not inherent in the sound waves' (1996:32). While I make no claim to know more than the average phonologist about how speech is parsed into words, phrases, and sentences by the listener, like Yngve, I remain as yet unconvinced that phonemes are real units in the physical world (or perhaps even real in cognition; but see below). However, Yngve may be missing a key point here. Although researchers have met with considerable difficulty in attempting to segment sound pressure waveforms, laboratory phonologists around the world have met with considerable success in decomposing signals derived from the articulatory movements of people engaged in the act of talking. This being the case, I believe that it is possible to build a model of phonology that conforms to – and can be tested against – real-world patterns of human speech articulation. This is exactly what my colleagues at Haskins Laboratories have been doing in recent decades. I have been privileged to take part in some of that research. In the present chapter, I take the reader on a brief tour of this work. Along our way, we will consider the scientific status of our work and the nature of the objects that we study.

2 Gestural events in the real world

2.1 Coordinative structures

Scholars have attempted to parameterize speech into individually manipulable features for as long as there have been phonologists. Although a feature-based approach to speech is indeed ancient in origin, the parameterization effort received a major boost when linguistic anthropologists and their colleagues began transcribing the speech of unfamiliar peoples into alphabetic notation for taxonomic, lexicographic, and pedagogical purposes. Even today, descriptivists outnumber theoreticians, though their work is no longer as well represented in the leading linguistics journals. Interest in features received another boost when linguists turned their attention to computational modeling of speech using symbols that could be entered from a standard keyboard, for example, for projects in machine translation, automated speech recognition, automatic speaker verification, speech synthesis, etc.

In recent decades, phonologists have emphasized the structuralist interest in contrast as a key to finding universal patterns in phonological (cognitive) systems. Most have not been particularly interested in the physics of speech except insofar as it can corroborate independently motivated theoretical stances. The nature/nurture controversy has driven the quest to find universals in the handsome collection of phonological data we have amassed as a community of scholars, which has further driven an interest in parameterization.

A number of my colleagues at Haskins Laboratories have been rethinking the problem of parameterization of speech in recent years. After observing the physiological properties of people in the act of moving their vocal organs, they have adopted a viewpoint that originated in work on visual perception within the framework of specificity theory which has evolved into the ecological approach to perception (Gibson and Gibson 1955; Gibson 1979; Gibson and Pick 2000). Ecological psychologists proceed from the understanding that, like other animals, we live in environments that we have to know about in order to function effectively. To know about our environment, we must perceive whatever is in it – at least whatever in it exists at roughly the human scale. These theorists hold that we learn to perceive the layouts (that is, permanently arranged surfaces), objects, and events (that is, movements and actions of objects) in our environment without constructing intermediary mental representations of them. In this sense, perception is believed to be direct.

The notion that we visually perceive objects rather than patterns of light may not strike the reader as odd. However, some objects move or are moved and therein generate sounds. When they do, the ecological psychologist says that we hear objects in motion, as well. The assertion that we hear objects in motion rather than patterns of sound often strikes us as counterintuitive. I believe our discomfort with the notion that we directly perceive the sources of structure in sound waves follows from our biological proclivity to trust what we see over and above what we hear. We are visual believers and auditory skeptics by nature. Even so, if the reader will consider the parallels between optical and auditory signals, the parallels in perception will make sense.

For example, consider a windchime. Ecological psychologists will argue that, even when the chime is still, we perceive (that is, see) it directly, not a prototype of it, or a cognitive representation of it, or cues that suggest it, or codes from which we must infer the presence and properties of the chime. The situation is no different in the realm of perception by ear. Sound is normally generated by an action or collision that sets objects into motion. The windchime is an object given in advance that generates a sound when struck by wind in space over time. Such dynamic (spatio-temporal) events are as clearly given in advance as the objects involved. We perceive the windchime directly by eye and we perceive its movement by eye and ear just as directly. The movement of the chime's colliding parts structures the patterns of light and sound that reach the human retina and eardrum. These patterns of light and sound contain abundant information that specifies the properties of the source of the disturbance. Thus the proximal stimuli (patterned light and sound waves) convey information about distal events (the causal source of the patterns of light and sound) to the visual and auditory perceptual systems respectively.

An ecological approach to speech perception begs the question 'What is out there when we speak?'. What events structure the air? The answer must begin with production. Speech is generated by the coordinated movement of human objects: the articulators of the talker's vocal tract: tongues, lips, jaw, etc. Such speech events are abundant in our ecological niche. However, as early as the 1950s, investigators were noting difficulties inherent in segmenting waveforms and in synthesizing invariant phonetic percepts across contexts on the basis of acoustics. (For discussions of early findings within a Motor Theoretic perspective, see work by Liberman, *et al.* 1967 and Liberman and Mattingly 1985.) Evidence that the listener can perceive articulatory stabilities was also emerging. Thus those among my colleagues at Haskins who work within the Direct Realist theory of speech perception have concluded that patterns of coordination in vocal organ movement are exactly the real-world events that are out there (see Fowler 1991; Surprenant and Goldstein 1998). Articulators can be seen even when people are not moving them, but patterns of coordinated movement among articulators in space over time (also known as coordinative structures) can be seen and heard.

The specific attributes of the coordinative structures relevant to speech (that is, speech events or articulatory gestures) have been formalized in what has become the gestural theory of speech production (see Saltzman 1986; Browman and Goldstein 1995). Over the past two decades, my colleagues at Haskins and elsewhere have tested gesture-based hypotheses and amassed considerable evidence suggesting that gestures are indeed the public, real-world, task-directed, spatio-temporal events of production and perception.

The Haskins group has developed a model of gestures – in our view, a model of real-world events, not purely a model of theoretical events. The gestural model successfully predicts the spatial and temporal properties of gestures observed when the coupled articulators of real people work together synergistically to bring structures in the vocal tract into approximation (at present, along the two-dimensions of the midsagittal plane only). In most cases, the computational component of the gestural model plots to a computer screen the coupled articulator trajectories that correspond to the synergistic constricting action of two or more articulators. For example, in outputting a bilabial closure gesture, the model plots lip aperture curves involving the coordinated action of the upper lip, lower lip, and jaw. The model does not simply produce the spatio-temporal trajectories of the individual articulators. Therefore, the model can be used to test predictions about events against the events themselves.

As indicated by the example of the bilabial closure gesture just given, it is important for the reader to bear in mind always that gestures differ from raw movement curves. In the gestural model, two gestural events are deemed equivalent if they share the same spatio-temporal target, even though they may actually be achieved by different relative contributions of the articulators involved. In the example given above, with a goal of achieving a target such as bilabial closure, in one instance the jaw might contribute more than the lower lip and the upper lip remain nearly still, but in another instance, the upper lip might do nearly all the work. The stability is in the goal. Instance-by-instance differences in gestural movement curves observed in space over time can occur as a consequence of differing degrees of overlap between neighboring gestures (coarticulation) due to different speaking styles or rates. Or, two articulator trajectories for a unitary gesture might vary because the gestures are produced in differing gestural contexts. Differences might even occur simply because observed combinatorial gaps among gestures make speech so redundant that undershot gestural targets are, in many cases, recoverable by the listener. Even though the gestural movement curves may vary from instance to instance, the gesture is identical to both talker and listener. The same cannot be said of purported acoustic correlates of, or cues for, phonemes, for which stable acoustic patterns have been difficult to identify in speech records, and for which complex rules of phonetic realization have been even more difficult to formulate. In gestural terms, there is neither derivation, nor generation, nor implementation. There are no abstract underlying units that must be realized – the gestures are at once units of perception, action, and cognition. They are always present during the act of talking and listening. Gestural movement curves lawfully produce acoustic consequences, but we seek invariant patterns in the synergistic behavior of real-world articulators.

The Haskins computational model has been applied successfully in testing numerous hypotheses about gestures for well over a decade. The program uses task dynamics (Saltzman and Munhall 1989) to model gestures. While much remains to be understood about the physiology behind coordinated human movement, task dynamics does appear to do a reasonably good job of approximating complex control of the anatomical structures believed to be most directly relevant for speech. The mathematics are beyond the scope of the present chapter, but see Hawkins (1992) for an accessible introduction to the equations involved. Although the mathematics are somewhat complex, conceptually, the model is fairly straightforward. Here is how it works.

Gestures have their own internal equations modeled after the workings of a critically damped point-attractor system. Gestures are not sequenced. Rather, a certain point within one gesture (corresponding, say, to achievement of target) is phased temporally with respect to a certain point within another gesture (corresponding, say, to release of target). The researcher wanting to test a prediction about gestural organization lays out the predicted gestures in a non-linear fashion on a multi-tiered grid (minimally, one tier for velic gestures, one for oral gestures, and one for laryngeal gestures). This grid is known as a gestural score. Once the user has composed a gestural score, the score is run through the computational model where gestural movement curves are generated. Under an analysis-by-synthesis strategy, these movement curves can be compared with actual curves derived from individual-articulator trajectories collected, for example, as articulometer 'subjects' (real people) talk with transducers affixed to flesh points along the midline of the vocal tract (Perkell *et al.* 1992). Finally, the movement curves may be input to an articulatory synthesizer for generation of sound that can be played for listeners in naturalness or perceptual tests. Articulatory synthesis can also be used in a more exploratory way. The configurable articulatory synthesizer is essentially a midsagittal talking head. The head's two-dimensional articulators can be manipulated geometrically on the computer monitor, and cross-sectional vocal tract area functions can be computed and acoustic signals generated for the listener.

At this relatively early stage of development, the model may be overly simplistic in the details of the way it specifies the internal dynamics of gestures, as may be the patterns of intergestural coordination that we specify (see Mattingly 1990). For instance, it is possible that some parameters of off-midline articulation about which we know very little are actually important in the formation of gestural events. It is also possible that we have constrained our initial observations of speaker behavior too narrowly even in the mid-line and have therefore missed relevant aspects of vocal tract constrictions. It is also possible that our theory is essentially right-headed, but that our mathematical-computational model will need to be tweaked in order to produce correct output with respect to a particular prediction. However, no matter how far we are from having captured an accurate picture of gestures and gestural organization, it is my belief that gestural events do exist in the real world, and that we will get better and better at modeling them. It is also possible that we are mistaken in asserting that gestures are events for the speaker and hearer, but it seems to me extremely unlikely that gestures do not exist at all.

I have used 'gestures' to refer to real-world events and to phonological units in our theoretical representation of those events. The scientific justification for our work as a theory of the real world and not a theory of theories lies in our ability to test the articulatory output of the computational model against gestural movement curves derived from articulatory events in the real world. In the next section, I describe the nature of the data we consider in deriving such gestural movement curves.

2.2 What count as data

Within mainstream phonology, new theories are minted and fall almost instantly into wide circulation on average every decade. In the 70s we had generative phonology. In the 80s we had autosegmental and metrical phonology, which evolved into a very popular nonlinear framework: feature geometry. In the 90s we saw the adoption of optimality theory and of related logical-domain theories involving constraints on output. Each theory emerges out of the insufficiency of an older model to deal with a particular set of data elegantly. However, with each round of new theories, the frenzy that follows has been the same: reanalyze everything (or at least everything of interest within the new model). We dig through old papers, extract the data that were once well 'explained' and apply the new model to the data hoping to discover whether the new model is indeed just powerful enough.

Articulatory Phonology, the arm of the gestural school that concerns itself with universal and nonuniversal patterns in gestural organization, has followed a different path. While it is true that Articulatory Phonology also arose to account for a specific set of problems (especially postlexical assimilations, epenthesis, and elisions in casual speech), its proponents have generally addressed novel questions on the basis of novel data. This is as it must be. Traditional phonological 'data' are simply transcriptions of acts of speech. Transcriptions are highly problematic. First, they are observer-dependent. Second, transcriptions impose phonemic (that is, letter-sized) units on streams of speech. We have yet to find firm evidence in acoustics or physiology for a phonemic unit of analysis. Interestingly, even the universality of the phoneme as a 'mental' object has been called into question by what little data there are on phonemic awareness among illiterates and among adults literate only in nonalphabetic orthographies. To be fair, a lack of phonemic awareness does not necessarily mean that phonemes are not 'psychologically real'; it may be the case that people who do not read alphabetic orthography are simply unaware of units that they 'know' in cognition. (See Read, et al. 1986; Adrian et al. 1995.)

Nongestural, phoneme-based theories require complex, *ad hoc* rules of phonetic interpretation (interpolation, translation, instantiation, realization, implementation) to predict the phonetic quality of segments in output and to imbue segments extrinsically with temporal information so that they can be realized in production (Fowler 1980). It has long been a working assumption of standard structuralist grammar that such rules for phonetic realization of static segments can be written successfully, though few researchers have bothered. If solid evidence for a unit akin to the phoneme does emerge some day, it may be entirely possible to reconstruct something like (but not identical to) the notion of the phoneme as a constellation of gestures. Goldstein and Fowler have suggested the chemical term 'ion' for such a possible set of bonded gestures (Goldstein and Fowler, in press). Ions would be available to recombine with other ions into a large number of compounds (words or syllables). Such a gesture-based treatment of the segment would not require rules of phonetic interpretation – a definite plus. However, the key point is that, if it ever becomes necessary to posit an ion to account for apparently phonemic behavior, we would, nevertheless, not be justified in counting phonemic transcriptions as data. Goldstein's argument is that, just as the evidence for ions in chemistry comes from empirical investigation of chemicals, not from our intuition that sodium carbonate and calcium carbonate have something in common, so the evidence for gestural 'ions' in speech would have to come from real-world investigation of speech. The difference in the nature of the data in Articulatory Phonology versus traditional structuralist phonology cannot be overemphasized, particularly given that the Haskins work on casual speech, and more recently on speech errors, reveals how transcriptions can be systematically misleading as to the actual real-world properties of some speech events (Pouplier 2003). Clearly, even if we do someday find ourselves adopting a phoneme-like unit as a construct, we will not simply turn to digging up old transcription 'data' and reanalyzing them without collecting articulatory data. Gesture theory considers only real-world movement as data.

While, for us, data are observed in the real world, they are not necessarily observed under as natural a circumstance as are some of the data Yngve has collected. In other words, although we study people in the act of talking, we do not generally study people in the act of communicating spontaneously. Our movement data are collected in the laboratory, though our experimental designs do not exactly simulate what Yngve would call linkages. In our designs, talkers are usually asked to produce multiple repetitions of gestural constellations, often by reading aloud. These constellations might correspond to units of analysis from traditional grammar (which are rather easy to elicit from literate talkers) or they might be constellations that the subject has never before produced (nonsense utterances). The repeated acts of speech (no matter how variable from repetition to repetition) form the basis of discrete, replicable, observer-independent spatial and temporal measurements, for example at articulator velocity peaks or zeros, at peaks in articulator acceleration, or at extrema in articulator displacement. These measurements are subsequently subjected to conventional statistical testing. Here, as in all hard sciences, statistics provide a basis for testing the null hypothesis, and for drawing conclusions about an individual's behavior that may, in principle, with a large enough sampling of the population, generalize to the group.

2.3. Physiological data acquisition

Some gestures can be seen with the naked eye – those produced in the anterior regions of the vocal tract – but most gestures are hidden from view. However, even gestures that we cannot easily see can be studied and measured with the right tools. The measurements made depend on the data collection device used. Gesturalists have tended to acquire laboratories full of unusual instruments for use in physiology experiments. Collectively, we have used video cameras, SELSPOT optical motion analysis systems (Innovision Systems, Warren, MI/ USA), the velotrace (Horiguchi and Bell-Berti 1987), magnetic resonance imaging, ultrasound imaging, cineradiography (where local jurisdiction allows), electromyography, point-source tracking (x-ray microbeam [Nadler et al. 1987]), and, especially, electromagnetic articulometry (e.g., Perkell et al. 1992, etc.). There are also laboratory techniques for measuring laryngeal activity such as electroglotto-graphy (see Scherer et al. 1988) and laryngoscopy (direct and technology-assisted) and subglottal coordination indirectly (Pneu-motach Mask [Glottal Enterprises, Syracuse, NY/USA]) or some-what more directly (Respitrace [Ambulatory Monitoring Inc., Ardsley, NY/USA]). Some of the foregoing techniques and devices are borrowed from, or inspired by, clinical practice. A few have even been designed specifically for purposes of speech research. A further step removed from movement, but sometimes also instructive, are contact patterns between articulators such as can be measured through palatography. Wandering even further from the direct observation of movement, we routinely examine the lawful acoustic consequences of gestures. Finally, the effects of gestures on listeners can be measured – listeners themselves being real-world objects.

3. Slow but steady progress

3.1 Coarticulation and individual variation

Considering the relative youth of the gestural endeavor, the techniques we have available to us are truly impressive, and, yet, they are nevertheless crude in comparison to the task of studying the complexities of speech physiology. Perhaps that is why we collect so many new devices; the old ones do not suit our purposes. Because our instruments are so crude, we often come close to wrongly accepting the null hypothesis. There certainly are repeating patterns in speech to be found, but those patterns appear to be hidden in a mire of coarticulation – necessary 'noise' that our crude instruments alone cannot always see through. In order to give our data collection devices a leg up, we often must collect pilot data several times before we have analyzable data – data that allow us to tease apart the effects of gestural co-production well enough to find evidence of an individual gesture. Some combinations of gestures obscure each other in output so badly that we must simply give up and ask another question.

Even once we have a well-designed stimulus set, we are often faced with the hairy problem of inter-speaker variation. As happy as we are that we can identify the voice of a familiar caller on the telephone, in the laboratory idiosyncratic differences in speech habits can make it difficult to draw conclusions quickly. Some of these individual talker differences in behavior can arise from genuine idiolectal (that is, 'personality') differences. We try to screen talkers for membership in homogeneous populations with respect to at least the style of speech the experimental instructions imply. However, in my experience in the laboratory, the extent of individual variation even among well-screened subjects is surprisingly high. Collecting data from many subjects often helps idiosyncrasies to 'wash' in the statistics, but physiological data collection and analysis are time-consuming and costly. Conventional funding structures simply do not encourage it. Even when we do have a large number of subjects, variation remains the rule. Yngve shows tremendous clarity in joining the sociolinguists to call into question the logical-domain notion of the ideal speaker-hearer. Perhaps we must content ourselves to study the individual in multiple linkages more often than we study the group until our technologies speed up the research process.

3.2 Convergence

Although studying gestures does present special practical problems that slow down the entire enterprise, we are making genuine progress – producing occasional results that may even outlive our own productivity as researchers. Even some of the longstanding puzzles of traditional grammar have been addressed very elegantly by articulatory phonologists (Browman and Goldstein 1991). Chances are, intuitions about how people communicate cannot all be wrong. It is therefore not surprising that gesture-based findings and logical-domain phonology have converged on occasion, and that ideas found in literature authored by traditional phonologists have provided fodder for successful gestural investigation. Given that traditional grammar is not a hard science, convergence with it does not argue for or against the rightheadedness of a gestural approach.

However, there are other areas of convergence between the Haskins work on gestures in speech and work in other sciences that is very encouraging. Because the gestural model is rooted in ecological and task-dynamic approaches to the production and perception of human movement in general (locomotion, grasping, etc.), convergence there does meaningfully corroborate our findings. In addition, we see parallels between our findings on the gestural organization of speech and findings on the spontaneous emergence of order and complexity in other self-organizing systems in nature – systems that make potentially unlimited use of finite, discrete units in building larger structures (physics, chemistry, genetics, etc.). For example, without necessarily committing to any particular units of traditional grammar, Haskins researchers have begun to consider how a finite set of discrete gestural units might be organized into larger stable configurations such as consonant-clusters and syllables (Browman and Goldstein 1988; Honorof and Browman 1995; Studdert-Kennedy and Goldstein 2003). Such larger, stable configurations of gestures may be structured by real-world functional constraints. For example, some such patterns may naturally emerge from the competing requirements that a) speech events be sequential in order to be recoverable by the listener, and, b) speech events overlap in order to hasten the flow of information through parallel transmission (Mattingly 1981; Browman and Goldstein 2000). Any convergence between the findings of gestural research and findings in other physical-domain fields (biology, physics, etc.) only serve to shore up the status of gestural work as a hard science (Ohala, 1990).

4. Does gestural research weigh in as a hard science?

4.1 Yngve's two criteria for weighing hypotheses or theories

I have introduced the reader to a theory in which spatio-temporal events in the vocal tract are held to be real-world events in production and perception. Let us now consider how well the gestural approach holds up to the two standard criteria of acceptance of hypotheses or theories in hard science laid out by Yngve (1996:99–100).

> Criterion 1. Theory driven, hypothesis-generated predictions 'pass tests against the real world by means of careful observations and experiments'.

We do subject our predictions about gestures to careful experimental testing. We expend considerable effort refining and calibrating our data collection devices, screening subjects, and presenting tasks to them in ways that do not prejudice behavior. We collect a large number of data points, measure them, and analyze them statistically. We reject hypotheses that do not stand up to testing.

> Criterion 2. Observational and experimental results are reproducible when questioned.

Our measurements are, whenever possible, automated, which makes them observer-independent. Even where algorithmic measurement is not possible, very strict measurement criteria are followed and published, allowing for replication by other research groups. There is not much funding for studies that aim solely to replicate results of other researchers, and the work we do often makes use of instrumentation that exists at very few other laboratories, but replication and extension of our studies certainly can be undertaken, and sometimes are. In any case, there are less costly devices on the market that can be used for confirming our articulometric findings using slightly different designs. Confirmation through similar means is even better than confirmation by replication, after all; true replication can duplicate methodological error.

4.2 Yngve's four assumptions underlying scientific work

Yngve also lays out the four, time-tested, commonsense presuppositions of hard science that we must take on faith (1996:101–02). Let us now examine whether we have made only the same four assumptions, or introduced any special assumptions.

> Assumption 1. 'There actually is a real world out there to be studied.'

Our procedures are based upon this ontological assumption. Gestures, though partly conventional (learned), are indeed out there. They are produced and perceived because they exist, and are not just convenient fictions. Gestural events take place independent of our theories and observation.

> Assumption 2. 'The real world is coherent so we have a chance of finding out something about it.'

Because we study human individuals as well as gestural events, and because individual behavior can be difficult to constrain even in simulated communicative situations in the laboratory, the world sometimes seems a little more chaotic to the experimenter than it actually is, especially when our sample size is small. This is a matter of frustration specifically because we share the regularity assumption with other scientists.

> Assumption 3. 'We can reach valid conclusions by reasoning from valid premises ... We can trust our ability to calculate predictions from our theories for comparison with the real world.'

We assert that gestures are real-world events (dynamical objects) produced by talkers and perceived by listeners. The mathematical definition of gestures under task-dynamic modeling allows us to calculate predicted movement curves that can be compared with actual movement curves obtained from talkers in the laboratory. So far, so good. However, there is a third element to the model: gestures are held to be units of production, perception, and phonology. This is where, at first glance, it might seem that we inch close to the edge of the hard science-traditional grammar border. We accept the rationality assumption, but, having tested our predictions against the real world, step back from the communicating individual and go on to ask questions about formal phonological patterning among the units of analysis themselves. The gestural model itself together with the phonological patterns we arrive at through informal observation of speech and by reading the writings of scholars of traditional grammar inspire new hypotheses. We then subject predictions so derived to further laboratory testing. In this sense, we allow formalist work to inspire our prediction-generating process, but our commitment to behavioral data forces us to test our predictions against the real world. Our experiments rarely produce entirely unambiguous results, but even in the traditional hard sciences, this is to be expected.

Because gestural events exist, it is reasonable to assume that people have conscious or subconscious knowledge of them. We do not rely on 'native-speaker intuitions' to investigate that knowledge, however. The gestural units of which people have knowledge are spatial and temporal, so our knowledge of them is reflected directly in dynamic behavior. Even when we are looking at phonology, our predictions are tested in the laboratory.

Yngve warns us against assuming blindly that units such as phrases, words, phonemes, etc. exist and that people use them to communicate. He notes that such grammatical units belong to the logical domain until proved otherwise. However, we believe we have found strong evidence for gestural units in the physical domain, in particular in acoustic and, especially, physiological speech records. Thus we are on sound scientific footing in asserting that talkers and listeners learn to use such coordinative structures to communicate.

Once we have admitted to consideration the gesture as a spatio-temporal 'object' (that is, an event) that can be used by people in accomplishing a task, we are inclined to ask how such events are learned by the child and how they might have evolved. These questions bring us to the point where we can more meaningfully contribute to the nature/nurture dialog. Given that gestural units are subject to physical constraints, phonological learning need not necessarily imply language-specificity. To be sure, some gestural patterns are used by some groups of talkers who are able to communicate with each other (that is, who share some phonological knowledge), and not by others. But other gestural patterns may turn out to be universal. Gestural universals are bound to follow from the functional demands the real world places on the evolution of gestural communication over time (Studdert-Kennedy and Goldstein, in press), and in the individual user attuning to the environment (Goldstein and Fowler, in press). This is not to say that the environment always structures the human organism. Some real-world demands on gestural communication may emerge from our own species-specific auditory and neurological anatomy and physiology, in which case we may be structuring the environment of the learner of spoken gestural systems of communication by placing constraints on the evolution of gestural events.

Yngve has criticized prominent linguists for their skin-deep allegiance to hard-science linguistics – an allegiance born of a desire to appear scientific, but lacking in the commitment to build models that can be subjected to external validation. The idea is that linguists are not honest in admitting that they are logicians, and that they go so far as to borrow scientific rhetoric to argue points based on intuition or on purely logical assumptions about language. At Haskins Laboratories, if anything, we suffer from the opposite type of confusion of identity. We actually borrow logical-domain rhetoric to talk about hard science. Although we test our theories in the physical domain, we are constructing a phonological theory that resembles, in some respects, the soft science of the traditional logical-domain structuralist. Furthermore, we report our results in mainstream linguistics journals using many terms borrowed directly from the traditional study of language. Doing so allows us to engage the larger Linguistics community, and to benefit from the insights of its great minds, even though we may make different assumptions about what count as data, how predictions may be generated, and what counts as a good test of a model.

Given that our explanations tend to be very tightly constrained by the real world, our peers in traditional linguistics often think of us as functionalists. In my view, form and function are related, but the forms themselves are also of interest; we treat phonetics *and phonology* in a unified manner. Doing so may, in fact, make us *structuralists*, but clearly we are structuralists with a difference. The Haskins work involves units of analysis that are at once theoretical constructs and mathematical predictors of real-world, gestural movement curves – not special-purpose, theoretical objects from the logical domain. Our units are given in advance, but can also serve as playthings for logicians.

Assumption 4. 'Observed effects flow from immediate real-world causes.'

We observe movement curves and infer gestural organization. Clearly, we accept the causality assumption.

5. Summary

The present chapter does not aim to enlist support for gesture-based work over Human Linguistics or vice-versa. Rather, I have simply described my personal perspective on a laboratory-based research program that shares important features with Human Linguistics. The gesturalist approach I describe meets the two criteria and four assumptions of hard science set forth in Yngve's 1996 book. Our work has proved to be slow going at times, but nearly always profitable.

At the crossroads of behaviorism and structuralism, we sidestep the mind-body and performance-competence dichotomies. To my way of thinking, the ideal linguistics uses hard-science methodology to discover events in the real world that also help structure human perception and cognition. If linguistic events occur in the physical domain and we are able to perceive them, it only makes sense that learners should use them to build cognitive structure. In working both top-down and bottom-up, my colleagues have found ample empirical evidence for just such a real-world (spatio-temporal) object given in advance – the gesture. These gestural units of perception and action were discovered by studying the behavior of objects given in advance – people.

Nevertheless, we gesturalists sometimes frame our arguments in terms borrowed from traditional structuralist grammar. At times, structuralist techniques are even borrowed to help us manipulate variables in the laboratory as we attempt to simulate measurable and quantifiable communicative behavior within individuals.

Quantifiable communicative behavior shared by groups may be another matter. In this connection, Yngve rejects the traditional notion of the ideal speaker-listener – a notion summed up by Chomsky as follows:

Linguistic theory is concerned primarily with an ideal speaker-listener, in a completely homogeneous speech-community, who knows its language perfectly ... This seems to me to have been the position of the founders of modern general linguistics, and no cogent reason for modifying it has been offered. [1965:3–4]

Perhaps Chomsky intends this statement as an idealization meant to simplify the linguist's job in eliciting the grammar from informants, not as a literal endorsement of the notion that all members of a speech-community share exactly the same grammar. In any case, Yngve would encourage us to study the individual as an individual or as a member of more than one communicating community. Through my own gesture-based research and through my reading of variationist literature, like Yngve, I have come to question the notion of the ideal speaker-listener. In my case, I do so entirely without glee. I wish my experimental subjects were more alike in their properties as communicators. Cross-speaker similarities in behavior would make interpretation of experimental results much tidier. In any case, having found a real-world event that is at once serviceable as a unit of production, perception, and phonology – the gesture – it would certainly be very comforting to find that individuals who routinely communicate with each other share at least minimal elements of a gesture-based system of communication. After having served on the front lines of speech physiology research, I will not easily be persuaded that neatly bounded, homogeneous speech communities exist, but I certainly hope that our work produces a clearer picture of the sorts of communicative behaviors that are shared between people who sometimes talk with each other.

Acknowledgements

I acknowledge the support of NIH Grant DC-03782 to Haskins Laboratories from which I received funding during the preparation of the present chapter. I thank Carol Fowler, Louis Goldstein, and Vic Yngve for very helpful comments.

References

Adrian, J. A., Alegria, J., and Morais, J. (1995), 'Metaphonological abilities of Spanish illiterate adults'. *International Journal of Psychology*, 30 (3), 329–353.
Bloomfield, L. (1933), *Language*. New York: Holt.
Browman, C. and Goldstein, L. (1988), 'Some notes on syllable structure in articulatory phonology'. *Phonetica*, 45, 140–155.
Browman, C. and Goldstein, L. (1991), 'Gestural structures: Distinctiveness, phonological processes, and historical change', in I. G. Mattingly and M. Studdert-Kennedy, *Modularity and the Motor Theory of Speech Perception*. Hillsdale, NJ: Lawrence Erlbaum, pp. 313–338.
Browman, C. and Goldstein, L. (1995), 'Dynamics and articulatory phonology', in R. F. Port and T. van Gelder, *Mind as Motion: Explorations in the Dynamics of Cognition*. Cambridge, MA: MIT Press, pp. 175–193.
Browman, C. and Goldstein, L. (2000), 'Competing constraints on intergestural coordination and self-organization of phonological structures'. *Bulletin de la Communication Parlée*, 5, 25–34.
Chomsky, N. (1965), *Aspects of the Theory of Syntax*. Cambridge, MA: MIT Press.

Fowler, C. A. (1991), 'Auditory perception is not special: We see the world, we feel the world, we hear the world'. *Journal of the Acoustical Society of America*, 89 (6), 2910–2915.

Fowler, C. A. (1980), 'Coarticulation and theories of extrinsic timing'. *Journal of Phonetics*, 8, 113–133.

Gibson, E. J. and Pick, A. D. (2000), *An Ecological Approach to Perceptual Learning and Development*. Oxford: Oxford University Press.

Gibson, J. J. (1979), *The Ecological Approach to Visual Perception*. Boston: Houghton Mifflin.

Gibson, J. J. and Gibson, E. J. (1955), 'Perceptual learning: Differentiation or enrichment?' *Psychological Review*, 62, 32–41.

Goldstein, L. and Fowler, C. A. (in press), 'Articulatory Phonology: A phonology for public language use', in A. S. Meyer and N. O. Schiller, *Phonetics and Phonology in Language Comprehension and Production: Differences and Similarities*. Mouton de Gruyter.

Hawkins, S. (1992), 'An introduction to task dynamics', in G. J. Docherty and D. R. Ladd, *Papers in Laboratory Phonology 2*. Cambridge: Cambridge University Press, pp. 9–25.

Honorof, D. N. and Browman, C. P. (1995), 'The center or edge: How are consonant clusters organized with respect to the vowel?', in K. Elenius and P. Branderud, *Proceedings of the XIIIth International Congress of Phonetics Sciences*, *3*, Stockholm, Sweden, pp. 552–555.

Horiguchi, S. and Bell-Berti, F. (1987), 'The velotrace: A device for monitoring velar position'. *Cleft Palate Journal*, 24 (2), 104–111.

Liberman, A. M., Cooper, F. S., Shankweiler, D. P., and Studdert-Kennedy, M. (1967), 'Perception of the speech code'. *Psychological Review*, 74, 431–461.

Liberman, A. M. and Mattingly, I. G. (1985), 'The motor theory of speech perception revisited'. *Cognition*, 21, 1–36.

Mattingly, I. G. (1981), 'Phonetic representation and speech synthesis by rule', in T. Myers, J. Laver, and J. Anderson, *The Cognitive Representation of Speech*. Amsterdam: North Holland, pp. 415–420.

Mattingly, I. G. (1990), 'The global character of phonetic gestures'. *Journal of Phonetics*, 18, 445–452.

Ohala, J. J. (1990), 'There is no interface between phonology and phonetics: A personal view'. *Journal of Phonetics*, 18, 153–171.

Nadler, R. D., Abbs, J. H., and Sujimura, O. (1987), 'Speech movement research using the new x-ray microbeam system', in *Proceedings of the XIth International Congress of Phonetic Sciences (1)*. Tallinn, Estonia: Academy of Sciences of the Estonian S.S.R. Institute of Language and Literature, pp. 221–224.

Perkell, J. S., Cohen, M. H., Svirsky, M. A., Matthies, M. L., Garabieta I., and Jackson, M. (1992), 'Electromagnetic midsagittal articulometer (EMMA) systems for transducing speech articulatory movements'. *Journal of the Acoustical Society of America*, 92, 3078–3096.

Pouplier, M. (2003), *Units of Phonological Encoding: Empirical Evidence*. Doctoral dissertation, Department of Linguistics, Yale University. (To become available via free download from ProQuest Digital Dissertations, http://wwwlib.umi.com/dissertations/gateway.)

Read, C., Zhang, Y.-F., Nie H.-Y., and Ding, B.-Q. (1986), 'The ability to manipulate speech sounds depends on knowing alphabetic writing'. *Cognition*, 24, 31–44.

Saltzman, E. (1986), 'Task dynamic coordination of the speech articulators: A preliminary model'. *Experimental Brain Research*, 15, 129–144.

Saltzman, E. L. and Munhall, K. G. (1989), 'A dynamical approach to gestural patterning in speech production'. *Ecological Psychology*, 1 (4), 333–382.

Scherer, R. C., Druker, D. G., and Titze, I. R. (1988), 'Electroglottography and direct measurement of vocal fold contact area', in O. Fujimura, *Vocal Physiology: Voice Production, Mechanisms and Functions*. New York: Raven Press, pp. 279–91.

Studdert-Kennedy, M. and Goldstein, L. (2003), 'Launching language: The gestural origin of discrete infinity', in M. H. Christiansen and S. Kirby, *Language Evolution*. Oxford: Oxford University Press, pp. 235–254.

Surprenant, A. M. and Goldstein, L. (1998), 'The perception of speech gestures'. *Journal of the Acoustical Society of America*, 104 (1), 518–29.

Yngve, V. H. (1970), 'On getting a word in edgewise', in M. A. Campbell *et al.*, *Papers from the Sixth Regional Meeting, CLS 6*, Chicago: Chicago Linguistic Society, pp. 567–78.

Yngve, V. H. (1996), *From Grammar to Science: New Foundations for General Linguistics*. Amsterdam/Philadelphia: John Benjamins.

Chapter 7

An Outline of Hard-Science Phonetics-Phonology

Victor H. Yngve

Galileo, in his *Dialogue Concerning the Two Chief World Systems – Ptolemaic & Copernican* (1632), has his spokesman Salviati say that 'in the natural sciences, whose conclusions are true and necessary . . . one must take care not to place oneself in the defence of error'.[1] The pioneering work of Galileo and his contemporaries four centuries ago exposed errors inherited from Aristotle and the ancients and led to the spectacular rise of science and the vast increase of our knowledge of the natural world. The work of Galileo in laying the foundations of modern science deserves close study by all serious linguists.[2] The founders of modern linguistics, also wishing not to place themselves in the defense of error, joined the scientific revolution about two centuries ago and today linguistics is defined in its textbooks as the scientific study of language.

1. Linguistics and science

It is usual in linguistics to start with an assumption that speech is structured or patterned into phonemes, phones, features, syllables, or some other units, or in terms of some 'non-segmental' structure with segments no smaller than the syllable, or what is essentially equivalent, an initial transcription of speech by symbols on paper, such as the International Phonetic Alphabet (IPA) or some other phonetic script. The founders of modern linguistics, however, have generally realized that such an assumption is actually false, but have tentatively accepted it anyway, perhaps due to the force of tradition and the lack of an alternative (e.g. Bloomfield 1933).[3] But what was once tentative has become permanent. Could this reflect ancient errors not yet removed from a linguistics striving to be scientific?

Actually, phonemes, which Twaddell (1935) characterized as

convenient fictions, do not exist in nature, nor do any other purported segments of speech such as features or syllables. They are not part of the real physical world: they have been introduced into linguistics only by assumption. The false assumption of their reality stems directly from the ancient Aristotelian and Stoic semiotic-grammatical theory of signs relating sounds and meanings handed down to us through the ages in philosophy and normative grammar.

The false assumption of the segmental nature of speech has then served as the basis for postulating phonetic and phonological or syllabic structure for the assumed segments. This and other serious difficulties in received linguistic theory have led to the unwelcome conclusion that phonology, and with it the rest of linguistics, has been built on fatally flawed foundations. A careful search has found no brand of linguistics that avoids these difficulties. It leads one to wonder how one can avoid placing oneself in the defense of error.

In order to eliminate such problems, new foundations for linguistics have been developed that adhere only to the criteria and assumptions that have been standard in science since Galileo's time (Yngve 1986, 1996, 2000). These new foundations make it possible to reconstitute linguistics as a natural science cognate with biology, chemistry, and physics, a true hard science that in its foundations no longer places us in defense of error.

The primary question of hard-science linguistics is, 'How do people communicate?'. This paper outlines in a general way a properly reconstituted phonetics-phonology within hard-science linguistics that fills out the new theory in this important area and thus helps to unify linguistics in a seamless and scientifically acceptable fashion all the way from social and pragmatic phenomena down to physiology and physics.

Although much of what is already known in linguistics is relevant, it is often destructively misleading. We need to move completely away from the usual criteria and assumptions of a semiotic or grammatical linguistics. We need to accept instead only the standard criteria and assumptions of the hard sciences. Then we can proceed and do good science.

To refresh your memory, the standard criterion for accepting theory in the hard sciences is that its predictions must agree with the results of observation and experiment and the standard criterion for accepting observational and experimental results is their reproducibility. No other criteria are honored. The four standard assumptions of the hard sciences are that there is a real world out there to be studied, that it is coherent so we can find out something about it, that from valid premises we can calculate valid conclusions, and that observed effects stem from immediate real-world causes. All other proposed assumptions are converted into hypotheses and are subject to test using the above criteria. If they do not pass the tests or if they cannot be tested, they are rejected. These two criteria and four assumptions of science have been developed by scientists over the past four centuries and have become quite stable and standard everywhere in the hard sciences. They are at the basis of its ability to make scientific advances.[4]

2. The physics of sound

Let us start by considering the sound waves and the surroundings through which they propagate. These are physically real and are studied in a hard-science discipline that accepts, like the other hard sciences, only the two standard criteria and the four standard assumptions of all science. When we come later to include the people who communicate, in addition to the sound waves and the surroundings, we can treat them, too, in a standard hard science, since people, too, are objects of nature and part of the real physical world.

Sound waves and the surroundings through which they propagate are aspects of communicating external to speakers and hearers. They are usually neglected in the linguistics of language, which lives in the logical domain, not the physical. But their consideration would seem to be necessary for understanding the interaction of people with each other and with their physical environment. Such studies could lead to an ecological biological evolutionary understanding of the development of mankind's ability to speak.

When a person speaks, the sound energy produced is distributed over a range of frequencies. It's as if there were multiple sound sources, each at a different frequency. What is recorded, then, from a microphone placed close to the mouth, is a complex wave form representing the sum at each instant of time of the sound pressures from the multiple sources.

Speaking is inherently broadcast in nature. When a person speaks, all others within a certain region of the surroundings can hear it. But the intensity of the sound generally decreases with distance from the source. However, because the human ear is sensitive over a rather large range of sound intensities, this decrease in intensity with distance becomes important only at large distances.

The intensity and character of the sound may be affected also by other aspects of the surroundings. There may be absorption and scattering of the sound by the ground, by foliage, or by sound-absorbent materials in a room. There may be diffraction around trees or other obstructions and through doorways and the effects of the sound shadows of buildings and features of the landscape. There may be significant reflections from walls and buildings and natural obstructions. There may be effects of echoes in enclosed places such as ravines, canyons, or caves, or in a gymnasium or indoor swimming pool. These effects will vary with the frequency or with the wavelength, which varies inversely with the frequency.

There may be severe interfering effects of other sounds in the surroundings. It may be difficult to hear a person speak on a beach where a surf is running, or when leaves are rustling in a moderate wind or the wind is howling around obstructions such as trees, branches, corners of buildings, and architectural protrusions and cavities. It may be difficult to hear a person speaking in a city over loud traffic noise or in a moving vehicle.

In a small group at a dinner table, other people speaking may interfere with understanding what one of them is trying to say. If there are many people speaking as in a large restaurant, especially if there is a bad echo, each person may speak louder so as to be heard and the noise level can easily increase to the point where carrying on a conversation becomes difficult or impossible.

The various sound pressures from the multiple sources at different frequencies and from the various differently affected reflections, etc. will add to and mix with one another resulting in a complex sound field where the sound pressure with time measured at any listener's position will generally include much more than, and be much different from, the sound waves measured at a speaker's mouth.[5]

Since people often talk and are understood in noisy and acoustically degraded surroundings, we conclude that resistance to noise is a characteristic of human communicating by means of sound waves. We will want to account for how a person can extract a speech signal from noise so effectively.

3. The biology of hearing

When I began reading in the area of neuroscience in the late 1960s under the excellent tutelage of Dr. Joel Murray of the University of Chicago Department of Neurology, she shared with me her surprise and amazement that there were a large number of nerve fibers going from the brain back to the ear. This seemed counterintuitive. Isn't the ear simply a passive sense organ that transduces sound into nerve impulses which are then sent on to the brain for processing? It turns out that this puzzling observation provides a crucial clue to how hearing works.

The widespread but misleading view that first there is sensation and then perception and then propositional knowledge has its origin in the ancient Greek semiotic-grammatical theory of how a perfectly rational wise man could ideally come to perfect knowledge about the world and distinguish truth from falsity.[6] But imagining that this ancient philosophical theory of knowledge has anything to do with the actual physical functioning of the ear involves a serious confusion between the logical and the physical domains.

It is more likely that land creatures through the eons have not been much interested in ideally coming to perfect knowledge about the world and distinguishing truth from falsity. Instead they were actively searching their environments for food, danger, mates, and other objects important to their survival and these were the factors that mainly drove the evolution of their hearing organs.

In the 400-million-year evolution of hearing since the first land animals crawled out of the sea, it is thought that initially auditory papilla developed from the vestibular system devoted to balance. These had a few hundred sensory hair cells. From the very beginning of land animals there were both afferent and efferent nerve fibers transmitting impulses from and to the ear. And from the very beginning the hair cells had electrical tuning and active processes for frequency selectivity and amplification (Manley 2000a, 2000b).

From about 120 million years ago all placental and marsupial mammals have had inner ears with coiled cochleas that are divided along their length by a basilar membrane, which in humans is about 34 mm long. The incoming sound energy produces mechanical traveling waves moving along the basilar membrane, which is so shaped and designed that each incoming frequency will produce a maximum amplitude of vibration of the traveling wave at a different place along the length of the membrane, with the higher frequencies closer to the base and the lower frequencies closer to the apex.[7]

Arrayed along the length of the basilar membrane are 12,000 outer hair cells in three rows which sense its vibrations through their hair-like stereocilia that contact another membrane parallel to the basilar membrane called the tectoral membrane. These hair cells have both efferent connections from the brain and afferent connections to the brain and serve functions of amplification and frequency selectivity. There is also one row of 3500 inner hair cells that send the resulting signals to the brain.

For a long time it was not clear how a human could distinguish so accurately between different frequencies because the maxima of vibration along the basilar membrane were thought to be very broad. The answer has emerged mainly only since about 1985 and is a topic of current intensive research activity. It hinges on a growing understanding of the amazing properties of the outer hair cells.

When an outer hair cell detects motion in the basilar membrane at its particular frequency it responds by actively lengthening and shortening at that frequency thus feeding mechanical energy back into the basilar membrane so as to increase its amplitude of vibration at that place and at that frequency. A hair cell coupled to the basilar membrane in this way exhibits the sharp tuning characteristics of a resonant feedback system (compare Kössl 2000:109). Consequently the mystery of how a person can distinguish so well between different close frequencies is solved. The hair cells are sharply enough tuned to make this possible and they cover the sound spectrum like many radio receivers tuned throughout the broadcast portion of the radio spectrum. The analogy to the old regenerative radio detectors is even closer.

Another important characteristic of this system is that it is massively parallel. Each hair cell is doing its own thing, looking for and responding actively to vibrations of the basilar membrane at its own particular frequency.

What could be the function of nerve fibers going from the brain to the ear? Some have suggested they may serve as negative feedback to protect the ear from damage from very loud sounds while maintaining small-signal sensitivity, and indeed they seem to be inhibitory in nature. They could also adjust the gain individually for each hair cell to prevent its breaking into oscillation like a public address system with the volume turned up too high or to increase the gain of hair cells tuned to frequencies for which the animal is actively listening.

What is the function of sound and hearing in the wild? An animal that is subject to predation is actively listening for the sounds of predators and for other dangers and distinguishing them from background noises. A predator hunting for prey or lying in wait is actively listening for the sounds expected of prey. In many species there is a large role of sound and hearing in attracting and finding mates and in defending a territory. There would be survival value in being able to carry out several of these and other important hearing tasks actively and at the same time.

Could the outer hair cells also be directly involved in matching incoming sound with the sounds expected from food sources, danger, mates, and other objects important for survival? Could they be intimately involved in actively searching for particular sounds and distinguishing them from the general background noise rather than in passively sensing the whole surrounding sound field with all its irrelevant sounds as would be implied by the tradition? Perhaps in some cases, but I think more likely not in the cases of interest to us.

An organism takes into account the differences in sound in the two ears to determine its direction and correlates and unifies the several related frequencies from each source; and for each source, it takes into account systematic differences in pitch, sound quality, intensity, and position of the source for different sources of the same type, as for example the sounds of footsteps of animals of various sizes and weights and types of foot.

There is obvious evolutionary utility for animals in coping with the environment in being able to unify the various sounds from the same source in this way and relate them all to the same set of expectations. The neural mechanism for this must have evolved over millions of years and probably extends back at least to the earliest vertebrates. A hypothesis that some levels of the corticofugal (efferent) system higher up in the brain might serve the purpose of actively matching incoming sounds with expected sounds would seem quite likely.[8]

So with this heritage a person is even able to separate out the sound of a clarinet from an orchestra and separate out different voices talking at the same time in a small group even though the sound energy from the different voices overlaps extensively in frequency. These are tasks that instruments, lacking expectations, cannot carry out.

Consequently phoneticians are reduced to recording voices and audiologists to testing the hearing of persons individually in sound-proof and anechoic chambers. In fact, audiologists have found that they can only get reliable and repeatable measurements of thresholds of hearing if the subject is actively listening for the particular pitch of test tone to be presented.[9]

4. Expectations

Though humans are assuredly more complex communicatively than other species, there does seem to be some continuity even in understanding speech. A pet dog may come running excitedly whenever someone says 'out'. He must have been actively listening for it.[10]

Is an active listening hypothesis really credible in humans? A mother is especially sensitive to the cry of her infant. One might say she is actively listening for it even if she is sleeping. Perhaps this is innate in both the mother and the child. It is thought that the evolutionary transition of reptiles to mammals is marked by the nursing of infants, a separation or isolation call when an infant is separated from its mother, and that mammals play.

Your friend hears a strange noise and says 'What was that?'. You listen and try to play back and search through the sounds you recently heard. 'What?' you say. After a pause he says 'That'. This time you hear it and can tell him what you think it was. This would seem to require a short-term echoic or playback memory that can retain a record of the uninterpreted sound energy heard (Neisser 1967). Then there would have to be some kind of a search task carried out in the individual for comparing this with predictions of what would be expected from various possible known source types. An echoic memory would also serve well for animals listening to sounds from their environments and learning to make predictions about their environments that are important for their survival.

There is evidence that hearing and understanding speech operate by matching incoming sound with the sounds expected from others speaking. In a crowd of voices, a person is particularly sensitive to someone across the room speaking his name but does not take particular notice of other names being spoken. Undoubtedly this is a learned sensitivity.

A customer going up to a salesman in a store expects to hear something like, 'May I help you?'. And since, when one asks a question one actively expects the other person to answer it or deal with it in some way, the salesman, in turn, expects to hear the customer say something like 'Do you have ...?' or 'How much is ...?'.

'Well', you might object, 'suppose the sounds heard do not match the expectations, what then? People are not as predictable as that.' But remember that in communicating a person regularly relies on being able to predict how what he says will be understood by others. And when a person listens to someone speaking, there is usually a set of several or more expectations lying in wait and the incoming sound chooses among them. Often a person in a conversation can even predict and volunteer the very next word that the other person was about to say but cannot remember at the moment.

Comparing what is heard with expectations is part of a feedback mechanism for error detecting leading to taking corrective action.

This is the normal case. When one hears something that is not expected, a different task is invoked to analyze further what was heard. This will involve searching for other possible expectations that might be satisfied by the incoming sound. And if a serious failure in communicating is detected, the listener can always ask for clarification: 'What?', 'What did you say?'.

When a syntactic example out of context is presented in class, the student will search desperately for a context in which it can be understood, or in the case of claimed ambiguity, to find a match with another context in which it can be differently understood.[11]

Operating with expectations would be a great assistance in understanding rapid or slurred speech or someone speaking with a foreign accent. One could fill in from expectations what was not distinctly heard. People hear what they expect.[12] We can now understand how a person can extract a speech signal from noise so effectively. People expect to hear the sound of their language even though heard in noisy or acoustically degraded surroundings.

People learning a foreign language bring the expectations of their own language to the task and hear the distinctions of their own language. Then when they speak, they inevitably make the distinctions they have heard and they end up speaking with a foreign accent. It is well known that in learning a foreign language one first has to learn to hear the foreign distinctions before one can produce them.

And switching expectations can take some time. A friend of mine, a native speaker of French, looked at me blankly after I had come up and spoken to him briefly in English. 'Oh', he said after a pause, 'I though you were speaking French.'

What is the source of expectations? In some cases they would seem to have their source in the outside world in what someone says. In other cases they would seem to come from something internal to the person, such as wanting to ask a question. On closer consideration we must conclude that in each case, since the expectations determine in part what a person does or says or understands, they must be internal to the person no matter what their original source.

What a person does or says or understands depends on the context. But the operative context is revealed as simply a continually changing web of expectations. We need to find out how these expectations are structured and how they change.

In order to carry our analysis further we need a body of theory that can deal with organisms actively matching incoming sounds against expectations. We need a body of freestanding theory at a higher scientific level than neuroscience that is capable of accounting in detail for observed high-level communicative behavior, much of it learned, and that is capable of eventually explaining the high-level functioning of low-level neural mechanisms now known or that may be postulated in the future.

Hard-science linguistics theory, designed to replace the ancient semiotic-grammatical tradition as a foundation for linguistics, is general-purpose enough to replace also our ancient static theories of sensation and perception by a dynamic theory of hearing involving expectations as part of the active processes of organisms struggling to survive in their environments. In this theory expectations are analyzed internally in terms of scientifically justified lower-level properties and elementary procedures that are potentially reducible to neuroscience.

A full exposition of this theory is given in Yngve (1996), where close attention is paid to questions of its scientific justification. But a simple example can serve to indicate its general architecture.

5. The structure of expectations

In science we regularly distinguish between the part of the real physical world modeled and our testable model or theory of that reality, which we can formalize as a *system*.

Consider a formal meeting following parliamentary procedure.[13] The assemblage of persons attending the meeting can be represented or modeled in theory as a system called a *linkage*. We can call this particular linkage system [meeting].

Systems are characterized by *properties*, some of which may be *task procedures*. The internal structure of task procedures, expectation procedures, and other types of procedures are given in Yngve (1996). When the meeting is transacting business, we can say that the [meeting] linkage is carrying out a task procedure <transact business>. When the meeting is transacting business, we say it is open. We model this as the [meeting] linkage having a property <open>.

Consider a person attending this meeting as a member. We set up a system called a *role part* to represent in theory the part that this member plays in the meeting. We can call this role-part system [member].

The task procedure executed in the [member] role part when the member is attending the meeting can be called <attend>. This <attend> task in the [member] role part is carried out by carrying out a sequence of subtasks:

<time> involving waiting for the time for the meeting to start;
<take seat> involving the member taking a seat in the hall;
<come to order> involving the member's part in the meeting coming to order; and
<transact business> involving the member's part in transacting the business of the meeting.

There is no problem in using the same name 'transact business' for the linkage task procedure and for the role-part task procedure as they are properties of different systems. Similarly, the [member] role part can have a state property called <open> to represent the member's part in the [meeting] linkage state property <open>.

We can write this analysis of the <attend> task in the [member] role part as:

<attend> = <time> -> <take seat> -> <come to order> -> <transact business> ? <open>

Let us now look at the member's task <come to order>. This involves parallel expectation procedures. Having taken his seat the member expects either the presiding officer to stand <expect stand> or to hear the sound of the rap of the gavel <expect rap> or the assemblage to become quiet <expect quiet>. When any of these occurs, the member becomes quiet <be quiet> and expects to hear the presiding officer call the meeting to order <expect call to order>.

Using commas to separate parallel expectation procedures, we can write this as:

<come to order> = <expect stand>, <expect rap>, <expect quiet> -> <first done> -> <be quiet> -> <expect call to order>

Note how the influence of context is handled. It is manifested in the expectations. If the presiding officer in the context of a formal meeting, as here, stands when he is expected to open the meeting, the assemblage becomes quiet.[14] If he were to stand in some other context or in this context at some other time when not expected, it would probably be ignored.[15]

Note that this type of analysis is not just invented on the basis of whim or intuition. Expectation procedures, although they do make intuitive sense, are carefully introduced as constructs in a scientifically justified physical-domain theory. This stands in stark contrast with various grammatical theories and notations that it may appear superficially to resemble. The resemblance can be a guide in reconstituting linguistics as a hard science, but one must beware at every turn of the many pitfalls connected with domain confusions and the lack of scientific justification within the grammatical tradition.

Now consider the member's task <expect call to order> in which the member expects to hear the presiding officer call the meeting to order. This involves hearing the sound of the presiding officer calling the meeting to order and trying to match it with expectations. Turning to the standard manuals (Robert 1990:24; Sturgis 1993:109) for examples of what might be expected, and using + to indicate an attempt to match a sound with expected sounds, we can model this in the [member] role part as:

> <expect call to order> = <(sound heard from presiding officer)> +
> <expect sound of 'The meeting will come to order'>,
> <expect sound of 'The meeting will be in order'>,
> <expect sound of 'The meeting will please be in order',
> <expect sound of 'The Eighty-third Annual Meeting of the House of Delegates of the American Dental Association is now convened'>
> -> <match> N <try again> Y ->

The task <expect call to order> involves the member actively listening for the presiding officer to call the meeting to order. It can be seen as involving the focus of attention of the member on the presiding officer and what the presiding officer might say, which can be seen as a lower level of the member's focus of attention on the meeting through his task <attend>.

The task procedure <(sound heard from presiding officer)> involves the evolutionarily advantageous ability of animals being able to localize and unify the various sounds from the same source and relate them all to the same set of expectations taking into account systematic differences in pitch, sound quality, and intensity of the source for different sources of the same type, such as the men's or women's voices of different presiding officers.

The results of no match, N, lead to executing a task procedure <try again>, the details of which could be analyzed at a lower level, and the results of match, Y, lead on to the next task after the completion of <expect call to order>, which is the <transact business> subtask of the <attend> task as above.

Consider now the several parallel subtasks <expect sound of '...'>.

It may be that one or another of the possibilities will be remembered and recognized as a whole as in rote memory. But it is likely that the longer ones or perhaps all will not be remembered as a whole, but recognized in terms of separate sequential and possibly hierarchically structured expectations.

This sort of recognition is a version of analysis by syntheses as explored in considerable detail in Neisser (1967), but here it is freed from grammar and consequently the domain confusions have been removed that were revealed in attempts to test the depth hypothesis of Yngve (1960),[16] and the needed ability to handle all contextual and pragmatic effects has been added.

The question then arises: for each of the possibilities, what is the structure of the expectations different people might have or the same person might have at different times that would lead to recognition? How far down would the structure of tasks and subtasks go?

We can measure the capacity of the evolutionarily advantageous short-term echoic memory discussed earlier that can retain a record of the uninterpreted sound energy heard.

Many writing systems around the world are based on the syllable. That casts some doubt on the psychological reality of phoneme-sized expectations.

The intuition that speech is segmented is an observational phenomenon about people, and particularly about linguists and about literates. Any structuring projected on heard speech is in the person's task hierarchy and its expectations. Consequently, these intuitions can provide us with information on expectations, but it must be used with the utmost care. Remember that we're not studying people's intuitions, a logical-domain enterprise; we're studying how people communicate, a physical-domain enterprise. We must be extremely careful to avoid the domain confusions lurking here.

In one family that I knew, a child, after a long silence said, 'Mommy, Daddy, I know why they call it the fourthajuly. Because it's the fourth of July!'[17] Other such hints of learning in terms of fairly long segments are easily available.

We can't ignore hints from phonemic theories. Within these, problems have arisen that have led to considerable work relevant to hard-science linguistics, particularly in the study of prosodic effects, vowel harmony, consonant harmony, and 'suprasegmental' phenomena, e.g. Lehiste (1970), Hansson (2001) and many others.

6. Speaking and learning to speak

We have seen that all or nearly all of the properties of hearing needed to support speech were well in place a hundred million or more years ago. A modern larynx and vocal tract that can support speaking, on the other hand, have evolved only within the last few hundred thousand years (Lieberman 1991:73).

An ability to speak is not needed for understanding speech. Some animals can learn to understand a bit of speech. It has been reported that a child physically unable to speak can learn to understand the speech of others. It is well known that children need to learn to understand before they can speak.[18]

Giving a child the breast after crying is not only a nutritional act promoting the survival of the child: it is a significant communicative act as well from which a child normally equipped can begin to learn complex communicative skills. Crying gradually becomes more differentiated and there is learning in the mother-infant linkage directed toward the necessary giving of care to the infant.

Play is characteristic of all mammals. Babbling is an aspect of play. It gives the child practice in controlling the vocal tract in a nonsocial setting where the child has auditory feedback and can compare the sounds he makes with his memories of sounds he has heard. This requires a short-term or echoic memory by which the child can remember the sound he has just produced. It also requires a longer-term memory for uninterpreted sounds for matching and the ability to compare incoming sounds to this and to make judgments of same or different. This supplies the feedback necessary for learning.

A child is embedded in a physical and social environment, its circle of linkages, from which it can learn. This circle of linkages can be quite complex with overlaps of different people playing different role parts in different linkages. There may be linkages with parents, other adults, siblings, playmates, and eventually in many cases school.

Linkage theory is equipped to handle this social interactive complexity and the relation of individuals to groups. Linkage theory also includes mechanisms for handling the communicative effects of real-world objects and the surroundings as well as sound and other forms of communicative energy flow including writing, a fairly recent and still not universal communicative skill. It allows the representation of complex overlappings and interactions of groups and of groups of groups all the way up to the largest complexly structured communities and their various observed interactive overlaps.

Learning to speak is a social process involving pragmatic real-world consequences for a child at every turn as he interacts in the various linkages of his circle. The large effect of social context is included in the properties of the various individuals and linkages making up the child's circle. In these linkages the child experiences the social and real-world consequences of his own attempts at speaking and of the speaking of the others he observes. And from this he learns to understand and to speak.

Speaking tasks are parallel to hearing tasks in that the child or the adult hears himself speak. This allows for the very important facilitating effect of monitoring by which a person can judge the results of his attempts to speak. Again, hearing is necessary for speaking. It is difficult for a hearing-impaired child to learn to speak due to the poor quality of the acoustic feedback for monitoring. This kind of monitoring, more advanced than the child's monitoring of his babbling, requires a memory for two plex structures, that is, for the structure of tasks and expectations involved in the child's attempt and the structure of tasks and expectations involved in his hearing and understanding the monitoring feedback, and of course a mechanism for comparing the two and making judgments of same or different. This is a memory for interpreted speech in contrast to the memory for the uninterpreted speech of babbling. Thus we account easily for the difference well-known to language teachers between imitating and repeating the speech of another person.

Other mammals imitate their mothers in matters important for survival such as where to go, what to eat, and what to be afraid of. The child's attempts at imitating the speaking of others may be rewarded by success in the child-mother linkage and in linkages with other persons.

However this is much more than just imitation. Analogy is involved as is the child's gradual learning of the distinctions that make a pragmatic difference in its life.

Thus children use much more evidence than, as has sometimes been alleged, just the sounds they hear.[19]

I strongly suspect that also involved in the dynamic processes of speaking and understanding is a memory covering the function of the temporary memory in the depth model (Yngve 1960) but that includes much more than just syntactic expectations. This may become evident as hard-science linguistic plex structures are further elaborated and their relation to the type of phrase-structure grammar assumed in the depth hypothesis is more clearly understood. But we have to be careful of the analogy. That model was purely syntactic; in hard-science linguistics we must include everything that might condition what a person says or understands at any given time.

The exciting work on task dynamics promises a hard-science method for analyzing the control of the physical gestures of speaking. Task dynamics describes motions such as reaching for a cup or closing the lips in a speech gesture not in terms directly of physical movements in space but in terms of the targets of the tasks, with the interaction of various overlapping gestures being automatically coordinated by the theory. Coarticulation effects fall out automatically. For further details see Docherty and Ladd (1992), particularly the introductory chapter by Sarah Hawkins (1992); and Munhall and Jones (1995) and other papers in the same volume.

Task dynamics is inherently pragmatic and would fit well in human (hard-science) linguistics which is pragmatic from top to bottom. Although much of the current work in task dynamics accepts logical-domain (phonemic) assumptions about the higher-level commands leading to speaking, the theory is completely physical-domain in nature and task-dynamic models could easily be embedding in a hard-science phonetics-phonology. This may be particularly important to the further development of task dynamics in offering a compatible way of modeling the sequencing and timing of speech gestures. The tasks of task dynamics would be seen as subtasks of hard-science-linguistics tasks and this would work well since hard-science linguistics has a built-in method of handling time delays.[20]

7. What is innate?

Evolution operates on species but in the first instance it operates on individuals and their reproductive success in their environments. For humans that involves also in part speaking and understanding in their social environments. In order to understand the effects of social forces on evolution and to confront the phenomena in their entirety, we need two orders of linguistic theory, individual and social. Hard-science linguistics provides those two orders of theory built on a scientifically justified foundation.

It is only properties of real-world organisms in the physical domain that can be innate, i.e. inherited in the genes. Hard-science linguistics moves the question of what may be innate into the physical domain where it can actually be investigated scientifically.

We have seen that ears and the related neurological equipment are not passive devices. They are active dynamic organs and have been from the very beginning of land animals. They are biologically adapted to scan, search for, and analyze significant environmental sounds in a complex and ever-changing sound field that has come to include even the sounds of other persons speaking. An impressive evolutionary continuity is revealed.

Let us now consider Chomsky's so-called 'innateness hypothesis' and his 'UG'.[21] It is formulated not in the real-world physical domain where ordinary biological evolution takes place, but in the non-real logical domain where there is no possibility of testing theories or hypotheses scientifically. We can say with certainty that Chomsky's 'Universal Grammar' is not innate because it is formulated in the logical domain where nothing is real and nothing can be innate. It is not a scientific hypothesis at all and cannot be taken seriously by scientists.

I can say no more about Chomsky's assumed power to confer biological reality on UG and other of the theoretical constructs he creates and names than to quote Galileo in *The Assayer* in his dispute with the philosophers of his own day:

> I am not so sure that in order to make a comet a quasi-planet, and as such to deck it out in the attributes of other planets, it is sufficient for Sarsi or his teacher to regard it as one and so name it. If their opinions and their voices have the power of calling into existence the things they name, then I beg them to do me the favor of naming a lot of old hardware I have about my house, 'gold'. [Drake 1957:253]

Chomsky's powers would have to be even greater, for Sarsi was concerned only with physical-domain objects such as comets and planets. He never attempted to materialize real-world objects out of freely invented logical-domain constructs. But in this Chomsky has had a lot of practice stretching back at least to his 'systematic ambiguity' (1965:25), of which he says:

> Note that we are again using the term 'theory' – in this case 'theory of language' rather than 'theory of a particular language' – with a systematic ambiguity, to refer both to the child's innate predisposition to learn a language of a certain type and to the linguist's account of this.

Notice how Chomsky slips the word 'innate' into this logical-domain discussion thus purposefully muddying the distinction between the logical and the physical domains and completely ignoring the well-understood distinction between philosophy, which proposes theories of theories that cannot be tested, and science, which proposes theories of the real world that can. This surprisingly explicit and admitted equivocation foreshadows the double-talk of 'mind-brain' which invites the reader to disregard the many domain confusions throughout Chomsky's writings.[22]

8. Conclusion

How far has science come since Galileo? There is no hesitation today in accepting the methods and findings of modern science in the physics of sound, the biology of the ear and the vocal tract, and related ecological and evolutionary considerations even including animal communication. But it seems that at the mere mention of a person speaking or understanding speech, suddenly standard science goes out the window. Such questions tend inevitably to introduce scientifically unacceptable assumptions of unreal objects of language and signs and grammars. Our best efforts to build a science are frustrated and we find ourselves not much beyond the philosophical speculations of Aristotle and the ancient Stoics.

It is unacceptable in what aspires to be a science to continue to study the convenient fictions of classical phonology and support an approach to linguistics that embraces false assumptions and invents its own objects of study. In the logical domain anyone can freely invent and introduce competing fictions and there is no good way to decide among them. We can do better than that. Science does not introduce its objects of study by assumption; it finds them already existing in the real world. In studying the real world, individual scientists decide for themselves what theories to accept. In this they honor only the standard criteria and make only the standard assumptions of all science. Four centuries of experience has shown that this leads in the end to agreement.

I am not arguing for yet another brand of grammar but only that after two centuries we finally accept modern standard science. I am arguing that we follow Galileo and not place ourselves in the defense of error. Galileo worked to replace the ancient and inadequate Aristotelian philosophical tradition as a foundation for physics and astronomy by a modern scientific foundation.[23] We must now work to replace the ancient and inadequate Aristotelian-Stoic semiotic-grammatical tradition as a foundation for linguistics by a modern scientific foundation. We must reconstitute linguistics as a standard science. That means it must be a hard science focused on real-world objects such as people and sound waves rather than philosophy or a soft science focused on unreal immaterial objects such as language or grammar or segmented and structured utterances.

To argue for standard science should not be controversial among linguists: our goal for two centuries has been to build a linguistic science. And to maintain intellectual integrity and openly defend the search for scientific truth against a false but widely held and strongly entrenched ancient philosophical tradition should not take nearly as much courage in the twenty-first century as it took Galileo in the seventeenth.

Notes

This is an updated version of a paper presented as a plenary lecture at the 2002 SLE (Societas Linguistica Europaea) meeting in Potsdam, Germany. Although I take full responsibility for this paper, I want to thank Laura Koenig for feedback and discussions in the beginning and for many valuable leads to the literature, Sean Fulop for discussion and valuable leads, David Powers for discussions on acquisition, Joanna Lowenstein for a most valuable lead, Jeanne Perkins for feedback regarding audiology, valued colleagues, particularly Mojca Brezar, Lara Burazer, Bernard Sypniewski, and Douglas Coleman, and members of the email list.

1. This appears shortly before the middle of *The First Day* (pp. 53–54 in the excellent English translation by Stillman Drake).
2. The widely available paperback by Drake (1957) is probably the best place to start for an introduction to Galileo's writings. It's thrilling to read first-hand Galileo's own description of his first discoveries with the telescope in *The Starry Messenger* (1610), appearing here with his most important early works including his influential *The Assayer* (1623), skillfully abridged. Interesting biographical and historical information is also included. All Galileo's works are easily accessible to the general public, for whom he wrote, and for whom he wrote in Italian for the most part rather than in Latin for the academics of his day.

   Galileo was his own popularizer of science. His contributions did not need to be interpreted for the public as did the works of later scientists like Newton and Einstein: yet his important lessons for the academics were always abundantly clear. His sometimes polemical style adds interest for the reader, and was probably required to convince the majority of the intellectual leaders of his day to move from a dependence on a deeply entrenched philosophical tradition and the writings of ancient authors such as Aristotle to an acceptance of a modern scientific approach to deciding what to believe about the natural world. Having served this purpose of changing the criteria for accepting or rejecting statements of presumed fact about the natural world, a polemical style soon went out of favor in science to be replaced by dispassionately laying out the scientific merits of a case.

Drake and O'Malley (1960) gives English translations of several works in Latin and Italian figuring in the controversy on the comets of 1618. It pits Galileo and a colleague against a traditional philosopher. Galileo's final answer *The Assayer* (1623), included here in its entirety, played a pivotal role at the beginning of the modern scientific revolution and has been called his scientific manifesto. It is important for understanding how modern science differs from the Aristotelian philosophy that came before. Galileo's works are also deservedly valued for their beautiful prose style and literary excellence, which shines through in Stillman Drake's excellent translations. The wide acclaim that *The Assayer* received led Galileo to seek permission from Rome to write his famous dialog (1632) on the two chief world systems, which then got him into trouble with the Inquisition and led to his house arrest for life. His most significant work scientifically, however, is his later work on the *Two New Sciences* (1638), in which the foundations of modern physics are laid. Stillman Drake truly calls this the 'first great work in modern physics'.

3. Bloomfield was carefully explicit about a conceptual problem that afflicted all approaches to linguistics. He wrote:

> The study of language can be conducted without special assumptions only so long as we pay no attention to the meaning of what is spoken. This phase of language study is known as *phonetics (experimental phonetics, laboratory phonetics)*. [1933:75]

> The study of *significant* speech-sounds is *phonology or practical phonetics*. Phonology involves the consideration of meanings. The meanings of speech-forms could be scientifically defined only if all branches of science, including, especially, psychology and physiology, were close to perfection. Until that time, phonology and, with it, all of the semantic phase of language study, rests upon an assumption, the fundamental assumption of linguistics: we must assume that *in every speech-community some utterances are alike in form and meaning*. [1933:78]

Such a false assumption is not needed in hard-science linguistics, which is conceived in the modern scientific tradition and studies people and sound waves in the real-world physical domain rather than being conceived in the ancient semiotic-grammatical tradition concerned with assumed logical-domain objects such as language and utterances and meanings that are not real objects and thus cannot be studied scientifically. For a further analysis of Bloomfield's assumption and a discussion of the problems surrounding it, see Yngve (1983, 1986, 1996).

4. A widely available and easily accessible introduction to science is Feynman (1995). Written by the renowned 1965 Nobel Laureate in

Physics who was famous also for his clear explanations and brilliant teaching, this book selects six lectures from Feynman's introductory course at the beginning college level. One should read all the material in the book written by Feynman except Chapter 3, which is vastly out of date and where Feynman was out of his element.

5. Relevant theory is found in the science of acoustics in physics. The sound energy from a spherical source in an otherwise unobstructed region propagates out from the source in all directions so as to flow uniformly through the surfaces of ever larger spheres centered on the source. The analogy already known to the ancients is to the ripples in a pond expanding in ever increasing circles when a stone is tossed in. The sound intensity J radiating from a spherical source falls off as the square of the distance r from the center, $J_r = k/r^2$, where k is a constant. This law follows simply from the law of the conservation of energy and the fact that the area of a sphere varies as the square of its radius.

Theory is available for calculating the behavior of sound in other simple geometries. The resonances of a room of given width, length, and height can be calculated. The scattering of sound from a cylinder can be calculated, and how it varies with the wavelength of the sound in comparison with the radius of the cylinder (Morse 1948). But if the sound is obstructed in the many complex ways we have been discussing, many theoretical considerations would have to be invoked if one wanted to calculate the sound intensity at any point and at any given frequency. Such calculations might be rather complex and difficult to carry out. Calculating the effect of a tree trunk on the sound field would probably have to involve the simplifying assumption of a cylindrical tree trunk with perfectly reflecting bark. For complex cases of many obstructions one would probably have to resort to a computer simulation program that reproduced the physical situation point by point and there would still be such problems as how to represent the tree in the simulation.

6. Much of the literature on the sense organs tacitly follows the assumptions of the ancient Greek philosophical and epistemological semiotic theory dating to Aristotle and before that dealt with the question of how we ideally know what there is in the world. For a good outline of the very influential Stoic version of about 300–150 BC see the account in Diogenes Laertius (Hicks 1925). There were logical-domain levels of sensation, perception, and propositional logic that have often mistakenly been assumed as appropriately underlying modern physical-domain biological and psychological theories of hearing, sight, and other sensory modes. The serious domain confusions introduced has taken the work completely outside of science.

7. Suggested readings on hearing include Ashmore (2000), Flock, Ottoson, and Ulfendahl (1995), Geisler (1998), Gelfand (1998), and Yost (2000).

8. See Suga, Enquam, Zhang, Ma, and Olsen (2000).

9. It is standard practice in audiology (Travis 1971:356) when measuring the threshold of hearing for a pure tone, to first present the subject with a burst of the test tone of about one second duration at a level that he can easily hear 'to assure that the subject is fully aware of the experience for which he is to listen' (Carhart and Jerger 1959:331) and then present bursts of test tone starting at a level below threshold and then at gradually increasing levels until the subject reports he can hear it.

10. A number of colleagues assure me that their dogs are much more talented than this in understanding speech.

11. The problem is that grammatical theory cannot handle these cases because the semiotic-grammatical tradition on which it is based has no mechanism for handling context or contextual expectations. So it inevitably operates by unrealistically abstracting away from the context.

12. And when they read they see what they expect. Although I should have foreseen it, it caught me completely by surprise that my 1996 book, which had been carefully composed to be clear and unambiguous, would be regularly misunderstood in quite different ways by different people with different backgrounds and sets of expectations. This is undoubtedly connected to their not switching expectations or not realizing to what extent they would have to switch expectations. It has to be read with great care and no parts skimmed over hurriedly, because it likely will not be saying what one might expect. Those having the easiest time understanding it have been beginning students without highly developed expectations in relation to the subject matter covered.

   Perhaps the greatest intellectual obstacle to understanding and working with hard-science linguistics that is faced by those coming to it with extensive linguistic or philosophical training is to discount their familiar expectations and learn to identify and reject nonscientific criteria and unsupported assumptions lurking among their preconceptions. This is not easy for most people. It requires extensive work in questioning what one has always assumed.

13. I follow here the paper 'Rules of Order' that has been presented at meetings and has been widely available as a memorandum. An updated version appears above as Chapter 4.

14. Note also that although we are focusing on sound in this study, we are not restricted to sound in hard-science linguistics. We can easily handle the communicative relevance of standing and of rapping with a gavel. And we can distinguish this instance of standing from a member standing to be recognized during the course of the meeting.

15. It has long been realized that context is important: it figures dynamically in what people do and understand when they communicate. The semiotic-grammatical tradition does not offer a mechanism for taking the context into account. That lack has always been there. It can be traced back to ancient Greek philosophy that was concerned with eternal truths independent of the context. We have inherited a

foundation based on triadic signs relating sounds, concepts, and things that has no place for the context. Hard-science linguistics corrects the lack by incorporating context right in its very foundations in terms of the conditional properties in elementary procedures.

16. This is the widespread confusion between grammar in the logical domain and what people actually do in the physical domain when they speak and understand. Unfortunately this domain confusion not only infested the depth hypothesis but apparently also infests most of the current work in psycholinguistics and related disciplines. People do not 'use' grammar when they speak or understand nor do they 'have' internal grammars that they so use. It is to be hoped that progress in hard-science linguistics will make it possible for such confusions to be gradually eliminated from linguistic theory.

17. US Independence Day.

18. Although communicating is a cooperative endeavor, the usual account, that assumes phonemes or other segments, starts with a discussion of producing these segments in speaking and then moves on to consider the listener and the distinctions he can hear. This makes sense if one assumes phonemes as given and follows the flow of causality and the direction of the arrows in Saussure's famous illustration of the speech circuit (1955:27).

    But in hard-science linguistics we are freed from this assumption. We can follow evolution in our account and start with hearing. And if we were to follow the development of the child, we would again have to give priority to hearing since a child has to learn to hear the distinctions of speech before he can learn to produce them.

19. This idea goes back in history, but more recently it has been reduced to the absurd. Since the semiotic-grammatical tradition has no formal way of handling either context in the broad sense or the social side of communicating, linguists like Chomsky have apparently been led to believe that children learn to speak simply by hearing others speaking out of context and using that as data. Consequently, Chomsky claims he cannot conceive of how a child, with this restricted 'impoverished' data, could learn his form of grammar in the time available. So he concludes that grammar must be innate – the poverty of the stimulus argument that has been widely criticized. But it is not poverty of the stimulus, it is poverty of the conception. And this oversimplified and idealized view of the child 'learning language' by exposure only to the sounds of people speaking has encouraged others to try to model language learning by a purely statistical procedure on texts or recorded sound waves.

20. I first heard about task dynamics around 1970 from my colleague at the University of Chicago, Peter H. Greene. His example was of a person signing his name first with a pen on paper and second in chalk on a blackboard. Although their sizes are quite different, still there is a resemblance as both are the person's signature. How can this be as the

motions and muscle groups involved in the signing are quite different in the two cases? Task dynamics addresses this.

21. See almost any recent work of Chomsky, for example 1986:3 *passim*.
22. A discussion of some of the controversy surrounding Chomsky's innateness claims may be found in Fischer (ms.).
23. Albert Einstein expressed it this way: 'The *leitmotif* which I recognize in Galileo's work is the passionate fight against any kind of dogma based on authority. Only experience and careful reflection are accepted by him as criteria of truth' (Drake 1967:xvii).

References

Ashmore, Jonathan (2000), 'Hearing' in Patricia Kruth and Henry Stobart, *Sound*. Cambridge: Cambridge University Press, pp. 65–88.

Bloomfield, Leonard (1933), *Language*. New York: Holt (Reprint: Chicago: University of Chicago Press, 1984).

Carhart, Raymond and Jerger, James F. (1959), 'Preferred method for clinical determination of pure-tone thresholds', *Journal of Speech and Hearing Disorders*, 24:330.

Chomsky, Noam (1965), *Aspects of the Theory of Syntax*. Cambridge, MA: MIT Press.

Chomsky, Noam (1986), *Knowledge of Language: Its Nature, Origin, and Use*. Westport, Connecticut: Praeger.

Docherty, Gerard J. and Ladd, D. Robert (1992), *Papers in Laboratory Phonology II: Gesture, Segment, Prosody*. Cambridge: Cambridge University Press.

Drake, Stillman, ed. and tr. (1957), *Discoveries and Opinions of Galileo: Including The Starry Messenger (1610), Letter to the Grand Duchess Christina (1615), and excerpts from Letters on Sunspots (1613), The Assayer (1623)*. Garden City, New York: Random House Anchor Books.

Drake, Stillman, tr. (1967), see Galileo (1632).

Drake, Stillman and O'Malley, G. D., eds and trs (1960), *The Controversy on the Comets of 1618: Galileo Galilei, Horatio Grassi, Mario Guiducci, and Johann Kepler*. Philadelphia: University of Pennsylvania Press.

Feynman, Richard P. (1995), *Six Easy Pieces: Essentials of Physics Explained by Its Most Brilliant Teacher*. Reading, MA: Helix Books (Addison Wesley).

Fischer, Olga. (in press) 'Grammar Change vs. Language Change: Is there a Difference?' Plenary presentation read at the 12th International Conference on English Historical Linguistics. *New Perspectives in English Historical Linguistics 1: Syntax and Morphology* edited by Christian Kay, Jeremy Smith, and S. Horobin. Amsterdam: Benjamins.

Flock, Å., Ottoson, D., and Ulfendahl, M. (1995), *Active Hearing*. Wenner Gren International Series. Vol. 65. Kidlington, Oxford: Elsevier Pergamon.

Galilei, Galileo (1610), *The Starry Messenger ('Sidereus Nuncius')*, Venice. See Drake (1957).

Galilei, Galileo (1623), *The Assayer ('Il Saggiatore')*. Translated by Stillman Drake, in Drake and O'Malley (1960).

Galilei, Galileo (1632), *Dialogue Concerning the Two Chief World Systems – Ptolemaic & Copernican*. Translated by Stillman Drake, foreword by Albert Einstein. Berkeley: University of California Press (1967).

Galilei, Galileo (1638), *Dialogues Concerning Two New Sciences ('Discorsi e dimostrazioni matematiche intorno a due nuove scienze')*. Translated by Henry Crew and Alfonso Se Salvio. New York: Dover, 1954.

Geisler, C. Daniel (1998), *From Sound to Synapse: Physiology of The Mammalian Ear*. New York: Oxford.

Gelfand, Stanley A. (1998), *Hearing: An Introduction to Psychological and Physiological Acoustics* (3rd edn). New York: Marcel Dekker.

Hansson, Gunnar Ólafur (2001), 'The phonologization of production constraints: Evidence from consonant harmony,' *CLS 37*. Chicago: CLS, pp. 187–200.

Hawkins, Sarah (1992), 'An introduction to task dynamics', in Docherty and Ladd (1992), pp. 9–25.

Hicks, R. D., tr. (1925), *Lives of Eminent Philosophers*, by Diogenes Laertius (2 vols). Cambridge: Harvard University Press; London: William Heinemann.

Kössl, Manfred (2000), 'Otoacoustic emissions and cochlear mechanisms in mammals', in G. A. Manley, H. Fastl, M. Kössl, H. Oeckinghaus, and G. Klump (2000), *Auditory Worlds: Sensory Analysis and Perception in Animals and Man*. Weinheim, Germany: Wiley-VCH Verlag GmbH., pp. 106–120.

Lehiste, Ilse (1970), *Suprasegmentals*. Cambridge, MA: MIT Press.

Lieberman, Philip (1991), *Uniquely Human: The Evolution of Speech, Thought, and Selfless Behavior*. Cambridge, MA: Harvard University Press.

Manley, Geoffrey A. (2000a). 'Design plasticity in the evolution of the amniote hearing organ', in G. A. Manley, H. Fastl, M. Kössl, H. Oeckinghaus, and G. Klump, *Auditory Worlds: Sensory Analysis and Perception in Animals and Man*. Weinheim, Germany: Wiley-VCH Verlag GmbH., pp. 7–17.

Manley, Geoffrey A. (2000b), 'Cochlear mechanisms from a phylogenetic viewpoint'. *Proceedings of the National Academy of Sciences of the United States* 97:11736–11743.

Morse, Philip M. (1948), *Vibrations and Sound*. New York: McGraw-Hill.

Munhall, K. G. and Jones, J. A. (1995), 'The spatial control of speech movements', in Fredericka Bell-Berti and Lawrence J. Raphael, *Producing Speech: Contemporary Issues for Katherine Safford Harris*. New York: American Institute of Physics, pp. 521–537.

Neisser, Ulrich (1967), *Cognitive Psychology*. New York: Appleton-Century Crofts.

Robert, Henry M. (1990), *The Scott Foresman Robert's Rules of Order Newly Revised, a new and enl. ed. by Sara Corbin Robert, with the assistance of Henry M. Robert III, William J. Evans*. N.p.: Scott Foresman.

Saussure, Ferdinand de (1955) [1915], *Cours de Linguistique Générale*. Paris: Payot.

Sturgis, Alice (1993), *The Standard Code of Parliamentary Procedure, Third Edition, New and Revised*. New York: McGraw-Hill.

Suga, N., Enquam, G., Zhang, Y., Ma, X., and Olsen, J. F. (2000), 'The corticofugal system for hearing: recent progress'. *Proceedings of the National Academy of Sciences of the United States of America*, 11807–11814.

Travis, Lee Edward (1971), *Handbook of Speech Pathology and Audiology*. New York: Appleton-Century-Crofts.

Twaddell, W. Freeman (1935), *On Defining the Phoneme* (= *Language Monograph* no. 16). Baltimore: Linguistic Society of America. (Reprinted in Joos and Martin (1957), *Readings in Linguistics*. Washington: American Council of Learned Societies.)

Yngve, Victor H. (1960), 'A model and an hypothesis for language structure'. *Proceedings of the American Philosophical Society* 104:444–66.

Yngve, Victor H. (1983), 'Bloomfeld's fundamental assumption of linguistics', in John Morreall, *The Ninth LACUS Forum 1982*, Columbia, SC: Hornbeam Press, pp. 137–145.

Yngve, Victor H. (1986), *Linguistics as a Science*. Bloomington and Indianapolis: Indiana University Press.

Yngve, Victor H. (1996), *From Grammar to Science: New Foundations for General Linguistics*. Amsterdam/Philadelphia: John Benjamins.

Yngve, Victor H. (2000), 'The depth hypothesis and the new hard-science linguistics', in Irena Kovačič, Milena Milojević-Sheppard, Silvana Orel-Kos, and Janez Orešnik, *Linguistics and Language Studies: Exploring Language from Different Perspectives*. Ljubljana: Filozofska fakultete Univerze v Ljubljani, pp.191–202 (revised here as Chapter 1).

Yost, William A. (2000), *Fundamentals of Hearing: An Introduction* (4th edn). San Diego: Academic Press.

PART III

IN SEARCH OF CONTEXT

Chapter 8

Reconstituting Notions of Reference

Lara Burazer

The treatment of reference in traditional grammar and discourse analysis is compared with a human linguistics treatment.

The notion of reference is associated with a number of disciplines. In general, it denotes some sort of relationship between two items under consideration. In philosophy it is defined as a naming relationship that exists between words and the real world. In traditional linguistics, words do not name or refer to objects around us, they primarily create relationships intra-textually between various textual items. Thus reference is transferred from a relation holding between language and the real world to a relationship within language alone.

Through examining the concept of reference in cohesion and coherence as understood in discourse analysis, the traditional text-bound treatment of reference is compared with the human-linguistics treatment of referring, which accentuates the importance of the real world in its concepts of participants, channels, props, settings, and linkages. In human linguistics, the notions of reference and referring are no longer defined even partly in terms of language and text in the logical domain, but rather in the physical-domain terms of people and sound waves. It is people who refer, not words, and we speak of 'referring behavior'.

1. Notions of reference and referring

The notions of reference and referring appear in many different fields of research, especially those dealing with humans and their behavior. Most philosophers define them as concepts having to do with the relationship between a linguistic unit and the extralinguistic entity referred to by this unit:

'... a range of semantically significant relations that hold between various sorts of terms and the world.' [*Encyclopedia of Philosophy* 1998, 8:153]

Or, in the words of Frege and Russel, 'a name refers to a certain object because that object is picked out by the name's associated description' (*ibid*. p.154).

The selected citations both associate the concepts of reference and referring with language. They represent some sort of common ground for all human languages, or any code of human communication. What is also pointed out in these definitions from philosophy is that it is the *words* that refer to or point out objects and other worldly phenomena. In these definitions it is not *people* who refer or point to something, which is the case in human linguistics.

In traditional linguistics, the notions of reference and referring are defined in terms of devices used *in texts* to create the relationship of referring between two *textual* elements. The relationship of *word toward the world* has been transferred into a relationship of word toward text. The role of reference has been assigned to textual elements, as if words and other textual entities were conveying messages on their own.

In the more recent field of text linguistics, reference has been given a prominent role as a grammatical cohesive device, some sort of textual glue in the form of various grammatical forms.

In the developing field of human linguistics, the notions of reference and referring are no longer associated with logical-domain terms like language, text, or textual elements. In the hard-science physical domain, it is not these logical-domain terms that refer: it is people who refer. Therefore, in order to keep the two concepts separate, we reserve the terms *referring* and *referring behavior* for the realm of human linguistics, and the term *reference* for traditional linguistics.

2. Text linguistics faces human linguistics

In discourse analysis, the most frequent linguistic representation of reference occurs through personal pronouns, demonstratives, and comparatives (and in English at least, the definite article; although all reference has the semantic property of definiteness or specificity). These textual entities refer to other textual entities in the text. The type of reference depends on the order of occurrence of the referent and the reference unit, as well as the accompanying textual and non-textual environment.

In accordance with Halliday and Hassan's discourse analysis treatment of reference (1976) we speak of various *phoric* relationships:

Endophoric reference, which deals with intra-textual referential relationships, i.e. reference within the text;
Exophoric reference, which deals with extra-textual, situational referential relationships that occur between a textual item and an entity outside the text.

Endophoric reference is further divided into *anaphoric* reference, which points backwards to preceding text, and *cataphoric* reference, which points forward to following text.

The above traditional treatment of reference

tends to think of a referential domain as static and given in a lexicon, so reference selects from entries in the lexicon. But in human linguistics a referential domain is dynamic. It is not lexical entries that are accessed from a static lexicon, but dynamically changing concepts in the plex accessed through the dynamically changing domain of control. [Yngve 1996:330]

In human linguistics, participants do not refer to elements or words in the text. It is concepts in the hearer's or reader's domain of control that are accessed. They are concepts of items in the external reality or in the imagined external reality or abstract concepts. A certain given communicative behavior may trigger access to different concepts at different times depending on the domain of control.

The following example illustrates the above statements:

(1) *The boy* (the author) had noticed the ring when *she* (his aunt) had read to *him* (the author) as a child.

Using the definitions and vocabulary of traditional grammar, one could claim that in our example, the personal pronouns in italics refer to the male and female protagonists in the short story 'Secrets' (Mac Laverty 1997) respectively. The reader *automatically* knows exactly who the referents are. But in human linguistics, referring behavior is concerned with the 'triggering of procedures in dependence on the context rather than with people using words' (Yngve 1996:277), as in traditional linguistics.

In a human-linguistic analysis of communicative behavior, one would have to point out the importance of the domain of control for the interpretation of the personal pronouns above in italics. Here the author is referring to the *concepts* of the appropriate male and female protagonists respectively, both accessible in the reader's domain of control, based on personal perception and interpretation of previous knowledge.

Personal pronouns shift their referents depending on the domain of control and thus constitute a valuable area of investigation in analyzing referring behavior.

Some of the questions that arise at this point are:

How does the reader extract the intended meaning from text? How does the reader *access the appropriate referent or the intended concept*?

What is the *automatism* behind human understanding? What are the *expectations* in communicative behavior?

What are the reasons for *misunderstandings* in human communication? What are the monitoring and search processes involved?

In the logical domain, these questions may not represent a serious problem, since it operates at the level of text. A possible analysis of the above text is as follows.

In example (1) the pronoun *him* endophorically anaphorically refers to *the boy*, and *she* endophorically anaphorically refers to *the boy's aunt*. This means that the reader presupposes the existence of these elements in the preceding text on the intrasentential as well as the intersentential level, which makes the text cohesive. In terms of Halliday and Hassan's theory, 'the concept of cohesion is a semantic one; it refers to relations of meaning that exist within the text, and that define it as a text' (1976:4). Relations between various textual elements set up a *tie* whose interpretation depends on a presupposition and the presence of another element which resolves the presupposition. It is obvious that the selection of an individual word has no cohesive force by itself unless there is some explicit referent for it within reach (*ibid.* p.5).

In the physical domain, one looks for answers in the physical world. This means that one can no longer rely on text itself making sense through explanations or explications, but must explore the relevant physical reality. In the physical domain, one no longer speaks of textual elements and textual phoric relationships, on the access of which human communication depends. Hard-science linguistics introduces the execution of *procedures* and the accompanying changes in *properties* in the *plex structures* of human-linguistic systems such as participants, role-parts and linkages, in which human communicative behavior is analyzed.

3. Defining reference in cohesion and coherence

Halliday and Hasan discuss cohesion in terms of it being 'expressed through the stratal organization of language' (1976:5).

Meaning	(the semantic system)
Wording	(the lexicogrammatical system, grammar and vocabulary)
'sounding'/ writing	(the phonological and orthographic systems)

The above scheme of the stratification of language already reveals some of the problems of traditional linguistics. Namely, all three levels of text cohesion are presented as independent procedures. What is being left out is the overarching *domain of control* (possibly compared to the traditional notion of the context of situation) that human linguistics is largely involved with. It is the domain of control that 'changes so that anaphoric and other references operate to access the appropriate concepts and not others' (Yngve 1996:282).

Accessing appropriate concepts is the basis of successful communicating, and accessing inappropriate concepts is the basis of misunderstanding or humor (puns):

(2) a. When was the last time you saw your mother-in-law?
    b. I haven't yet seen her for the last time. (I intend to see her again.)

or

(3) a. Time flies.
    b. You can't. They fly too quickly. (Halliday and Hasan 1976:4)

In traditional terms, what happens in example (3) could be described as the hearer's intentional interpretation of the word *time* as an imperative form of the verb rather than a noun, and the word *flies* as a noun rather than a verb.

In human-linguistics terms, our communicative behavior is *sufficiently redundant to allow detection of a failure of reference*. A search activity is then set up in *an ever widening domain* in an effort to find the appropriate context for the referring behavior (Yngve 1996:283).

What is again interesting in the latter example is the pronouns. The imperative verb forms are usually directed at specific referents (the hearer or the reader), whereas in our example the recipient chooses to interpret the imperative in more general terms. Therefore the speaker uses the generic you, with reference to the human race, to express the meaning of general impossibility of the task.

The second instance of a personal pronoun, *they*, anaphorically refers to *flies*, thus providing significant information for correctly interpreting and understanding the response. Without it, the intended (or misunderstood) meaning would be veiled.

This is another instance of personal pronouns shifting their referents in dependence of the context of situation, which in this case may result in misunderstanding.

The definition of reference has been a much discussed topic in traditional linguistics as well as in the more recent realm of text or discourse linguistics. It has been difficult to establish a narrow scope that would cover reference in its 'pure' sense (personals, demonstratives, the definite article: i.e. grammatical words with relatively small lexical values) without bringing into the discussion items carrying considerable lexical weight (e.g. general words and combinations of reference items with lexical ones). Even the discussion of verbal phrases involves referential treatment, although its place in verb structures is not clear.

Thus we find in Halliday and Hasan (1976:126) the following:

> The general verb do is anaphoric only by lexical cohesion, in that it stands as a synonym for a set of more specific verbs, as in do sums, do an essay, do the vegetables, or combines with them in their nominalized form, as in do the cooking, do the writing, and therefore coheres with such items if they have occurred in the preceding text. All such instances of general verb or pro-verb do are instances of reference, not of substitution.

The beginning of this citation treats the verb *do* in terms of *lexical cohesion*, while towards the end the authors claim it to be an instance of (anaphoric) *reference*, and not *substitution*, although the verb *do* is discussed in the chapter on substitution. In one short paragraph, the verb *do* is associated with *lexical cohesion, reference*, and *substitution*, which in discourse analysis represent separate areas. This may create an impression that this type of analysis cannot fully account for the numerous and manifold linguistic phenomena without causing a certain degree of confusion.

Even as lay readers we can sense a certain confusion, which arises from the fact that human language is dependent for its interpretation on a number of cognitive and other mental processes each utterance triggers in our minds. These are complex and intertwined to the degree that renders all three of the above analyzes for the function of the verb *do* possible. Its meaning is interpreted in the *co-text*, which is then interpreted in *the context of situation*. The former is the subject of cohesion, a notion belonging strictly to the logical domain, since it operates on the level of surface text clues. The latter is the subject of coherence; it includes the reader's and the writer's knowledge and mental processes needed to access that knowledge. This is close to the physical domain concept of the *domain of control*. It is where human linguistics reaches beyond the traditional scope and digs deeper into the core of human understanding. Coherence touches upon human linguistics by presenting itself as a result of the actualization of meaning whose purpose is making sense.

'Making sense' would correspond in human linguistics to triggering, monitoring, and search processes accessing the appropriate concepts in the domain of control.

One basic drawback of traditional linguistics is that it tries to place a demarcation line between the functions of various language elements on the intrasentential level, and text linguistics on the intersentential level. Human linguistics, on the other hand, relies on the properties of people responsible for how they communicate.

In text linguistics, de Beaugrande and Dressler (1981, V 44) have discussed the concepts of '*making sense*' and '*activation of knowledge*'. They describe making sense as the purpose of the *actualization of meaning*, which results in text *coherence*.

As for activation of knowledge, the authors claim the textual world to be made up of cognitive elements (knowledge) which are being compared to our convictions about the 'real world'. Instead of saying that 'words refer to objects', we say that 'utterances activate knowledge' (*ibid.*).

In their discussion of cohesion and coherence, de Beaugrande and Dressler introduce the notion of *active storage* (1981, IV 2), which is defined as temporary storage for textual (visual or audio) input where it is interpreted in some sort of organizational scheme. This process is a short-term one. Therefore this part of text analysis cannot afford a thorough inspection of the participant's world knowledge, but rather of a sub-system with a narrowed-down scope of choices and patterns, i.e. syntax. This assessment is in accordance with the finding that surface structures, which serve as clues to cohesion, are kept longer and investigated in the 'short-term memory', while meaning, which is a clue to coherence, stays longer in the 'long-term memory' (Wright 1968).

The above definition of active storage offers the explanation for the somewhat vague expression 'within reach' (Halliday and Hasan

1976:5). At first glance it would appear that this means that the reader's making sense of a text occurs in stages: first cohesion, then surface clues within reach, then coherence. But that might not accurately describe the way our minds operate.

The proof lies in the fact that one can produce a text with perfectly valid textual-grammatical surface clues which makes no sense at all. And, on the other hand, one can make perfect sense of a stretch of text with no surface clues at all.

Let us consider the following two examples (the following examples (4) and (5) were used in a workshop by Cvetka Sokolov 'Essay writing – creating coherence' at the Faculty of Arts in Ljubljana in November 1998):

(4) a. 'Goodness, darling, I never heard such a fearful noise in all my life! You can hear *it* all the way down the street.'
   b. 'Were you trying to kill *it* and we interrupted you?' the man said. (Vine, 1986:159)

(5.1) KK: (lifts the receiver and sings out the number)
   GF: Hello. Is this Kitty or Judith?
   KK: Yes.
   GF: (pause) This is Gerald Faulkner. Please tell your mother I managed to get the tickets, and the film starts at eight.
   KK: Oh.
   GF: Thank you. (pause) Goodbye.
   KK: (silence)
   GF: (hangs up). (Fine 1989/90:16–17)

Example (4) represents a text with surface clues, yet it is difficult to determine the meaning of the second *it*. At first sight, the second *it* seems to have the same referent as the first *it* (i.e. a fearful noise). However, the co-text would reveal quite an astonishing referent, namely a *child*. The stages before reaching this conclusion would probably be:

grammar (personal pronoun) *cohesion* (reference item anaphorically referring back to noise) *general linguistic* knowledge (it is usually used with reference to inanimate nouns) *coherence* (the only possible referent in the co-text is Jamie, the child).

The text continues:

The way I was carrying poor *Jamie* must have inspired this. I hoisted him on to my shoulder where he hung, sobbing.

Without the appropriate amount of co-text, one cannot determine the referent of *it* in (4), yet in example (5) one can, without too much pondering, determine the addresser and the addressee in the dialog, the relationship between them, the topic and the purpose of the exchange, and the time and place of the conversation. More extensive co-text would not considerably influence our decisions. This was shown by the results of the task in the workshop which required filling in the unspoken thoughts of KK and GF. They approximated the following expansions, in spite of the fact that the participants of the workshop did not share the same linguistic background, nor were they familiar with the source of the dialog:

(5.2) KK: (lifts the receiver and sings out the number)
     GF: Hello. Is this Kitty or Judith?
     KK: Yes. (*I won't tell you which of the two.*)
     GF: (pause) (*Whoops! Handle with care.*) This is Gerald Faulkner. Please tell your mother I managed to get the tickets, and the film starts at eight.
     KK: Oh. (*She is going out again? With you? But she can't! She has to help Jude with her school work. She promised!*)
     GF: (*I expect you'll pass on my message.*) Thank you. (pause) (*Well, obviously you've decided to be difficult.*) Goodbye.
     KK: (silence) (I *don't feel like being polite. I refuse to talk to you. Let's see how you'll cope with this one.*)
     GF: (*Suit yourself. I don't have to take this.*) (hangs up).
     (Fine 1989/90:16–17)

Cases where coherence is displayed without cohesion are mostly instances of spoken language or dialogs, where other important factors like intonation, gestures, facial expressions, the addresser's and the addressee's common knowledge, logical reasoning, etc. contribute to successful communication.

In human linguistics, the concept of *expectations* is introduced, which may be tested in different ways. The above example may serve as an instance of testing expectations experimentally. Not by means of interrupted text where subjects are asked to guess the completion, in accordance with Yngve's suggestion (Yngve 1996:285), but by filling in the implicit content.

In their discussion of cohesion, Halliday and Hasan (1976:20) determine *the context of situation* in terms of 'relations between the language and the relevant features of the speaker's and the hearer's (or the writer's and the reader's) material, social and ideological environment'. In human linguistics we could say that the authors establish the importance of the physical world around the communicating individuals, but they separate from it the properties of the participants, which in discourse analysis correspond to the speaker's and the hearer's (or the writer's and the reader's) knowledge of the world. What is interesting is that the knowledge of the world is treated as part of coherence, but not as part of the context of situation, since it is considered to be more relevant to the analysis of cognitive processes.

H. P. Grice (1971) introduces the notion of the 'cooperative principle', where he speaks of four *maxims*: the maxim of quantity (say no more than needed), the maxim of quality (tell the truth), the maxim of manner (be perspicuous), and the maxim of relation (be relevant). The latter justifies the *assumption of coherence*, which represents another important factor in human communication. The participants in the discourse *want* to make sense of it and are therefore *looking* for clues to justify its textuality. On the part of the participants, it is 'the normal expectation ... that the discourse will be coherent' (Brown and Yule 1983:66).

In their work, Brown and Yule also discuss interpreting indirectness (1983:256). They call it *making inferences* and further define it as 'that process which the reader (hearer) must go through to get from the literal meaning of what is written (or said) to what the writer (speaker) intended to convey'. This aspect of human communication can also be related to the assumption of coherence, the participants' willingness to extract a meaningful message from the text.

Regardless of their linguistic background, participants will always recognize some *language function* in the utterance. This means that people communicate through language with the main purpose of achieving a certain goal. Austin (1962), and later Searle (1969:23) defined these various language functions in terms of *speech acts*. They are the following:

> *utterance acts* referring to the use of words and sentences;
> *propositional acts* referring to the use of content and reference;
> *illocutionary acts* referring to the use of sentences to perform various functions, i.e. a promise, a threat;
> *perlocutionary acts* referring to the linguistic behavior focusing on achieving a desired effect on the addressees.

In order to achieve a successful transfer from writer or speaker to reader or listener, the writer or speaker needs to take into account the group of people the text in question is targeted at. We speak in the well-known terms and phrases used in discourse analysis: *target reader, background knowledge, reading into text*, etc. They also influence the form and the content of the message.

The above stated factors (the context of situation, the cooperative principle, making inferences, and recognizing language functions as well as target readers, background knowledge, and reading into the text) all inevitably bring into the discussion *cognitive processes* that underlie successful human communication. The task of human linguistics is to decompose these processes down to their atomic units and find not linguistic rules but the clue to human understanding.

4. A practical representation

Let us take a closer look at example 5:

(5.3) KK: (lifts the receiver and sings out the number)
       GF: Hello. Is this Kitty or Judith?
       KK: Yes.
       GF: (pause) This is Gerald Faulkner. Please tell your mother I managed to get the tickets, and the film starts at eight.
       KK: Oh.
       GF: Thank you. (pause) Goodbye.
       KK: (silence)
       GF: (hangs up). (Fine, 1989/90:16–17)

Example (5) represents an extract of written text, which is actually a fictional instance of spoken language. The context of situation is a telephone conversation. This information is accessible to the reader by a quick glance at the form of the text, which exhibits the turn-taking phenomenon characteristic of conversations. No overlapping might lead the reader to conclude it is a telephone conversation (although no overlapping is not a rule in telephone conversations). The writer's comment in parentheses, namely *lifts the receiver and sings out the number*, triggers the reader's knowledge of the world involving telephone conversations.

The action of 'lifting the receiver' is associated with telephones, and 'singing out the (telephone) number' with the beginning stage of telephone conversations. Also, certain conventions of telephone communication *are* followed, such as greeting (*hello, this is Gerald Faulkner*). These conclusions are all based on the reader's knowledge of material environments.

In the first exchange, the reader learns about two female characters involved in the story, Kitty and Judith (or assumes these are female names) who are related. The introduction of their names tells the reader that the voice is high pitched, characteristic of females.

In the second exchange, the reader is warned about the somewhat rude or at least not very talkative nature of the female participant. Once the other speaker introduces himself, the reader knows it is a male voice on the other end of the line. Another concept is introduced here, namely the one of film, cinema (*tickets, film, starts*). *Managed to get* would imply popularity or newness of the film in question, standing in line at the ticket office, crowds, efforts, money exchange. *Tell your mother* brings in the concept of family relations (obviously the two girls are sisters, daughters of the woman Gerald Faulkner is involved with). It also reveals the purpose of the call (either informing the mother of the plans for the evening or confirming the plans), and the outcome (leaving a message with one of the daughters. Of course, by now the reader knows that the girl involved in the conversation is Kitty, since the writer used the initials KK in signaling turn-taking).

The third and the fourth exchanges further exhibit the relationship between the speakers, which is not a friendly and warm one. The reader is led to believe that Mr. Faulkner is the mother's partner, but not the daughters' father. This is probably due to some unfortunate events in the family (divorce, death, or disappearance of the father, or even cheating).

These conclusions are due to the reader's social and ideological environment.

In the above analysis, we can already perceive the dynamics of the referential domain:

> It appears that the domain of control provides a dynamically changing access structure to a limited number of temporarily interconnected concepts available to reference through anaphora, deixis and other devices. (Yngve 1996:282)

In this brief exchange, the reader's train of thought frequently changes direction: from formal telephone greetings, to female siblings and family relationships, to cinema. This change of direction is in human linguistics referred to as the dynamics of the domain of control.

The assumption of coherence or looking for clues to justify discourse textuality brings us to the human linguistics 'search for evidence of expectations, tasks and subtasks' (*ibid.* p. 283). Since the reader is automatically trying to make sense of the text, trying to access those concepts that would fit into this particular piece of the referential net, the task of the linguist is to obtain hard scientific evidence of such assumptions.

In the case of making inferences, we can say that in human linguistics these procedures would relate to *precontext* and *postcontext* (*ibid.* p. 284). Precontext would roughly correspond to the literal meaning of the text, and postcontext to the meaning the writer intended to convey.

The illocutionary act or the language function of the above exchange is to get in contact with a certain person or leave a message about the plans for the evening. This analysis would roughly correspond to the human linguistics search for evidence of tasks and subtasks (*ibid.* p. 283).

In traditional terms, by using language, we are communicating a great deal more than just that piece of language. For instance, by using the word *mother*, we are communicating the attributes female, grown up, with children, with partner (at one time at least); we are also communicating certain social norms, such as family as a form of organization in society or single-parent household. In matriarchal societies, we are also communicating head of organizational unit, leader. We are communicating emotional connotations of unconditional love and nurturing; also experience and wisdom. And each of these attributes reaches further to other relating concepts, thus creating an endless network of interrelated notions. No concept is an island that can be treated on its own. Therefore, even in traditional terms the sentential treatment of grammatical entities does not suffice. Lexis and grammar, for example, cannot account for communication through sign language, where participants communicate concepts without explicitly using traditional grammatical structures. Children learn to communicate successfully without having mastered the complexities of grammatical structures.

In the human-linguistics view, the scope of referring is so extensive it seems to cover the whole realm of what has been called language communication. All language only makes sense when it refers to some accessible entity in the reader's knowledge of the world.

In human linguistics, communicating individuals are the participants in the process of communicating, and their linguistic, social, and emotional properties are involved in their understanding of referring behavior. Traditional analysis of grammatical structures and lexis reveals the surface layer of the message. It does not, however, explain the phenomena behind successful communication in cases such as two friends using unfinished sentences and cue words, or in cases where the message carries double meaning, yet the receiver extracts the correct one, suitable to the particular context of situation. Or even humor, except in puns. In order to be able to account for how people communicate, a much wider framework needs to be considered – one that reaches beyond surface grammatical structures, or even the context of situation – one that takes into account all factual elements playing a role in encoding and decoding a message. This requires that we move from the logical to the physical domain of investigation.

Note

This paper is based on a paper presented at the 34th Annual Meeting of the Societas Linguistica Europaea (SLE) August 28–September 1, 2001 in Leuven, Belgium.

References

Austin, John (1962), *How to Do Things with Words*. Oxford: Clarendon.

Beaugrande, Robert A. de and Dressler, Wolfgang U. (1981), *Introduction to Text Linguistics*. Harlow, UK: Longman Group Limited. A Slovene translation is available (Ljubljana: Park, 1992) by Aleksandra Derganc and Tjaša Mikliä, with added analyzes of examples from Slovene literary works.

Brown, Gillian and Yule, George (1983), *Discourse Analysis*. Cambridge: Cambridge University Press.

Fine, Anne (1989/90), *Goggle-Eyes*. Harmondsworth: Hamish Hamilton.

Grice, Paul (1971), 'Meaning', in Danny Steinberg and Leon Jakobovits (eds) (1971), *Semantics: An Interdisciplinary Reader in Philosophy, Linguistics, and Psychology*. Cambridge: Cambridge University Press, pp. 53–59.

Halliday, M. A. K. and Hasan, Raqaiya (1976), *Cohesion in English*. London and New York: Longman. Reprinted in 1997, London and New York: Longman.

Mac Laverty, Bernard (1997), *Secrets and Other Stories*. Reading, UK: Vintage at Random House.

Searle, John (1969), *Speech Acts*. London: Cambridge University Press.

Sokolov, Cvetka (1998), *Pisni sestavek – ustvarjanje koherence* (What makes a text coherent). A workshop at 'Novosti stroke za učitelje'; Ljubljana, Faculty of Arts.

Vine, Barbara (1986), *A Dark-Adapted Eye*. Harmondsworth: Penguin.

Wright, Patricia (1968), 'Sentence retention and transformation theory'. *Quarterly Journal of Experimental Psychology*, 20, 265–272.

Yngve, Victor H. (1996), *From Grammar to Science: New Foundations for General Linguistics*. Amsterdam/Philadelphia: John Benjamins.

Chapter 9

Reconstituting Austin's Verdictives

Bernard Paul Sypniewski

J. L. Austin (1975) described a 'performative utterance' as speech that affects or performs 'extra linguistic' behavior. His twelve lectures, given in 1955, form a prolonged attempt to delimit the linguistic features that definitively distinguish performative utterances from other types of language. By the end of the last lecture, Austin realized that his efforts did not achieve the results that he wanted. By recognizing the importance of context, Austin came tantalizingly close to some of the key insights of hard-science linguistics (HSL) (Yngve 1996). Austin's project produced limited results because he tried to see performative utterances as completely understandable within the scope of traditional linguistics. In terms of the major distinction between traditional linguistics and hard-science linguistics, Austin tried to understand utterances as part of language in the logical domain rather than to understand people as part of nature in the physical domain.

We wish to know whether Austin's theory of performative utterances can be profitably reconstituted in hard-science linguistics. Since a consideration of all of Austin's performative utterance types will unnecessarily enlarge this paper, we will only discuss the type of performative utterance that Austin calls a 'verdictive'. Austin never defines verdictives except by example. The closest he comes is, 'Verdictives ... are typified by the giving of a verdict, as the name implies, by a jury, arbitrator, or umpire. But they need not be final' (Austin 1975:151). A little later, he says, 'Verdictives consist in the delivering of a finding, official or unofficial, upon evidence or reasons as to value or fact, so far as these are distinguishable. A verdictive is a judicial act as distinct from legislative or executive acts' (Austin 1975:153).

Austin considered mid-twentieth century British law in his

examples. I will use examples from contemporary New Jersey criminal law. In order to understand verdictives, I examine both a jury's finding of guilt and a defendant's entry of a guilty plea. In the last third of the twentieth century, the guilty plea hearing has taken on a significant role in American criminal jurisprudence, becoming the resolution method of choice in the vast majority of criminal cases. A jury verdict is an obvious example of one of Austin's verdictives, but guilty plea hearings raise some interesting problems for Austin's theory. Comparing jury verdicts that find a defendant guilty of some crime to hearings in which a defendant enters a guilty plea will show us some details of performative utterances that might otherwise be obscured. Although different types of communicative behavior occur in jury verdicts and guilty pleas, and the assemblages and linkages are somewhat different, the result is the same: a defendant is found guilty of one or more crimes.

1. Informal descriptions of a jury verdict, a guilty plea, and a sentencing hearing

In American jurisprudence, the purpose of a criminal trial is to determine whether the State's charges against an indicted defendant are justified. The indictment is a formal document containing a summary of charges against the defendant. Each charge is contained in a separate, numbered 'count'. A defendant can be found guilty in either of two ways. A defendant may be found guilty of one or more counts of the indictment by a jury after a trial or the defendant may plead guilty to one or more of the counts of the indictment at a separate plea hearing. Other than these two methods, a defendant may not legally be found guilty of a crime. The next three sections give descriptions of typical cases of the return of a verdict, a guilty plea hearing, and a sentencing hearing. These are described in only enough detail for us to examine the performative utterances in each situation.

1.1 The return of a jury verdict

In the case of a jury verdict, a defendant is found guilty of count x but not guilty of count y when, after a trial, the jury unanimously decides that the defendant performed the acts described in the count number x but not the acts described in the count number y of the indictment. The jury foreman announces the decision of the jury in a courtroom with the judge, prosecutor, defense attorney, defendant, court reporter, and other jurors present. Other persons may also be present but, for our discussion, their presence is irrelevant. This announcement ceremony is known as 'returning a verdict'.

A jury, through its foreman, returns its verdict at the very end of a trial. The judge sits at his desk; the jury foreman stands in front of his seat in the jury box; the defendant and his attorney stand at the defense table. The judge asks the jury foreman if the jury has reached a unanimous verdict. The jury foreman acknowledges that they have. The jury foreman, at the judge's prompting, reads the verdict from a completed verdict form 'onto the record', meaning that the decision of the jury becomes publicly known and recorded by the court reporter. The jury verdict form is a document prepared by the court for the jury to unambiguously record their decision. It contains the name of the case, a short description of each count of the indictment, and a place to check off either 'Guilty' or 'Not Guilty' after the description of each count.

1.2 The entry of a guilty plea

In the case of a guilty plea, a defendant may, if he chooses, plead guilty before or sometimes during a trial to one or more counts of the indictment. A guilty plea occurs at a hearing before a judge without a jury, with the prosecutor, defense attorney, defendant, and court reporter present. Others are present as well but are irrelevant for our discussion. The defendant's attorney and the prosecutor describe any inducements (plea agreement) that encouraged the defendant to plead guilty. The judge briefly reviews the indictment, any plea agreement that has been entered into, and the defendant's description of the acts that the defendant claims makes him guilty of a crime. If the judge finds these elements to be acceptable, the judge accepts the defendant's plea. The reader should be careful to distinguish between a guilty plea, which is a statement of certain facts, and a plea agreement, which is a binding agreement between the State and the defendant that creates expectations for each party about the occurrence of certain communicative behavior at a sentencing hearing.

1.3 A sentencing hearing

A sentencing hearing takes place either after a trial that results in a guilty verdict or after the entry of a guilty plea by a defendant. In between the entry of the verdict or guilty plea and the sentencing hearing, a presentence report is prepared for the sentencing judge to review. The contents of the presentence report need not concern us here. After reviewing the presentence report, the judge will take one of two courses of action depending on whether the sentencing results from a jury verdict or a guilty plea. If a jury verdict was entered, the judge sentences the defendant according to law. If the defendant previously entered a guilty plea, the judge must decide whether to accept the plea agreement before he sentences the defendant. If the judge rejects the plea agreement, he gives the defendant the option of retracting his guilty plea and going to trial or to accept sentencing in a manner that the judge thinks fit regardless of the plea agreement. We need not concern ourselves here with how or why a judge sentences a defendant in a particular way or why a judge might reject a particular plea agreement. We are interested only in what the acceptance or rejection of a plea agreement tells us about performative utterances.

2. A hard-science linguistics analysis

We now turn to a hard-science linguistics analysis of the return of a jury verdict, the entry of a guilty plea, and a sentencing hearing. This will allow us to see clearly that what Austin called performative utterances, and in particular his verdictives, cannot be understood solely in terms of traditional linguistics.

If some named person such as John Doe is accused of one or more crimes, he becomes a participant [John Doe] in a [Proceedings]. Among the tasks of this linkage are <Decide the guilt of named persons charged with one or more particular crimes against the state>. In this linkage [John Doe] will play the [Defendant] role part. There will be a prop part [Indictment] with properties <count 1>, <count 2>, etc., which enumerate the crimes with which John Doe has been charged. Correspondingly, there will be linkage properties <guilty of count 1>, <guilty of count 2>, etc., each with an initial value of 0 to reflect the presumption of innocence. Of course the linkage properties <guilty of count 1> etc. will be reflected in similar properties at a lower level in the [Defendant] role part played by the participant [John Doe].

2.1 The return of a jury verdict

To analyze a case going to trial, we set up a [Trial] linkage that is subordinate to the [Proceedings] linkage. The top-level task of the [Trial] linkage is <try the case>. The final subtask of the <try the

case > task is the < return the verdict > subtask. For this we set up a [Verdict return] linkage as a sublinkage of the [Trial] linkage.

A trial always takes place in a courtroom, so there will be a [Courtroom] setting. The [Trial] linkage has role parts [Defendant], [Judge], [Prosecutor], [Defense attorney], and [Court reporter], and the prop part [Case record]. A jury is empanelled, so we set up a [Jury] sublinkage of the [Trial] linkage, having 12 jurors playing [Juror] role parts. One of these is designated also as the foreman of the jury, so we also set up a [Jury foreman] role part. These functional parts of the [Trial] linkage are also functional parts of its [Verdict return] sublinkage. Other people may be present in the courtroom but their presence is irrelevant to the proceedings at this point. The indictment is also present in court as a matter of custom, so we include the [Indictment] prop part.

The jury foreman has a verdict form in which he has entered for each count of the indictment whether the jury has unanimously decided, for example, that the defendant John Doe is guilty of count 1, not guilty of count 2, etc., that is, that John Doe performed the acts described in count number 1, did not perform the acts described in count number 2, etc. Thus we have a [Verdict form] prop part with properties such as < the jury finds John Doe guilty of count 1 >, < the jury finds John Doe guilty of count 2 >, etc.

The verdict is not returned until the required participants and objects are all present together in the courtroom. Returning the verdict is a simple process. The judge is seated at his desk. The defendant, the defense attorney, and the jury foreman stand at their places. At the appropriate time the judge asks the jury foreman whether the jury has reached a unanimous verdict on all counts of the indictment. The jury foreman says that they have. The jury foreman has the verdict form in his possession. At the prompting of the judge he reads the verdict from the jury verdict form. For each count of the indictment he reads either 'guilty' or 'not guilty'. A jury may not return any other verdict.

To model this crucial moment in the trial, and taking care to leave behind the baggage of ordinary-language folk theory implicit in the above (Yngve 1996:118–119), we say that the task < return the verdict > is executed in the [Verdict return] linkage. This involves at a lower level the subtask < read verdict > executing in the [Jury foreman] role part.

This is modeled in HSL as procedures executing in the [Jury foreman] role part that result in the sound waves of his reading these replies. The executing of these reading procedures in the [Jury foreman] role part are also represented by the executing of associated procedures in the [Verdict return] linkage that result in appropriate changes of linkage properties. This models what is called 'reading onto the record'. Specifically, the linkage properties <guilty of count 1> etc. have their values changed from 0 to 1 by the associated linkage procedures for each count when the jury foreman reports 'guilty' and not changed when the foreman reports 'not guilty'.

This is of course reflected in associated changes in the [Defendant] role-part properties (that he has been found guilty of count 1, etc.) and also in the properties of others in the courtroom reflecting their understanding of the verdict. Furthermore, the changes in the guilt properties are also reflected in the properties of higher-level linkages all the way up to the level of the society (see Yngve 1996:236–242), for not only is the trial open to the public but procedures in [Court reporter] make a transcript of what transpires so that the appropriate official can make an entry in [Case record], a prop part of the [Proceedings] linkage to change its properties to indicate in a permanent manner that John Doe has been found guilty of count 1 etc. of the indictment. Thus the verdict is 'made public' and [John Doe] is recorded as having been judged guilty by the Criminal Justice System of New Jersey of the specified counts in the indictment.

While more happens in court after the jury returns its verdict, this is all that is relevant here.

2.2 The entry of a guilty plea

If a defendant decides to enter a guilty plea, he does so after his attorney and the prosecutor have negotiated a plea agreement. A plea agreement describes, among other things, communicative behavior that will take place later if certain conditions are met.

The defendant is called before a judge into court to enter his guilty plea. A guilty plea may occur anywhere, such as a room in a jail or in a hospital, but usually occurs in a courtroom. After the attorneys describe the plea agreement to the judge and present him with the necessary paperwork, including a plea agreement form, the defendant tells the judge that he understands the plea agreement and what acts he performed that make him guilty of the crimes to which he pleads. The defendant's statements are known as his allocution.

Once the defendant completes his allocution, the judge makes a preliminary assessment of whether the defendant's statements constitute an adequate basis for a finding of guilty of the crimes referred to in the plea agreement, whether the defendant voluntarily entered his guilty plea, and whether there is anything obviously amiss with the plea agreement. If the judge is satisfied as to each of these elements of the guilty plea, the judge accepts the guilty plea, orders a presentence report, schedules a sentencing hearing, and ends the guilty plea hearing.

Let us call the linkage that we set up to model a guilty plea [Guilty plea hearing]. The top-level task, the subtasks, and role parts sketched in this paper include only enough detail to discuss the relevance of a guilty plea to verdictives. The relevant role parts of the linkage [Guilty plea hearing] are [Judge], [Defendant], [Defense attorney], [Prosecutor], and [Court reporter], as above. There are two relevant prop parts: [Indictment], as above, and the plea agreement prop part, [Plea agreement]. The top-level task in the linkage [Guilty plea hearing] is the <plea entry> task, which has several subtasks: <agreement acknowledgement>, <allocution>, <guilty plea acceptance>, and <sentencing hearing scheduling>.

In <agreement acknowledgement>, certain tasks in [Defense attorney] execute that communicate the contents of [Plea agreement] to [Judge].

In <allocution>, tasks in [Defendant] execute that describe to [Judge] the acts that he performed that make [Defendant] guilty of the crimes referred to in [Plea agreement].

The task <guilty plea acceptance> has several subtasks. The first <elements suffice?> models the judge's preliminarily deciding whether the description legally suffices as proof of the crimes referred to in [Plea agreement], among other things (see above).

If the decision is that [Defendant]'s statement suffices, tasks in [Judge] set certain guilt properties to 1 and tasks in [Court reporter] result in the appropriate official making entries in [Case record] and the subtask <sentencing hearing scheduling> is executed, which is the last subtask of <plea entry>.

If the decision is that the defendant's statement is not legally sufficient, procedures execute in [Judge] that model his informing the parties of the rejection of the guilty plea. At this point <plea acceptance> and consequently <plea entry> end and we say that the judge rejected the plea agreement.

The parties may decide to restart the <plea entry> task, i.e., to perform the aforementioned acts once again with the contents of [Defendant]'s communicative behavior during the <allocution> subtask being different.

2.3 A sentencing hearing

A sentencing hearing usually takes place in a courtroom. The judge, the defendant, the defense attorney, the prosecutor, and the court reporter must be present. Others may be present but are irrelevant to our discussion. The communicative behavior at a sentencing hearing depends on how the defendant was found guilty. A judge who sentences a defendant who was found guilty by a jury only needs to review the presentence report (prior to the hearing) and sentence the defendant as he deems proper, after hearing any comments from the defendant, his attorney, the prosecutor, and, in some cases, the victim. The judge cannot alter a jury verdict at a sentencing hearing. A judge who sentences a defendant after a guilty plea hearing can do one of two things. After a review of the presentence report, the judge may decide to either accept or reject the plea agreement. If the judge rejects the plea agreement, the judge gives the defendant the option of retracting his guilty plea and going to trial or allowing the judge to sentence him as the judge thinks is proper. If the judge accepts the plea agreement, the judge will sentence the defendant according to the terms of the plea agreement.

We will only model those aspects of a sentencing hearing which come into play when there is a guilty plea and which are relevant to our discussion of verdictives. We set up a linkage to model a sentencing hearing in the relevant part and call it [Sentencing]. Although a full model of a sentencing hearing would require more role parts and subtasks than those we describe here, we can adequately model a sentencing hearing for our discussion with only two role parts, [Judge] and [Defendant]. [Sentencing] also includes three prop parts: [Indictment] and [Plea agreement] as above, and PSR [Presentence report]. PSR is important because, prior to the sentencing hearing, the judge reviews it to determine whether he should accept or reject the plea agreement. A sentencing hearing cannot take place without a PSR.

In the top level task of [Sentencing] (not discussed here) we focus on two subtasks. In the first, < plea acceptance >, the procedure < acceptable? > executes in [Judge] to model whether he has found [Plea agreement] acceptable or not and to produce the sound waves by which he announces his decision.

If the plea agreement is found unacceptable, then the subtask < retract plea > in the linkage [Sentencing] executes. This involves a subtask < go to trial? > executing in the [Defendant] role part that models whether the defendant decides to go to trial or to continue with the sentencing.

If the defendant decides to go to trial, then procedures execute in [Judge] that reset to 0 the values of any linkage properties <guilty of count 1> etc. that have been set to 1 during [Guilty plea hearing], the linkage task <retract plea> ends, and the top level task of [Sentencing] ends.

If the defendant does not wish to go to trial, the properties <guilty of count 1> etc. that have been set to 1 are not reset, the linkage task <retract plea> ends, and the judge sentences the defendant according to the plea agreement.

3. Discussion

During the history of the trial, the value of each property <guilty of count 1> etc. in the [Trial] linkage is 0 (not guilty) because of the presumption of innocence unless the value changes at the end of some subtask of [Trial] due to appropriate communicative behavior. The purpose of a criminal trial, restated in HSL terms, is to determine whether, after certain communicative behavior occurs in [Trial], any or all properties <guilty of count 1> etc. change value from 0 to 1.

Assume the jury decides to alter the value of <guilty of count 1> to 1 but to leave the value of <guilty of count 2> at 0, that is, the jury finds the defendant guilty on count 1 but not guilty on count 2. Then the subtask <read verdict> in the role part [Jury foreman] of the [Return verdict] linkage, a sublinkage of the [Trial] linkage, will execute modeling the jury foreman responding 'guilty' when the judge prompts him for the jury's decision as to count 1 and procedures will execute that set <guilty of count 1> in the [Trial] linkage to 1.

Although the jury decided to change the value of <guilty of count 1> during its deliberations, the value of <guilty of count 1> in the [Verdict return] linkage, and thus also in the [Trial] linkage, does not change until it is changed by the <read verdict> task executing in the [Jury foreman] role part which models him responding 'guilty' at the judge's prompt for the jury's unanimous decision as to count 1 as part of the <return the verdict> subtask in the [Verdict return] linkage.

Because trials are 'public', the [Trial] linkage includes not only [Prosecutor], [Defendant], and [Judge] role parts but also role parts for jurors and others including [Court reporter], and it is also open to role parts for members of the public. This models the defendant's right to a public trial.

Because <guilty of count 1 > etc. in the [Trial] linkage is a 'public' property, i.e., a property that is 'visible' to participants in the trial besides the defendant, the values of <guilty of count 1 > etc. must be altered in a 'public' manner. The [Verdict return] linkage is such a public method for altering the values of <guilty of count 1 > etc. of the [Trial] linkage.

The jury may change its decision at any time up until it is delivered in open court (in <return the verdict>) but it cannot do so once <read verdict> has executed in the [Jury foreman] role part.

The verdict must be communicated by the jury foreman to the judge while the other necessary participants in the [Verdict return] linkage are present in the courtroom. If the jury foreman delivered his verdict in an empty courtroom, the values of <guilty of count 1 > etc. would not change. If someone other than the jury foreman said the same words as the jury foreman would say when he delivered a verdict, the values of <guilty of count 1 > etc. would not change. In an emotionally charged case, the victim's or the defendant's friends or family often attend the trial. Many times, they vocally disagree with the jury's verdict and shout out their disagreement. Members of the audience cannot alter the values of <guilty of count 1 > etc. Even the jury foreman cannot do so. Although one of the functions of the [Jury foreman] role part is to announce the decision of the jury to participants in [Verdict return], he cannot unilaterally make the jury's decision.

A jury verdict is clearly one of Austin's verdictives (Austin 1975:151). We should note that a jury verdict is delivered 'upon evidence or reasons as to value or fact, so far as these are distinguishable' (Austin 1975:153). The communicative behavior in [Trial] prior to <return the verdict> concerned itself with just this evidence.

At first blush [Defendant] appears to alter the value of his own <guilty of count 1> etc. in [Guilty plea hearing]. A careful examination of the situation will show that actually it is [Judge] rather than [Defendant] that alters the value of <guilty of count 1 > etc. When [Defendant] finishes his communicative behavior during the <allocution> subtask, he does *not* alter the value of any properties <guilty of count 1 > etc. He merely states a series of 'facts'. [Judge] does not accept or reject the agreement outlined in [Plea agreement] until the sentencing hearing. [Judge] alters the values of the <guilty of count 1 > etc. referred to in [Plea agreement] when he accepts the communicative behavior of [Defendant] in the <allocution> subtask. Recall Austin's comment that a verdictive is based on evidence or reasons. The communicative behavior of [Defendant] during <allocution> is just such evidence. We see that this is so by observing those cases in which a judge rejects the plea agreement at a sentencing hearing. By 'rejecting the plea', we mean that [Judge] refuses to perform those acts of communicative behavior expected of him because of [Plea agreement]. He also resets the value of <acceptable?> to 0. [Judge] also resets to 0 the value of <guilty of count 1> etc. referred to in [Plea agreement] if [Defendant] wishes to go to trial but not if [Defendant] wishes to be sentenced according to [Judge]'s suggestions. Although [Defendant] has an option, his option determines whether [Judge] resets the value of a property. We may observe additional evidence to support this claim by observing those cases in which [Defendant] wants to retract his guilty plea before he is sentenced. He must ask permission to do so at a separate hearing (a motion to retract a guilty plea). The judge has the option to allow the defendant to retract the guilty plea. Usually, a judge does not exercise the option. If [Defendant] were able to alter the value of <guilty of count 1> etc. by himself, he would not need permission from [Judge] to do so. If [Defendant] had the ability to alter the values of <guilty of count 1> etc. by himself, the legal system could only require some notice to retract a guilty plea to publicly announce [Defendant]'s decision; [Judge] could not rule on [Defendant]'s decision because [Judge] could not alter <guilty of count 1> etc. These hearings give us clear evidence to support the claim that [Judge] in [Guilty plea hearing] and [Sentencing] controls the value of the appropriate <guilty of count 1> etc. properties and not [Defendant].

4. Austin's domain confusion

Austin noted the importance of the assemblage. In Lecture I, he said:

> Speaking generally, it is always necessary that the circumstances in which the words are uttered should be in some way, or ways, appropriate, and it is very commonly necessary that either the speaker himself or other persons should also perform certain other actions, whether 'physical' or 'mental' or even acts of uttering further words [Austin 1975:8]

Austin stayed within the logical domain. All 12 lectures were devoted to finding a complete theory of performative utterances *in language*. Austin saw but did not attach sufficient importance to the fact that merely uttering a verdictive is not enough. This is so easy to see that it is surprising that Austin did not make more of it. Suppose that the jury has notified the judge that it has reached a verdict. Because of the hour, the judge decides that the foreman will deliver the verdict after lunch. The jurors discuss the case at lunch, as they are admonished not to do but are widely suspected of doing. At lunch, the jury foreman says the exact same phrase that he will later say in the courtroom. Uttering the words at lunch does not alter the value of < guilty of count 1 > etc. The defendant cannot be punished because of the utterance of the jury foreman in a cafeteria. If the jurors deliberate further and come to a different conclusion than they did before lunch, it is the jury's conclusion announced in court that matters. In HSL terms, sound waves are not sufficient to alter the values of < guilty of count 1 > etc. The appropriate sound waves must be uttered by the appropriate participant in the process of fulfilling a certain function in a specific linkage subtask.

Austin did not consider the results of a performative utterance. For him, the utterance was important, not the role of the utterance in a larger context. If we look at the effect of the utterance, we can see that the utterance, as here described in HSL terms, may have considerable importance for future communicative behavior. Examples are not too hard to find. If, as is usual, a defendant pleads guilty before trial, there is no trial. In HSL terms, the communicative behavior of [Defendant] causes [Judge] to set the value of < guilty of count 1 > etc. from 0 to 1. The value of < guilty of count 1 > etc. determines whether the tasks and subtasks in [Trial] execute. If the value is 1 and other conditions, not mentioned here, are met, there is no need to set up the [Trial] linkage. If the values of all < guilty of count 1 > etc. are 0 after the preliminary subtasks in [Proceedings] are completed, then [Trial] must be set up. If, after the tasks and subtasks in [Trial] are completed, the values of all < guilty of count 1 > etc. are 0, the top-level task of [Proceedings] ends. On the other hand, if the values of one or more < guilty of count 1 > etc. are 1 after the subtasks of [Trial] are completed, [Defendant] is subject to further activity in [Proceedings] (sentencing).

5. Conclusion

Using the observations above, we may say that some tasks or subtasks, e.g. < read verdict >, require that the communicative behavior take place in certain physical locations (a courtroom). Other tasks or subtasks do not. For example, [Guilty plea hearing] may occur in a room in a jail, in effect a temporary courtroom. All tasks and subtasks require that certain props, role parts, or participants be present while the communicative behavior takes place.

Role parts and participants must be distinguished because it may only be necessary that, in some cases, a certain task be executed not that a specific individual execute that task. A good example is [Court reporter]. There must be a court reporter taking down testimony but the individual court reporter may be different from one linkage to another. On the other hand, it is vital that the individual who fills the role part of [Defendant] be the same throughout all tasks in the linkage.

While the communicative behavior of [Jury foreman] rarely varies from case to case, we should not be lulled into believing that the exact words uttered by [Jury foreman] are solely what changes the values of < guilty of count 1 > etc. A thorough examination of the communicative behavior during [Guilty plea hearing] is beyond the scope of this paper but an examination of that communicative behavior causes us to question whether specific language is required for a performative utterance. It is the resulting changes in properties that are important.

Austin's theory of performative utterances moved linguistics a step away from its concern with the abstractions of grammar toward concerns with the real world. Austin, however, did not go far enough. Austin could not shake loose from the notion that linguistics should decontextualize language in order to study it. HSL provides the additional theory that Austin needed to resolve many of the difficulties he experienced in his lectures.

Note

This paper is based on a paper presented at the 34th Annual Meeting of the Societas Linguistica Europaea (SLE) August 28–September 1, 2001 in Leuven, Belgium.

References

Austin, J. L. (1975), *How to Do Things with Words* (2nd edn). Cambridge, MA: Harvard University Press.
Yngve, Victor H. (1996), *From Grammar to Science: New Foundations for General Linguistics*. Amsterdam/Philadelphia: John Benjamins.

Chapter 10

Analysis of a Business Negotiation

Mojca Schlamberger Brezar

The purpose of this paper is to show how the whole process of negotiating can be represented in terms of hard-science linguistics. What are the major tasks in the task hierarchy and what are the tasks the participants of a linkage have to accomplish in order to come to agree?

An analysis of a negotiating session will be presented. We chose a video-recorded negotiation. In fact, when analyzing communication, a video-recorded conversation shows the output from all nonverbally expressed communicative tasks, for example nods and gestures, as will be seen in the following analysis. Nonverbally expressed tasks cannot be taken into account when working on a simple transcription. The negotiating session in the Slovene language was transcribed and translated into English. It is included here in the Appendix.

1. Background

It has been usual in the analysis of dialog and conversation to start with a definition. Negotiation has been defined as an exchange that leads to an agreement (Roulet 1985:8).

But we will take a different tack here and start instead with the people who are negotiating and examine in detail what they are doing when they negotiate. Negotiating is not only related to business or political negotiating but is a part of everyday life. Each individual in his everyday activities, as he enters into different linkages with different people, continuously accommodates to other individuals (Yngve 1996:298). Negotiating concerns not only facts and opinions, but also themes and forms of communicating, participants' identities, power, and even their opinions about the negotiation itself (Kerbrat-Orecchioni 1985).

So negotiating is seen as a general component of communicating. It is a process between two individuals, linkage participants in terms of hard-science linguistics, accommodating their behavior to reach a consensus in a matter that is important for both of them. Negotiating in a linkage is triggered by a problem that influences the individuals involved to accomplish tasks in order to produce the sort of changes in their communicative behavior that make possible an agreement.

Since it is very difficult to record authentic business negotiations because they are usually secret, our negotiating session is in fact a simulation of a negotiation recorded on videotape in 1994, including the roles of a buyer and a seller involved in a linkage, as will be seen below.

2. Analysis in terms of hard-science linguistics

According to Yngve (1996), if two people are in conversation, there are three distinct physical things: person A, person B and the flow of energy that passes between them. Communicating is in fact the result of specific properties (inputs and context) that trigger procedures.

In terms of hard-science linguistics, people, individually, are represented in theory as systems called communicating individuals. An assemblage of people, together with the sound waves and other real objects involved in their communicating, is represented in theory as a system called a linkage. A communicating individual that participates in a given linkage is analyzed as a system called a participant. The functional part or role that a person plays in an assemblage is represented in theory as a system called a role part.

Our linkage of two negotiators is a temporary linkage involving two participants playing the two role parts of [buyer] B and [seller] S. The buyer and the seller are both representatives of and participants in two larger linkages, namely the [buyer's enterprise] and the [seller's enterprise] that are referred to during the negotiation as a part of a larger context represented in the conditional properties. The negotiation is about a prop, a representation of a real object, a computer that broke down.

The relevant part of the surroundings is the room where the negotiation was recorded. This is represented in theory as a system called the setting. Since the setting includes just those properties that are required to account for its communicative relevance in the assemblage (Yngve 1996:129), we excluded the man with the camera that recorded the negotiation because he had no impact on the action.

The channel is represented mostly by sound waves and sometimes by light waves that reflect nonverbal behavior such as nods, smiles, and grins.

The analyzed negotiation is triggered by a problem: the computer that the buyer bought from the seller broke down two weeks after the manufacturer's guarantee had expired. The seller has repaired it and charged the buyer for it and now the bill causes a problem. That bill represents the initial conditions (Yngve 1996:215) or inputs that trigger the negotiation. Both the negotiators are given the instruction 'get an agreement under the best possible conditions'. That is a task for them, the completion of which represents the final conditions (Yngve 1996:215) or outputs.

Usually, the negotiation will proceed to a point where both participants agree on a conclusion. That means when a consensus has been reached on both sides, a property of the linkage. The participants may also both agree that a consensus cannot be reached. A consensus at the linkage level is thus the final condition that ends the negotiation.

Conditional properties change during the negotiating – evidence for the conditional properties can be seen at the following points: the linkage of the buyer and the seller is referred to as a 'long-time relationship' and 'in the past, we were cooperating'. Those properties of a linkage surely influence the behavior of both participants. As we know from business communications, conditional properties of being involved in a long-time relationship may bring a better deal.

Already at the beginning of the analysis we can state the following linkage properties (which would be represented in the domain of control, covering what has often been called the context of situation):

A common agreement on the language used: the participants are native speakers of Slovene, so they are able to understand conversational implicatures, metaphors and metonymies of the language they are speaking;

A common acceptance of the participant roles: 'I am the buyer, you are the seller, we are both responsible for what we are doing ...';

A common agreement on politeness rules: when one is talking the other is listening and vice-versa.

3. Description of the analyzed linkage

The description of the linkage, as is evident from the analyzed videotape, is as follows: it is a linkage lasting over a certain time – the participants, namely the buyer and the seller, have known each other for a certain time. They have common business in mind; it seems that the linkage of the participants playing the role parts of the [buyer] B and [seller] S represents a long-lasting linkage because in the transcription they refer to previous actions and also some expectation of future cooperation. They are willing to maintain the relationship under certain conditions, so the seller S is willing to negotiate with the buyer B. The presence of the prop is relevant since the change of the prop's properties and problems related to it represent initial conditions or inputs for the negotiation.

Evidence for the context of the negotiation is given at the beginning of the communication in example (1). This constitutes evidence that the buyer B bought a computer at S's firm, that they were satisfied with it and will need more computers, but after about a year the computer broke down and this constitutes a problem for the buyer. (The italicized part of this example will be analyzed further in a later section.)

Example (1)

S1: Good afternoon, you phoned me that you'll come today, you seem to have a problem, don't you?

B1: Yes, well, unfortunately, we've met several times, haven't we?

S2: Yes.

B2: ... for our common business ... but now I am here because of a completely different problem. I don't know if you are concerned, *but a while ago we bought a computer at your shop.*

S3: *Yes, I think it was about two years ago, wasn't it?*

B3: *No, it was about a year ago, I think it is exactly one year now.*

S4: *Yes, you are right, it should be about one year.*

B4: *Yes, one year.* And we've been using that computer, haven't we, for graphics and all that stuff, and we were really satisfied with it, weren't we, and then we had a meeting, because we are working in marketing and PR and we need a lot of that stuff, don't we, and we had a meeting that we would need some more computers, and after a few days the thing broke down.

4. Tasks, subtasks, and task hierarchies

4.1 Basic procedures of every task

4.1.1 At the linkage level

When communicating, participants execute tasks. A task is a communicative activity that can be expressed verbally or nonverbally. The execution of a task is based on the following sequence of linkage procedures:

> \< emission – reception \> ->
> \< execution – recognition \> ->
> \< expectation – reaction \>

We can explain this with an example of a greeting: when we see a friend or acquaintance for the first time that day, we will greet her or him. Who will greet first is normally a question of minimal negotiation. This task is executed by the emission of sound waves (or light waves if we do it by gestures). When we have greeted, we expect an answer. When a participant executes a task by speaking or gesturing (that means verbally or nonverbally), he expects a reaction to it.

But the other person has to confirm the reception of our greeting and recognize (and interpret) our communicative task as a greeting to be able to react properly. Reception means hearing or seeing the outputs of a task executed by the other participant. At the same time or immediately after that, the recognition procedure becomes active. We do not mean by this only the recognition of a person or a situation that will change the communicative behavior of the participant (Yngve 1996:294–296), but the recognition of a task as such. The participant should recognize the task to react properly.

There follows the reaction to the task. The reaction may end the task or may begin a new task. The latter can be seen in example (1) above (in B3 where the participants negotiate about the time of buying the computer). If the expectations are satisfied and completed, a task may end, if not, it will be prolonged until a consensus of both participants is reached, because a task should be completed at the linkage level. In example (1), we have a consensual solution in S4 / B4 and then the conversation goes on.

4.1.2. At the role-part and participant levels

At the participant level in the linkage, the execution of a task is as follows in the speaking (or acting) role part:

<emission> -> <execution> -> <expectation>

In the addressee role part it is:

<reception> -> <recognition> -> <reaction>

The tasks executed by the two participants are not symmetrical but complementary.

These procedures are somehow basic and, since they are present all the time, we could say that they represent a part of the conditional properties. A task always functions in a context, named conditional properties in terms of hard-science linguistics. A task once executed changes the properties of the linkage: in our examples that means that when the greeting is finished, the conversation is open, and when a negotiation is completed, it is over. According to Yngve (1996:284), in terms of hard-science linguistics, we speak of a precontext and a postcontext. The postcontext of one task contributes to the precontext of the following task. We thus have a dynamic description of conditional properties.

4.2. Sequencing of tasks and subtasks; parallel tasks

A task becomes active at a certain moment of the communication when a certain pulse triggers it. A task is completed when certain conditions are satisfied. The task <negotiate> is triggered by exposition of certain points that are important for the relationship; each exposition represents a task. It remains active until an agreement is reached on the points discussed. That means the tasks are completed.

The tasks are usually not executed in sequences, but in parallel. Parallel tasks are tasks executing at the same time. If we look at the first part of the analyzed negotiation, presented in the example (2) below, we can see that 9 tasks are opened, some of them are negotiated about and closed. The tasks <greet> and <phatic> are not negotiated, they belong to different groups of tasks concerning politeness formalities and monitoring, as we will see below (in section 4.3).

Example (2)
   S1: Good afternoon, you phoned me that you will come today, it seems that you have a problem, don't you? *Tasks:* <greet> | <introduce the negotiation> | <expect a list of problems>
   B1: Yes, well, unfortunately, we've met several times, haven't we? *Tasks:* <greet> *(nonverbal - completed)*| <answer to expectation of problems> | <mention a long-time relation-

       ship = we are good partners > | <phatic >

S2: Yes. *Tasks: < affirmative answer to the assertion above >*

B2: ... for our common business ... but now I am here because of a completely different problem. I don't know if you are concerned, but a while ago we bought a computer at your shop. *Tasks: <mention a long-time relationship = we are good partners > | <introduce the problems > | <we bought a computer >*

S3: Yes, I think it was about two years ago, wasn't it? *Tasks: <we bought a computer – time location >*

B3: No it was about a year ago I think it is exactly one year now. *Tasks: <we bought a computer – new time location >*

S4: Yes, you are right, it should be about one year. *Tasks: <we bought a computer: agree with the new time location >*

All the tasks above are subtasks of a general task, <negotiate to get an agreement >. That task is active throughout all the analyzed discourse and is closed at the end with double agreement as in example (3) below. The final agreement leads to evaluating and greeting that finish the negotiation.

    Example (3)

B61: Well, that is nice. I am very pleased that we managed to make such a good deal, and I hope that we will cooperate in the future. *Tasks: <agree >, <evaluate the agreement >*

S62: Well, I share your point of view. We are very pleased with your cooperation and I hope that there will be no misunderstandings in the future. *Tasks: <agree >, <evaluate the agreement >*

B62: Well, good-bye. *Tasks: <greet at the end >*

S63: Good-bye. *Tasks: <greet at the end >*

As we said before, some of the tasks will be closed throughout the discourse, and some of them will be suspended and postponed, as for example the task T2, <maybe we will buy some more computers >. This is possible because the linkage of the [buyer] B and the [seller] S will probably continue in the future. The agreement in this task is made under condition; the task is active and confirmed every time when the participants of the linkage meet.

4.3. The nature of tasks

Tasks, realized verbally or nonverbally, can be analyzed down to the phonetic and phonological level of communicating on the one hand and up to basic cognitive activities on the other hand. We will present the tasks of the negotiation first on a macro-level and then on the micro-level of communicating.

The major linkage task resulting from the analysis is negotiating with the intention of reaching an agreement. Tasks to be completed to reach agreement within the negotiation have the status of subtasks. The division into tasks and subtasks is not arbitrary; it depends either on the place that a task takes within the general tasks or on the scope of research. When we are interested in the analysis of a part of the communication, the tasks that could appear as a part of a discourse and therefore as subtasks can be viewed as major tasks.

In the task analysis, we cannot establish a word-to-task or an utterance-to-task relationship. Tasks and subtasks describe activities of participants. They are represented at the participant or the role-part levels and at the linkage level. At the role-part level, they appear to be asymmetrical, they are active in pairs. When one is talking, the other is listening (if both participants follow the politeness rules). When one participant carries out a certain task, such as, for example, <greet>, the other has to confirm the reception of that task and complete the task <answer the greeting>.The tasks follow a cause/consequence logical sequence – when a task is completed, it will provoke a change in the other participant's behavior.

So, for example, the task of negotiating <negotiate> can appear as a major task and at the same time as a subtask (for example, <negotiate about the bill>, <negotiate about the date>, etc.), as can be seen from example (4) below (italics B2 to B4). Here, the two participants negotiate the exact date of buying the computer.

Example (4)

B2: ... for our common business ... but now I am here because of a completely different problem. I don't know if you are concerned, *but a while ago we bought a computer at your shop.*

S3: *Yes, I think it was about two years ago, wasn't it?*

B3: *No it was about a year ago, I think it is exactly one year now.*

S4: *Yes, you are right, it should be about one year.*

B4: *Yes, one year.*

In the analyzed conversation, there appear to be three major groups of tasks:

(1) tasks concerning politeness formalities

(2) monitoring – also called 'phatic' tasks
(3) tasks related to negotiation activities

4.3.1. Tasks concerning politeness formalities

4.3.1.1 THE GREETING TASK

There are <greet> tasks at the beginning and at the end. They are
in fact social rituals. See example (5) and schemes in 4.3.1.1.1,
4.3.1.1.2, and 4.3.1.1.3 below. Tasks concerning politeness formalities usually do not need to be negotiated, and in the present analysis,
they are not. Other tasks are negotiable and are negotiated to a certain
point, as we will see.

The greeting at the beginning of the analyzed negotiation is
presented in example (5):

Example (5)
S1: *Good afternoon,* you phoned me that you will come today,
you seem to have a problem, don't you?
B1: /nod/ Yes, well, unfortunately, we've met several times,
haven't we.

Greeting in this part is expressed verbally by 'good afternoon',
uttered in S1 by the participant playing the role part S, [seller]. As
can be seen from the videotape, the participant playing the role part
B, [buyer], greets nonverbally, when entering the room, by a mere
nod. The task <greeting> is composed of two separate subtasks,
<greet>, executed by the participant S, and <answer the
greeting>, executed by the participant B. Each of the two subtasks
consists of basic procedures, mentioned before, that are represented
in the schemes 4.3.1.1.1, 4.3.1.1.2, and 4.3.1.1.3 below.

4.3.1.1.1. Role part S
<see a person B> -> <recognize the person B> -> <greet> ->
<expect answer>

When the participant S sees the participant B as he enters the room,
he recognizes him, greets him and expects an answer to his
greeting.

4.3.1.1.2. Role part B
<see a person S> -> <recognize the person S> -> <hear the
greeting> -> <greet>

When the participant B sees that S has entered the room and greeted him, he recognizes the greeting and answers it, but he does it nonverbally.

4.3.1.1.3. Linkage level
<see each other> -> <recognize each other> -> <greet – hear> -> <answer>

Greeting at the linkage level of description takes into account everything that happens in the linkage during the greeting. Greeting is represented as a subtask of a larger task and is, in turn, composed of several subtasks: the two participants see each other and recognize each other and expect greeting, then one greets first and the other answers the greeting.

The presentation of the greeting task is not symmetrical either at the role-part level or at the linkage level. As we can see from the example above, in the greeting task, the only verbal element is 'good afternoon', uttered by the participant S. All the other tasks are completed by nonverbal elements.

4.3.2 Monitoring
Monitoring is another task going on throughout the whole negotiation. This task represents the contact between the two linkage participants and the contact with the channel; we could also call it 'phatic'. According to Yngve (1996:272–273), this task 'operates in parallel with tasks of speaking'. By executing this task, the participant that is not talking gives evidence of his presence, listening, and interest. This task can never appear independently, only in parallel with other tasks.

Evidence for monitoring can be seen throughout the whole negotiation and it consists of the following points:

(1) eye contact (movement) or its absence
(2) phatic agreement
(3) tags, signaling that one participant is taking the other participant into account.

4.3.2.1. EYE CONTACT
Eye contact or its absence can be seen at several points in the videotape. In general, the participant playing the role part S tries to maintain eye contact and the participant playing the role part B avoids it at some important points, for example, when expressing disagreement.

4.3.2.2. PHATIC AGREEMENT

Phatic agreement is expressed in Slovene by the participant playing the role part S as *ja, ja, mhm,* which equals *yes* with growing intonation in English; phatic agreement by the participant playing the role part B is expressed as *no* with falling intonation, which equals *yeah,* something between agreement and disagreement. In the analyzed transcription, phatic agreement is marked as <confirm> when we have the task <confirm>, because it confirms the reception of the sound waves. Thus it is separated from the subtask <agree> that stands for 'I heard you and I agree with you' and represents a sort of 'act' of agreement. The task <confirm> is a task concerning monitoring, giving signs 'I am here, I understand, you may continue', and indicates that the other participant recognized the task as active. These tasks can be distinguished from each other by replacing the answer 'yes' by 'no' – when 'yes' represents agreement it is possible to replace it by 'no', which is impossible when it is phatic and represents monitoring.

4.3.2.3. TAGS

The third evidence for monitoring is tags, as for example *haven't we, don't you, aren't you.* They are quite frequently used by both participants, especially in the first part of the negotiation when the participants are repeating the important parts from previous linkages, as for example *haven't we, weren't we* and *don't we* in example (6) below.

Example (6)
    S4: Yes, you are right, it should be about one year.
    B4: Yes, one year. And we've been using that computer, *haven't we,* for graphics and all that stuff, and we were really satisfied with it, *weren't we,* and then we had a meeting, because we are working in marketing and PR and we need a lot of that stuff, *don't we,* and we had a meeting that we would need some more computers, and after a few days the thing broke down.

By tags, the participant is testing mutual agreement in the linkage and seeking a consensual position of the other for what he is saying. He wants the other to confirm his statement.

4.3.3 Tasks concerning the negotiation

Generally, the number of tasks and subtasks is indefinitely large. The name of a task suggests what is going on. In the analysis of the negotiation, the tasks, which were in fact the subtasks of the negotiation, are listed as:

(T1)   < are S's computer's good >
(T2)   < maybe we will buy some more computers >
(T3)   < are we good partners >
(T4)   < warranty problem >
(T5)   < computer broke down >
(T6)   < computer repaired >
(T7)   < bill too big >
(T8)   < give us a new computer >
(T9)   < distance problem >
(T10) < faulty computer replacement >
(T11) < evaluating >

These tasks are composed of several subtasks. We will show the functioning of the task T1 < are S's computers good >.

4.3.3.1 TASK T1: < ARE S'S COMPUTERS GOOD >

The task < are S's computers good > is introduced in B4 (see the translation of the transcript in the Appendix, section 7 below), asserted and argued in S5, opposed in B5, then in S6 introduced as apologizing, but it is not really apologizing, it is only conceding. The participant is saying 'we sold them ... they were satisfied' and by this gives evidence for the quality of computers. This is answered and countered in B6. In S7, the task T1 is asserted and in B7 we have a partial agreement from the participant playing the role part B.

This part can be presented as follows: at the level of the participant playing the buyer role part B, we have the following subtasks:

(1)   < introduce a task >
(2)   < listen to S's answer >
(3)   < oppose S's answer >
(4)   < listen to S's explanation >
(5)   < concede, argue >
(6)   < listen to S's explanation >
(7)   < confirm reception, express (a sort of) agreement >

At the level of the participant playing the seller role part S we have:

(1)   < listen to the task introduction >
(2)   < answer >
(3)   < listen to B's opposing >
(4)   < explain >

(5) < listen to B's arguing >
(6) < explain >
(7) < listen to B's confirming >

At the linkage level:

(1) < introduce the task T1 (express – listen to) >
(2) < answer (express – listen to) >
(3) < oppose (express – listen to) >
(4) < explain (express – listen to) >
(5) < argument (express – listen to) >
(6) < explain (express – listen to) >
(7) < confirm / agree >

In this part, there is no definite answer to the question 'are S's computers good'. The buyer B partly agrees with the seller S; it is more like a concession 'in spite of my problem I'll let you defend the quality of your computer'. The answer in fact is *well, yes* – in Slovene *no, saj*, which means that we do not agree completely, but we'll let it go, because there is no use arguing about it at this point – we can see that complete agreement is not reached because the task reappears later with B12. The task is only closed for a time and that enables the participant B to introduce a new task, namely the tasks T2 and T3 in our case.

The task T1 < are S's computers good > is reintroduced in B12 in a form of a question. It is implicitly asserted in S13 (our computers are good) and in B13 there is a complaint about the quality, which continues in B14. In S15, the seller S is asking about information concerning T1 'The computer was good for a year ...'. That is answered in B15 where T4 is confirmed. S16 is a repetition of S15. B16 and B17 are a complaint about T1, S17 between the two is phatic and S18 introduces opposition to B16 and B17. In B18, the complaint is continued. S19 asserts T1, the tasks appear in B20, and in S21 negotiation is proposed about it. B21 takes the task T1 for the basis for asserting other tasks and in B23 the task is inquired about. The task T1 appears here as a complaint, which is a part of a task T4.

The whole process can be seen at the levels of both the role parts and at the linkage level:

At the level of the buyer role part B:

(1) < reintroduce the task >
(2) < listen to phatic agreement >
(3) < continue the complaint >

(4) <listen to S's assertion that the computers are good>
(5) <answer>
(6) <listen to S's question>
(7) <interrupt S, complain>
(8) <listen to S's confirming>
(9) <a new beginning of a complaint>
(10) <listen to S's assertion that the computers are good>
(11) <continue the complaint>
(12) <listen to S's apologizing>
(13) <accept>
(14) <listen to S's opposition to the bad quality of computers>
(15) <state a demand on the basis of T1 >
(16) <listen to S's question about the task T4 based on T1>

At the level of the seller role part S:

(1) <listen to the task T1 again>
(2) <confirm>
(3) <listen to the complaint>
(4) <assert that the computers are good>
(5) <listen to the answer (that their computer broke down)>
(6) <inquire about the computer>
(7) <listen to the interruption, listen to the complaint>
(8) <confirm/listen to the complaint>
(9) <assert that the computers are good>
(10) <listen to the complaint>
(11) <apologize for the exception in the quality of their computers>
(12) <listen to the confirming>
(13) <negate that the computers are bad>
(14) <listen to the demand>
(15) <inquire about the demand>

At the linkage level, we have the following subtasks:

(1) <reintroduce the task/listen to the task T1 again>
(2) <listen to phatic agreement/confirm>
(3) <continue the complaint/listen to the complaint>
(4) <listen to S's assertion that the computers are good/assert that the computers are good>
(5) <answer/listen to the answer>
(6) <listen to S's question/question about the computer>
(7) <interrupt S, complain/listen to the interruption, the complaint>
(8) <listen to S's confirming/confirm>
(9) <a new beginning of a complaint/listen to the complaint>

(10) <listen to S's assertion that the computers are good/assert that the computers are good>
(11) <continue the complaint/listen to the complaint>
(12) <listen to S's apologizing/apologize for the exception in the quality of the computers>
(13) <accept/listen to the accepting>
(14) <listen to S's opposition to the bad quality of the computers/ negate that the computers are bad>
(15) <state a demand on the basis of T1/listen to the demand>
(16) <listen to S's question about the task T4 with the basis of T1/ question the demand>

The task T1 is reintroduced once again, at S34, as a question about general quality, it is agreed in B35 and then reappears in S35. The part introduced by S35 is not answered. It represents a sort of a dead end of the task.

The two participants playing the role parts of the buyer B and the seller S do not agree on the task T1 <are S's computers good>. It seems more that it was not a point to be negotiated, but a part of B's strategy to get a better deal.

The task changes during the negotiation because the whole process of communicating is dynamic – the conditional properties are changing all the time, the task that was introduced at the beginning gains in strength. Every reaction changes conditional properties of the task and makes new initial conditions.

4.3.3.2. TASK T2: <MAYBE WE WILL BUY SOME MORE COMPUTERS>
Task T2 <maybe we will buy some more computers> is first introduced in B7 and confirmed in S8. At this point, B utters the task and S confirms it as a task. The task reappears in B16 where it is asserted and confirmed in S17. At the role-part and linkage levels we have the same structure as above.

The task appears in B21 as asserted and conditioned with tasks T1 and T4. It is implied in B23 and confirmed in S24. Then it is answered under the condition – if T2 then T4 – in S25 and resumed by the buyer B in B26. It is confirmed by S27.

The task is reintroduced in B33 and confirmed; its representation at the participant and the linkage level is the same as above. It appears then at S40, where it is asserted under a condition and it continues in S41, B41 (asking about condition). It is then confirmed by S42 and agreed by the buyer B. That part is a micro-negotiation, which is completed.

The task T2 <maybe we will buy some more computers> is not really completed: it is in fact a purpose of the negotiation. Both participants agree on better conditions for future purchasing that are conditional or even virtual. The fact that the task T2 is not completed can indicate that the linkage between B and S will go on in the future and whenever they meet in the role parts of a buyer and a seller, the task T2 is going to be discussed.

4.3.3.3. TASK T3: <WE ARE GOOD PARTNERS>

The negotiation begins by the task T3 <we are good partners> in the following forms, as implied in B1 and agreed in S2. It reappears in B7 as asserted and argued and is confirmed in S8. The task <we are good partners> is again active from B10 to S14.

In S19 and S20 the partnership is a sort of a subtask for negotiation and this is also the case in B20 where the buyer B demands negotiation based on <we are good partners>. That condition is agreed in S21.

The task <we are good partners> appears again in B33 to B35. It is implied in B52, confirmed in S53, and agreed in B54.

The task T3 <we are good partners> never appears on its own and is never discussed, it is just a 'seal' for the bargain – or maybe a procedure to reach the bargain. It is represented as a sort of initial condition for a 'good' bargain.

4.3.3.4. TASK T4: <WARRANTY PROBLEM>

The warranty problem is raised in B8 and B10 and is answered in S12 and S13. The task is then postponed until B21 and B23 when the buyer B complains about the warranty. The complaint is answered in S24, the task is inquired about in B25 and in S25 the conditions of the task T4 are laid out. In B25, the participant B agrees conditionally with the task T4. The task is once again asserted in S26, resumed in B26, and completed in S27.

In S40, the participant S begins once again with the task T4 as a basis for negotiation. There follows the buyer's conceding in B40. The task T4 <warranty problem> is argued in S41, agreed in B41, and then confirmed in S42 and B42.

The task T4 <warranty problem> is one of the major tasks of the negotiation and ends in double agreement.

4.3.3.5. TASK T5: <COMPUTER BROKE DOWN>

The task T5 represents an introduction to the general negotiation. It is asserted in B4 with 'the thing broke down'. Then in S5 and S6 the [seller] asserts non-T5, that usually the computers do not break down like that, and tries to show this particular example as an exception to the general rule. The task is then implied in B8. The [seller] S answers in S13 as he did in S5 and S6. In B16, the task T5 <computer broke down> represents a condition for partnership (if T5, non-T3 <we are good partners>). In S18, the fact that the computer broke down is once again shown as an exception. The task T5, asserted as a fact not taken into account by S, is once again presented in B27.

The participant S, the seller, does not mention the T5 task possibility, except once as its negation – but does not overtly oppose B's assertion about the broken-down computer, nor does he agree that it has anything to do with him.

4.3.3.6. TASK T6: <COMPUTER REPAIRED>
The fact that the computer has been repaired is mentioned as task T6 in B9 and then in B27 by the buyer B. The seller S does not take it into account. The expectation of the buyer B is not fulfilled; the sequence is blocked at this point.

The task T6 <computer repaired> is a small task that serves only as an introduction to a bigger negotiation about the bill being too high. It is not a point to be negotiated but a mere fact.

4.3.3.7. TASK T7: <BILL TOO HIGH>
When agreement is reached about T7 <bill too high>, the seller S reduces the bill. It is the major point of the negotiation. The negotiation is completed between B49 and B51. What follows is expressions of feelings and an evaluation of the deal.

4.3.3.8. TASK T8: <GIVE US A NEW COMPUTER>
The task T8 <give us a new computer>, which is a demand, is an example of negatively answered negotiation.

The buyer B wants to get a new computer as compensation for the bill after the warranty period in B21, but the negotiation is rejected at the very beginning by the seller S in S22. The buyer B opens the same question in B27, but after a few negative responses by the seller S in S28, S29, and S31 accepts the negative outcome.

4.3.3.9. TASK T9: <DISTANCE PROBLEM>
The task T9 <distance problem> is a subtask of the negotiation about the bill and presents a small negotiation. It is asserted in B44, accepted in S45 (with demand of verification), and then asserted in

B45. In S46 the seller S proposes negotiation about it. In B46, the buyer adds an argument about why to negotiate about the task and in B47 he demands reduction of the bill which is a part of the task T7.

4.3.3.10. TASK T10: A HYPOTHETIC TASK: <FAULTY COMPUTER REPLACEMENT>
The task T10 appears in B54 in a hypothetic form *if T10* as a subtask of the major task of negotiation then the central negotiation is finished. The seller S agrees with it under condition. Then the buyer B corrects his expression and both agree in S56, B56, and S57.

4.3.3.11. TASK T11: <EVALUATING>
The task T11 represents the evaluating of the whole negotiation and appears in B61 and S62. It consists of expressing satisfaction with the negotiation.
    At the end of the negotiation, the following changes have been achieved: the bill has been reduced, the warranty prolonged, and the relationship maintained. All the major tasks that were negotiated about were agreed on before the end of the negotiation which led to a final agreement and a bargain. The seller S reduced the bill in order to maintain the relationship. Only the task long-time relationship was not really negotiated and remained active for further transactions.

4.4. The forms of tasks

As we can see from the above description of the tasks, a task always appears in a certain form:

(a) introducing a task
(b) asserting a task
(c) inquiring about a task
(d) asking about information
(e) answering
(f) agreeing
(g) disagreeing
(h) arguing
(i) conceding
(j) opposing
(l) proposing negotiation (about the task)

We can see this in example (7) below. The task T5, <computer broke down>, is realized in the following form:

Example (7)

B4:   T5 (*assert*) Yes, one year. And we've been using that
      computer, haven't we, for graphics and all that stuff, and
      we were really satisfied with it, weren't we, and then we
      had a meeting, because we are working in marketing and
      PR and we need a lot of that stuff, don't we, and we had a
      meeting that we would need some more computers, *and
      after a few days the thing broke down.*

S5:   *non*-T5 (*assert*): Well, *I must say that it is a shame, isn't
      it, because, you know, we've sold a lot of those computers, and
      then, well, and they are really good computers, I must assure
      you.*

S6:   They were very satisfied with them. We sold them also to
      the ministry of education *and not one broke down.*

B6:   *confirm:* Well, yes.

B8:   T5 (*implied, continues*) Well, and unfortunately, after that,
      to tell you the whole story, *when the thing broke down*, and
      we had an important project going on at the same time, we
      said 'good, we will have it repaired, since the computer
      must still be within the warranty period', and then we
      discovered that the warranty has just expired.

S9:   *confirm (phatic agreement)* Yes ...

S12: *answer non*-T5 Yes, of course, you did the right thing, just
      let me look at the bill ... Yes (looking for the bill in the
      drawer), I remember, I have to tell you the following: it is
      a normal procedure *that if the machine breaks down one
      week after the warranty has expired, it is the same as if it
      broke down one year after it.* Generally, we assume that the
      warranty has expired. But it is true that ...

B16: *if* T5, *not* T3 Well, we are talking now ... We intended to
      buy some new computers. And now, *if we know that after a
      year the machine'll break down and that the repair'll cost as
      much as a new computer, we do not want such a business,* you
      know.

S18: *answer (non*-T5, *exception)* Yes, I understand all that, but
      I have to say once again that it is the first computer that
      broke down after one year.

The seller S mentions the T5 <computer broke down> task
possibility only once as its negation – but does not overtly oppose B's
assertion about the broken-down computer, neither does he agrees
that it has anything to do with him.

Here, we can see the different possibilities of appearance of the task T5 <the computer broke down>. There are other possibilities than asserting T5 and its negation, non-T5, namely asking about T5 (When did your computer break down? How did your computer break down? Why? etc.), argue about T5 (That is why your computer broke down) and so on. Although we stated at the beginning of this section that the number of tasks and subtasks is indefinitely large, we can argue at this point that each task can appear only in a limited number of forms. We listed the majority of forms that were typical for the analyzed negotiation. There should be some more (for example, wonder about the task), but not as many forms of tasks as one might imagine.

Tasks change during a negotiation because the whole process of communicating is dynamic – the conditional properties are changing all the time, the task that was introduced at the beginning gains in strength. Every reaction changes the conditional properties of the task and creates new initial conditions.

Tasks and forms of tasks differ in basic characteristics: the tasks are named by the role they accomplish and their number is unlimited. The tasks listed above are specific to the present analyzed negotiation. The task forms are general, applicable to every task. Their number is limited.

5. Tasks as basic cognitive activities

When a task is expressed verbally, we can adopt two points of view: one represents the energy flow, represented by sound waves, analyzed in traditional grammar in terms of so-called phonetic features concerned with uttering sounds and producing sound waves.

The other point of view is cognitive. We are curious about what cognitive activities are basic to each task. We have already presented a macro-analysis of the tasks and forms of tasks. But every task, as we have found for greeting in example (5) above, can be divided into basic cognitive activities. We will discuss some of these tasks in terms of the cognitive activities that were found in the analysis of the negotiation. These are: referring, describing, identifying and, within the interpersonal dimension, also monitoring, expressing agreement, explaining, arguing, and giving orders.

5.1. Referring

Referring in the analyzed dialog can be taken as the basis of everything: if we look at the first task, S1: *you phoned me that you will come today*, we have referring to the context *you* refers to the addressee, *phoned* to a past action, *me* to the speaker, *today* to the moment of speaking. If we go a little further, *It seems that you have a problem* refers to a referent with an indefinite article that has not been mentioned yet – once being introduced, it will become *the problem*.

Then, the task that we called in the negotiation analysis < introducing a problem >, and transcribed as 'We bought a computer at your shop last year', can be seen as composed of several basic cognitive 'subtasks' that are related to the context of speaking, namely the conditional properties in terms of hard-science linguistics. The basic subtasks in the latter task were: referring to the speaker (*we*), referring to a past action (*bought*), introducing a new concept (*a computer*), time (*last year*), and location description (*at your shop*). Referring is thus the most basic task, bringing the outer world into the conversation. We can distinguish two sorts of referring – to a known or to an unknown referent (definite versus indefinite article).

Referring is not only related to the world outside but also to the speaker's attitudes: if we look at the task < introducing a problem > *It seems that you have a problem*, we see that *it seems* refers to the personal attitude of the speaker of 'uncertainty' or 'probability'. Also in the answer, *unfortunately*, the speaker refers to a problem and evaluates it. In this part, we have two other examples of referring to personal attitude (*Yes, I think*; *No, I think*). Expressions of personal attitude are found throughout the negotiation. Here we are already in the interpersonal dimension that we will discuss later.

5.2. Describing

In the part discussed above, we saw the describing of circumstances: *we bought a computer, one year ago, at your shop*. Later, we have the describing of procedures. See example (8) below:

Example (8)

    B4: ... And we've been using that computer, haven't we, for graphics and all that stuff, and we were really satisfied with it, weren't we, and then we had a meeting, because, we are working in marketing and PR and we need a lot of that stuff, don't we, and we had a meeting that we would need some more computers, and after a few days the thing broke down.

And also describing the quality:

Example (9)
S5: Well, I must say that it is a shame, isn't it, because, you know, we've sold a lot of those computers, and then, well, *and they are really good computers*, I must assure you. *Tasks: are S's computers good – asserted.*

Describing is a more complex task than referring and is done after the referring – the participant is referring to some particularities of the referent or to what happened to it.

5.3. Identifying

Identifying as a basic task was rarely used, namely in the examples *That is the computer we have bought* and *That's it*. As with describing, identifying is also based on features the participant attributes to the referent and comes after referring.

5.4. The interpersonal dimension

5.4.1. Phatic tasks or monitoring
In phatic tasks, the participant is giving signs of 'being with it' that means that he is participating in the conversation, that the conversation is open and is going on. We have already discussed this task among the other basic tasks.

5.4.2. Expressing agreement and disagreement
Expressing agreement or disagreement is another personal attitude, it can be seen in S3, B3, S4 and so on.

5.4.3. Explaining
Explaining is a task that consists of giving reasons for something (it may refer to known or to possible reasons) and contributes to a higher task of arguing. An example can be seen in B21 in example (10) below. The word *because* triggers the expectation procedure of explaining.

Example (10)
B20: Well, we said, if it is an exception, this computer, well, it would be better, for your reputation and our feelings, that . . .
S21: Of course, normally. . .

B21: That, either you exchange the computer for us, or you do something else for compensation. We counted on the possibility that the computer would be repaired within the warranty period. *Because I think that there were a lot of problems with the computer, and, now, I don't know, we said that if you take it into account and repair it within the warranty period, then we would somehow trust you and will in the long-term buy other computers.* But otherwise, we don't know, if every computer breaks down after the warranty term and the repair costs half of the price of a new one ... it is not a trifle. So, if you could make an exception, we would be very pleased.

5.4.4. Arguing

Arguing is an even more complex task than explaining; all the sequence B21 represents arguing, which is a subtask of a larger task, computer problem. As mentioned before with *because*, we can also argue that *but* triggers the expectation procedure of introducing a counter-argument, as can be seen in example (10) above.

5.4.5. Giving orders

This task is expressed verbally and anticipates what should be done nonverbally. It is treated separately because it was not directly formulated in the analyzed negotiation: for example, it is difficult to be polite and say *Give us a new computer!*

Those tasks try to describe the basic cognitive activities in the analyzed negotiation.

6. Conclusion

We have tried to show how spoken communication can be analyzed in terms of hard-science linguistics. We have analyzed a negotiation simulation with a special stress on tasks.

A task/subtask analysis offers us a better insight into discourse because it takes into account the linguistic and nonlinguistic elements of communicating, as we have shown on the example of a greeting.

The marking of the tasks and the giving of task names is determined by their semantics – there is an indefinitely large number of possible tasks. There seems to be a limited number of the forms in which those tasks appear. A task can be, for example, asserted, inquired about, negotiated, rejected, and so on.

The task representation at the linkage and at the role-part level is asymmetrical. It normally follows the order 'cause–consequence': a given impulse causes a reaction and thus a change in the communicative behavior of a participant.

Tasks appear in parallel: usually there are several tasks going on at the same time. The tasks can be closed at a certain moment in the conversation, but their execution can also be postponed for another conversation if the participants remain in a linkage. The agreement of participants helps to finish a task.

Task analysis can be carried out down to the phonetic-phonological level as well as up to the cognitive level, as we have tried to show above. These issues can be tested against the real world.

7. Appendix

English translation of the Slovene transcription of the negotiation.

S1: Good afternoon, you phoned me that you'll come today, you seem to have a problem, don't you?

B1: Yes, well, unfortunately, we've met several times, haven't we?

S2: Yes.

B2: ... for our common business ... but now I am here because of a completely different problem. I don't know if you are concerned, but a while ago we bought a computer at your shop.

S3: Yes, I think it was about two years ago, wasn't it?

B3: No, it was about a year ago, I think it is exactly one year now.

S4: Yes, you are right, it should be about one year.

B4: Yes, one year. And we've been using that computer, haven't we, for graphics and all that stuff, and we were really satisfied with it, weren't we, and then we had a meeting, because we are working in marketing and PR and we need a lot of that stuff, don't we, and we had a meeting that we would need some more computers, and after a few days the thing broke down.

S5: Well, I must say that it is a shame, isn't it, because, you know, we've sold a lot of those computers, and then, well, and they are really good computers, I must assure you.

B5: Well, we were also ...

S6: They were very satisfied with them. We sold them also to the ministry of education and not one broke down.

B6: Well, yes.

S7: So that I have to say, it is a big shame.

B7: Well, it is all right, isn't it. We found out while considering the information about your firm, that we could buy some more computers from your firm, since we've been good partners, and thus head for a long-term relationship.

S8: Yes, of course ...

B8: Well, and unfortunately, after that, to tell you the whole story, when the thing broke down, and we had an important project going on at the same time, we said 'good, we will have it repaired, since the computer must still be within the warranty period', and then we discovered that the warranty had just expired.

S9: Yes ...

B9: We knew that fact, we called for your service and the computer has been repaired. And now, to explain why I have come here, the fact is that the bill you charged us with is somewhat too high.

S10: Yes ...

B10: First, we counted on the fact that we've been cooperating for a long time and that the computer broke down a week after the warranty has expired and we thought that you will count it as if it were within the warranty period, because, finally, it shouldn't be such a big repair. We negotiated that point and after that the bill you charged us with surprised us, and now we are considering, first, if we pay it or not ...

S11: Yes ...

B11: and second, are we still willing to cooperate in the future. But I said, before the others in the firm begin with some new draconian measures about it, OK, I'll travel to Maribor to talk to you, won't I, because otherwise there could be some misunderstandings.

S12: Yes, of course, you did the right thing, just let me look at the bill ... Yes (looking for the bill in the drawer), I remember, I have to tell you the following: it is a normal procedure that if the machine breaks down one week after the warranty has expired, it is the same as if it broke down one year after it. Generally, we assume that the warranty has expired. But it is true that ...

B12: So your computers do break down?

S13: Well, it happens that a machine breaks down. We have been in business for a long time, and it has happened before. But it is true that in such a case that it is only, wait a second, I'll take a look (looking at the paper for the exact date), only two weeks after the warranty has expired, we haven't yet had such a case, I must admit, where there would be such a big repair just after the warranty has expired. There were smaller things, you know. It is normal, it happens. But I don't think we have had such a case. I have to explain that it is our usual practice that after the warranty expires we do not take it into account, but it is true that, considering our long-term relationship, we could talk about it. And considering our relationship, I think that we could discuss certain things.

B13: Well, yes, all that bothers me in this affair, is, that those spare parts you needed for your repair are so numerous. That, in general, should not happen with a machine that is only one year old – or, otherwise, it means that the whole machine was out of order. Because then the computer as a whole is out of order and it worries me that it has one year of warranty and then breaks down. It seems to me also, if we talk business, that from your point of view it is not completely correct. And now I have to say, in our firm, people were disappointed, not to say shocked, first, because of all the parts ... and then, the sum of the repair, because, finally, who is going to trust your computers ...

S14: Mhm ...

B14: And it seems ...

S15: Well, but the computer worked well for a year...

B15: Yes, of course.

S16: There was not any major repair needed for a year?

B16: Well, we are talking now ... We intended to buy some new computers. And now, if we know that after a year the machine'll break down and that the repair'll cost as much as a new computer, we do not want such a business, you know.

S17: Yes.

B17: For such ...

S18: Yes, I understand all that, but I have to say once again that it is the first computer that broke down after one year.

B18: Well, that's why ...

S19: It is a real shame, on one hand, and I think that it concerns us, doesn't it, because we want to preserve our good reputation. So, I think we could negotiate some points.

B19: Well, yes, at our firm ...

S20: We couldn't negotiate everything, but for some points, I think it would be possible.

B20: Well, we said, if it is an exception, this computer, well, it would be better, for your reputation and our feelings, that ...

S21: Of course, normally ...

B21: That, either you exchange the computer for us, or you do something else for compensation. We counted on the possibility that the computer would be repaired within the warranty period. Because I think that there were a lot of problems with the computer, and, now, I don't know, we said that if you take it into account and repair it within the warranty period, then we would somehow trust you and will in the long-term buy other computers. But otherwise, we don't know, if every computer breaks down after the warranty term and the repair costs half of the price of a new one ... it is not a trifle. So, if you could make an exception, we would be very pleased.

S22: Well, as for the spare parts, those spare parts are imported and cost us quite a lot, so that we could get by without the profit margin and I think... So that the spare parts should be paid for. But we could talk about the work costs; it means our technicians, and the costs of travel. We could discuss those matters. It means, as for the spare parts, hm, for the computer, as for the spare parts we could namely debate that we sell them without the profit margin.

B22: Well, ...

S23: and you pay only the price we paid for those parts when we imported them, because our computers are imported, we have to pay for those parts. Then, about the work, about the repair I think we could go down to about 50 per cent.

B23: Well, you know, I think that as far as I am concerned, there is still a basic dilemma. How will you guarantee that all the computers we buy in the future will not break down. Because you'll offer us something now for the future, won't you, for other computers, namely cheaper spare parts or whatever, but first I would like, before going into the future deals or longtime relationships, that you confirm whether it was a rare mistake ... Because for me, the warranty is if you repair the computer not for free but for a little sum of money, don't you think. Because I assume that two weeks after the warranty period has expired is still the same as the warranty period.

S24: Yes, but it is true that it is also a question of principle. It is our usual practice that after the warranty expires, you understand. But I think that we could make a deal that if we are going to start a longtime relationship, we could extend the warranty period up to two years.

B24: That means if we buy ...

S25: If you buy a new computer at our firm, the warranty period would be for two years.

B25: Yes, well, we ...

S26: For our computers I can guarantee that in those two years you won't have any problems.

B26: So, if we buy your computers in the future, you offer us a two-year warranty.

S27: Two-year warranty, yes.

B27: Ah, so. Well, how about ... You mentioned something related to the computer that broke down, well, because the sum of the repair that is in front of us represents about half the price of the computer at this moment. So we were thinking about ... how about exchanging the old computer for a new one?

S28: Aha. That means that we would exchange the computer, your computer, for another one?

B28: Yes, because, we thought that why don't we, for example, for the money that you would charge us for the repair, why wouldn't we return the computer and get a better one, you know, technical changes appear every day and we find it stupid to pay for a one-year old computer half of the price for its repair, if we could, for example, make a better deal. We would like to order a better computer if you take this computer back, considering that we do not pay for it, that you take this sum of repair into the price.

S29: Yes, but in that case you should pay everything that ...

B29: Well, yes ...

S30: For a better computer. Better computers are now pretty expensive. And we must take into account that your computer has been used and that it is about one year old.

B30: Well, yes ...

S31: So that, all the facts taken into consideration, I would be obliged to make a deal and to calculate what would be the price of a new computer.

B31: Well, I just tried to ...

S32: Yes ...

B32: think, to consider if there are any other possibilities, you know, the problem is that I have to explain those amounts in my firm, ...

S33: Yes, yes ...

B33: They are going to discuss the dilemma if we are going to cooperate at all, so that it would be good, well, ... It is in my interest to cooperate with you in the future. And up to now, everything was all right, wasn't it?

S34: Well, how about the other products that you got from our firm, are you satisfied with them? Because I know that you have been ...

B34: Of course, of course ...

S35: buying ... computer hardware and software ...

B35: I think that until now there has been no problem in our cooperation. That is why we were so shocked now. Well, we said, that if we cooperate, and if we buy a computer, why do you give us such a bill ...

S36: Yes ...

B36: with such high prices. And we said, well, some of our colleagues are quite irascible, they fly off the handle easily, and we have a board deciding those things, because we are a small firm ...

S37: Yes ...

B37: and everything goes public ... so ...

S38: there is a mess everywhere.

B38: Everybody wants to control ... and everybody asks other firms, we do collaborate also with others, we offer them our marketing service and then ...

S39: Then, if you should, for example, we are talking about the repaired computer, if you should pay the price of the spare parts and 50 per cent of the work of our technicians, do you still find the price too high?

B39: Well, we should take a better look at this.

S40: Because I'll offer you, for the products you buy here, I'll offer you a two-year warranty ...

B40: Well, concerning ...

S41: to avoid such cases, because, after one year ... I'm really sorry, but it is a great pity.

B41: Yes, yes, well, that cooperation, it is still a point to negotiate. But if you could now really promise us a two-year warranty ...

S42: Yes, we could do that, our longtime relationship taken into consideration and possible future cooperation. It would be to avoid such cases that we could agree on a two-year warranty.

B42: Well, as far as I'm concerned, it's all right. I would be at ease presenting it in my firm and giving arguments that if we decide to buy something in the future, well, then, you mentioned that you would charge us only for the spare parts without the profit margin ...

S43: Yes, we could do that, so that we do not have any profit at all.

B43: Yes.

S44: We would charge you only for the cost of the spare parts. And include the payment of the 50 per cent of the service.

B44: Yes. And I wanted to say, you are in Maribor, we are in Ljubljana. The travel is a pretty large amount here in your bill. If we consider that it takes time, because we need the computer, it seems to me that the travel charge should be left out of the bill. It is your problem that you are in Maribor, we could have taken a computer seller from Ljubljana. And I think that Maribor is not that far from Ljubljana that it could generate such expenses.

S45: Well, if we check it again ... and we do not charge you for the real expenses of the travel but only for the fuel ...

B45: Well, you know, such travel ...

S46: We could diminish that ...

B46: You know, we count the travel in the price of the employee.

S47: Yes ...

B47: Our mode of work ... In our firm an employee costs a certain amount of money per hour wherever he is. So we are willing to pay for the hours the technician needed for the repair, because we think you should take care of the other things.

S48: Well, that would be possible, because I know that the technician had some more repairs to do at that time, not only in your firm, and I have to take a look, so that I think we could make a bargain about the travel.

B48: Well, if you ...

S49: Well, if we take into account other services, we are obliged to charge you for that 50 per cent.

B49: Good.

S50: Is it all right?

B50: Yes, it is all right.

S51: Does it suit you?

B51: Well, I think it is quite suitable. It would reduce the sum indicated on the bill and it would enable me to talk at ease in the future.

S52: Also for the future, yes.

B52: I'll tell you frankly, I was a little bit, not to say, surprised, when we got the bill. I said 'what do these people think?'. First, I said, it must be a mistake. It must have been a mistake, because we cannot do business that way.

S53: Yes.

B53: And as I can see, there was a little mistake.

S54: Well, you know, it was the normal procedure and our bookkeeper wrote the same sort of bill as for the others. He didn't taken into account our cooperation.

B54: Well, yes, it is like that. I would like to suggest another thing to you . We need that computer all the time. And we said that it would be fine, in case the computer breaks down, that you would offer us for that time a computer that would replace the one that is out of order, because that would diminish the problems and the costs due to the lack of a computer. I think we would appreciate it if you would put that into your offer.

S55: Yes, we could do that, but you know, our service is very quick. We usually come within the same day or at least the next day, because we . . . Here, we have a greater distance and we came the next day. And let's say, if there would be a larger problem, a more important one, that couldn't be repaired at once, if there would be more repairs needed, we would surely give you a computer. If it were after the warranty term, we would offer you a computer for a small rent.

B55: Well, yes, for a rent.

S56: That's true. For a small rent.

B56: Mhm.

S57: But within the warranty period, normally, free of charge.

B57: Yes, well, that would be nice, you know, because people cannot work when we are without a computer. It would be very nice, also for us, if we are going to buy the computers at your place, because you are in Maribor and we are in Ljubljana, that we have one thing that compensates the two hours' travel.

S58: Certainly, and with our bad roads . . .

B58: So that we could talk about those things.

S59: Anyway, I can guarantee that in the two-year period you will be given, in case of bigger repairs, a new computer for free for the time of the repairs, and after that time you will be charged a small rent.

B59: Well, all right.

S60: Because it costs. But we have to make an arrangement by phone first . . .

B60: Of course.

S61: that we'll bring another computer.

B61: Well, that's nice. I am very pleased that we managed to make such a good deal, and I hope that we will cooperate in the future.

S62: Well, I share your point of view. We are very pleased with your cooperation and I hope that there will be no misunderstandings in the future.

B62: Well, goodbye.

S63: Goodbye.

Note

Earlier reports on this work have been presented at meetings of Societas Linguistica Europaea (SLE) in 2000, 2001, and 2002.

References

Kerbrat-Orecchioni, C. (1985), 'Les Négociations conversationnelles'. *Verbum*, VII, 1984/2–3, 223–243.

Roulet, E. (1985), 'De la conversation comme négociation', in *Le Français aujourd'hui*, 1985/71, pp. 7–13.

Yngve, V. H. (1996), *From Grammar to Science: New Foundations for General Linguistics*. Amsterdam/Philadelphia: John Benjamins.

Chapter 11

Lottery Betting

Bernard Paul Sypniewski

Austin used the phrase 'I bet you sixpence it will rain tomorrow' (Austin 1975:5) (hereinafter 'the betting performative') to illustrate his notion of performative utterances as language types that have nonlinguistic effects on the world. While in places Austin said that performative utterances relied, in part, on the context for their effect, in other places, he gave the role of context lip service, at best. When briefly discussing the betting performative, Austin does not mention the effect of context at all. Hard-Science Linguistics (HSL) theory can easily demonstrate the effects of the surroundings, i.e. Austin's context. This study looks at the effect that the surroundings have on people who perform a simple task (lottery betting) in a 'controlled' environment where Austin's betting performative would be expected to be used. The study shows that the task could be successfully completed regardless of utterance and, indeed, with no utterance at all. As such, the study challenges the traditional claim that it is the language that performs the act.

1. Description of the study

The state of New Jersey operates a statewide lottery that is administered through private vendors in stores in local communities. Because the lottery is state controlled, there is a small range of variation in the operation of individual lottery sales from store to store or community to community. A lottery player[1] may purchase a lottery ticket at any vending location throughout the State in the same way. The State requires every lottery location to make certain materials available to players, e.g. lottery slips, pens, etc., to display certain signs and advertisements, and to have certain equipment available to account for sales. The real-world surroundings in any one store are unlikely to change in any linguistically meaningful way over the short term. A lottery purchase involves only two people: the person authorized and trained to sell lottery chances, the 'seller', and the lottery purchaser, the 'player'. Lottery betting in New Jersey thus allows us to see a 'minimal' linguistic situation with a limited scope occurring with the smallest possible number of people. State control creates what is, in effect, a series of linguistic laboratories.

The reader may wonder whether the purchase of a ticket or the filling out of a lottery slip is actually a bet, in Austin's sense. Austin does not describe a bet. He merely states the betting performative. Austin's bet can best be described as 'informal'; a bet perhaps between friends. The State of New Jersey considers the lottery a form of betting. The preprinted forms that players use that are supplied by the Lottery Commission to sellers are referred to as 'bet slips' (hereinafter 'slips') in the instructions for each game, printed on the back of each slip. The back of every slip and instant game ticket (hereinafter 'tickets') contains the admonition: 'If you or someone you know has a *gambling* problem, call: 1-800-GAMBLER'. In the 'Prizes' section on the reverse side of the 'Jersey Cash 5' slip, for example, players are told, 'Fifty per cent of all money *bet* is placed into the prize pool' (emphasis added). In addition, the lottery was created not only as a source of revenue for the State but as a way to eliminate or control the type of illegal gambling formerly referred to as 'the numbers'.

The State directs the vendor to offer lottery chances in certain ways, going so far as to require certain standardized types of displays, supplies, and equipment for the seller and player to use. Lottery bets are made in stores that sell other merchandise, in a prescribed area of the store set aside exclusively for lottery betting. In some stores, this area is very small but in CamPark Liquors (the store in which the observations were made), the lottery area is large and elaborate. Except for the selection of winning numbers for certain games, which is broadcast on television, radio, and other media, the entire lottery betting process is conducted in the store in public view. The type of game generally referred to as an 'instant game' or a 'rub-off' in which the player purchases a ticket with spots to rub off with a coin can be completed from bet to payoff in the store.

The study consists of the analysis of 25 recorded observations of lottery betting in one store in the town of Woodbine, New Jersey. In each instance, a player was observed approaching the lottery counter to either play a slip or to purchase one or more lottery tickets, or both. In the case of CamPark Liquors, several different employees are authorized to accept lottery bets. Because lottery bets are made in stores, players sometimes combined betting with other purchases. In many locations, the lottery sales area is immediately adjacent to the checkout area. Because of the noise level in the store, the details of every conversation could not be recorded with absolute fidelity. However, enough information was recorded for each transaction to indicate the type of lottery game the player wished to play, the gross details of the method of play (handing a slip to the seller, purchasing a ticket, etc.), and any other gross activity that occurred during the purchase. Conversation not part of the actual purchase was ignored for the purpose of this study. In most cases, there was no conversation unrelated to lottery betting. Players often made more than one lottery purchase, e.g. a slip and a ticket. No additional interviews with either players or sellers were carried out.

There are two broad categories of lottery game. In the 'traditional' game, a player bets a player-determined amount of money that three or more digits (depending on the game) will be drawn in a certain order in a publicly held procedure at the Lottery Commission's headquarters at a certain time and on a certain date. A player approaches the counter and either tells the digits and the other details of the bet to the seller or, more usually, fills out a bet slip with the necessary information and hands the completed slip to the seller. The seller records the lottery bet in a machine connected to Lottery Headquarters, collects the money for the bets, and hands the player the appropriate receipt(s). Traditional games have names like 'Pick 3', 'Jersey Cash 5', or 'The Big Game'. A bet slip has room for up to five bets for the same game. Therefore, a bet slip may represent between one to five individual bets. When a player has the seller check a previously played slip to determine whether he or she has won a prize, the player may replay the same numbers by so indicating to the seller and paying the new bet amount without filling out a new bet slip.

The Lottery Commission also sponsors a large number of 'Instant Games', which are games whose tickets have a number of 'rub-off' spots, thus accounting for a colloquialism for 'Instant Games': 'rub-offs'. If the player uncovers matching spots, the player wins a prize as mentioned on the game ticket. The player may rub off the spots in the store immediately after purchase and determine whether he or she has won a prize, hence the name 'Instant Game'. Instant Games have names like '2002 and Beyond' and 'Baseball Bucks'. Each ticket contains one bet. To place more than one bet on the same instant game, a player must purchase a ticket for each bet he or she wishes to make. Rolls of unsold instant game tickets are displayed in transparent boxes, stacked to form a divider on top of the lottery counter. Each box holds tickets for only one instant game. Each game has only one box. The store labeled each display box with a store-assigned number in a small blue circular label for players' convenience.

For the purposes of the study, each player was assigned a number starting with B1 and continuing in chronological order to B25.

2. Analysis of the observations.

In 21 out of 25 instances (84 per cent), players purchased at least one instant game ticket. In 8 out of 25 instances (32 per cent), players bought at least one instant game ticket and played a traditional game, thereby placing lottery bets in two different ways on the same occasion. In two out of three instances where a player recited the digits of a traditional game to the seller, the player did not purchase a ticket. In 16 out of 21 instances (76 per cent) in which a player purchased one or more tickets, the same player did not play a traditional game. No betting instance lasted more than about 2 minutes. On occasion, a queue formed with one player making lottery purchases at a time (turn-taking behavior).

Three players (B10, B14, and B15) pointed at a transparent box holding the instant game ticket that he or she wished to purchase. B14 did not name the instant game that he wanted to play but referred to it in a general way ('I'll take one of these rub-offs'). Two players (B10 and B15) both named the desired instant game and pointed at it. One player (B21) replayed a losing ticket and only used the words 'Give me one of these' to refer to the desired ticket. During one observation (B5), both player and seller were completely silent during the transaction which was resolved through the use of a completed betting slip and the exact amount of payment necessary for the purchase. Another player (B25) silently placed his bet but engaged in some small talk regarding previously purchased slips and tickets that he wanted checked. Most of his quips were with another store patron but he did answer the seller's question about whether he wanted his slips back. Three players (B7, B9, and B23) told the seller what numbers they wished to bet on by reciting a series of digits to the seller.

A traditional linguist using Austin's performative theory or speech act theory would look at the language used to determine what acts were performed. ·A surprisingly wide variety in language occurred during the observations, summarized in Table 11.1. Counting silence, there were eight different ways that players made lottery bets.

Table 11.1. Language use

None	2
'Give'	10
Referring to instant games by number only	2
Referring to instant games by name only	7
Reciting digits to be played	3
Amount only	1
'Take'	1
x on y	2

In these observations, no instance of 'bet' was recorded. Thus, there was no instance of any variant of Austin's betting performative *per se*. Using traditional speech act theory, a linguist would need to either explain away the lack of Austin's performative, perhaps by questioning whether lottery betting was *really* betting in Austin's sense, whatever sense that may have been, or by suggesting that Table 11.1 contained surrogates for the betting performative. Either approach would lead a traditional linguist into attempts to save the theory and away from the real-world observations. As we will see, HSL provides a more accurate analysis of the case.

If we examine the data, we find that players successfully placed lottery bets in five ways, counting Austin's performative as a theoretical possibility. Some of these are nonverbal. Table 11.2 shows the number of instances in each category. The tradition would discount the nonverbal instances as being 'uninteresting' but HSL can account for them in a meaningful way and demonstrate their importance.

3. The [lottery sales] linkage

We assume that the buyer is legally able to make a lottery purchase, the sales person is legally authorized to sell lottery chances, and the buyer has sufficient money to pay for the purchases. Since the lottery is State regulated, these assumptions are warranted; no observation

Table 11.2. Types of lottery betting

Present slip to seller	7
Recite numbers to seller	3
Name instant game (by name or number)	21
Point to an instant game (ostension)	3
Austin's performative	0

negates them. Therefore, we will not model these aspects of actual situations.

We set up a linkage called [lottery sales] that we will only partially describe in this paper. The lottery signs both inside and outside the store are the first objects that we model. Some signs change, e.g. the signs announcing the top prize in certain games change frequently; some signs are temporary, e.g. signs announcing new games or recent local winners; and some signs are more or less permanent. It would be cumbersome in this chapter to enumerate them as individual props. Because the aggregate of lottery signs on the exterior of the store or meant to be visible from outside the store (in windows, etc.), regardless of their actual number, effects a single expectation procedure, they may be treated as one prop, [outside signs], with the property <outside signs visible>. Similarly, we shall treat the aggregate of lottery signs inside the store as one prop, [inside signs], with an <inside signs visible> property. We must always model [inside signs] and [outside signs] in [lottery sales] in a complete description of [lottery sales]; this is verified by having observed the collection of interior and exterior signs at CamPark Liquors and many other lottery sales locations. In a more complete description of the [lottery sales] linkage, we would also describe the channels associated with the signs since, communicatively, the visibility and readability of the signs is important. Here we will simply assume that the signs are clearly visible.

In the real world, both sets of signs play an informative purpose. However, for [lottery sales] the informative function of the signs is secondary and will not be considered. Instead, we model the interplay of signs and expectation procedures. Recall that not every store in the State of New Jersey sells lottery chances and, further, lottery sales are not made in all parts of a store. Someone who wishes to play the lottery must be able to determine which stores sell lottery chances. The lottery signs are indications of a place where lottery bets can be made. In a complete description of [lottery sales], we would model expectation procedures that interact with [outside signs] and [inside signs]. We can, if we wish, expand the linkage to include observations as 'far back' as the selection of the store that a player enters to place a lottery bet using an expectation procedure and [outside signs]. Since lottery sales take place within restricted areas inside a store, we could use another expectation procedure and [inside signs] to model the player's moving toward the lottery counter.

We model two participants in [lottery sales], [Bettor] for the player and [Agent] for the seller. [Bettor] has five tasks: <enter store>, <approach counter>, <see Agent>, <place bet>, and <leave>, to be executed in that order. [Agent] has one task: <serve>. The tasks <enter store> and <approach counter> model the obvious but important observations that all lottery players who were observed played the lottery in a particular place, i.e. inside the store and at the lottery sales counter. We model the surroundings with props such as [tickets], [slips], [sales counter], etc. The task <see Agent> models the fact that lottery bets are not self-service. Players cannot retrieve tickets from a vending machine but only from an authorized individual. If a seller is not within the lottery sales area, a lottery sale cannot take place. Once the seller is at the counter, the player may place a lottery bet <place bet>. Once this task is accomplished, the player's job is done; we model this with the <leave> task in which the player physically leaves the lottery sales area. This task allows us to model a queue of players placing lottery bets.

[Agent] has one task <serve> that models the seller's responses to the player's actions. <serve> consists of a number of subtasks that interweave with [Bettor]'s tasks. We will discuss this below.

[Bettor] has a property that we may call <at counter>. No store in New Jersey sells only lottery chances.[2] Every lottery venue sells other merchandise. The <at counter> property accounts for [Bettor]'s physical location. If −<at counter>, the tasks in [lottery sales] cannot proceed. When the player is at the counter, he waits for the lottery sales seller to indicate his or her readiness to accept the sale. Once the player gets a suitable response, the player may begin to indicate his purchase. The <see Agent> task that models this may be written as follows: <see Agent> = <at counter> x <expect response from Agent> -> <ready to order>. Note that we may have to include a time delay along with <expect response from Agent> to account for the possibility that the seller may be somewhere other than at the lottery counter.

The reader may say that the player may begin to fill out slips before the seller arrives at the counter and that this should be accounted for in the <see Agent> task. Indeed, this was observed, e.g. in B10. The player arrived at the lottery counter while the seller was talking to her boss and another employee. The player removed a lottery slip from the carousel containing uncompleted slips and filled it out. However, it wasn't until the seller stepped to the lottery sales counter that the player was able to hand the completed slip to the seller. The player cannot place a bet until the seller is present, i.e. the player cannot place the bet until he gives the slip to the seller. This behavior concerns us here. Perhaps, in a more complete description of [lottery sales], we might model the completion of a slip but, for now, it is unnecessary. The < see Agent > task accounts for the communicative behavior observed. The name of the expectation procedure, < expect response from Agent >, should not suggest that this is an expectation procedure that requires a particular kind of response. It may be satisfied simply by the seller's physical presence behind the lottery sales counter, as was seen in B10 and other observations.

Once the seller acknowledges his or her readiness to proceed, the player expects the seller to accept the bet < expect Agent to accept >.[3] The player tells the seller what his bet will be < place bet >. Since there are two types of games, traditional games and instant games, we model the possibility that a player may place one or both types of bet in some combination. Furthermore, there are several possibilities within each type. There are at least five traditional games and at least 32 instant games.[4] There were several ways of placing a bet on each type of game, see Table 11.2. Rather than listing all of the possibilities here (a list that may be outdated by the time this chapter is read), we will model two broad possibilities. The player may name or otherwise indicate an instant game < indicate game > or may in some way indicate the digits of a particular traditional game on which to bet < complete digits >. We may write < place bet > = < expect Agent to accept >[5] x (< indicate game > v < complete digits >), in which 'v' (or) is to be understood inclusively, as a partial description of < place bet >. In observation B5, both the player and the seller were silent during the observation. There was not even a greeting or a farewell, yet a lottery bet was placed. In observation B25, the player silently placed his bet[6] and the seller only stated the amount due. In observation B23, the player asked for a 'Big Game', a traditional game but, rather than giving the seller specific digits, said 'You surprise me with the number'.[7] As Table 11.2 shows, players pointed at an instant game in three instances. In traditional speech act theory, there is no way to account for the effect of nonverbal communication on a nonlinguistic act.[8] Using HSL theory, if we set up a linkage to model each observed instance of lottery betting, we could use the same model for B5 and B25 or for the instances of ostension as for any other instance.

Once he has placed his bet, the player pays for his bet < pay >, a subtask of < place bet >. The player needs to know the total amount due < get total >. He tenders an amount equal to or exceeding the total to the seller < give money to Agent > and, after doing so, he expects to get back a record of his purchases, either receipts for the slips or the actual instant game tickets <expect receipt>. We write <pay> = <get total> -> <give money to Agent> -> <expect receipt> x <get receipt>. The player may calculate the amount due since the player has control over the amount to be bet. Furthermore, all instant games have fixed prices.[9] In some cases, e.g. B5, the player tendered the exact change to the seller; in other cases, the seller announced the amount due. In the <get receipt> task, we see two expectation procedures, <expect entry> (the player anticipates that his bet will be properly recorded) and <expect paper record> (the player expects to receive a receipt for the completed lottery slip or the actual instant game ticket). Player takes the receipt(s) from the seller <take receipt>. The <pay> subtask completes the <place bet> task. The player leaves the lottery sales area <leave>.

The seller responds to the player's actions. In a broad sense, their interaction can be seen as a type of turn-taking behavior. [Agent]'s single task, <serve>, consists of several subtasks. The seller observes a customer entering the lottery sales area to place a lottery bet <see Bettor>. The seller prepares to accept the bet <greet>, takes the order from the player <accept order>, fills the order by entering the traditional game information into the lottery machine or getting the indicated instant game ticket(s) <get order>, gets the payment from the player <get payment>, gives the receipts or tickets to the player <give receipt>, and terminates the sale <farewell>. We write <serve> = <see Bettor> -> <greet> -> <accept order> -> <get order> -> <get payment> -> <farewell>.

We have seen above that, at times, the mere presence of the seller behind the lottery counter is sufficient to indicate the seller's readiness to accept lottery bets. When the seller observes a player in the lottery sales area and indicates her readiness to accept a bet <indicate readiness>, the seller anticipates that the individual in the lottery sales area will place a bet <expect order>. However, since the store sells more merchandise than just lottery chances and since the lottery sales area is adjacent to other sales areas, a person who is physically located in the lottery sales area may actually be present for some purpose other than placing a lottery bet. On March 23, 2002 there was a queue for lottery tickets. Players B12 and B13 placed lottery bets. Player B14 began a conversation with B12 who lingered in the area.[10] The seller was not certain whether B14 was a lottery player or simply an acquaintance of B12's. The seller asked B14 'Are you just here with' B12 'or can I get you something?' In terms of our model, [Agent] attempted to determine the value of <expect order>.[11] In a more complete description of the [lottery sales] linkage, we would model a subtask that would determine whether a person, physically at the counter, was a player or not. This subtask sets the value of < expect order > .

The above description is sufficient for our discussion of expectation procedures and Austin's betting performative. We have seen that both a player and a seller anticipate the behavior of the other that is created by the surroundings. The player anticipates that the seller will accept the bet and the seller anticipates that the player will place the bet. While the details of the bet vary from player to player, they vary over a very small range, due to the surroundings. A player cannot walk into a store and expect the seller to accept a $10,000 bet on the outcome of a football game. In New Jersey, this behavior may result in a crime being committed.

The State of New Jersey limits acceptable bets and says that it, through its sellers, will accept any bet within those limits. What we see is that there are three parts to a bet:

(1) the offer of a bet
(2) the subject (and amount) of the bet and
(3) the acceptance of the bet.

The lottery system says that sellers will accept (3) certain bets (2) placed by any and all players (1). By limiting the subject of lottery bets (2), the State of New Jersey has limited the scope of behavior needed to place a bet. By saying that its sellers will accept (3) all bets of a certain type (2), the State limits the need to discuss whether a bet is acceptable. We have observed that only the offer of the bet (1) need occur.

What of Austin's performative? Once again, Austin's performative is 'I bet you sixpence it will rain tomorrow' (Austin 1975:5). Austin says that the verb 'bet' performs the act of betting. There are several problems with this. First and most obvious, there is no acceptance of the bet. A bet, as we have seen, requires at least two people. Austin's performative occurs in isolation.[12] While there is a subject matter of sorts (rain tomorrow), we do not know what would satisfy the subject matter and how much is being risked, if anything. Indeed, Austin's performative may be merely rhetorical in the proper situation (think of Noah). The reader may claim that the betting performative was merely an illustration and not completely described. If we read Austin's lectures as a whole, we see that he initially mentioned the role of context in performatives but placed less and less emphasis on context as his lectures proceeded. By the end of his lectures, context disappears as a factor in his performative theory. Austin approaches a major insight and then backs away from it because the tradition only looks at language.

The reader from the speech act school may object that these explanations do not explain why the verb 'bet' was not used in lottery situations or whether the observations were, in some way, equivalent to the betting performative. To answer the objection, we informally consider a better-developed situation similar to Austin's in which the verb 'bet' might be used. Consider two friends, Tom and Jerry, who watch a football game in Jerry's living room.[13] Each person roots for a different team. At one particularly interesting point in the game, Tom says to Jerry 'I bet you $1.00 that my team makes the first down on the next play'. Jerry says, 'You're on'. Tom loses, as usual, because, to make matters short, his team is incompetent. In this situation, we have explicitly stated the three parts of a bet that we have seen. The offer of the bet is 'I bet you $1.00 that ...'. The subject matter of the bet is that 'my team makes the first down on the next play'. The acceptance is 'You're on'.

In the case of a lottery bet, very little is left to chance (other than the outcome of the bet). Prior to the offer of the bet, Jerry had no reason to anticipate that Tom would make the offer or, even if he did, he would not know what the subject matter of the bet would be. Games are spontaneous events. While there is certainly reason to believe that a team would attempt a first down sometime during the game, Tom and Jerry could not have predicted before the game that a first down attempt would occur at the precise moment that it did. Tom made the offer but had to wait (for however long) to see whether Jerry would accept the bet. Jerry might have accepted the bet or perhaps he wouldn't. The player had a virtual certainty that the seller would accept the bet. If we set up a linkage for the Tom and Jerry type of bet, there would be no expectation procedures that one person would offer a $1.00 bet on the outcome of certain events in a particular televised football game or that the other would accept the bet because we could not predict the outcome before the offer of the bet occurred. In short, the difference between the two situations is the collection of expectation procedures that exist in one but not the other.[14]

On the other hand, a lottery-betting linkage is full of expectation procedures. We have seen some of them above but a fuller description of the linkage would need to include others. The player believes that the prices are accurate, that the seller is authorized, etc. In many cases, the values of these expectation procedures only become negative in unusual circumstances so the need for expectation procedures is not obvious. Because the surroundings in lottery sales are so standardized, we may speculate that task completion is also the subject of an expectation procedure. We actually have evidence for this. The players and the sellers knew what to do. They knew what each other anticipated, and complied with those anticipations. Perhaps, then, in a fuller model of [lottery sales], we should couple a task completion expectation procedure with each task. For example, [Bettor] not only has a < pay > task but both [Bettor] and [Agent] expect [Bettor] to have (and complete) the < pay > task.

4. Conclusion

From what we have seen above, we may make certain predictions. Perhaps the strongest prediction that we can make on the evidence produced by this study is that when people participate in repetitive tasks, the tasks include large numbers of expectation procedures that occur in a more or less 'fixed' setting. We may describe 'narrow contexts' as situations with significant expectations,[15] such as at ticket booths, gas pumps, toll booths, checkout counters, and the like, in which the occurrence of certain aspects of the surroundings is predictable. Indeed, what may be seen as efficiency[16] in these areas may be due to the fixed nature of the anticipations of all parties that participate in these kinds of behavior.

Expectations in limited circumstances are ubiquitous. Expectation procedures guide the completion of tasks. This study suggests that expectation procedures arise from the design of the surroundings or, if viewed from the perspective of the surroundings, that the design of the surroundings promotes certain expectation procedures. A parallel area of research that may prove useful is the study of 'custom', i.e. repetitive and originally unplanned activity that may also create expectations, e.g. preparations for religious services, 'pickup' games, or visits to relatives.[17] This paper has not set forth the full description of the [lottery sales] linkage. A complete description would demonstrate the role that expectation procedures play in controlling tasks in [lottery sales].

Studies such as this one make it obvious that linguistics needs to examine much more than grammatical relations or language in order to explain how humans communicate. Linguistics has stalled because of the outmoded beliefs that everything about language can be explained through grammar and that the only interesting area of communications is language.

Notes

This chapter is based upon research for a paper given at the 2002 Conference of the Societas Linguistica Europaea in Potsdam, Germany.

1. In this paper, 'player' means the person who places a bet; 'seller' means the person who accepts the bet.
2. Some states have 'betting parlors', e.g., New York's Off-Track Betting stores (OTB), whose sole 'merchandise' is betting.
3. There were no observed instances in which < expect Agent to accept > would have a negative value. It might have a negative value if the player was underage or the lottery machine was not acting properly. A sign might indicate the latter occurrence.
4. These numbers may vary with different promotions. Furthermore, new games may be added and old games may be retired.
5. The location of the expectation procedure should not be understood as requiring the expectation procedure to be satisfied before the tasks. A player might hand a slip to a seller who may try to enter it into the lottery machine only to find that the lottery machine will not function properly. In such a case, the task would be performed before the expectation procedure would change value from positive to negative. No occurrence such as this was observed.
6. He did, however, exchange quips with another customer.
7. New Jersey lottery machines, into which all traditional games purchases are entered, are capable of generating a set of random digits appropriate to different games.
8. We could claim that some nonverbal acts are actually instances of language and therefore satisfy speech act theory. We could also claim that a much wider variety of language performs nonlinguistic acts. The latter seems to be what the tradition has done. In this way, it seems as though nearly everything is an act, including 'having' or 'being'. Speech act theory has moved away from Austin's tight coupling of language to acts performed ('bet' performs the act of betting; 'we find the defendant guilty' performs the act of rendering someone guilty of a crime, etc.) in either an excess of enthusiasm or in an attempt to save the theory by so broadening the notion of the nonlinguistic act as to make it meaningless.
9. The prices vary from game to game over a range of $1.00 to $5.00 at the time of this writing.
10. He was talking on a cell phone.
11. This little observation also indicates that individuals in close proximity to each other may be in different 'contexts' as far as communicative behavior is concerned. Sometimes it is not easy to see just what context they are in. When this difficulty occurs, we can predict that some sort of clarifying communicative behavior will occur.
12. It is an utterance 'out of context' unlike some of Austin's other examples. See my chapter on verdictives.

13. We should assume that the usual football-gazing accoutrements are present: a television set, a comfortable couch or chairs, liquid and solid refreshments, etc. We can see these as parallels to pens, signs, slips, etc. at the lottery counter.

14. While I do not wish to pursue this point, we may speculate on whether certain expressions are used to 'create contexts', thereby limiting communicative behavior and creating certain expectations.

15. This is obviously not a satisfactory definition. However, it may serve to point the way toward fruitful future work.

16. Or routine. Routines are repetitive behaviors with fixed goals (and fixed expectation procedures).

17. Human-animal communications, e.g. communications with a pet, may be 'customary' in the sense that interspecies communication may rely more on expectations than intrahuman communications do since the ameliorating effects of verbal language are generally not available.

References

Austin, John L. (1975), *How to Do Things with Words*. Cambridge, MA: Harvard University Press.

Yngve, Victor H. (1996), *From Grammar to Science: New Foundations for General Linguistics*. Amsterdam/Philadelphia: John Benjamins.

PART IV

VARIATIONAL AND HISTORICAL LINGUISTICS

Chapter 12

Moving a Classic Applied Linguistics Study into the Real World

Douglas W. Coleman

The work of William Labov has been *extremely* influential in the field of applied linguistics. One of the reasons is that his work has tended to be very well designed from a research standpoint. This paper focuses on his classic study 'The social stratification of (r) in New York City Department Stores' (1972). In it, he identifies what he refers to as 'the linguistic variable (r)' – 'the presence or absence of consonantal [r] in postvocalic position' – and attempts to correlate it with the social status of New York City speakers. The particular strengths of Labov's investigation into this issue are outstanding. But there are also a few elements of the research which present weaknesses. I will deal with both below.

Yngve (1996) argues convincingly that 'business as usual' in linguistics falls within a philosophical, rather than a scientific, domain. In examining Labov's study of '(r)', I will place special emphasis not only on typical considerations of research design, but also on the degree to which Labov escapes the philosophical traps of 'business as usual' in linguistics and successfully conducts a study wholly within the physical domain of science. In doing so, it will be my intention to show that at least some of what Yngve has metaphorically called the territory of the 'old country' of linguistics in the logical domain can, in fact, be taken along as we undertake the task of 'emigrating from the logical domain to the physical [the new world]' (Yngve 1996:105).

1. The focus of Labov's research

Labov (1972) presents a sociolinguistic study conducted of New York City speakers. He identifies this immediately at the outset of his paper (p. 44). As Labov begins to narrow down the topic, we see that, on the basis of exploratory interviews with New York City residents, he has noted that '(r)' seems to be not only a feasible, but easy, measure of linguistic behavior to observe. Hence, we are told right away that his study will involve '(r)'. What is not immediately clear, however, is the precise nature of '(r)', and thus whether it is in the physical domain. This is a key point, and I will return to it below.

Now an aside: I am aware that some of my readers will have their training primarily in theoretical linguistics (TL), and others in applied linguistics (AL). I apologize in advance to readers conversant with the social-science terminology and quantitative research frameworks of applied linguistics. To make myself clear to readers whose backgrounds are in theoretical linguistics, I have found it advisable to spend time clarifying much terminology that must already be familiar to those in AL. I hope they do not find these explanations too tedious.

1.1. Labov's research hypothesis

Labov at first states his hypothesis in a fairly general way, as follows:

> If any two subgroups of New York City speakers are ranked in a scale of social stratification, then they will be ranked in the same order by their differential use of (r). [Labov 1972:44]

As is typical in much writing in the social sciences, Labov thus offers a broad statement of intent early in the paper, and presents the hypothesis in a more precise (testable) way only later on. Such a general statement of hypothesis is typically offered by way of letting the reader know what the researcher believes the larger implications of the work to be. It also allows the researcher to give the reader an idea of what the hypothesis is before getting down to details in terms of subjects and investigative methods.

Labov's particular research hypothesis *suggests* that a correlation is being sought, and that it will be a correlation by pairs of rankings. However, we cannot really take that as a serious restriction on where the paper will proceed or what Labov's approach to a statistical analysis should be. We can tell by its placement in his paper and its very general wording that the above is only a broadly-worded 'research hypothesis', not yet intended to be a statement directly testable by the analysis of specific data.

Only as we read further do we find Labov explaining why he feels department store salespeople are ideal subjects for this research. The identification of who the subjects are in a study is a key issue. It reveals a great deal about how broadly the results can be applied (their 'generalizability', in textbook terms). In getting to this point, Labov has cited some prior work done by Barber (1957) and Mills (1956). Much of this Labov presents not in the main body of text, but in footnotes (fn. 2–5, pp. 45–48). Normally, a researcher would cite even more work than this in order to contextualize his own study within his discipline. He might even cite a long procession of previous books and papers to explain why his own research topic arose and how his research fits in with broader work done in the field. Because this paper is Chapter 2 of a book, rather than a free-standing paper in a journal, Labov has already presented some of this background material earlier, in Chapter 1. So we see a less substantial review of the literature than we would normally expect in a free-standing paper in any branch of AL.

1.2. Labov's restatement of hypothesis in testable form

Near the bottom of page 45, just above the footnote, Labov presents his hypothesis restated in a form he intends to test:

> Salespeople in the highest-ranked store will have the highest values of (r); those in the middle-ranked store will have intermediate values of (r); and those in the lowest-ranked store will show the lowest values.

This hypothesis is now being stated in a testable form in the sense that it now includes an explicit prediction about what form relevant observable data will take. Labov is saying this: when the data is collected, suppose he tallies it in three columns. The left-hand column will be for Saks (the highest-ranked store), the middle column for Macy's, and the right-hand column for S. Klein (the lowest-ranked store). Thus the columns go from highest-ranked on the left to lowest-ranked on the right. Suppose that in each column he puts the percentage of '(r)' observed at that store. Labov's restated hypothesis simply says that the percentage in the left-hand column will be the greatest, that in the middle, the next-greatest, and that in the right, the least, i.e. Saks employees will use '(r)' the most, Macy's employees will use it somewhat less, and Klein employees will use it the least.

2. Research validity

To determine whether or not Labov's study can be couched fully in terms of the physical domain, we need to consider the nature of the entities he purports to observe. If they are physical-domain entities, then the study can be considered to reside fully in the real-world, rather than the logical, domain. The correspondence of variables under study to properties of real-world entities is broadly subsumed under the notion of their validity. In the most general terms, the validity of a measure depends on how accurately a variable of a study represents an observable (real-world) property of an object under study. Various types of validity are often mentioned in social-science research, and two are of particular relevance here: *construct validity* and *face validity*.

Construct validity is the degree to which measures obtained by a particular method of observation in use correspond to the theoretical property purportedly being measured. This sounds fine until we closely examine the nature of the theoretical objects of linguistics. Nearly half a century ago, for example, Whorf (1956) places 'atomic structures and cosmic rays' on a theoretical parallel with 'meaning ... and the structure of logical propositions' (p. 223). He clearly considers all of these to be abstractions. Whorf refers to the latter as 'strictly linguistic phenomena', separating them from the 'physical ... phenomena' which exist on a lower plane (p. 248). More recently, Gee (1993) presents a similar but complementary confusion of the logical and physical domains. He places 'cats and water, and the sentences one hears and understands' within the same domain (supposedly that of concrete objects), contrasting these with theoretical entities. In Coleman (2001), I have noted a consistent confusion in TL literature and textbooks in TL spanning the whole of the twentieth century (pp. 77–79).

Perhaps surprisingly, the same confusion can be found in AL works as well. Take, for example, these two passage from Hatch and Lazaraton's highly influential textbook in AL research methods (1991). They say (p. 541), 'there are many constructs in our field for which we have no direct measures – constructs such as motivation, need achievement, attitude, role identification, acculturation, communicative competence, and so forth'. In regard to construct validity, they say (p. 37):

> Since constructs are abstract (constructs such as proficiency, motivation, self-esteem, or academic success), particular care is needed in evaluating operational definitions.

That is, they seem to equate not having a direct measure (way of observing directly) for something with the abstractness of that thing. This is not the case in science, where all theories are taken to be theories of things in the real world. For example, even before molecules were 'directly' observable with any sort of imaging technology (such as electron microscopes), they were theoretical entities of chemistry and physics. This does not mean that chemists and physicists regarded them as abstractions; they were regarded to be physical entities which at that time could not (yet) be directly observed. The difference between an abstraction, on the one hand, and a physical entity which cannot be directly observed, on the other, is not a trivial one.

So, construct validity is key insofar as we will want to know whether the constructs associated with Labov's variables are necessarily abstractions (existing only in the logical domain) or are potentially real-world properties of entities in the physical domain.

Face validity is validity of the 'if-it-quacks-like-a-duck-it-must-be-a-duck' sort. The notion is not very reliable as typically applied, because of its dependence on researcher intuition (read 'potential researcher bias'). However, face validity is still relevant here. If a researcher regards a construct as a mere abstraction *per se*, rather than a model of something in the physical domain, then the researcher is working in the logical domain, not in science.

2.1. Labov's definition of the variables under study

Labov has – in his restated hypothesis – identified the two main variables that he is interested in (in a scientific study, these are properties of observable entities). One is '(r)', which he has defined as 'the presence or absence of '[r]'. It has two values, which he labels '1' (present) and '0' (absent). The other variable is the social ranking of groups of New York City speakers, based on the department stores where they work. To this variable he has assigned three possible values: high (Saks), middle (Macy's), and low (Klein). They are conventionally called 'variables' because they are properties of the entities under study which *vary* across a given range of possible values.[1]

Labov does not go into any detail in regard to the definition of '(r)', as if to say 'the presence or absence of [r]' were sufficient. It is not, as I will explain below. The subjects in Labov's study, department store employees, clearly exist within the physical domain (and are thus real-world entities corresponding to theoretical entities referred to as *communicating individuals* and *participants*, in the terminology of Yngve 1996 pp. 124 and 125 respectively). So do the stores (corresponding to the elements of theory referred to as *settings*, p. 129).

Only from the bottom of page 45 on does Labov begin to lay out his selection of the three department stores and to explain why they were selected. This section of Labov's paper contains both some of the strongest elements of his study and one of its weakest. Note how he defines the stratification of the three stores in terms of easily-measurable factors which reasonably should correlate with social ranking. The factors relate to *various* contributors to social class, all of which correlate in producing the same ranking of Saks (high) → Macy's (middle) → S. Klein (low). The weakness of this section lies in a failure to point explicitly to all of the previous research that established these factors as independent measures of social class. Labov could have done this in virtually every case, but for some reason, chose not to in some cases. In the footnote on page 46, he cites (but with disappointing vagueness) a survey of newspaper readership in New York City and anecdotal 'common knowledge' in footnotes on pages 47 and 48. Because research existed on which he could have based these measures, this lack of explicitness does not represent a weakness in the research design, but could certainly be regarded as one of presentation.

In using several independent measures of social stratification, Labov avoids introducing a circularity into the definition of the social strata (in this case, high-low strata). This is very worthy of note. A typical example of a failure in this regard is found in Swales (1990). He states that discourse communities are to be defined in terms of six 'necessary and sufficient ... characteristics' (p. 26), one of which is the set of genres its members employ. A problem arises when Swales later defines genres in terms of the discourse communities which employ them (p. 58). In fact, his problem of circularity is by no means new. Bloomfield (1933) defines speech communities in terms of the similarity of the speech of their members (pp. 42 ff.), even while recognizing that boundaries of speech communities are immune to precise demarcation. Yet his 'fundamental assumption of linguistics' states 'that *in every speech community some utterances are alike in form and meaning*' (emphasis his, p. 78). Thus, Labov escapes this pitfall. The approach he uses has been set out explicitly in Saville-Troike (1989:17). She suggests that such circularity can be avoided only if researchers begin 'with an extra-linguistically defined social entity'.

Labov also introduces a number of other variables, including race, age, sex, and the casualness of an utterance. Most of these, like '(r)', are never precisely defined, but are taken to be self-evident. The casualness of the utterance is defined fairly precisely, in terms of the order of occurrence of the utterance within his interaction with the department store employee: the employee's first response is labeled 'casual', the second, 'emphatic'.

2.2. Labov's data collection method

Labov collects his data by approaching department store employees and asking for directions to a particular department that he had predetermined was located on the fourth floor. He asks, for example, 'Excuse me, where are the women's shoes?'. After receiving a response, he leans forward and says 'Excuse me?' and thus receives a second response. He treats the first response as casual, the second as emphatic. Moving out of the subject's view, he makes notes and moves on to the next available subject (p. 49).

On pages 49–50, Labov explains his data-collection method in detail. It is one which has come to be called a type of 'rapid-and-anonymous data collection'. It is *rapid* in that Labov does not need to assemble his subjects in a laboratory or develop a complex test instrument (such as a survey questionnaire), and the time taken with each subject is very minimal. It is *anonymous* in that Labov does not have any way to tie his subjects' responses back to them individually, nor do they even know they are taking part in a research study. The approach has the additional advantage of focusing on natural communication. The characteristics of *rapidity* and *anonymity* are there only because the data collection phase takes place entirely in a natural setting, with what is (from the point of view of the subjects) an ordinary communicative interaction. It is only the researcher who sees it otherwise. The naturalness obtained via the rapid and anonymous technique arises due to the fact that data is taken from linkages (Yngve 1996:126 ff).[2]

Most data-collection procedures lack this naturalness, and try to make up for it in other ways. Some experimental procedures which simulate natural communicative interactions seem to succeed *at least in part*. Other experimental procedures which distract subjects from the actual experimental task by suggesting that it is something other than what it is, and then requiring subjects to engage in a communicative task as well also succeed, *at least in part*. Some (so-called *post hoc*) studies collect real-world data on human communication after the fact (e.g. from existing tape or video recordings, from printed texts, and so on); these involve natural data on human communication. Most other experimental approaches, all questionnaire-based ones, and most interview-based ones, *lack* this naturalness which Labov's study on (r) possesses.

By the same token, this 'rapid-and-anonymous' data-collection procedure has certain weaknesses. One is precisely its anonymity. Labov has no way to *reliably* measure individual subject responses and their personal characteristics, such as gender, race, age, and so on. He can obtain highly reliable data on his subjects' personal characteristics only from employment records, and thus only in aggregate – at the level of the department store (but this confounds levels of description; see below). Another weakness arises from the rapidity. Labov, you will recall, records the subjects' responses as soon as he walks away from each, by jotting down the values for '(r)' in each of the four possible slots (casual *fourth floor* and emphatic *fourth floor*), so he may record a particular interaction as '0-0-1-1', meaning no [r] in the subject's first (casual) response, but [r] both times in the same subject's second (emphatic) response.

The problem with this approach to recording the data is two-fold. First there is the question of accuracy. Labov does not record his subjects' responses in an audio format, given the technology of the day. In the late 1960s high-quality tape recording is available only on bulky reel-to-reel machines. Such equipment cannot be used in the type of data-collection Labov employed. So, he is forced to settle for making notes on paper based on what he hears. If we want to be very careful about our data collection today, we use a pocket-size analogue or digital recorder to obtain the acoustic production of each subject in electronic form. We can then use speech spectrogram software to analyze the actual waveforms the speaker produces.

2.3. Labov's data

Labov identifies *all* of the variables of interest only within his 'Method' section, which begins on p. 49. Here he lists his 'independent variables' (pp. 49–50) and 'dependent variable' (p. 50 – there is actually more than one dependent variable; see below). The distinction of 'independent' and 'dependent' variables is, of course, sometimes one of assumed direction of causality, sometimes merely one of the direction of a statistical prediction. In Labov's restated hypothesis (p. 45, see above), 'the store' is his independent variable, 'the use of (r)' is his dependent variable. If we look back at this hypothesis, we see that in it he claims to be able to predict 'the use of (r)' on the basis of 'the store'. Hence, the predictor variable ('the store') is the one called 'independent', while the predicted variable ('the use of (r)') is the one called 'dependent'; i.e., its value is seen to be dependent on that of the other variable. Labov does not explicitly state whether the correlation he seeks is, in fact, theorized to be causal in nature.

Here is something very important to note. When he lists several more independent variables, Labov is establishing a new set of additional hypotheses, each with a new independent variable: 'floor within the store', 'sex', 'age (estimated in units of five years)', 'occupation (floorwalker, sales, cashier, stockboy)', 'race', and 'foreign or regional accent' (pp. 49–50). For example, since one of these variables is identified as 'race', Labov is implicitly hypothesizing that the variable 'race' will permit prediction of the variable 'the use of (r)'.

There is an additional complication in that Labov does not consistently treat 'the use of (r)' as a single variable. To understand this, we need to consider two of his figures, Figure 2.1 (p. 51) and Figure 2.2 (p. 52). I will try to describe the key elements of these figures so that the reader will not have to have them in hand.

His Figure 2.1 shows 'Overall stratification of (r) by store'. For each subject, Labov has noted the total number of occurrences of '(r)'. (This is the total out of four possible occurrences of (r) in each subject's two *fourth floor* responses.) He then uses these totals to count what percentage of the subjects at each store fall into the categories of 'all (r-1)', 'some (r-1)', and 'no (r-1)' (his sample sizes are as follows: $n_{Saks} = 68$, $n_{Macy's} = 125$, $n_{Klein} = 71$). (Recall that Labov records the presence of [r] as '(r-1)', its absence, as '(r-0)'.) In this case, 'the use of (r)' is a single variable. If a subject's responses have been recorded as 1-1-1-1 ([fo:r̠θflo:r ... fo:r̠θflo:r]), he/she is assigned the value 'all (r-1)', for example. If the subject's responses have been recorded as 1-0-1-1 ([fo:r̠θflo:r ... fo:r̠θflo:r]), 0-0-1-1 ([fo:r̠θflo: ... fo:r̠θflo:r]), etc., he/she is assigned the value 'some (r-1)'. If the subject's responses have been recorded as '0-0-0-0' ([fo:θflo: ... fo:θflo:]), then he/she is assigned the value 'no (r-1)'.

In contrast, the four possible occurrences of '(r)' ('casual: fourth floor, emphatic: fourth floor', p. 50) are treated separately in his Figure 2.2. Here each line on the graph shows 'the use of (r)' for a given store, each point along the line, one of the four positions – '(casual) fourth', '(casual) floor', '(emphatic) fourth', '(emphatic) floor'. Each of these variables has a percentage value (ranging from 0 to 100, therefore). We might call the first of these variables 'casual use of (r) in *fourth*', the second, 'emphatic use of (r) in *floor*', and so on. Note that these values have been rounded off to integers, but they might have been reported as fractional percentages, e.g. 29.5 per cent.

Labov's Table 2.1 (p. 53) similarly breaks down 'the use of (r)' into four separate variables, each of which has a whole-number value, not a percentage. Here, the values reported are of the number of salespeople in a given store who provide a given response. This table shows that there were 17 Saks salespeople whose response on '(casual) fourth' is assigned the value '(r-1)', 31 Saks salespeople whose response on '(casual) floor' is assigned the value '(r-1)' and so on. The values here must be in whole numbers because they are a raw count of the number of people in each store who were identified as having made each particular response.

Remember that Labov records each response of each of his subjects with a '1' or a '0'. He simply notes whether or not he can detect '(r)' in the speech of that person: '1' means he can detect it, '0' that he cannot. Yet he is not limited to treating the data thus obtained as 'present' or 'absent'. By aggregating the data in different ways (as in Figure 2.1 vs. 2.2), he displays quite different information from the same data.

3. Possible confounding of different levels of description

A basic question of Labov's study surrounds the basis for the differential appearance of '(r)' under different conditions. In his original hypothesis (p. 45), the independent variable is identified as the social ranking of the store. When we try to move this hypothesis into the physical domain, we find that the independent variable *social ranking of the store* is a property of linkages associated with this setting (Yngve 1996: 129). The original hypothesis, above, states how a property of the setting is connected to properties of a particular linkage type. It is strictly a hypothesis formulated at the linkage level. However, recall that there are the subsidiary hypotheses presented on pp. 49–50 involving the additional independent variables 'floor within the store', 'sex', 'age (estimated in units of five years)', 'occupation (floorwalker, sales, cashier, stockboy)', 'race', and 'foreign or regional accent'. While the first of these ('floor within the store') is likewise an aspect of the setting (a linkage property), the others involve categorial properties of a communicating individual ('sex', 'age', and 'race'), a combination of a participant's categorial and procedural properties ('occupation'), and some general procedural properties of a communicating individual ('foreign or regional accent'). The casualness of the subject's response ('casual' vs. 'emphatic') could be associated with a property of an individual resulting from a linkage state (a role-part property) or with the relevant property of the linkage. It is sometimes not clear whether each hypothesis concerns properties of a communicating individual or properties of a linkage (this is discussed further in section 5 below). The two system levels sometimes seem mixed within a given hypothesis. Still, despite these possible confusions, there is no clear problem so far that prevents the hypotheses from referring to real-world entities.

4. The nature of 'the linguistic variable (r)'

This leads us to the separate but related issue of the nature of the linguistic variable (r). This is what Labov was attempting to record on paper as 1's and 0's. Recall that he identifies the linguistic variable (r) as the presence or absence of [r]. So, more to the point, how does Labov view [r]? Is it (1) a *speech sound* as perceived by the department store employee, (2) a *speech articulation* that person performed, (3) the *acoustic energy* produced by that speaker's articulation, or (4) the *speech sound* as perceived by Labov?

To know the first, Labov would have to either (a) have mind-reading talents or (b) lose the advantages of the naturalness of the 'rapid-and-anonymous' technique by asking – and even then he would not have any reason to trust his subjects' conscious judgments about what they were perceiving.

To know the second, Labov would have to be able to observe what was going on inside the person's vocal tract. But he has no way to see whether or not tongue retraction was occurring, so he has no way to see if there was the specific articulation one could associate with (r). To know the third, Labov would have to have access to equipment of the kind we have today – a mini-recorder that could be kept out of sight and turned on and off on cue. He probably had access to a speech spectrograph, but without recordings of the subjects' speech, it would not have helped.

Clearly, then, what Labov notes on paper is (4), the 'speech sound' as he perceives it. This raises two questions. The first is whether or not the listener's perception of the sound is the appropriate thing to be recording. It is, after all, quite a different thing from that of the acoustic energy, which does *not* map one-for-one onto what a person perceives. The second question is whether or not Labov's perception could unconsciously be affected by his own expectations. Did he perceive more occurrences of [r] at Saks because he expected to? We know that such things *do* happen – they fall under a set of events known as 'researcher bias'. Labov himself recognizes this as a potential problem (see his fn. 11 on p. 66). Applied linguists would categorize this problem as one of *internal validity* arising from a potential weakness in instrumentation.[3] Labov's variable '(r)', then, does not unambiguously lie within the physical domain.

Let us assume that we could define [r] in terms of articulations and the acoustic waveforms they produce (by repeating Labov's experiment, but this time recording subjects' speech for spectrographic analysis). This would place [r] within the physical domain as a procedural property of a communicating individual. Let us further suppose that we could identify 'postvocalic' [r] in real-world terms on the basis of the presence of vowel formants immediately before the part of the spectrogram we associate with the [r] articulation. Recall that Labov defines the variable '(r)' as 'the presence or absence of *consonantal* [r] in *postvocalic* position' (p. 44 – emphasis mine). Together these would place the linguistic variable (r) in the physical domain as a conditional property of a communicating individual. Its value would condition the triggering of the procedural property [r] (the [r] articulation) in the communicating individual.

Although Labov's (r) does not unambiguously lie within the physical domain, it might. It is his dependence on his perception in the data-collection process which weakens the claim to (r) being a real-world property. There are without question the objects and events present in his study to allow it to be moved fully into the physical domain of science.

5. Labov's model building

All people who are engaged in scientific research are performing the task of building models. Model building usually occurs in several steps. It typically begins with informal observation of some aspects of the world. For a linguist, this may involve personal experiences in communicative interaction with others. For an astronomer, 'informal observation' may involve the use of highly technical instruments. In either case, it seems fair to call the observation 'informal' if observers have not pinned down exactly what they are looking for and have not precisely defined the entities they are interested in. The scientist's intuition generally comes into play next to suggest possible ways of organizing personal experience. It may provide the basis for formal definitions of entities to study. It may offer up possibilities about how to describe the relationships among these entities. It doesn't really matter how a scientist comes up with possible models as long as the models are models of real-world entities. If they are, then they can be tested by observation in the real world. Labov's treatment of social stratification of stores is based on real-world properties described in terms of linkages and communicating individuals. His 'linguistic variable (r)' is not unambiguously within the physical domain – but may closely correspond.

Labov's hypotheses confound levels of description in mixing properties of individuals with those of settings and linkages. His mixing of levels of description indeed raises one serious practical question. Suppose the variable of social ranking involves a property of the linkage that occurs in a particular setting (the store) that would set a conditional property in the role part (the employee). Then if an S. Klein employee, for example, quits his job and goes to work at Saks, Labov's hypothesis predicts his linguistic behavior in regard to the variable '(r)' will change. On the other hand, suppose the variable of social ranking instead involves a categorial property of the communicating individual (who would possess a given value for '(r)'). Then Labov's hypothesis predicts no such change. Rather, it would predict that a majority of S. Klein employees would simply be unable to get a job at Saks. In this case, there would be a prior bias in the selection of subjects able to obtain employment at each store, based on each one's categorial property in regard to '(r)'. So we do not know if there is a *concurrent* causal factor in the environment or a *prior* biasing factor in subject selection. Labov's observations would yield the same differences among Saks, Macy's, and S. Klein employees in either case. A different experimental design would be able to avoid the problem or resolve the question.

Labov's testing of his hypothesis is otherwise basically sound, because he has invoked a customer-employee linkage to obtain his data. Weaknesses noted above arise primarily from specifics of his implementation.

6. How much of Labov (1972) can be moved into the real world?

In each of the three department stores, recall Labov asked a question about the location of a department that he knew was located on the fourth floor (e.g. 'Excuse me, where are the women's shoes?'). In this way, he had a very good idea what the employee's response would contain. He expected the employee to respond with something like 'fourth floor'.

Figure 12.1 shows the speech spectrogram made from a recording of my saying 'fourth floor' two times – the first time performing the articulation [fo:θflo:], the second time the articulation [fo:rθflo:r].

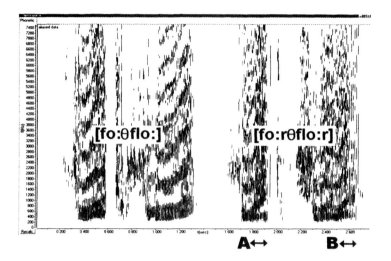

Figure 12.1

This is a conventional speech spectrogram showing frequency on its vertical axis (0 to 7500 Hz), time on its horizontal axis, and the relative intensity of the sound at a given frequency in the darkness of the graph at that point. Note the two lowest-frequency formants, (F1 – bottom) and (F2 – second from the bottom). Since F1 and F2 correlate closely with tongue height and the part of the tongue at which the greatest constriction of the airflow occurs, respectively, by examining them, it is possible, of course, to get a pretty good idea of what the tongue is doing at any particular point. We can see, in the spectrogram made from the recording of my [fo:rθflo:r] articulation (right half), a sharp rise in F2 clearly visible above each of the double-ended arrows A and B which is lacking in the corresponding sections of F2 for [fo:θflo:] These formant transitions indicate that the tongue retraction associated with an [r] articulation did occur in those two cases. Although Labov did not record and spectrographically analyze the responses from his department store subjects, we can see that what he was *trying* to observe does correspond to a real-world phenomenon, both in articulatory and acoustic terms.

In Labov's department store study, he entered into an assemblage which we can represent in terms of a customer-employee linkage (Yngve 1996:126). He did so in order to elicit a certain type of response from the employee. In the following, I will not examine the larger elements of the linkage, nor the properties of the communicating individuals (Labov and the employee) as they pertain to the whole linkage. I will focus specifically on one aspect of what Labov himself was trying to study (the 'casual-emphatic' variation), and focus merely on the properties relevant to the tongue retraction articulation [r], treating it as a socially-stratified communication behavior.

Figure 12.2 shows in rough form the articulatory sequence [fo:rθ]. Note that each articulation subtask (T1 – T3) does not represent an equal, or even discrete, time-slice. Contrary to what is implied by traditional treatment, articulations do not consist of sequences of discrete, neatly-timed 'speech sounds' like beads on a string. If we recognize that such complexity is a part of an accurate picture, Figure 12.2 can help show what is going on without distorting things too much.

Figure 12.2 therefore shows only a very small segment of the relevant plex structure of an S. Klein employee who never produces a postvocalic [r] articulation. It shows the speaker's properties relevant to the articulation [fo:θ] in the responses to Labov in the linkage he employed. The primary task in this articulation is labeled 'FOURTH' in the top-most box. When a pulse comes down its input line (the arrow on the left of the box), the task initiates. It sends a pulse to subtask T1. The line going down from the T1 subtask box sends a pulse simultaneously to four additional subtasks. The top-to-bottom ordering among their subtask boxes does *not* indicate time order; all receive the pulse at the same time. Note that each of the four subtasks sends an output pulse to the AND gate to their right. When all four subtasks are complete, the receipt of all four pulses sends a pulse back up through the AND to the line reentering T1. When this feedback pulse is received, T1 is complete, and a pulse is sent on its output line leading to T2. The subtask structures of T2 and T3 are so similar to that for T1 that I will refrain from describing them in detail. Suffice it to say that when T3 is completed, a pulse is sent on its output line back up to FOURTH, satisfying that task, after which time a pulse is sent on via the output line from the right side of the FOURTH task box.[4]

Figure 12.3 shows a part of Figure 12.2, but with an added subtask, T2A. This subtask provides for the tongue retraction produced by the typical Saks speaker, who always produces the [r] articulation. Elements not shown (T1 and T3) are the same as in the plex structure of the S. Klein speaker.

Now for something a bit different. Figure 12.4 shows the relevant portion of the plex structure for a typical Macy's speaker (a selection procedure; see Yngve 1996). The difference is in the T2A subtask. As before, T2A receives a pulse along the input line on its left side. There

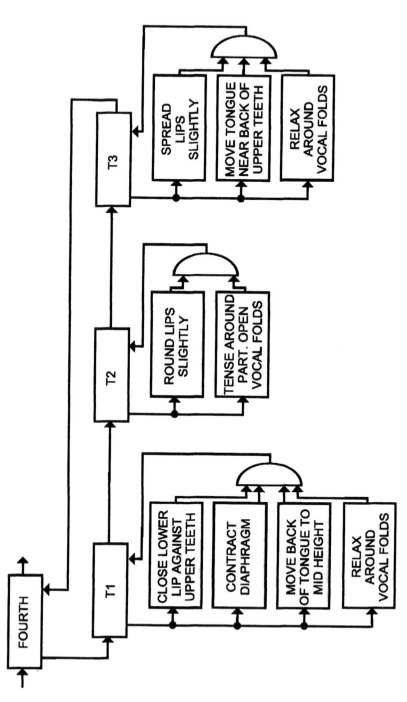

Figure 12.2

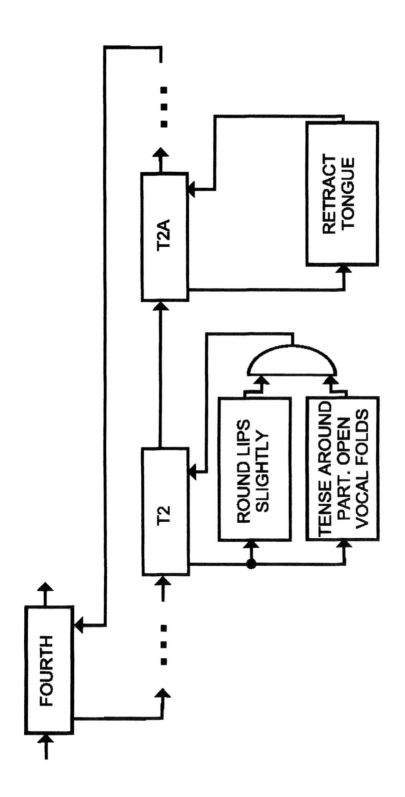

FOURTH

T2

ROUND LIPS SLIGHTLY

TENSE AROUND PART. OPEN VOCAL FOLDS

T2A

RETRACT TONGUE

Figure 12.3

are then two possible additional input levels, each one determining a separate output pulse. If the T2A subtask also receives a level on C1, the output pulse will be on S1. If T2A receives a level on C2, the output pulse will be on S2. Hence, if the conditioning environment is CASUAL, then the RETRACT TONGUE subtask will be bypassed; however, if the conditioning environment is EMPHATIC, then the subtask RETRACT TONGUE will be invoked.

How is the 'conditioning environment' referred to above different from one in a grammatical description? The above shows general procedural properties of communicating individuals. The participant task properties that are relevant to the employee role part in a customer-employee asking-giving directions linkage in all three cases include a state just after the employee has been asked to identify the location of a department and another state (which can only arise slightly later) just after the employee has responded, and the customer has indicated the response was not understood. The first of these is indicated in Figure 12.5 by the task 'State location'. This task invokes a set of subtasks which include those shown in any one of the above plex segments (in Figures 12.2–4). It also sends a level on the line here labeled as the property 'casual'. The task 'Clarify' invokes the same subtasks as does 'State location', but it simulta-neously sends a level on the line labeled here as the property 'emphatic'. In the plex segments in Figures 12.2 and 12.3, neither level ('casual' or 'emphatic') has any effect on the subtasks shown. However, in Figure 12.4, either C1 or C2 is affected on T2A, resulting in subsequent pulses out S1 or S2, respectively. Hence, changes in the linkage state result in changes in the employee's participant task properties, in turn affecting certain general condi-tional properties of the same communicating individual. This account differs from a grammatical treatment in that it describes real-world properties of a person and how they are affected by changes in the person's environment. As the linkage changes state, its state changes trigger changes of state in people via channels (Yngve 1996:128) – light waves, sound waves, and so on.

7. Conclusion

Labov's classic study is not completely framed in terms of the physical domain, and thus is not completely amenable to scientific treatment. However, in many respects it is an ideal of mid-twentieth century linguistics in that it has the potential to be translated fully into physical-domain terms.

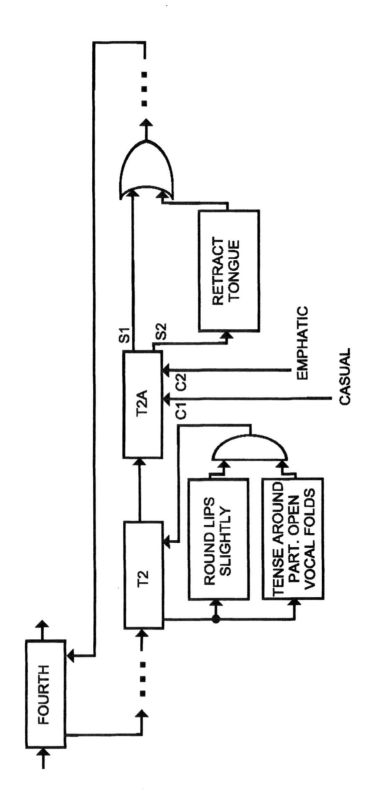

Figure 12.4

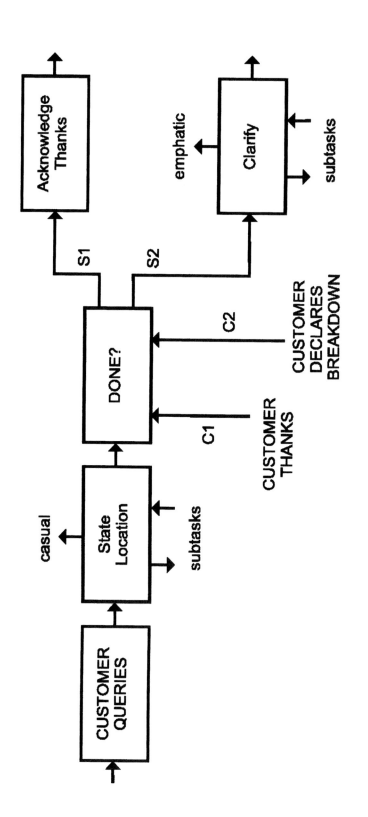

Figure 12.5

I am willing to suggest at this point that a major effort of early twenty-first century applied linguistics should be to review past work, to determine which aspects of it can be moved fully into the real world, and to leave behind the baggage of that which cannot.

Notes

A draft version of this paper was presented at the Workshop in Scientific Linguistics, a LACUS XXIX pre-conference tutorial, July 29–30, 2002, University of Toledo, Toledo, Ohio. I would like to thank those who made very helpful comments on the paper at that time, especially Carl Mills of the University of Cincinnati.

1. Note that by 'values' of course I do not necessarily mean 'numerical values'. The frequency of '(r)' will be a numerical value, but each store (or its rank from high to low) has been assigned no numerical value, only a label. The use of the term 'value' in this sense is conventional in statistical studies.

2. Of course, although the rapid-and-anonymous technique is strongly associated with its participant-observer (first-person) variant as used by Labov, it is also possible to perform rapid-and-anonymous data collection with the researcher in the role of a detached third-person observer. The latter technique (third-person) gives the researcher less direct control over certain interactional variables. At the same time, however, it greatly reduces certain risks of researcher bias.

3. The term 'instrument(ation)' does not have to imply that 'instruments' in the everyday sense (e.g. mechanical or electronic) are involved. In social-science research it refers to the procedure and any devices used by the researcher in observing and recording data on a variable.

4. Note that in this regard, a task box logically resembles an R-S flip-flop, with S and R inputs and Q and $\bar{Q}$ output levels (see Figure 12.6). An initial pulse to the S line, from the previous task, simultaneously is sent to the first subtask. The flip-flop is also toggled 'ON', meaning the $\bar{Q}$ line is forced high. The last subtask outputs a pulse which comes back in on the flip-flop's R input and, simultaneously, is logically anded with the $\bar{Q}$ output level before being passed on. (The Q output level in effect loops back to help toggle the flip-flop's state, but has no output *per se*.) Thus the task must be in an 'ON' state (toggled by an input on S) in order for a pulse on R to have any effect. In this way, some or all of the same subtasks might be shared by other tasks without confusion as to which task they are serving.

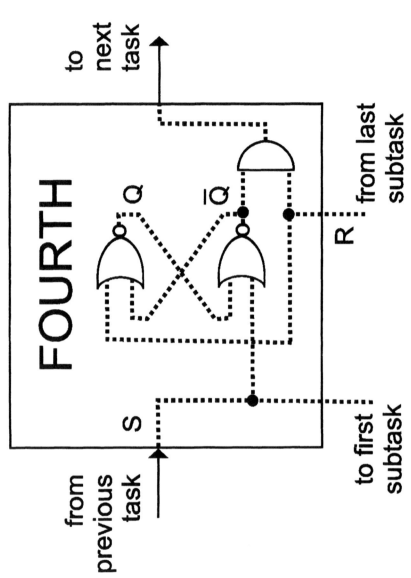

Figure 12.6

References

Barber, Bernard (1957), *Social Stratification*. New York: Harcourt Brace.

Bloomfield, Leonard (1933), *Language*. New York: H. Holt and Co.

Coleman, Douglas W. (2001), 'DATA and SCIENCE in introductory linguistics textbooks'. *LACUS* 27:75–85.

Gee, James Paul (1993), *An Introduction to Human Language: Fundamental Concepts in Linguistics*. Englewood Cliffs, NJ: Prentice-Hall Publishers.

Hatch, Evelyn and Lazaraton, Anne (1991), *The Research Manual: Design and Statistics for Applied Linguistics*. New York: HarperCollins/Newbury House.

Labov, William (1972) 'The social stratification of (r) in New York City department stores, Chapter 2' in *Sociolinguistic Patterns*. Philadelphia: University of Pennsylvania Press, pp. 43–69.

Mills, C. Wright (1956), *White Collar*. New York: Oxford University Press.

Saville-Troike, Muriel (1989), *The Ethnography of Communication: An Introduction* (2nd edn). New York: Basil Blackwell.

Swales, John M. (1990), *Genre Analysis*. Cambridge: Cambridge University Press.

Whorf, Benjamin Lee (1956), *Language, Thought, and Reality: Selected Writings of Benjamin Lee Whorf* (ed. John B. Carroll). Cambridge, MA: MIT Press.

Yngve, Victor H. (1996), *From Grammar to Science: New Foundations for General Linguistics*. Amsterdam/Philadelphia: John Benjamins.

Chapter 13

Describing Frisian Communities in Terms of Human Linguistics

Elżbieta Wąsik

1. Preliminary remarks

This paper is based on my previous investigations of Frisian (Wąsik 1999a, 1999b). These followed a theoretical model coming out of certain language minority studies. However, its methodological apparatus has been largely enriched following my participation in the workshop devoted to *Exploring the Domain of Human-Centered Linguistics from a Hard-Science Perspective* at the SLE Meeting in Poznań (cf. Wąsik 2000). As a result of my recent experiences, I became aware that the domain of my studies should encompass the interrelationships between linguistic properties of individuals and groups with the surroundings in which they function as communicating individuals, and to which they refer their expressions. While focusing on people (in accordance with Yngve 1996), I have confined myself to treating their communicative behavior as observable links that mediate between communities and their surroundings within a span of years, in a certain territory, in a given country, and/or in the relationship between states.

2. Linguistic communities of West Frisians as a set of long-lasting coupled linkages

My studies have aimed at showing how various forms of verbal and nonverbal behavior link social groups that function as ethnic communities. As an analytical example, I have taken the Frisian-speaking community in the Dutch province of Friesland (Fri. *Fryslân*). Elements expressing national identity of West Frisians (from the viewpoint of individuals and collectivities) have been searched for according to the principles of human linguistics among the properties of communicating individuals as participants in various types of linkage systems.

My data come from sociological investigations (cf. Gorter *et al.* 1984:3ff) in the province of Friesland under the auspices of the Frisian Academy. Alluding to the *dictum* 'Who speaks what language to whom and when' (Fishman 1965), I have been interested, rather, in finding an answer to a standard sociolinguistic question: 'Who speaks what language to whom, about what, and why?'. The identity of Frisians, however, except for the use of the Frisian language constituting a specific property of the members of this ethnic group, has been revealed also by other concretely observable physical phenomena. These are considered in terms of human linguistics as channels, props, or settings (which constitute other constituents of the Frisian linkages apart from the communicating individuals). I have contrasted the presentation of selected linguistic-communicative properties of the Frisian-speaking linkage as a whole and the subordinate social linkages with the ecological approach to language as known from the naturalist tradition of language studies.

The ethnic group of West Frisians forms today a separate and relatively compact communicative minority within the state of the Netherlands. On the one hand, they are distinct from other Frisians, namely, the North Frisians and the East Frisians living in the Federal Republic of Germany. Their separateness is explained, e.g., by the fact that their direct connections with the members of the former tribal community has not existed for centuries because of their belonging to the Dutch national state. On the other hand, West Frisians have preserved their separateness from the Dutch-speaking inhabitants of the province of Friesland, and generally from the remaining inhabitants of the Netherlands. Their language – Frisian – is the second official language of the Netherlands. According to the principles of human linguistics, the community of West Frisians can be treated as a set of coupled linkages (as to the number of its constituents and to its temporal boundaries) with various central and peripheral linguistic properties forming through the ages a *large* and *long-lasting* linkage. West Frisians form a community associated with a geographical, political and/or cultural unit. The number of the participants in the West Frisian linkage is about 400,000 if we include in this group those inhabitants of the province who can speak Frisian. However, the total population of the province is 600,000 (cf. the statistical data of, e.g., Gorter 1997a:1152).

Traditionally, Frisians were distinguished, at least by Frisian speakers within the province, because they knew Frisian and spoke it in various communicative situations. The knowledge of the Frisian language against the background of Dutch was considered as the most important property of Frisians expressing their identity. However, recently the language seems not to be as important for the determination as Frisian as, for example, the place of birth. (See more about such criteria for the Frisianness of individuals as the linguistic criterion, the criterion of kinship, or of the place of birth or habitation, or of self-determination in Gorter 1997b:287ff, especially 288.)

To explain how Frisians managed to preserve their ethnic identity for ages, one should recall the theory of tasks and subtasks modeling the communicative behavior of individuals and linkages (cf. Yngve 1996:186 and 265). It has to be stated that the main task of the activity of the West Frisian linkage as a whole has always been to keep their separateness as a group. This has led in fact to the creation by individuals of a group formation, which distinguishes itself from other groups. At present, as in the case of many ethnic or linguistic minorities, the principal task of West Frisians is to strive for equality of rights in relation to the majority group within the state. They have striven to possess a unique position within the framework of Dutch culture, referring in this respect to their own history and their own verbal forms of expressing communicative tasks (cf., e.g., Breuker and Janse 1997b:11; Jonkman 1997:258). Subtasks of groups and particular linkages communicating in Frisian have in great measure been subordinated to the main task of expressing their ethnic identity.

Frisians, taken individually, function within various subordinate, coupled, and mutually conditioned linkages. The basis for the distinction of typical Frisian linkages can create such traditionally distinguished settings of language communication as work, school, and public life. However, there is a claim that the essence of Frisianness does not manifest itself, in principle, through the adherence to political organizations or through religion. Actually, political organizations or political parties function in the political and religious life of Frisians as large and long-lasting linkages where Dutch-speaking and Frisian-speaking participants meet together. From the viewpoint of sociology, there is a noticeable relationship between language background and political preference. The small conservative religious parties, the Frisian National Party (FNP) and the Christian Democratic Party (CDA), are the parties having the most Frisian-speaking supporters. These parties also constitute the most autochthonous parties in character. The Social Democratic Party (PvdA) has an average number of Frisian and non-Frisian speakers. Frisian speakers in the FNP, the small left-wing parties, the PvdA and the CDA are more strongly pro-Frisian, while the Frisian speakers in the small right-wing parties and D'66 and VVD are pro-Frisian to a much lesser degree. Generally, Frisians in the Dutch province of Friesland do not constitute a compact group as regards political and confessional matters. The Frisian National Party (Fri. *Frysk Nasjonale Partij*), although not important in the number of its members and its spheres of influence (cf. Gorter 1997a:1152ff), can be considered as a specific Frisian linkage. Its main task is to support the Frisian vernacular in interpersonal communication. The representatives of this party communicate with other linkages, e.g. in the sessions of communal councils and in the Councils of Provincial States.

In the context of political and religious life in Friesland, one can point to the phenomenon of 'pillarization', i.e. segmentation of society, as being important there since the nineteenth century. As a result of the process of modernization in the fields of politics, economics, and culture, the citizens were divided, as in the Netherlands, into four pillars: Protestant-Calvinistic (also with internal compartmentalization), Roman Catholic, Democratic Socialistic, and Liberal. In the province of Friesland the Orthodox Protestant (Reformed Protestant) pillar was of great importance. The pillarization of society means that a person being born, for instance, as a Protestant-Calvinist went from kindergarten to university via denominational schools. Furthermore, he became a member of a denominational trade union and political party; he read a newspaper, listened to radio programs, and watched television programs of the same ideological position. Consequently, he would spend his free time (sports and recreation) as a member of a denominational association (cf. Jansma 1997:245ff).

The pillarization of Frisian society, as a typical phenomenon, had a great influence on communicative behavior, and we can conclude, furthermore, on the formation of linkages on various levels of social life (including examples of the interaction through the arrangement). Important in the same way was the succeeding process of secularization, which took place within Dutch society up to the 70s and the 80s of the twentieth century and was aimed at depillarization.

Among Frisian-speaking groups, it is hard to distinguish large and long-lasting academic linkages, although Frisian studies are represented at some larger universities in the Netherlands. Members of the

Fryske Akademy, existing since 1938, are linked through the tasks of organizing scientific conferences devoted to Frisian language, literature, and culture. There are also professional organizations, schools, corporations, or trade unions, where the employees meet regularly to perform their common tasks of promoting the idea of Frisianness. In the province of Friesland, two types of bilingual linkages are coupled through education, namely Frisian-speaking and Dutch-speaking linkages. Recently, there has been an opportunity for the majority of young inhabitants of the province to be educated in Frisian at the primary and secondary school level.

In the cultural life of the province, common enterprises on a national scale contribute to the formation of social groups of brief and long-lasting linkages. They focus on the organization of such social gatherings as sporting events, musical or theatrical performances, etc. Frisians participate in such typical group sports as sailing on coastal ships with one mast (barge-sailing) (Fri. *skûtsjesilen*), pole-vaulting (Fri. *fierljeppen*), searching for eggs (Fri. *aeisykjen*), or flicking up the ball (Fri. *keatsen*). Brass bands and choirs have grown in popularity, and several Frisian hard-rock groups and amateur theater groups play and sing in the Frisian language. Organizations of all sorts – including writers, correspondents, readership associations of a newspaper or magazine, and performers and audiences of a particular theater or stadium – are flourishing in villages, towns and cities, and their performances are even available on radio or television.

In sociological investigations, several concrete communicative situations have to be distinguished where understanding in the Frisian language takes place. They contribute to the formation of small and brief or longer-lasting linkages, such as conversation:

• with a salesman in a store,
• between close neighbors,
• with clerks at the local post office,
• between parents and teachers at a school meeting,
• with a local policeman,
• with a foreigner at the door,
• with an administrator of a group of villages in the communal offices,
• with a doctor paying a visit to his patient,
• with a foreigner in the town,
• with a doctor in the hospital, or
• with a Dutch-speaking neighbor living there for a year, as well as
• with a Dutch tourist who asks the way (Gorter and Jonkman 1995:24–26 and 72).

We can see how the observable communicative properties of the participants of the linkage and the settings can influence each other. Sociological data may provide a certain image of the extent to which the inhabitants of the province use Frisian in a number of settings along with other (social) properties of the communicating individuals, as well as with the properties of concrete settings connected with the choice of Frisian. It is obvious that the use of Frisian for communicative tasks is connected with certain social properties of the communicating individuals as well as with the properties of concrete communicative settings. Generally, it was stated that the use of Frisian by the inhabitants of the province decreases in the more formal domains of public life. It is determined by (1) whether Frisian has been learned as a first language at home or as a second language, (2) whether the attitude towards Frisian is positive or not, and (3) whether the speakers of Frisian live in the country or in the town. In particular, we can conclude that born-and-bred Frisian speakers having a higher occupational position or who are younger use Frisian relatively less. The difference in the use of Frisian is greatest between the rural population and the inhabitants of the cities, partially as a result of the relatively smaller number of Frisian speakers in the cities. However, the Frisian speakers themselves use their language less in an urban environment, particularly in urban public life. The use of Frisian is lowest in the provincial capital Leeuwarden. Frisian speakers use Frisian in the neighborhood, also in mixed neighborhoods. Frisian-speaking youth are strongly under-represented at higher levels of higher education, but more pupils speak Frisian or another dialect with each other than have acquired these as first languages in the home. Frisian speakers use their language at work relatively rarely. Many Frisian speakers at a higher level do not speak Frisian with their colleagues, but above all, they do not speak Frisian with those above or below them in the hierarchy. At lower levels, a large majority of the Frisian speakers do use Frisian with their co-workers. Frisian is used most often with customers. Frisian speakers and non-Frisian speakers are members of Frisian-speaking and non-Frisian-speaking associations respectively. The division is so sharp that one could speak of a linguistic border in association and club life, determined additionally by the domicile. The Frisian speakers in the city are on average less often members of a monolingual association, while the Frisian speakers in the country are more often members of such associations. A great diversity in language use is exhibited in public life. A great deal more Frisian is spoken with those employed in the assistance and service sectors that have a somewhat lower status than with persons who perform a higher function.

Moreover, one can observe that more than half of the school-age children use Frisian with their playmates, but many more persons in the youngest age group use a combination of Frisian and another language than in the oldest age group. Along with education, public administration, and the media, religion can be regarded as one of the highly developed domains of language communication. Although services in Frisian are only held sporadically (2 or 3 per cent of all religious services in Friesland), most of the inhabitants of the province who go to church regularly have attended a Frisian service at one time or another. In many congregations, services in Frisian are held a couple of times a year. Of those who speak Frisian at home not even half appear to pray in that language. Only a quarter of those who are religious-minded appear to have a copy of the Frisian Bible translation (completed in 1943), only one fifth use it. It seems, however, that the barriers between the language of the home and colloquial language and the language of religion are slowly being broken down among young people, who are beginning to use Frisian in their religious life.

The media of newspapers, radio, and television, which can be regarded as channels in the communication between the smaller Frisian linkages, uniting them into a large superordinate linkage, play a unifying role to a certain degree in relation to participants of Frisian-speaking linkages. Although the pieces in Frisian in the *Leeuwarder Courant* and the *Friesch Dachblad* occupy only 5 per cent of the editorial space, they are read regularly by half of the readers of both newspapers. One third of the population of Friesland regularly listen to the regional programs in Frisian emitted by the Regional Broadcasting Organization of Friesland *Radio Fryslân* and local television. Frisian books and periodicals play a role of props in communication within the groups of long-lasting and brief linkages, when estimated from the readership in the libraries or supply in the book market. Over 100 new books are published every year. Some books are translations (e.g. children books). Poetry and novels are mostly original Frisian books. Publishing in Frisian is stimulated by the Provincial government and professional councils and is available through the Frisian Literary Museum and the Foundation for the Frisian book. Moreover, volunteers carry out an annual promotional campaign for Frisian books by means of door-to-door sales. The books are carried in wheelbarrows (also to be considered as props) through the neighborhoods and villages. However, we can point to an important property of the participants of the Frisian linkage, namely that only 30 per cent of the total population of Friesland can read in

Frisian. In this state of affairs, one can observe that as the purchases of Frisian books increased, borrowing of Frisian books from lending libraries decreased. Periodicals, which appear primarily or entirely in Frisian and whose primary circulation area is Friesland, have generally a cultural Frisian character. They are aimed at a small group. 16 per cent of the Frisian population had occasionally read a Frisian-language periodical, the number of subscribers is most certainly well below that.

As was stated at the beginning, the Frisian-speaking community is a set of long-lasting linkages. Therefore, we should find out the mechanism of how the ethnic identity of Frisians has been transmitted through the interaction of individuals and linkages in the course of time. We could take into consideration, for example, the fact that in the early Middle Ages, Frisians were an important sea-faring and trading people. Thus, they were united through a common occupation. They were distinguished from the neighboring German tribes first by their own law. As a common task of Frisians in the past, one enumerates also their everlasting struggle with the sea. As props among the communicating individuals and groups coming from the ancient period, we could take into consideration the runic inscriptions (from the sixth–eighth century) and the oldest of the preserved Old Frisian texts, mainly legal sources (coming mainly from the thirteenth and fourteenth centuries). Starting in the seventeenth century, literary works written in Frisian have also played a certain role as props. There was also person-to-person communication, which has contributed to the long-lasting focused types of linkages: namely, the Old Frisian law which was transmitted through oral tradition for many years.

A well-known person who can be considered as a link joining many smaller Frisian linkages was, for example, the Frisian religious leader Menno Simons (1492–1559). The religious group of Mennonites (originally Anabaptists) being numerous in the sixteenth and seventeeth centuries constitutes today only a minority within the Frisian population. Myths of the origin of Frisians and stories about important historical events referring to Frisians and Frisian heroes can be treated as a kind of *rumor* uniting the Frisian linkage in time and space. As focused linkages, one can consider small groups with fuzzy boundaries to which such legends were transmitted orally. The groups of persons linked by stories could be extended to the scope of complete linkages. One has to consider also the settings in which these legends and myths were created, their creators, authors of works from the period of the Middle Ages and the Renaissance, who amended and modified these stories so that they won broader and broader circles of receivers. One could also include here mythical or historical personalities, as, e.g., the king of Frisians, Radbod, the king of Franks, Charles the Great, and the national hero Magnus. Similarly, among props or channels one could enumerate the written works within which these stories were published, and also paintings, pictures, or other illustrations of personalities or events mediating between their creators and receivers.

Among the well-known legends of the Frisians, for example, various versions of an old story are mentioned of how travelers arriving by sea from Asia to the northern countries became founders of new peoples. A certain Frisian personality, whose name was *Friso*, had seven sons, and to each of them he gave one part of *Frisia* to rule. Furthermore, a story was handed down about how Charles the Great had given freedom to Frisians. It found among others its reflection in the work of Jacob van Maerland of the thirteenth century – *Spiegel Historial*. Frisians under the command of Magnus had helped Charles the Great to capture Rome and therefore had received from him divers privileges (cf. more about this event in Janse 1997:77ff). To the Frisian tradition belong also the legends of the rumor kind, in which motifs connected with Christendom appear, as, e.g., 'Legends of King Redbad' (see Piebenga 1954, 'Sêgen fan kening Redbad'). They tell the stories of:

- how Frisians accepted baptism from the hands of Wilfryd, the archbishop of York from England;
- how Redbad while having assumed power expelled missionaries from the country and ordered the destruction of the churches and the restoration of paganism;
- how Redbad had to fight against Charles, the king of the Franks (Fri. *Karel Frankelân*);
- how Charles, as a ruler of Friesland, pointed out the place where the Frisians might gather at a folk meeting (the so-called *thing*) and ordered them to pass their own laws; and
- how Redbad, standing on one foot in the baptismal font, concluded that those who are not baptized, and notably his ancestors – Frisians – cannot be in heaven, and so decided to withdraw.

As relevant from the viewpoint of expressing the ethnic identity of Frisians one can also point out some linguistic properties of communication participants, such as, e.g., speaking in a standard variety or in a dialect, code-switching, linguistic interference, etc. (occurring in bilingual territories). Here Frisian vernaculars, with their intimacy, constitute a core element marking the ethnicity of Frisians in addition to folk habits and customs, history, and culture defined next to such components as the agrarian structure, the rural convivial atmosphere, and the landscape. Among the other factors embodying the concept of Frisianness also occupying a stable place are the nationality name, the myth of common descent, the unique culture, the association with a specific territory, the sense of solidarity, and intimacy.

3. Conclusion

Based on experimental techniques or investigative methods elaborated by sociologists, we obtain, in fact, a static community-related image of a given group of people. The application, however, of the perspective of human linguistics enables us to present multilingual linkages in a dynamic way. Heretofore, our knowledge of communicational processes within ethnic groups had to be supplemented by considering changes. Groups of people studied by human linguistics are not static in reality but dynamic, and their existence is conditioned only by communication among their members. For example, the number of speakers within a traditionally distinguished speech community is assessed in a static manner. Therefore, when taking into account the number of interacting linkages, statistical data always have to be modified.

References

Breuker, Philippus H. and Janse, Antheun (1997a), *Negen eeuwen Friesland-Holland. Geschiedenis van een haat-liefdeverhouding* [Nine Centuries Friesland-Holland: A History of a Hate-Love Relationship]. Zutphen: Fryske Akademy, Walburg Pers.

Breuker, Philippus H. and Janse, Antheun (1997b), 'Beelden' [Pictures], in Philippus H. Breuker and Antheun Janse (1997a), pp. 9–66.

Fishman, Joshua (1965), 'Who speaks what language to whom and when'. *La Linguistique*, I, 67–88.

Gorter, Durk (1997a), 'Dutch-West Frisian', in Hans Goebl, Peter H. Nelde, Zdeněk Starý, and Wolfgang Wölck, *Kontaktlinguistik/Contact Linguistics/Linguistique de contact*. Berlin and New York: Walter de Gruyter, pp. 1152–1158.

Gorter, Durk (1997b), 'Friezen als Europese taalminderheid' [Frisians as a European language minority], in Philippus H. Breuker and Antheun Janse (1997a), pp. 286–292.

Gorter, Durk, Jelsma, Gjalt H., Plank, Pieter H. van der, and Vos, K. de

(1984), *Taal yn Fryslân. Undersyk nei taalgedrach en taalhâlding yn Fryslân* [Language in Friesland: A Study of Language Behavior and Language Attitude in Friesland]. Ljouwert: Fryske Akademy.

Gorter, Durk and Jonkman, Reitze J. (1995), *Taal yn Fryslân op 'e nij besjoen* [Language in Friesland Seen Anew]. Ljouwert: Fryske Akademy.

Janse, Antheun (1997),'Graaf Willem II van Holland en de Friese vrijheid' [Count William II of Holland and the Frisian freedom], in Philippus H. Breuker and Antheun Janse (1997a), pp. 77–86.

Jansma, Lammert Gosse (1997), 'Onkerkelijkheid, orthodoxie en de regionale factor' [Churchlessness, orthodoxy and the regional factor], in Philippus H. Breuker and Antheun Janse (1997a), pp. 245–251.

Jonkman, Reitze Jehannes (1997), 'Op weg van onderschikking naar nevenschikking: gewijzigde verhoudingen tussen het Fries en het Nederlands sinds de Franse Tijd' [On the way from subordination to equality: modified relations between Frisian and Dutch since the French time], in Philippus H. Breuker and Antheun Janse (1997a), pp. 252–259.

Piebenga, Jan Tjittes (1954), 'Sêgen fan kening Redbad' [Legends about King Redbad] (on the basis of [Jacobus] [Pieter] Wiersma, *Friese Sagen*), in Jan Tjittes Piebenga, *Frysk Lêsboek* [Frisian Reader] Part 2. Grins, Djakarta: J. B. Wolters, pp. 110–117.

Wąsik, Elżbieta (1999a), 'Domänen und Aufgaben der externen Sprachbeschreibung. Am Beispiel des Friesischen', in Norbert Reiter (1999), *Eurolinguistik ein Schritt in die Zukunft. Beiträge zum Symposium vom 24. bis 27. März 1997 im Jagdschloß Glienicke (bei Berlin).* Berlin: Harrassowitz Verlag, pp. 303–316.

Wąsik, Elżbieta (1999b), *Ekologia języka fryzyjskiego. Z badań nad sytuacją mniejszości etnolingwistycznych w Europie* [The Ecology of Frisian. From the Studies on the Situation of Ethnolinguistic Minorities in Europe]. Wrocław: Wydawnictwo Uniwersytetu Wrocławskiego.

Wąsik, Elżbieta (2000), 'Towards redefining the concept of the ecology of language in the framework of human-centered linguistics (with special reference to Frisian-speaking linkages)', in V. H. Yngve and Z. Wąsik (2000), Workshop: 'Exploring the Domain of Human-Centered Linguistics from a Hard-Science Perspective', Societas Linguistica Europaea 33rd Annual Meeting: *Naturalness and Markedness in Synchrony and Diachrony.* Poznań: The School of English, Adam Mickiewicz University, Motivex, pp. 29–31.

Yngve, Victor H. (1996), *From Grammar to Science. New Foundations for General Linguistics.* Amsterdam/Philadelphia: John Benjamins.

Chapter 14

Mayday or m'aider. A Call for Help in Understanding Linguistic Change

Janusz Malak

1. Introductory remarks

'Mayday' as well as 'm'aider' are the international radiotelephone distress calls. While the former sounds a bit strange as a distress call, if one were to adopt the so-called 'folk-etymology' responsible for the introduction of, for instance, *cheeseburger*, the latter appears to be fully justified if it is taken into account that its literal meaning corresponds to French 'help me'. These calls sound similar but are produced by participant subsets of communicating individuals belonging to quite different linguistic communities. Nevertheless, the two variants have equivalent functions at the role-part and linkage levels. A similar situation seems to have been responsible for the development of what has been traditionally described as the personal endings of Middle English. The Middle English personal endings, especially in the majority of northern and north-eastern dialects of Middle English, bear little affinity to their Old English predecessors. What seems to be a particularly enigmatic phenomenon about those endings is the origin of the -*es* ending of the 3rd p. sg. present tense.

The ideas presented in Yngve (1996) as well as the notational apparatus introduced there appear to be helpful in attempts at explaining certain linguistic phenomena in the history of the English language. One such phenomenon is the above-mentioned origin of the ending of the 3rd p. sg. present tense indicative. Jespersen (1909–1949) remarks that: 'in the Northumbrian dialect of the tenth cent. *s* was substituted for *þ* (sg. *bindes*, pl. *bindas*)' (Jespersen 1909–1949, Vol VI:15). He also remarks that in the same dialect the second person singular also ended in *s*. This remark is not without significance for the analysis to be presented here. Linguists dealing with the history of the English language, following Jespersen (1909–1949), perceive the appearance of -es in the function of the 3rd p. sg. present tense ending as pure substitution of -es for the OE ending -þ. They also unanimously indicate the northern Middle English dialect as the homeland of this process (cf. Berndt 1982; Fisiak 1968; Sweet 1891; Wełna 1996; Wright 1928). Shields (1980) indicates that the ending -es is a variant of the suffix -eþ, which appeared in rapid speech. It was not until 1995 that it was postulated in Kroch *et al.* (1995) that the imperfect acquisition of Old English on the part of Old Scandinavian speakers in the northern part of Britain may have contributed to the development of the English inflectional morphology in the form of the ending -es in the sg. present tense. Adopting the methodological tools of human linguistics as presented in Yngve (1996) as well as data presented in numerous works on the history of the English inflectional morphology, we hope to indicate that the 'substitution' of -es for -þ was not solely sheer phonetic replacement, but also could have been the result of mutual contacts between members of two linguistic communities characterized by distant but genetically related linguistic properties.

2. The historical and sociolinguistic background

Human linguistics is the scientific study of how people communicate. It investigates: 'objects given in advance, namely people both individually in terms of their linguistic communicative properties and collectively as united in social linkages' (Yngve and Wąsik 2000). Thus in order to fully grasp the factors responsible for the substitution of the Old English -þ by the ending -es one has to take a closer look at the conditions which may have led to focused linkages between members of two linguistic communities with different linguistic properties. Linguists wishing to understand historical linguistic phenomena in terms of human linguistics must, of necessity, have recourse to traditional mixed-domain data. They can only make assumptions concerning the types of linkages that may have occurred at a given time and in a given area.

According to the *Anglo-Saxon Chronicle*, 787 is the date marking the beginning of the Scandinavian presence in Britain. Originally it was of no permanent character. The eighth century was mainly a period of looting and plundering. However, from 865 onwards the Danish invasions became Danish settlement, at first of temporary and later of permanent character (Wakelin 1972). At a later date Norwegian

Vikings came to Shetland, Orkney, and the Isle of Man. They later settled in the north-western part of England. In that region the density of the Anglo-Saxon population was low and the Scandinavian settlers, who may often have come as families, formed a majority of the population in many places (Ekwall 1936). Thus there were two phases of Scandinavian settlement in Britain, the Danish settlement preceding the Norwegian one. For long periods in the ninth and tenth centuries, the Danes and Norwegians occupied extensive regions in the north and north-eastern part of England, which is attested in place names in several shires (Wakelin 1972). According to Stenton (1967), the presence of Danish settlers, who had arrived in England during the first phase of Scandinavian settlement in England, resulted in a great number of intermarriages and intimate language mixture. However, there were also quite a number of immigrants who arrived later, after areas of foreign control were established. Most probably among these were many men and women. Therefore, it can be concluded that the linguistic effect of this combination of population movement and population mixture was extensive. As Wakelin puts it, 'by the time of the Norman Conquest the fusion of Scandinavians and English into one people was complete, notwithstanding pockets of Scandinavians who .... continued to speak their own native dialect until somewhat later' (Wakelin 1972:21).

The above remarks indicate that the intimacy of the contacts between Anglo-Saxons and the speakers of Old Danish and Old Norse may have resulted in numerous focused linkages, at least at the initial stage of the mutual contacts. The ideas set out in Kroch *et al.* (1995) imply that the linguistic properties resulting from such focused linkages, especially as regards Scandinavian (i.e. Old Danish and Old Norse) speakers, could be compared in some ways to linguistic properties resulting from the pidginization and creolization phenomena of more recent centuries. Thus the modifications which appear in the northern and north-eastern dialects of Middle English could be best understood as the remnants of the imperfect second language acquisition by the Scandinavian 'newcomers'. One cannot exclude the possibility that the modification in question was also adopted by other Anglo-Saxon speakers inhabiting the northern and north-eastern part of Britain at that period due to the alleged intimacy of contacts between the speakers of Anglo-Saxon and Old Scandinavian.

3. Analysis of the morphological data

From the traditional standpoint, personal endings are the morphological manifestation of the agreement between the subject and the verbal part of the predicate. However, apart from this formal agreement, the morphologically coded category of person plays an important informative role indicating the function of the referent of the subject noun phrase in the situation of speaking. Jespersen (1924) characterizes three persons as, respectively, 1st p. – the speaker, 2nd p. – spoken to, and 3rd p. – neither speaker nor spoken to. It is not hard to notice that the first two persons signal participants directly involved in the situation of speaking while the last person signals an element of the situation or a party which is not a participant in this situation. To this we must add the category of number. If the number is singular, the first person refers exclusively to the speaker. The same can be said about the 2nd and 3rd persons, as regards the roles they signal in the situation of speaking. Plurality in the case of the category of person roughly refers to groups which the three parties represent within a given situation. In other words, the 1st p. pl. refers to the group with which the speaker identifies himself, 2nd p. pl is the group of participants to which the utterance is addressed, and, finally, the 3rd p. pl is a group of people who are not participants in a given speaking situation, or simply objects. These remarks imply that, theoretically, there should be six morphologically distinct endings, each signaling the categories referred to above. As will presently be seen, the paradigm of the Old English finite verbal forms was characterized by a certain degree of syncretism. The person, in the case of the plural forms, was indicated by the presence of the nominative forms of pronouns or of noun phrases

The comparison of the Old English personal endings with the Middle English ones indicates that the changes were most extensive in the north, while users of the southern Middle English dialects appear to have been considerably conservative. In Old English dialects the personal endings seem to be little diversified. The overall pattern for the present tense indicative can be presented in Table 14.1 (Campbell 1959; Reszkiewicz 1973; Wełna 1996).

Table 14.1. The Old English personal endings.[1]

	Endings	Examples
		nerian 'to save'
1st p. sg	nWS -*u*, WS -*e*	*ic neriu/nerio; ic nerie*
2nd p. sg	nWS -*s*, WS -*st*	*þu neres; þu nerest*
3rd p. sg	both nWS and WS -*þ*	*he/heo/hit nereþ*
all persons pl	both nWS and WS -*aþ*	*hie neriaþ*

WS – West Saxon
nWS – non-West Saxon

Thus the personal endings for northern dialects of Old English (Northumbrian) will be something like:

1st p. sg. -*u* /-*o*
2nd p. sg. -*s*
3rd p. sg. -*þ*
all persons pl. -*aþ*

By around 1300, the Old English personal endings presented above were considerably restructured (Lass 1992). This restructuring was manifest in phonological/morphological modification. The result of this process was the loss of the more or less uniform Old English personal ending paradigm and its replacement by a number of morphologically distinct, dialectally diversified personal endings. The results of the modifications affecting the personal endings in Table 14.1 are presented in Table 14.2.

The analysis of the personal ending paradigms in the two tables indicates that the personal endings in the southern dialect are the direct continuation of the Old English ones (especially the WS personal endings). Midland dialects, both east and west, seem to be a compromise between the innovative north and the conservative south. The personal endings attested in texts written in northern dialects seem to be the most innovative. The innovation is mainly based on the simplification of the inventory of the endings. While the changes affecting the southern personal ending paradigm and partly the Midland one can be explained by the phonological tendencies responsible for the reduction of their manifestations (i.e. the reduction of the quality of the vowels in the endings under consideration, mainly *a, e, u* into schwa), the personal endings characteristic of the northern dialects of Middle English appear not to yield to this explanation.

Lass (1992), capitalizing on observations presented in Campbell (1959), presents two personal ending paradigms that can be found in late Northumbrian Old English texts: (a) conservative and (b) innovative. The two paradigms are presented in Table 14.3.

Table 14.2. The Middle English personal endings (Lass 1992)[2]

	North	West Midland	East Midland	South
1st p. sg.	-(*e*)	-*e*	-*e*	-*e*
2nd p. sg.	-*es*	-*es*(*t*)	-*est*	-*est*
3rd p. sg.	-*es*	-*eþ*/-*es*	-*eþ*/-*es*	-*eþ*
all pers. pl.	-*es*	-*en*/-*es*	-*en*/-*es*	-*eþ*

Table 14.3. Innovations in the personal ending paradigm in late North-umbrian Old English

	Conservative	Innovative
1st p. sg.	o, -e	-o, -e
2nd p. sg.	-s(t)	-as
3rd p. sg.	-eð, -að	-es, -as
all persons pl.	-eð, -að	-es, -as

The analysis of the contents of Table 14.3 shows that the innovation seems to be purely phonetic. While the conservative manifestations form a three-element paradigm, i.e. -o/-e : -s(t) : -e/að, which could be said to be the reflex of the previous system, the innovative system is a two-way system, i.e. -o/-e : -as/-es. The data presented above point to the growing degree of syncretism in the personal ending paradigm, which is quite a surprising phenomenon if one takes into account the function of the endings alluded to at the beginning of this section.

4. Previous attempts at analysis and explanation of the origin of the 3rd p. sg. ending

The data presented in Table 14.3 may have led Jespersen (1909–1949) to the conclusions presented in section 1. However, the data presented in this table point to one more aspect of the problem under consideration, i.e. the considerable degree of syncretism of the Middle English personal ending paradigm in comparison to its OE pre-decessor. Those simplifying changes of the personal ending paradigms have been attributed to a Scandinavian origin (e.g. Campbell 1959; Kroch *et al.* 1995; Lass 1992; Wełna 1996). Kroch *et al.* (1995) explain the simplification of the paradigm as the result of imperfect second language learning of Northumbrian Old English by Scandinavian invaders. This imperfection was to be manifested in the failure on the part of the Scandinavian invaders as well as their descendants to properly render the voiceless interdental fricative in the final position.

The Scandinavian simplification of the paradigm due to imperfect second language acquisition of Northumbrian Old English becomes plausible in light of the historical remarks presented in section 2. Old Danish and Old Norse speakers coming to live in the area inhabited by Anglo-Saxon speakers must have had contacts with them, the extent of the contacts determined by their needs. Therefore, it could be concluded that utterances produced by Old Danish and Old Norse speakers in contact situations must have been the result of their learning abilities as well as of a kind of compromise between the speech of the Scandinavian speakers and that of the users of the northern dialects of Old English. At this point, however, a question could be posed whether only perceptual strategies, mainly responsible for second language acquisition, were responsible for the simplification by Northumbrian Old English speakers. The answer to this question is to be looked for partly in the speech of the Scandinavian newcomers, which has been classified as genetically related to Northumbrian Old English but, at the same time, fairly distant.

The innovative changes can be roughly explained by phonetic similarity, however this does not seem to be an adequate explanation for the process under investigation. It appears strange that the voiceless interdental fricatives should have been replaced by voiceless alveolar fricatives (see Table 14.3). This fact appears even stranger if one takes into account the fact that the Old Norse as well as Old Danish consonantal systems had the interdental fricative phoneme, whose positional realization was almost the same as in Old English (Faarlund 1994).[3] Kroch et al. (1995) postulate that this substitution was mainly due to the markedness of distinctive features, i.e. according to the distinctive feature account, the two phonemes differ from one another in the specification ± Anteriority. The marked phoneme, i.e. /θ/ is characterized as [+ Anterior], while its unmarked counterpart /s/ is characterized by the negative specification of this feature. Kroch et al. (1995) additionally remark that late Old Northumbrian scribes often use the grapheme <s> to render the voiceless interdental fricative /θ/ unlike scribes writing in earlier Northumbrian and other Old English dialects.[4] In order to fully assess the possible impact of the imperfect command of Northumbrian Old English on the part of Scandinavian speakers on the evolution of the Middle English personal ending systems, one should also have a look at the personal ending system characteristic of Old Danish and Old Norse. It must be borne in mind that the northern and north-eastern part of Britain was invaded and subdued by speakers of two large dialect groups stemming from Ancient Scandinavian, i.e. West Old Scandinavian (Old Norwegian and Old Icelandic) and East Old Scandinavian (Old Danish and Old Swedish).[5]

According to Faarlund (1994), the two groups differed from one another mainly in phonology, which implies that their morphology was more or less the same. It can be assumed that the speech of the Old Norse invaders of the British Isles in the eighth century and later was characterized by the personal ending paradigm presented in Table 14.4.

Table 14.4. The personal ending paradigm in Old Norse (West Old Scandinavian) (Faarlund 1994)[6]

Person and number	Endings	kalla 'to call'; velja 'to choose'; vaka 'to be awake'		
		kalla	vel	vaki
1st p. sg.	Ø	kalla	vel	vaki
2nd p. sg.	-r	kallar	velr	vakir
3rd p. sg.	-r	kallar	velr	vakir
1st p. pl.	-um	kollum	veljum	vokum
2nd p. pl.	-ið	kallið	velið	vakið
3rd p. pl.	a	kalla	velja	vaka

Old Danish personal endings differed from those in Old Norse only in the first person singular and the second person plural. The former was the same as the 2nd and 3rd persons sg., i.e. -r, while the latter was -n/ -en/ -æn (Brøndum-Nielsen and Nielsen 1973; Faarlund 1994).

The analysis of the data in Table 14.4 as well as the data presented above indicate that the personal endings of East and West Old Scandinavian are different from those found in late Northumbrian Old English texts as well as those found in texts written in the north of England during the Middle English period. Given the observation presented in Kroch *et al.* (1995), the conclusion of the imperfect command of that part of Northumbrian Old English by the newcomers appears inescapable. However, a more careful analysis of the personal endings presented in Tables 14.2, 14.3 and 14.4 as well as data concerning the Old Danish personal endings reveals something more than the imperfect rendering of the Old English paradigm by the inhabitants of the invaded and occupied territory. The northern personal ending paradigm presented in Table 14.2, i.e. occurring in the speech of descendants of the mixed speech communities, reveals, among other things, the syncretism of the 2nd and 3rd persons sg. endings. Strangely enough it correlates with the personal ending syncretism of Old Norse and Old Danish 2nd and 3rd persons sg. (cf. Table 14.4). Moreover, the imperfect command of the Northumbrian Old English features manifest in a failure to make a distinction between /s/ and /θ/ must be attributed to the descendants of the mixed linguistic communities rather than the invaders themselves since, as Table 14.4 indicates, the interdental fricative appears as the final segment in the 2nd p. pl. element as regards Old Norse. Therefore, it could be concluded that the 2nd p.

sg. present tense ending was the first element that was internalized during the second language acquisition process on the part of the Old Danish and Old Norse speakers. The personal ending paradigm presented in Table 14.3 presents two sets of elements in late Northumbrian Old English, one conservative and the other innovative. In light of the above it could be assumed that the conservative elements were a part of the speech of the Anglo-Saxon speakers and their descendants and the innovative ones formed a part of the speech of the Scandinavian invaders and their Anglo-Scandinavian descendants. The innovative elements replaced the conservative ones in the north in the course of the Middle English period and spread slightly modified as regards the plural number southwards in the course of Middle and early Modern English.

5. A human-linguistics analysis and explanation

The data presented in the previous sections has traditionally been treated merely as a trace of processes attested in texts dating to the end of the Old English and the beginning of the Middle English periods. Whereas only Kroch *et al.* (1995) try to point to the sources of the phenomena dealt with in the sections above, none of the linguists dealing with the history of the English language has tried to reconstruct the process itself. The lack of any explanations concerning the possible causes of the replacement of the Old English system of personal endings by a simplified personal ending system characteristic initially of the northern dialects of Middle English can be attributed to the lack of any adequate explanatory model. One fact which seems to be ignored in accounts of linguistic historical processes is that the locus of the linguistic change is human beings. Therefore, it would be interesting to look at all the facts and interpretations presented in the sections above from a perspective taking human beings as the source of any linguistic phenomena.

Human linguistics appears to provide an alternative perspective for the analyzes of linguistic phenomena. Speaking and interpreting the sounds of others who are speaking are social phenomena arising under specified circumstances. In order to be able to take part in a linkage, a person must be a communicating individual whose ability to function within a given linkage is regulated by his plex. While speaking, a number of procedures within the participant's plex are executed, of which the task procedures of the lowest rank result in sounds being produced by the participant who is speaking. Energy flow activates the membranes in the inner ear of the participant of the linkage to whom the participant is speaking. The stimuli generated in the inner ear of this participant are the input to procedures responsible for the recognition and interpretation of the sounds produced by the other participant. The recognition and interpretation is possible due to the plex of the participant receiving the sounds. This model presupposes the similarity of the plexes of the two participants of the linkage. The similarity of two plexes implies similar linguistic properties. Without the similarity of plexes, verbal communication between members of a given community would be impossible. It can be assumed that this model has been relevant for as long as human beings have been communicating by means of sound waves.

The data presented in section 2 indicate that at the end of the Old English period, two large linguistic communities came to live beside one another. The contact between the two communities was characterized by considerable intimacy. The two communities differed in their linguistic properties. This, in turn, implies that if members of the two communities came into linkages with each other, members of one linguistic community had to modify their plexes in order to be able to cooperate with the member of the other in focused linkages. Therefore, it could be assumed that Scandinavian speakers were forced to develop alternative plexes in order to be able to communicate with Old English speakers. The problem to be addressed in this section is whether the modifications in the alternative plexes affected only one level of procedures or whether some other, higher-level procedures were also affected.

The data presented in section 4 imply that the modification of the Old English personal ending system in the northern areas occupied by two linguistically diversified communities is the result of pure phonetic substitution. Phonetic substitution takes place at the linkage level. As has already been mentioned, if two persons from two linguistic communities come into a focused linkage, one of the participants of this linkage will use his modified alternative plex in order to communicate with the other participant of the linkage. This modification is based on the data coming from previous linkages with members from the other linguistic community. Thus this modification will consist in the imitation of the role-part properties of the participants coming from the other community taking part in previous linkages. This imitation, however, will be slightly colored by the properties of his first plex. Thus *mayday* appears to be the distortion of the original *m'aider* resulting from the imitation of this French phrase due to the anglophone plex. Let us refer to this phenomenon as the 'mayday scenario'. The data then presented in sections 3 and 4 would comply with this scenario and the substitution of an alveolar fricative for the interdental fricative seems to be quite plausible.

Despite the plausibility of the 'mayday scenario' for the changes of the Old English personal endings, the modification of the plex as regards the Old Norse and Old Danish speakers does not provide the only explanation for the change in question. The analysis of the data presented in Table 14.4 shows that an interdental fricative also appeared in Old Norse personal endings (2nd p. pl.). It is also noteworthy that this fricative was also a part of the Old Danish consonantal system. This implies that there must have been a procedure in the Scandinavian plex responsible for producing this sound quite similar to the procedure in the Old English plex. Therefore, it can be assumed that hearing Old English speakers pronouncing an interdental fricative in an utterance, Scandinavian speakers may have recognized it as a sound produced by a procedure in their own plex and accordingly would have been able to pronounce it without any difficulty. The question remains why they failed to produce it during the same subtasks as Old English speakers.

The answer to the question posed above will be hypothetical due to the lack of adequate data coming from the physical domain. An attempt at resolving this problem will be based on the suspicion presented in Yngve (1996) that 'there would be sentence tasks and that their task hierarchies might in some respects resemble phrase structure' (Yngve 1996:270). As is rightly noticed there, details are still to be worked out on the basis of physical-domain observational and experimental evidence. However, as there are as yet no adequate data coming from experimental evidence, we will stipulate that utterances are tasks consisting of a number of subtasks belonging to different levels. All of the tasks and subtasks are responsible for activating procedures at different levels present in the plex of a participant in a given linkage. Let us further assume that when participating in a given linkage and when in conversation and having the turn (*cvt* x −*cvn*), a participant may produce utterances concerning himself, or a group he associates himself with, his interlocutor or the group the speaker associates the latter with, or the persons or objects in some way connected with the linkage. The three categories will correspond to three different tasks which will be signaled at a lower level by a subtask denoting the agreement between subtasks of a higher level, i.e. a subject subtask and a predicate subtask.[7] At the lowest level the agreement subtasks referred to above are transformed into instructions for the articulators. Thus it could be assumed that what is presented in Tables 14.1, 14.2, 14.3, and 14.4 reflect agreement subtasks belonging to plexes of Old English, Middle English, and Old Danish as well as Old Norse speakers.

Adopting this hypothesis, it could be assumed that when Old Danish and Old Norse speakers came into focused linkages with speakers of northern dialects of Old English, they must have heard numerous utterances addressed to themselves. The prominent element of those utterances which may have come to their notice was the element -s which was recognized as the agreement subtask in the plex of their interlocutors. Trying to communicate with Old English speakers, Scandinavian speakers must have replaced the procedure for the agreement subtask from their native -r to -s, thus developing an alternative plex used only for focused linkages with Old English speakers. At this moment analogy comes into play, which may partly explain the adoption of -s as the agreement subtask in utterances concerning other persons or objects. In their native plex, Old Danish and Old Norse speakers had the same agreement subtask for utterance tasks concerning their interlocutor and persons or objects referred to in their utterances. Thus -s was extended to the agreement subtask in utterances concerning other persons or objects. This would be Scandinavian speakers modeling their alternative plexes on the basis of their native plexes.[8] Adopting this hypothesis would also explain why Scandinavian speakers failed to produce an interdental fricative in circumstances under which Old English speakers produced it despite the fact that the Old Norse as well as Old Danish plex had procedures for producing this sound. The fact that this procedure must have been a part of their plex implies that they must have recognized this sound, however for ease of communication they adopted the most salient feature as a part of their alternative plex and, due to the analogy with their native plex, extended it to subtask procedures different from those in the Old English speaker plex. In other words, it can be said that the 'mayday scenario' comes into play once more but this time at a different level which still remains to be examined in terms of human linguistics.

6. Conclusions

During the Middle English period the 3rd p. sg. ending -es gradually spread southwards sending -eth into oblivion.[9] The fact that in northern dialects of Middle English the ending -es was also used for all persons plural has led linguists to the conclusion that this ending was a pure phonetic substitution. This phonetic substitution is attributed mainly to Scandinavian speakers inhabiting the northern part of England at the end of the Old English period. However, such a conclusion appears to be somewhat hasty in light of the fact that the Scandinavian invaders had the interdental fricative in their idiolects and even had a personal ending comprising this sound. This conclusion can further be invalidated by the observation found in, e.g., Fisiak (1968) that the ending -es could also be found with the 1st p. sg., which would be the reflection of the Old Danish plex. Therefore it can tentatively be assumed that the ending -es in other than the 2nd and 3rd persons sg. cropped up in English due to some other, still poorly understood phenomenon than just phonetic substitution. The hasty conclusion alluded to above was reached due to slavish bondage to written documents. However, what are written documents? They are simply inaccurate reflections of the plexes of their authors who have been dead for a number of centuries. Therefore conclusions concerning linguistic change based exclusively on written documents may sometimes be misleading, as has been indicated in this article. Human linguistics provides anyone interested in linguistic phenomena with a wider perspective which may throw new light on phenomena which are believed to be fully understood. Such a phenomenon is the origin of the 3rd p. sg. ending. There is no reason to believe that the 'mayday scenario' applies only to members of two different linguistic communities coming into focused linkages. It may also be helpful to understand how human beings develop their plexes within the confines of their own linguistic communities.

However, linguists attempting to find answers to questions concerning manifold enigmatic phenomena accompanying linguistic change seem to be handicapped in their scholarly endeavors in that they do not have access to the people speaking their languages at different periods. The analysis postulated in section 5, apart from attempting to interpret the historical facts in a human-linguistic vein, also indicates the tentativeness of this analysis. This tentativeness results from the lack of the relevant data from the physical domain. This conclusion presupposes the superiority of synchronic analysis based on data acquired by observational and experimental methods. It will not be until sufficient data from the physical domain have accumulated that the observations and ideas presented in section 5 can be verified. Anyway, studying people and their communicative behavior, both verbal and nonverbal, from a physical-domain perspective will produce favorable conditions under which we will receive a reply to our 'Mayday'.

Notes

This article is a modified version of the paper presented at the SLE Meeting in Poznań (Poland) in 2000. Its abstract can be found in Yngve and Wąsik (2000).

1. It must be borne in mind that the endings presented in this table should be treated as a kind of idealization. While the consonantal final elements are invariable, the vocalic elements showed variability connected with the historical origin of each verb class. For instance Weak Verb Class One had the endings as presented in Table 14.1. The 2nd and 3rd person sg. and all persons pl. for Weak Verbs Class Two were -*ast*, -*aþ*, -*iaþ* respectively, as in *lufast* 'you love', *lufaþ* 'he/she/it loves'. Weak Verbs Class Three, the least numerous one, is characterized by the same consonantal elements with the vocalic elements elided in the 2nd and 3rd persons sg., accompanied by the change of the manner of articulation of the final consonantal element in the stem as in *ic hæbbe, þu hæfst, he hæfþ* but *we/ġe/hie habbaþ*. The above remarks apply, more or less, also to Strong Verbs. However, because of the limited space of this paper we are not going to deal with all the morphological intricacies of the Old English present tense endings since they are immaterial for the purpose of the analysis presented in this paper.
2. Because of the paucity of space, the analysis presented in this part of the paper does not take into account positional variants characterized by the fact that, for instance, in the north the verb appeared without any ending if it was followed by the pronoun functioning as the subject.
3. What distinguished the Old Scandinavian distribution of the voiced and voiceless fricatives from that in Old English is the fact that in the former the voiced fricatives were also found in the final position. Kroch *et al.* (1995) assume that this fact may have been responsible for the phonetic substitution of the voiceless alveolar fricative for the voiceless interdental one. However, taking into account acoustic features of the two sounds, they differ from one another in the level of stridency, which makes them quite different (cf. note 4).
4. However, Kroch *et al.*'s (1995) specification does not explain much. Actually, the specification [±Anteriority] seems to be of little explanatory value as regards the origin of the -*es* ending signaling the 3rd p. sg. present tense. The distinction between [±Anteriority] as regards the specification between /s/ and /θ/ conversely corresponds to the acoustic feature of [±Strident] as originally postulated by Jakobson and adopted in Chomsky and Halle (1968). Stridency is the feature

which refers to the level of noise which is perceived during the production of fricatives. Due to this specification /s/ would be perceived as [+ Strident], i.e. noisier, while /θ/, represented in spelling as <þ>, as less noisy, i.e. [−Strident]. This may also account for the fact that Northumbrian scribes were prone to graphically represent the phonetically less strident fricative by a grapheme representing a more strident one, i.e. /s/ (cf. Campbell 1959). In this case the markedness specification would be not the articulatory feature [+ Anterior], but the acoustic one, i.e. [+ Strident]. However, the interdental fricative seems to be in a way marked if one takes into account pidgin varieties of English, since this unit appears to be rendered by voiceless interdental fricative [s] or voiceless alveolar stop [t] (e.g. in Tok Pisin). It must be borne in mind that the varieties characteristic of Tok Pisin emerged due to the contacts between two speech communities where the phonology of the language of the community on which English was imposed was not characterized by anything corresponding to the Germanic inter-dental fricative and thus the feature [± Strident] was irrelevant.

5. West Old Scandinavian is also referred to as Old Norse (Faarlund 1994). Kroch *et al.* (1995) seem to apply the term 'Old Norse' indiscriminately in reference to East and West Old Scandinavian.

6. According to Faarlund (1994) Old Norse is the best attested variety of Old Scandinavian. 'Classical' Old Norse is the language attested in the Icelandic sagas from the twelfth and thirteenth centuries. Therefore the data in Table 14.4 present the personal endings characteristic of West Old Scandinavian.

7. The categories suggested in this part may appear rather intuitive. However, reducing utterances to the phonetic level only will render it impossible to answer the question posed at the end of the previous paragraph.

8. This observation is further corroborated by the possibility of using the ending -*es*/-*is* as the signal for the 1st p. sg. in the northern dialects (Fisiak 1968). It would reflect the Old Danish pattern with the ending -*r* for all persons in the singular.

9. The 2nd p. sg. ending disappeared from English along with *thou* in early Modern English.

References

Berndt, R. (1982), *History of the English language*. Leipzig: VEB Verlag Enzyklopädie.

Blake, N. (1992), *The Cambridge History of the English Language*, Vol. II. 1066–1476. Cambridge: Cambridge University Press.

Brøndum-Nielsen, J. and Nielsen, K. M. (1950–1973), *Gammeldansk grammatik i sproghistorisk fremstilling*, 8 Vols. Copenhagen: Københavens Universitets fond til tilvejebringelse af Iæremidler.

Campbell, A. (1959), *Old English Grammar*. Oxford: Clarendon.

Chomsky, N. and Halle, M. (1968), *The Sound Pattern of English*. New York: Harper & Row.

Darby, H. C. (ed.) (1936), *An Historical Geography of England before A.D. 1800*. Cambridge: Cambridge University Press.

Ekwall, E. (1936), 'The Scandinavian element', in H. C. Darby (ed.), pp. 133–164.

Faarlund, J. T. (1994). 'Old and Middle Scandinavian', in E. Kökig and J. van der Auwera, pp. 38–71.

Fisiak, J. (1968), *A Short Grammar of Middle English*. Warsaw: Państwowe Wydawnictwo Naukowe.

Jespersen, O. (1909–1949), *A Modern English Grammar on Historical Principles*. 7 Vols. London: George Allen & Unwin.

Jespersen, O. (1924), *Philosophy of Grammar*. London: George Allen & Unwin.

Kökig, E and van der Auwera, J. (1994), *The German Languages*. London: Routledge.

Kroch, A., Taylor, A., and Ringe, D. (1995), *The Middle English verb-second constraint: a case study in language contact and language change*. ftp://babel.ling.upenn.edu/papers/faculty/tony_kroch/papers/mev2-contact.pdf

Lass, R. (1992), 'Phonology and morphology', in N. Blake (1992), pp. 23–155.

Reszkiewicz, A. (1973), *A Diachronic Grammar of Old English*. Warsaw: Państwowe Wydawnictwo Naukowe.

Shields, K., Jr. (1980), 'Fast speech and the origin of the Standard English verbal suffix -s'. *Journal of English Linguistics* 14, 24–35.

Stenton, F. M. (1967), *Anglo-Saxon England*. Oxford: Clarendon.

Sweet, H. (1891), *A New English Grammar: Logical and Historical*. Oxford: Clarendon.

Wakelin, M. F. (1972), *English Dialects: An Introduction*. London: The Athlone Press of the University of London.

Wełna, J. (1996), *English Historical Morphology*. Warsaw: Wydawnictwa Uniwersytetu Warszawskiego.

Wright, J. (1928), *An Elementary Middle English Grammar*. London: Geoffrey Cumberlege Oxford University Press.

Yngve, V. H. (1996), *From Grammar to Science: New Foundations for General Linguistics*. Amsterdam/Philadelphia: John Benjamins.

Yngve, V. H. and Wąsik, Z. (2000)., *Naturalness and Markedness in Synchrony and Diachrony Workshop: Exploring the Domain of Human-Centered Linguistics from a Hard-Science Perspective. Societas Linguistica Europaea 33rd Annual Meeting*. Poznań: The School of English, Adam Mickiewicz University, Motivex.

Chapter 15

Linguistic Change as Changes in Linkages: Fifteenth-Century English

Carl Mills

Yngve (1996) states that 'the linguistic study of written texts cannot substitute for the study of face-to-face interaction in investigating how people communicate. ... Speech in dialog intimately involves negotiating behavior, while reading and writing usually do not' (p. 302). This distinction follows from Yngve's insistence that the proper objects of study in a hard-science linguistics are 'people from the point of view of how they communicate' (1986:38), not the logical-domain construct language, however language might be defined. Yet Yngve also asserts that writing is worthy of study in its own right (1996:302). And there are cases where written texts are all that the linguist has available for study. For example, written texts, where available, are invaluable in historical linguistics.

This paper is concerned with a chapter in the history of English, written about half a millennium ago. Specifically, we are concerned with ASSEMBLAGES of people and the letters they wrote. Yngve uses the term ASSEMBLAGE to mean a 'group of people together with their linguistically relevant surroundings involved in particular communicative behavior' (1996:86). Technically, a person participating in an assemblage is represented in theory as a PARTICIPANT and a communicatively relevant object, e.g. a letter, is represented as a PROP (Yngve 1996:129, 228). But since most communicative behavior involves at least two people – the communicative behavior here always involves at least two people, occasionally more – many such phenomena are better examined in terms of assemblages rather than in terms of single persons or objects.

The theoretical construct relevant to the study of the communicative behavior of an assemblage is the LINKAGE: 'A LINKAGE is a representation in linguistic theory of an assemblage that includes just those properties that are required to account for the communicative behavior associated with the assemblage' (Yngve 1996:126).

The physical objects involved in the assemblages here are letters, in nearly all cases letters written in the fifteenth century from one person to another. This results in 'linkages directly coupled through contact in a physical object' (Yngve 1996:228). A letter typically has a sender and an addressee or receiver.

> In the case of one person writing a message to another, the first linkage has as constituents the writer as a participant and the writing implements as props. Communicative activity in this linkage results in changes in the properties of some of the props constituting the written message. The second linkage has as constituents this legible message as a prop and the reader as a participant. Communicative activity in this linkage results in the reader understanding the message. (Yngve 1996:228)

Here is an example of such a prop:

> I grete *the* wyll, and I haue grete marvele that *ye* wryt not to me no letters of syche tydyngys as *ye* haue at Caleys, the weche ys meche speche of at London, for the weche I cannot wryt to *the* nothyng for lake of vnderstandyng how it stand in the pertys of the Dewke of Borgens londys and the Kyng of Franse, for here ys strange spekyng for the weche I pray *the* be wyse, and be not or-haste in sale and delyueryng of good into Flanders, for I fere me sore of ware, and the Dewke be dede, as it ys sayd, and the Kyng of Franse enterd into Pecardy, as men seye, for the weche I pray *the* se wyll to ... I wryt no more to *the* at thys time, but Jhesu kepe you. (Richard Cely the elder at London to George Cely at Calais, 26 January 1476/7. Emphasis added.)

In particular, we can note the variation in the use of sequences of letters constituting *thou*, *thy*, and *thee* versus *ye*, *your*, and *you*. The italicized sequences, these marks in ink on paper, are physical objects involving an energy flow via light through a CHANNEL (Yngve 1996:128). The linguistics of language typically refers to them as 'second person pronouns'. Earlier in history, e.g. between ca. AD 450 and ca. AD 1150, a speaker or writer would use *thou*, *thy*, and *thee* when speaking to a single individual. We shall refer to these as the English second person singular pronouns. When addressing more than one person, a speaker would use *ye*, *your*, and *you*. We shall call these the second person plural pronouns. The venerable historian of

English, Albert C. Baugh, notes that in this early period 'the distinction was simply one of number' (Baugh and Cable 1978:242).

After the Norman Conquest, however, linkages underwent a change. Properties of participants, heretofore irrelevant, became important. Part of 'the activities of linkages and also the behavior of participants' (Yngve 1996:186), the HIERARCHY OF TASKS AND SUBTASKS, were modified to include relations of power and solidarity (Brown and Gilman 1960) – or politeness and intimacy. At this point, according to Baugh, 'in the thirteenth century the singular forms (*thou, thy,* and *thee*) were used among familiars and in addressing children or persons of inferior rank' (p. 242). Baugh goes on to say that 'by the sixteenth century the singular forms had all but disappeared from polite speech' (p. 242). Increasingly, speakers and writers, beginning with the upper classes but extending ever downward in the social hierarchy, came to use the 'polite' plural forms *ye, your,* and *you* to address EVERYBODY.

A linguistics based on notions surrounding 'language' would say, essentially, that this communicative behavior represented a long process of language change that would eventually result in *thou, thy,* and *thee* being dropped from active use, probably in the late seventeenth century, with an attenuated survival persisting in self-consciously archaic poetry and the behavior of certain religious sects, notably the Quakers.

There are some things wrong with this view. First, the timing is probably distorted. Historical linguists, forced to take their examples where they find them, have tended to lump together examples from all sorts of linkages: plays, poems, sermons, school books, court testimony, private letters, business documents, etc. Elsewhere (Mills 1999a, 1999b), I have argued that such uncritical use of evidence has resulted in an exaggeration of the number of singular forms in use at any given point during the period of transition (ca. 1400–ca. 1700). In other words, Baugh is probably correct, and *thou, thy,* and *thee* probably disappeared earlier than most people think.

At the same time, describing the fate of *thou, thy,* and *thee* in terms of language tells us rather little about WHY *thou, thy,* and *thee* passed out of use. In Yngve's terms, what was going on during this period should be described in terms of changes in properties of participants and the linkages they participate in.

More important, our view of the disappearance of *thou, thy,* and *thee* is blurred by treating all cases of 'language use' as the same. Viewing what happened in terms of participants, linkages, props, channels, etc. allows us to explain not only why the use of *thou, thy,* and *thee* shrank but also why the use of these forms persisted where it did.

But now let us take a closer look at some particular props. Let us focus on letters, mostly written from one person to another, by members of two families in the late 1400s.

My earlier studies focused on letters written by members of the Paston family, an important part of the landed gentry of Norfolk (Davis 1971). The letters begin with those of William Paston I, born in 1378, and end with those of William Paston IV, who died in 1554, covering four generations of Pastons. The 421 letters written by members of the family amount to approximately 200,000 words of text, exclusive of headnotes and other modern textual apparatus. Later studies added the Cely Letters (Hanham 1975), written by and to members of an important London family involved in the wool trade. Although this study will avail itself of data obtained from the Paston Letters, the focus will be on the Cely Letters.

The props studied here are the full text – minus editorial notes, addresses, etc. – of the Cely Letters, as transcribed, edited, and published by Hanham, 247 letters written between 1472 and 1488 and constituting slightly more than 85,000 orthographic words. To prepare the study, Alison Hanham's (1975) EETS edition of the Cely Letters was scanned into a computer and organized into searchable word processor files, thus constituting a 'mini-corpus' that could be analyzed from a number of perspectives. While some of the Cely Letters appear in other corpora, this constitutes a reasonably complete Cely corpus.

Now that we have identified the props, we should, following Yngve (2000), identify the people who function as participants in these linkages.

As mentioned above, the authors of the Paston Letters were members of fifteenth-century England's upper classes. Letter writers included Justices of the Peace, Members of Parliament, knights, and other wealthy, powerful figures. The Paston men, but not the women letter writers, were literate individuals, some of them educated at Oxford and Cambridge. The business of the Paston family consisted of obtaining control of land – through both purchase and marriage – defending that land against hostile takeovers – usually in the courts, sometimes at the royal court, at times in armed combat – assigning farmers to work the land, collecting rents from farmers, and supervising and funding repairs and improvements to the land. Their wealth and power stemmed from the land they controlled.

In contrast, the Celys were merchants in London. Their education consisted of apprenticeships served in the family business or the businesses of relatives and business associates. The business of the Cely family consisted of moving wool from the English countryside, chiefly the Cotswolds, to the Low Countries. The head of the family business tended to work in London, and junior members of the business, often sons or other younger family members, handled the continental end of the business from bases in Calais but also traveled to Bruges, Antwerp, and other trading centers.

An important part of the wool trade also consisted of the movement of money. London-based members of the family had to buy wool in rural England and pay for it. Calais-based members had to arrange for the sale of wool and to collect payment and arrange for the transfer of payments back to England. In addition, customs, duties to the Staplers Guild, freight, and other charges had to be paid. Given the primitive nature of international communication and the rudimentary banking system, collection and payment involved transactions with attorneys, proxies, factors, Lombard bankers, *et al*. Much of the communicative behavior in these letters involves accounting for shipments, purchases, sales, collections, and payments.

The most important participants in these linkages involve Richard Cely the Elder, his brother John Cely, and an associate William Maryon, who was also godfather to William Cely, a junior member of the business. These three formed a loose confederation of business associates, but not a true company (Hanham 1975).

Here, in Figure 15.1, as far as they are known, are the family and business relations of the persons involved in these communications under analysis.

Richard Cely the Elder (d. 1482) and Agnes Cely (d. 1483) had three sons. Robert Cely the Elder (d. 1485) appears to have been a ne'er-do-well: in Letter 52, Richard Cely the Younger tells his brother George that the family had sent 30 shillings to Robert to pay for lodging, which Robert 'playd hyt at dys, euery farthing'. Richard contemplated having Robert arrested for the debt, but the family made other arrangements. Robert's marital affairs were equally messy. He appears to have been pensioned off and eased out of the business. Hanham (1975) says that Robert's problems may have been mental rather than moral but offers no details.

George Cely, the second son (ca. 1458–1489), was a major participant in the business and the linkages associated with it. The letters indicate that he was doing business for the family on the continent as early as 1476. He functioned as the chief continental

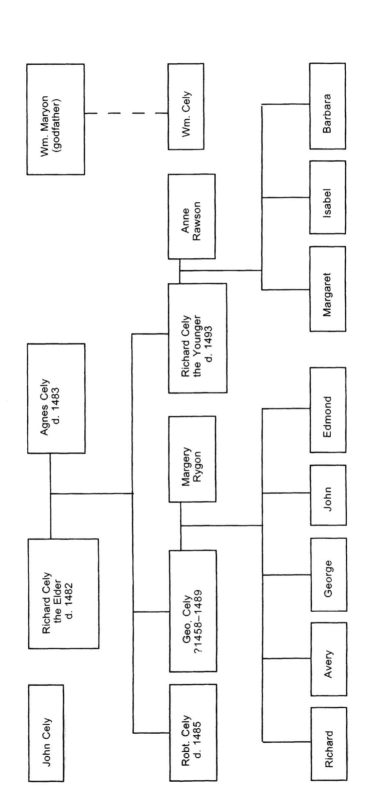

Figure 15.1

agent for the business until Richard Cely the Elder died in 1482. At that point, George moved to London, where he and the youngest son, Richard Cely the Younger (d. 1493), formed a true partnership. Richard the Younger was involved in the family business early on, though he appears never to have been as involved as George.

After George Cely moved to London, most of the business activities on the continent were conducted by William Cely. Presumably William Cely was a member of the family, but we do not know much about him, save that William Maryon, business associate of Richard the Elder and John Cely, was his godfather. Hanham points out, and inspection of the letters confirms, that William was always very deferential in writing to George and other members of the family.

Both George Cely and Richard Cely the Younger married relatively well-off widows in the 1480s, a fact that is material to this study. George had five sons, including one born after his death. Richard the Younger had three daughters. In 1489, after George's death, his widow and Richard the Younger became involved in a lawsuit over payment of the brothers' joint business debts. The letters we have were part of the evidence collected in connection with the suit and eventually came to rest in the Public Records Office. The Paston Letters cover more than three-fourths of a century and were preserved because they were the letters of an important family. The Cely Letters cover only the period 1472–1488, and were the letters of an unimportant family; they were preserved because they were evidence in a lawsuit.

We can tell a great deal about the linkages involved in the Cely Letters by examining the flow of energy in communicative activity as reflected in where letters came from and where they were directed.

We see from Figure 15.2 that the volume of letters is relatively low through 1477. In 1478 it rises sharply until it reaches a peak in 1479 and then declines somewhat through 1481. 1482 produced the greatest volume of correspondence, with a sharp drop in 1483, a smaller rise in 1484, no letters at all in 1485 and 1486, followed by a moderate volume in 1487 and still less in 1488.

We can get a different picture of the linkages if we view the letters by sending points and reception points, shown in Figure 15.3.

As we can see, more letters were sent from London than from any other location. This reflects the fact that London was the headquarters of the business, as does the fact that a large portion of the letters were sent to London as well. Almost as many letters were sent from Calais, and more letters were sent to Calais than any other destination.

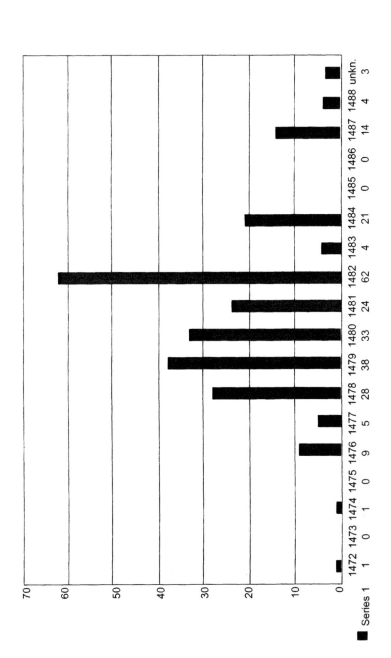

Figure 15.2

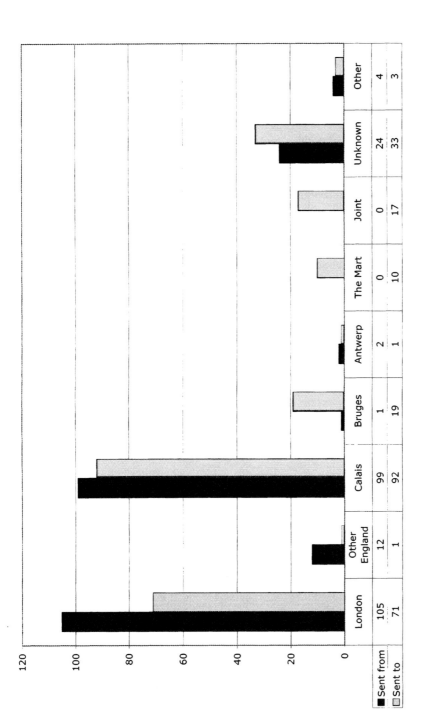

	London	Other England	Calais	Bruges	Antwerp	The Mart	Joint	Unknown	Other
Sent from	105	12	99	1	2	0	0	24	4
Sent to	71	1	92	19	1	10	17	33	3

Figure 15.3

Calais is where the company's continental representative was based. Except for letters from unknown locations, few letters were sent from locations other than London or Calais. However, a substantial numbers of letters were sent to Bruges, the mart, or to joint locations (usually, Calais or Bruges, when the whereabouts of the addressee was not known to the sender).

If, as in Figure 15.4, we group the letters into those sent to and from England and those sent to and from the continent, we can see that about the same number of letters were sent from England and the continent. But far more letters were sent to the continent than to England. Apparently, the most common communicative activity consisted of queries and directives from the head office to the field representatives.

Finally, we can examine who sent and who received letters, detailed in Figure 15.5. By a slim margin, William Cely was the most prolific letter writer. Most of his letters are reports from the field to London. Both Richard Celys sent quite a few letters.

George Cely is far and away the recipient of the most letters. This reflects the two pivotal positions he held in the company: early in his career he was the field representative in Calais, receiving queries and directives from Richard the Elder, Richard the Younger, and William Maryon; and after his father's death, he was the head of the company, receiving voluminous reports from William Cely in Calais.

Now, we turn to the occurrences of *thou*, *thy*, and *thee* in the Cely Letters. As reported in earlier studies (Mills 1999a, 1999b), the Paston Letters contain only seven occurrences of *thou*, two occurrences of *thy*, and three occurrences of *thee*, for a total of 12 tokens. And if we restrict our search to only the Paston Letters written after 1470, a period roughly the same as that of the Cely Letters, we find only two occurrences of *thou*, and none of *thy* or *thee*, out of 3482 second person pronouns.

On purely quantitative grounds we might be tempted to conclude that *thou*, *thy*, and *thee* had all but disappeared from the communicative behavior of English speakers – long before the disappearance is generally held to have occurred. But when we look at actual communicative behavior of the participants who use *thou*, *thy*, and *thee*, we see that the tokens of *thou*, *thy*, and *thee* in the Paston Letters occur only in reported speech, and reported speech of a particular kind, insults. In other words, the linkage of letter-writer to addressee contains within it references to other linkages, of insulter to insultee.

From these facts a sociolinguist would probably conclude that Baugh (1978) was right: *thou*, *thy*, and *thee* had disappeared from polite speech. Further, we could conclude that letters, which utilize a

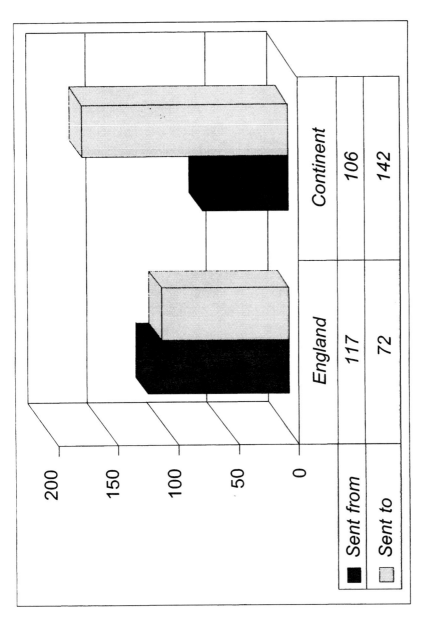

	England	Continent
Sent from	117	106
Sent to	72	142

Figure 15.4

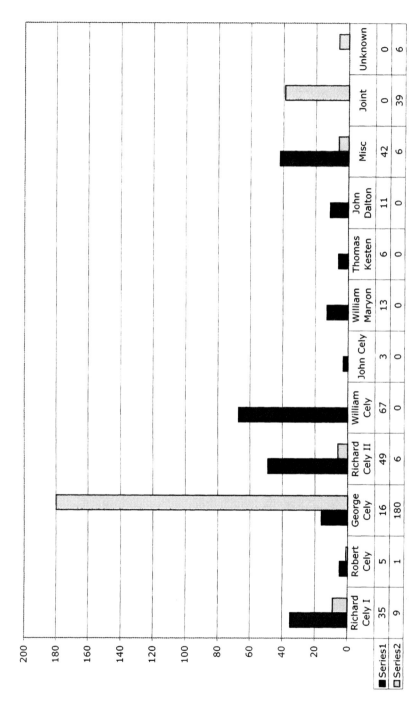

	Richard Cely I	Robert Cely	George Cely	Richard Cely II	William Cely	John Cely	William Maryon	Thomas Kesten	John Dalton	Misc	Joint	Unknown
Series1	35	5	16	49	67	3	13	6	11	42	0	0
Series2	9	1	180	6	0	0	0	0	0	6	39	6

Figure 15.5

different channel for energy flow, never allowed the use of *thou, thy,* and *thee.*

However, the Cely Letters yield a more complex picture. Here, we find no occurrences of *thou* (*ye* occurs in every position where we might expect *thou* except for a few occurrences of *you*), four occurrences of *thy,* 51 occurrences of *thee,* and two occurrences of *thyself*: a total of 57 tokens out of 3627 second person pronouns. Here again, a sociolinguist would point out that the society of merchants is nowhere near as 'polite' (*pace* Baugh) as that of the landed gentry.

But when we examine actual occurrences in terms of participants, linkages, and communicative activity, the picture becomes clearer. All of the tokens but one occurrence of *thee* occur in letters written by Richard Cely the Elder. One occurs in a letter to Robert Cely, a second in a letter to Richard Cely the Younger, and the rest in letters to George Cely. That is, nearly all occurrences of *thy, thyself,* and *thee* are in letters from the old man to his sons.

Hanham (1975) remarks that Richard Cely the Elder typically begins letters to George with *I grete the wyll* but that after 1479 he begins with *I grete you wyll.* Based on numerous factors, Hanham calculates that George was 21 in 1479 (p. 261, n.50). In Yngve's terms, Hanham's observations might be said to be a reflection of a major change in the properties of one of the participants, George, and a consequent change in the linkage involving letters from Richard the Elder to his son.

However, Hanham's conclusion is a bit simplistic. Letters 50 (1479) and 104 (1480) contain *thee,* and letter 116 (1481) has *thy,* though it turns out that Hanham was partly right.

The only occurrence of *thee* not written by Richard Cely the Elder is in letter 126 from Richard Cely the Younger to Joyce Parmenter. Viewing this in terms of the linguistics of language, in its social context, we could argue that Parmenter, as an employee, could be addressed as *thee,* but Richard the Younger never writes this way in other letters to junior members of the firm, and the Pastons never address employees as *thee* in letters.

It is when we look at the letter by Richard the Younger that we note that these linkages have other dimensions which may help to explain the distribution of *thou, thy,* and *thee* versus *ye, your,* and *you*:

> Geoos, I pray *the* send me the aulmen dagar that my brother gaue me, and send me whorde yefe Twesylton sellyd hony of my brothers hors whyll he wher heyr or not, and comende me to Twhessylton and aull good fellows.

Yngve (1996) points out that 'it is convenient to organize our understanding of the activities of linkages and also the behavior of participants in terms of a HIERARCHY OF TASKS AND SUBTASKS that are executed' (p. 186). Formalization of task procedures can be seen in Yngve 1996:264–267. Important for our purposes here are the notions of SUBTASKS (p. 266) and linear sequences of tasks (pp. 267–269). Thus, communicative activity can be viewed in terms of complex task hierarchies (pp. 270–271; 186–188).

If we view the communicative activity of sending a message by writing a letter in terms of tasks, it becomes apparent that such a linkage involves a number of subtasks that are typically sequenced. Examining Richard Cely the Elder's use of *thee*, we see that 14 occurrences (27.5 per cent) are of the form, *I grete the wyl*. In fact, he usually switches to *you* after the greeting, and as Hanham noted, he uses sequences like *I gret you wyll* (e.g. in letter 122) to greet George after 1479.

Another task that can occur in either speech or writing is making a request. In the Cely Letters requests typically begin with *I pray you* [do something]. There are 116 cases of *I pray you* in the Cely Letters – accounting for 7.4 per cent of the occurrences of *you* in the letters. In the example above by Richard Cely the Younger, he is requesting that his employee, Joyce Parmenter, send him a dagger, send him word whether Twesylton has sold any of his brother's horses, and 'comende me to Twhessylton and aull good fellows'.

Richard Cely the Younger is unique among these participants in his use of *I pray ye*, which occurs ten times (1.4 per cent of the occurrences of *ye* in the Cely Letters).

Richard Cely the Elder writes *I pray the* a total of nine times. The total (ten) occurrences of this particular way of commencing a request amounts to 19.6 per cent of the occurrences of *thee* in the Cely Letters. Thus, as set out in Figure 15.6, we can see that nearly half the occurrences of *thee* are devoted to the subtasks of greeting and requesting.

Since the other occurrences of *thy*, *thyself*, and *thee* are in the letters of Richard Cely the Elder, we can conclude that the distribution of these pronouns is governed chiefly by the hierarchy of tasks and subtasks and the properties of a single participant.

Note

An earlier version of this paper was presented at the meeting of the Societas Linguistica Europaea in Poznań, Poland, in 2000. This version has benefited greatly from editorial comments of Victor Yngve.

Uses of Thee in the Cely Letters

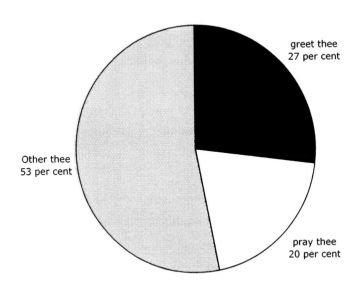

Figure 15.6

References

Baugh, Albert C. and Cable, Thomas (1978), *A History of the English Language* (3rd edn). Englewood Cliffs, NJ: Prentice-Hall.

Brown, Roger W. and Gilman, A. (1960), 'The pronouns of power and solidarity', in T. Sebeok, *Style in Language*. Cambridge, MA: MIT Press, pp. 253–276.

Davis, Norman (1971), *Paston Letters and Papers of the Fifteenth Century* (Part I). Oxford: Clarendon Press.

Hanham, Allison (1975), *The Cely Letters, 1472–1488* (EETS no. 273). New York: Oxford University Press.

Mills, Carl (1999a), 'Pronouns on the eve of modern English: evidence from letters'. Twenty-Eighth Annual Meeting of the Linguistic Association of the Southwest (LASSO 28), University of Texas at San Antonio, October 1999.

Mills, Carl (1999b), 'Discourse demands and language variation: pronouns in fifteenth-century English'. Twenty-Eighth Annual Conference on New Ways of Analyzing Variation (NWAVE 28), York University, October 1999.

Yngve, Victor H. (1986), *Linguistics as a Science*. Bloomington: Indiana University Press.

Yngve, Victor H. (1996), *From Grammar to Science: New Foundations for General Linguistics*. Amsterdam/Philadelphia: John Benjamins.

Yngve, Victor H. (2000), 'The conduct of hard-science research', in Victor H. Yngve and Zdzisław Wąsik, *Exploring the Domain of Human-Centered Linguistics*. Poznań: Adam Mickiewicz University, pp. 5–15 (appears here as Chapter 22).

PART V

SOCIAL AND PSYCHOLOGICAL ISSUES

Chapter 16

The Victorian Stereotype of an Irishman

Anna Cisło

The purpose of this article is to demonstrate how the phenomena of ethnic stereotypes can be understood in terms of human linguistics. More precisely, the phenomenon considered is the stereotype of the Irish Celt functioning in nineteenth-century Victorian society.

In existing definitions,[1] ethnic stereotypes are regarded as images of others formed in people's heads. In practice, they consist in projections of certain sets of traits – which are believed to be typical of a given ethnic group – onto individuals, i.e. members of this group. Such stereotypes either represent a great oversimplification of reality or simply are not true at all. Because they do not originate in the individual's experience of contact with the group whose members are stereotyped but from the individual's social environment, they are not likely to change over a long period of time. Ethnic stereotypes – often bordering on prejudice – may be treated as an important factor that integrates society in situations of conflict with a given ethnic group. Hence they are found in social ideology and political propaganda.

Speaking of the Victorian stereotype of an Irishman in terms of human linguistics we talk about a *large long-lasting linkage* (see Yngve 1996:126, 179) whose *participants* (Yngve 1996:125) share the stereotypical image of the Irish. It is obvious that the study of ethnic stereotypes and prejudice of over a century ago creates a number of problems, some of them resulting from the difficulty in gathering the data. However, the associations formed by the intolerant personalities in question may be considered on the basis of written evidence that some of them left behind.[2] What is meant here are mainly fragments of essays, speeches, and letters, some private and some printed in such newspapers as the *Times*. They played functional parts in spreading the stereotype and, in the light of the theory of human linguistics, can be regarded as *props* (Yngve 1996:129).

The first prop taken into account in our discussion of the nineteenth-century stereotype of the Irish Celt is a fragment of a letter written by Benjamin Disraeli and published in the *Times* in 1836. The Irish, wrote Disraeli,

> hate our free and fertile isle [England]. They hate our order, our civilisation, our enterprising industry, our sustained courage, our decorous liberty, our pure religion. This wild, reckless, indolent, uncertain and superstitious race have no sympathy with the English character. Their fair ideal of human felicity is an alternation of clannish broils and course idolatry. Their history describes an unbroken circle of bigotry and blood. (quoted in Curtis 1968:50–51)

A similar view about the Irish was expressed by Lord Salisbury in a speech published in the *Times* in 1886:[3]

> The confidence you repose in people will depend something upon the habits they have acquired. Well, the habits the Irish have acquired are very bad. They have become habituated to the use of knives and slugs which is wholly inconsistent with the placing of unlimited confidence in them. (quoted in Watson [1979] 1994:17)

A representative of the Celtic race – as portrayed in the above props – was semi-civilized and dangerous. What made spreading of such a stereotype easy was the fact that most Englishmen wanted to believe in the necessity of retaining the nineteenth-century Union between England and Ireland, whereas the Irish, internally colonized by the English (a term used by Hechter 1975), fought for their autonomy.[4]

The stability of anti-Irish prejudice in England resulted from its being almost independent of the actual experience of people. As pointed out by Curtis (1968:34),

> most educated Victorians derived their image of Ireland and the Irish either from limited contact with the Irish in Britain or from fiction, memoirs, history books, government reports, 'expert' accounts written by political economists and social reformers, and pure hearsay. In a relatively small number of cases Englishmen could lay claim to firsthand experience, however brief, of the country and its inhabitants.

In other words, the English formed their beliefs on the basis of available props, and not on actual familiarity with the Irish. E. W. T.

Hamilton's letter written to his nephew, Edward Hamilton, in 1878 illustrates the flimsiness of anti-Irish prejudice:

> I have never been in Ireland & I dislike the Irish so much that I have never made an effort to extend my sphere of knowledge in that direction. But one ought to see & learn – & it is only by personal observation that one can form sound conclusions about the many questions which are perpetually worrying Parliament in reference to that ill-fated country. (quoted in Curtis 1968:51)

Another prop which supports the argument that participants actively involved in the linkage had a very limited contact with the Irish is a letter that the English writer, John Ruskin, wrote to his wife during his first visit to Ireland in 1861:

> What I have seen of the Irish themselves in just the two hours after landing ... will, I suppose, remain as the permanent impression. I had no conception the stories of Ireland were so true. I had fancied all were violent exaggeration. But it is impossible to exaggerate. (quoted in Curtis 1968:50)

Still another recollection comes from Edith Balfour's 'A Week in the West of Ireland' published in the *National Review* in September 1905. Summing up her impressions of just one week's tour in the west of Ireland, she wrote that the Irish

> are like children still listening to old fairy stories while their bread has to be earned; they are like children who are afraid to walk alone, who play with fire, who are helpless; like children who will not grow up.
>   But, like children too, they have a strange ancient wisdom and an innate purity, and they appeal to the love and the pity of all who come in contact with them.
>   What would I not give ... to help them? But the task is very difficult, and if you give children complete freedom they will certainly stray. (quoted in Curtis 1968:53)

As is clear from the last sentence, the stereotype of the Irish supported the opposition to Irish Home Rule in England. The Union had to be retained and it was for the good of the Irish themselves.

Throughout the nineteenth century the general English stereotype of the Irish Celt underwent only slight modifications in detail, while its overall profile became sharper in focus. The epitome of that stereotype was 'Paddy', whose name was derived from a popular Irish name – Padraig (English Patrick). In its most often heard essentials, the image of Paddy was made up of the following adjectives: childish, emotionally unstable, ignorant, indolent, superstitious, primitive, dirty, vengeful, and violent. In English eyes, such traits made the Irish clearly unfit for self-government. At the same time, Englishmen tended to believe that the Anglo-Saxons possessed traits exactly opposite to those that made the Irish so unfit for the management of their own affairs, which in turn justified English political dominance.

The political belief in the higher race of the rulers was expressed even in contexts which, in theory, should have no place for political propaganda. What is meant here are books and articles written by the members of scientific societies, such as, for example, the London Anthropological Society. In 1850 in his *Races of Man* Robert Knox wrote:

> The Celt does not understand what we Saxons mean by independence; he understands a military leader, a faction fight, a fortified camp ... I appeal to the Saxon men of all countries whether I am right or not in my estimate of the Celtic character. Furious fanaticism; a love of war and disorder; a hatred for order and patient industry; no accumulative habits; restless, treacherous, uncertain: look at Ireland ... As a Saxon, I abhor all dynasties, monarchies and bayonet governments, but this latter seems to be the only one suitable for the Celtic man. (quoted in Curtis 1968:70)

The above image, however, was not reserved exclusively for the Irish. It concerned also other Celtic inhabitants of the British Isles. In 1866 in the columns of the *Anthropological Review and Journal*, Daniel Mackintosh published 'The Comparative Anthropology of England and Wales', in which he lists the traits of the Celt:

> Quick in perception, but deficient in depth of reasoning power; headstrong and excitable; tendency to oppose; strong in love and hate; at one time lively, soon after sad; vivid in imagination; extremely social, with a propensity for crowding together; forward and self-confident; deficient in application to deep study, but possessed of great concentration in monotonous or purely mechanical occupations, such as hop-picking, reaping, weaving etc.; want of prudence and foresight; antipathy to seafaring pursuits ... veneration for authority. (quoted in Curtis 1971:18)

The attitudes of people like Knox or Mackintosh were spread not only by representatives of just one academic discipline. It is worth noting that such ideas were reflected as well in contemporary cultural studies in England. Matthew Arnold's essay *On the Study of Celtic*

Literature (1867) contains a portrayal of the Celtic character easily paralleling the characteristics presented by Mackintosh:

> An organisation quick to feel impressions, and feeling them very strongly; a lively personality therefore, keenly sensitive to joy and sorrow; this is the main point. If the downs of life too much outnumber the ups, this temperament, just because it is so quickly and nearly conscious of all the impressions, may no doubt be seen shy and wounded; it may be seen in wistful regret, it may be seen in passionate, penetrating melancholy; but its essence is to aspire ardently after life, light, and emotion, to be expansive, adventurous, and gay ... The Celt is often called sensual; but it is not so much the vulgar satisfactions of sense that attract him as emotion and excitement; he is truly ... sentimental. (quoted in Curtis 1968:43–44)

In British anthropology the descriptions of the Celt extended beyond his character. The following prop is Mackintosh's comment on Celtic physiognomy:

> Bulging forward of lower part of face – most extreme in upper jaw. Chin more or less retreating ... (in Ireland the chin is often absent). Retreating forehead. Large mouth and thick lips. Great distance between nose and mouth. Nose short, upturned, frequently concave, with yawning nostrils. (quoted in Curtis 1971:18)

Such an appearance created a clear contrast with the archetypal Saxon, whose features, as perceived by Mackintosh, were a very regular round face, mouth well-formed, nose straight and neither short nor long, eyes blue or bluish grey, very prominent, flattened ears, hair light brown etc. (see Curtis 1971:18). Both in mental and physical traits the Celts were completely opposite to the Saxons. According to some nineteenth-century anthropologists, the British Isles were inhabited by two different races – the high and naturally civilized Anglo-Saxon race and the Celts, barbarous and incapable of changing their habits.

Another influential race theorist, mentioned by Curtis (1968:71–72), was John Beddoe, president of the Royal Anthropological Institute, Fellow of the Royal Society, Fellow of the Royal College of Physicians, and author of *The Races of Britain* (1885). Beddoe believed that hair and eye color were keys to ethnic and racial identity. He even developed a specious formula, which he called the 'index of nigrescence' and used it to 'prove' that the Irish were darker and more Negroid than the English. Speculating on the African genesis of what he called 'Africanoid' Celts, Beddoes's index of nigrescence provided apparent scientific justification for racial prejudice towards the Irish as an inferior race. One of the most explicit examples is found in a letter of an English writer and historian, Edward Augustus Freeman, who in 1881 wrote from America:

> This would be a grand land if only every Irishman would kill a negro, and be hanged for it. I find this sentiment generally approved – sometimes with the qualification that they want Irish and negroes for servants, not being able to get any other. This looks like the ancient human weakness of craving for a subject race. (quoted in Curtis 1968:81)

Besides the Africanoid Celt, still another modification of the stereotype of an Irishman constituted a simianized Celt. In 1845 an English historian, James Anthony Froude, wrote that the inhabitants of Catholic Ireland seemed 'more like tribes of squalid apes than human beings' (Curtis 1968:85), and in 1860 Charles Kingsley in a letter from Ireland to his wife reported:

> I am haunted by the human chimpanzees I saw along that hundred miles of horrible country. I don't believe they are our fault. I believe there are not only many more of them than of old, but that they are happier, better and more comfortably fed and lodged under our rule than they ever were. But to see white chimpanzees is dreadful; if they were black, one would not feel it so much, but their skins, except where tanned by exposure, are as white as ours. (quoted in Curtis 1968:84)

The image of the simianized Celt was even more explicitly presented in a different category of props, that is in caricatures published in the popular Victorian periodical *Punch*. The example in Figure 16.1 is John Tenniel's illustration of 'Two Forces' printed in *Punch*, 29 October, 1881. It depicts a confrontation between the forces of good and evil. Britannia is protecting her distraught sister Hibernia, i.e. Irish loyalists, from a stone-throwing Irish anarchist, whose repellent ape-like features, even including animal-like teeth in the jaw, underline the mistrust in which the Irish were held by the British.

Summing up, the presented selection of props[5] allows us to list the properties which the participants of the linkage believed to be true of all Irishmen: some nineteenth-century scientific theories 'proved' that an Irishman represented a lower race. Victorian caricatures

Figure 16.1

presented Paddy as a repulsive subhuman ape. His physiognomy was described in detail: he had dark hair and dark eyes, bulging face and thick lips, shallow lower jaw, short, upturned nose with yawning nostrils and fang-like teeth. He was dirty and poorly dressed. The image of Paddy connoted also his character traits. He was emotionally unstable, wild and dangerous, sociable but over-fond of whiskey and quick to reach for his sword, factious, easily irritable, impetuous and forward, inconsiderate, improvident, idolatrous, superstitious, over-sensitive, affectionate, sentimental, deceitful, incapable of creative work or logical thinking, deficient in application to deep study, reckless, imaginative, lazy, childish, and emotional. According to Curtis (1968:54), of all the Irishman's traits his reputation for emotionalism, instability, and the childish lack of self-control was probably most damning as far as the estimates of his political capacities were concerned. In general, the whole image – far from being flattering – contributed to the political discussion on the Irish Question, i.e. Irish autonomy.

The framework of human linguistics leads to identifying parts of the real physical world involved in the described phenomena. Since the people who in the nineteenth century were responsible for spreading the stereotype of the Irish Celt as well as the anti-Irish prejudice cannot be investigated, attention is focused on the existing props and only next on the reality behind them. Taken together, the props allow not only listing the alleged traits of the Irish but also speculating about the linkage of over a century ago.

The participants who originated the unflattering stereotype and passed it on to other members of Victorian society were usually pro-imperialists. The presumed receivers and supporters of their ideas were first of all people interested in politics or simply those English people who shared an ethnocentric attitude towards their country. But there must have been a lot of those who, at first politically neutral, accepted the negative stereotype of the Irish Celt passed on to them and who, consciously or not, participated in the linkage formed in relation to the political situation in the nineteenth-century British Empire.

Notes

The material data presented here were originally analyzed by the author of this article along the lines of available socio-psychological theories, including the concept of social construction of reality (see Berger and Luckmann [1966] 1973). The material was only later reconsidered within the framework of human linguistics to be presented at the workshop 'Exploring the Domain of Human-Centered Linguistics from a Hard-Science Perspective' organized by Victor H. Yngve and Zdzisław Wąsik for the SLE 33rd Annual Meeting in Poznań, Poland, 31 August–2 September, 2000.

1. It is generally agreed that, as a social scientific term, 'stereotype' was coined by Walter Lippman in *Public Opinion* ([1922] 1946). For details

and definitions see Allport ([1954] 1958), Schaff (1981), Aronson *et al.* ([1996] 1997), Berting and Villan-Gandossi (1995), and Macrae *et al.* (1996).
2. The sources come almost exclusively from two books of Lewis Perry Curtis, Jr. (1968, 1971).
3. Both politicians, Benjamin Disraeli and Lord Salisbury, were opposed to Irish autonomy, *Home Rule.*
4. It is worth noting here that in the nineteenth century the image of the Irish Celt was something more than a derivative of the stage Irishman who had cavorted in English plays for at least two centuries (see Christensen 1996:139–140). Primarily merely a figure of fun or even affection, the stereotypical Irish Celt gained a political significance, connoting to Victorians a collection of highly undesirable traits, which – according to the laws of racial inheritance – could not be changed.
5. For more props see Curtis (1968, 1971), Watson ([1979] 1994), Gibbons (1991), Young (1995), and Cheng (1995).

References

Allport, Gordon Willard [1954] (1958), *The Nature of Prejudice: A Comprehensive and Penetrating Study of the Origin and Nature of Prejudice. Abridged.* Reading, MA: Addison-Wesley; Garden City, NY: Doubleday Anchor Books (No. 149).

Aronson, Elliot, Wilson, Timothy D., and Akert, Robin M. [1996] (1997), *Social Psychology.* New York/Harlow: Longman.

Berger, Peter L. and Luckmann,Thomas [1966] (1973), *The Social Construction of Reality: A Treatise in the Sociology of Knowledge.* London, Fakenham, and Reading: Penguin Books.

Berting, Jan and Villain-Gandossi, Christiane (1995), 'The role and significance of national stereotypes in international relations: an inter-disciplinary approach', in Teresa Walas, *Stereotypes and Nations.* Cracow: International Cultural Centre, pp. 13–27.

Cheng, Vincent (1995), *Joyce, Race and Empire.* Cambridge: Cambridge University Press.

Christensen, Lis (1996), *A First Glossary of Hiberno-English.* Odense: Odense University Press.

Curtis, Lewis Perry, Jr. (1968), *Anglo-Saxons and Celts: A Study of Anti-Irish Prejudice in Victorian England.* Bridgeport, CT: University of Bridgeport.

Curtis, Lewis Perry, Jr. (1971), *Apes and Angels: The Irishman in Victorian Caricature.* Newton Abbot, Devon: David & Charles.

Gibbons, Luke (1991), 'Race against time: Racial discourse and Irish history', in Robert Young, *The Oxford Literary Review, Volume 13: Neocolonialism.* Huddersfield: H. Charlesworth, pp. 95–117.

Hechter, Michael (1975), *Internal Colonialism: The Celtic Fringe in British*

National Development, 1536–1966. London: Routledge and Kegan Paul.

Lippman, Walter [1922] (1946), *Public Opinion*. New York: [Harcourt Press] Penguin Books.

Macrae, C. Neil, Stangor, Charles, and Hewstone, Miles (1996), *Stereotypes and Stereotyping*. New York/London: Guilford Press.

Schaff, Adam (1981), *Stereotypy a działanie ludzkie*. Warsaw: Książka i Wiedza.

Watson, George J. [1979] (1994), *Irish Identity and the Literary Revival: Synge, Yeats, Joyce and O'Casey*. Washington, DC: The Catholic University of America Press.

Yngve, Victor H. (1996), *From Grammar to Science: New Foundations for General Linguistics*. Amsterdam/Philadelphia: John Benjamins.

Young, Robert (1995), *Colonial Desire: Hybridity in Theory, Culture and Race*. London and New York: Routledge.

Chapter 17

Needs as Expressed in Educational Discourse on the Basis of Textbooks in Linguistics

Piotr Czajka

This paper examines existing psychological work on human needs and explores the possibility of reconstituting it on the new foundations. Needs are understood as properties of participants that influence communicative behavior. Properties in didactic linkages are related to the needs of teacher and student and analyzed in terms of task hierarchies that reconstitute the educational discourse strategies of Stefan J. Rittel (1997) and the politeness strategies of Penelope Brown and Stephen C. Levinson (1978, 1990). Didactic linkages coupled through textbooks are investigated by examining three well-known Polish textbooks of linguistics (Furdal 1977; Milewski 1975; Bańczerowski, Pogonowski, and Zgółka 1982).

1. Human needs and communicative behavior

Let us begin by trying to find out if human needs may play any role in human communicative behavior.

1.1. The notion of need

The notion of need appears frequently in the works of such psychologists as Abraham Maslow (1959, [1954] 1964a, 1964b, [1954] 1970, 1971), Henry Murray (1938, 1951), or Kazimierz Obuchowski ([1965] 1967, 1977), who, as Kazimierz Jankowski ([1975] 1976:137) notices, were mainly preoccupied with the system of human needs and tried to analyze the connection between human needs and human behavior. The definitions of the notion of need formulated by Murray, Maslow, and Obuchowski vary. Murray, in Barbara Engler's (1985:223) interpretation, 'defines a need as a construct representing a force in the brain that organizes our perception, understanding, and behavior in such a way as to change an unsatisfying situation and increase our satisfaction ... It motivates us to look for or avoid certain kinds of press'. Maslow (1959:123) treats human needs as 'deficiencies which must be optimally fulfilled by the environment to avoid sickness and to avoid subjective ill-being'. Obuchowski states that 'a need for object Y may be generally defined as a property of individual X. This property means that individual X cannot function normally without object Y, i.e. individual X cannot acquire the optimal ability to preserve himself and his species and to develop himself' (quoted in Gajewska 1997:28).[1]

In spite of the fact that there are differences in the above definitions of the notion of need, one could assume that all the definitions refer to a psychical phenomenon which may stimulate any kind of human behavior, the purpose of which would be satisfaction of the perceived need. Therefore it seems conceivable to state that a subjectively perceived human need may well motivate and influence a particular instance of human communicative behavior which, in this case, would also be an instance of human action aimed at satisfying the perceived need.

1.2. Needs in human linguistics

If it is assumed that a subjectively perceived need may be a reason for the occurrence of communicative behavior and may also influence the shape of a particular instance of communicative behavior, it is possible to consider needs as properties of participants in a given linkage. Human linguistics (see Yngve 1986:53, 1996:141) distinguishes two kinds of properties: categorial and conditional. As to conditional properties, they 'reflect the momentary state or condition of the individual at any instant of time' and 'their changes accompany communicative behavior in regular ways' (Yngve 1986:53). Categorial properties, in turn, 'represent the categories or dimensions along which these changes take place' (Yngve 1986:53). Therefore, following the above distinction, the participant's ability to perceive a particular subjective need may be regarded as one of the participant's categorial properties in a given linkage, while the presence/absence of a given need could be a conditional property of a given participant.

The presence of a given need may cause an instance of communicative behavior aimed at a transition from the state in which the participant feels a given need into a state in which the participant feels the satisfaction of this need. It seems logical to claim that a given participant's need may be satisfied (1) directly by the output of the participant's communicative behavior, (2) by the changes that are caused by this output in the constituents of the linkage, (3) by the output/feedback of the other participant, or (4) by the changes in the constituents of the linkage that are caused by the other participant's output/feedback.

The needs of the participants of a given linkage may be distinguished on the basis of psychological tests. However, if the researcher has no immediate contact with the participants, he may first establish the type of the analyzed linkage, the role parts of the participants in this linkage, and then estimate the types of needs that may be satisfied by the participants performing these role parts. In order to enumerate the types of needs which seem to be characteristic of a given type of linkage, the researcher may again refer to the investigations of such psychologists as, e.g., Murray (see Hilgard [1953] 1972:193–194), Maslow ([1954] 1970), and Obuchowski ([1965] 1967:105–107), who worked out lists of needs that a human being is likely to experience.

1.3. Didactic linkages

Educational discourse seems to be a type of human communicative behavior present in a type of linkage that could be called didactic. One could characterize a didactic linkage as a typical instance of interaction between a teacher and a student. Using the words of Janina Labocha (1997:34), a typical interaction between a teacher and a student consists in 'the introduction of a ritualized situation which is based on a silently accepted agreement that one of the partners occupies a superior position having the right to steer the process of knowledge transmission and the right to evaluate the degree to which the knowledge has been acquired'. So, it is possible to state that a didactic linkage includes the role part of the teacher and the role part of the student. The role part of the teacher consists in transmitting knowledge to the student and checking if the student has acquired the knowledge. The role part of the student is to acquire the knowledge passed on to him by the teacher.

It is therefore feasible to state that a didactic linkage gives the student and the teacher a possibility of satisfying various needs requiring interpersonal contacts. One of them might be the need to teach (i.e. give instructions and guidance) noticed by Murray (see Hilgard [1953] 1972:194). It is postulated that the need to teach can be regarded as the typical need of the teacher. The typical need of the student could be another need which may, but need not, require interpersonal contacts, namely the need to know noticed by Murray (see Hilgard [1953] 1972:194), Maslow ([1954] 1964a:151–153), and Obuchowski ([1965] 1967:105–107). It also seems viable to state that apart from the need to teach and the need to know, a didactic linkage brings also an opportunity, both for the teacher and for the student, to satisfy some other needs requiring interpersonal contacts such as, e.g., the need to reject other people, the need to take care of others, the need to be supported by someone – all of them taken from Murray's list of needs (see Hilgard [1953] 1972:193–194).

1.4. Textbooks

The needs of the teacher and of the student may influence the communicative behavior of participants (and the outputs of that behavior) in any instance of a didactic linkage. This paper however concentrates on the phenomenon of textbooks, and in the case of textbooks, the contact of the teacher with the student may be treated as occurring in two linkages directly coupled by a physical object (i.e. by a textbook) which is the written output of the teacher and a possible input for the student (cf. Yngve 1996:228). This means that the student's need to know may be satisfied when the student has read the textbook (or a part of it), but the student's and teacher's other needs requiring interpersonal contacts, and the teacher's need to teach may be satisfied only when the student and teacher have the possibility of experiencing mutual feedback. For some teachers and students this possibility may never occur. Moreover, if the investigation of participants' needs in a didactic linkage is based only on textbooks, the researcher has no access to the student's communicative behavior, which means that the student as a participant of a didactic linkage is unavailable to the researcher. Thus, the researcher has to limit himself to the study of only the teacher's needs and their relations with the teacher's communicative behavior that influences the properties of the constituents of the didactic linkage. That is also why the following considerations will be devoted only to the teacher's needs requiring interpersonal contacts, namely (1) to the teacher's need to teach and (2) to the teacher's needs which are different from the need to teach but still require interpersonal contacts such as, e.g., the above-mentioned needs to reject other people, to take care of others, or to be supported by someone, all coming from the list of human needs proposed by Murray (see Hilgard [1953] 1972:193–194).

1.5. Needs and strategies

In this case the study of a given teacher's needs and their relations with properties of the constituents of a particular didactic linkage may be based on analyzing the properties of textbooks in search of those properties that may be regarded as the output of the teacher's instances of communicative behavior aimed at satisfying his needs. Instances of communicative behavior aimed at satisfying one's needs may in turn be described in reference to certain types of communicative behavior that could be called strategies of communicative behavior. In case of the need to teach, the teacher's communicative behavior could be a particular token of a type of a strategy aimed at transmitting knowledge. Such strategies are presented by Rittel (1997). As to the needs which are different from the need to teach but still require interpersonal contacts, the teacher's communicative behavior could be a particular token of a type of strategy aimed at creating a desired interpersonal situation. It is postulated that strategies of this kind may be the politeness strategies presented by Brown and Levinson (1978, 1990), who claim that following certain politeness strategies may cause definite effects influencing interpersonal relationships (see Brown and Levinson 1990:55).

Therefore, the analysis of the three selected textbooks in linguistics will consist of two parts. The first part will be devoted to examining the selected textbooks in linguistics from the point of view of Rittel's (1997) strategies of knowledge transmission. The second part will concentrate on searching for passages in the textbooks which might be considered as realizations of the politeness strategies described by Brown and Levinson (1990).

2. Analysis according to the need to teach

Beginning the first part of the analysis, let us first have a closer look at strategies of knowledge transmission.

2.1. Rittel's four strategies

Rittel (1997:55–60) distinguishes four such strategies: the strategy through acquisition, the strategy through solving problems, the strategy through action, and the strategy through experiencing problems.

The strategy through acquisition involves the following steps made by the teacher:

- signaling, which means that a person makes use of a kind of information such as optical, acoustic, sensory, abstract, or cybernetic,
- conceptualization, which means that a person makes use of their own concepts and connotations that express the way in which the person articulates the relation between the reality and its verbal/nonverbal shape,
- observing the reception of the transmission, which is to ascertain the character of the conceptualization of notions in the student's consciousness. (Rittel 1997:55)

In the case of the strategy through solving problems the teacher's activity embraces:

- noticing a problematic situation,
- formulating a problem which is put forward to be solved or formulating questions which are to lead to the achievement of understanding,
- verifying the outcome of applying the strategy through solving problems. (Rittel 1997:56)

The strategy through action followed by the teacher consists in:

- initiating action that is in this case connected with the occurrence of an idea or intention or is an assigned obligation, e.g. being a part of a teaching syllabus,
- projecting the action, which is connected with translating a general idea into a particular procedural scenario,
- controlling the results of action in reference to the aims which are to be achieved. (Rittel 1997:58)

As to the strategy through experiencing problems, the teacher's conduct comprises:

- arranging a set of factors to be considered from the viewpoint of the effectiveness of introducing one to the state of experiencing a problem,

- reinforcing the process of experiencing a problem,
- steering the process of initiating the state of experiencing a problem ... steering the process of experiencing a problem, and the process of leading one out of the state of experiencing a problem. (Rittel 1997:60)

2.2. Rittel's strategies in human linguistics

It has already been mentioned that Rittel's strategies of transmission of knowledge are treated in this paper as possible types of the teacher's communicative behavior aimed at satisfying the teacher's need to teach within a didactic linkage. Having this in mind and noticing that human linguistics, as Yngve (1996:186) points out, proposes to understand 'the activities of linkages and also the behavior of participants in terms of a hierarchy of tasks and subtasks', one could state that satisfying the need to teach may be regarded as a task of the teacher, who is a participant in a didactic linkage. Constructing educational discourse and following the strategies of the transmission of knowledge could then function as possible subsequent subtasks which the teacher may alternatively complete in order to accomplish the superior task, i.e. in order to satisfy the need to teach. An attempt to view these interdependencies as tasks and subtasks is presented in Figure 17.1.

It is worth noticing here that considering the steps of human communicative behavior in terms of task hierarchies imposes on the researcher the duty of stating clearly which steps are carried out in parallel and which in sequence. That is why the observations of Rittel (1997:55–60) connected with the strategies of transmission of knowledge had to be adapted to some extent for the purpose of fitting them into the model of description based on task hierarchies.

2.3. Observations of textbooks

As has been shown, Rittel (1997:55–60) distinguishes four strategies of transmission of knowledge, but the authors of the analyzed textbooks (Furdal 1977; Milewski 1975; Bańczerowski, Pogonowski, and Zgółka 1982) seem to follow only one of them, namely the strategy through acquisition. They all decided to make use of the optical kind of information and then, on the stage of conceptualization, they simply formulated successive parts of their textbooks trying to communicate the information that they regarded as indispensable for the student.

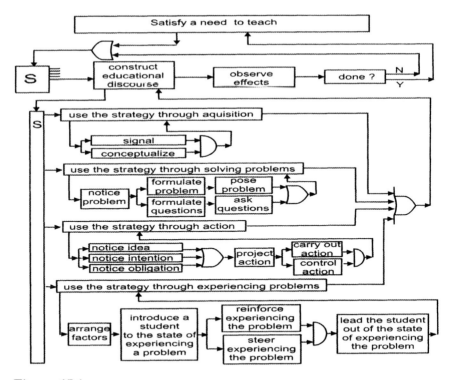

Figure 17.1

3. Analysis according to needs of interpersonal contacts

Passing on to the second part of the analysis, i.e. to the analysis of the three selected textbooks in terms of the model proposed by Brown and Levinson (1990), it seems necessary to recall some basic assumptions made by these researchers. Brown and Levinson (1990:62) assume that people communicating with each other, i.e. the speaker (S) and hearer (H), possess so-called *negative face*, which is the desire to preserve 'freedom of action and freedom from imposition', and *positive face*, which is the desire to be approved of and accepted. Next, Brown and Levinson (1990:65) introduce the notion of *face threatening act* (FTA), which refers to 'what is intended to be done by a verbal or nonverbal communication' and which runs 'contrary to the face wants of the addressee and/or the speaker'.

3.1. Brown and Levinson's strategies

In doing an FTA a speaker may follow so called *off-record* strategies using, e.g., irony, rhetorical questions, or understatements, which means that the speaker's intent is not communicated directly and that the speaker 'cannot be held to have committed himself to one particular intent' (Brown and Levinson 1990:69). Following *on-record* strategies means, in turn, that the speaker's communicative intention is clear and unambiguous (see Brown and Levinson 1990:68). Doing FTAs on record may be accompanied by redress/ redressive action, which is a kind of action 'that attempts to counteract the potential face damage of the FTA by doing it in such a way, or with such modifications or additions, that indicate clearly that no ... face threat is intended or desired, and that S in general recognizes H's face wants and himself wants them to be achieved' (Brown and Levinson 1990:69–70). A particular instance of redress represents a *positive politeness* strategy if it implies 'that S likes H so that the FTA doesn't mean negative evaluation in general of H's face', or it represents *negative politeness* strategies if it consists 'in assurances that the speaker recognizes and respects the addressee's negative face wants and will not (or will only minimally) interfere with the addressee's freedom of action' (Brown and Levinson 1990:70). FTAs may also be done using the *bald-on-record* strategy which involves doing FTAs 'without redress, ... in the most direct, clear, unambiguous and concise way possible' (Brown and Levinson 1990:69).

3.2. *Brown and Levinson's strategies in human linguistics*

Doing an FTA in Brown and Levinson's understanding is assumed here to be a way of satisfying the teacher's needs which are different from the need to teach but still require interpersonal contacts. Hence, it is conceivable to consider satisfaction of a particular need requiring interpersonal contacts but different from the need to teach as a task of the teacher in a didactic linkage. Doing an FTA might then function as a possible subtask of this task. The strategies of doing FTAs described by Brown and Levinson (1990) could therefore be regarded as alternative subtasks of doing an FTA. Figure 17.2 presents these interdependencies.

The assumptions made by Brown and Levinson (1990) limit the application of their model to the analysis of human communicative behavior which encompasses doing FTAs. Considering the role part of the teacher in the didactic linkage it is quite apparent that it consists firstly in instructing and telling the student how to understand or solve certain problems and secondly in persuading the student to accept and follow the way of reasoning presented by

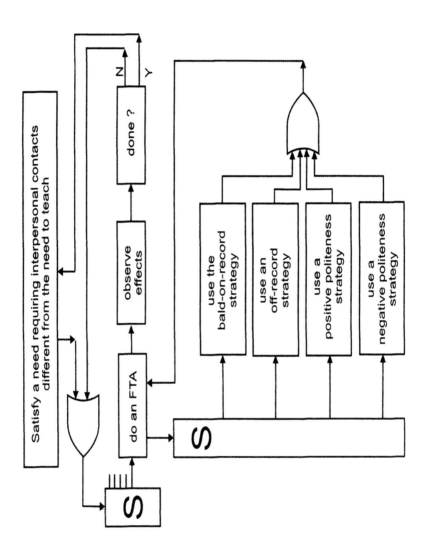

Figure 17.2

the teacher. So, typical activities of the teacher may be regarded as acts threatening the negative face of the student. One of the possible forms of the teacher's output may, of course, be a textbook. Therefore, it seems possible to state that in the case of textbooks one has to do with acts which are done by teachers (as the authors of the textbooks) and which threaten the student's negative face.

3.3. Observations of textbooks

Examination of the three Polish linguistics textbooks[2] revealed examples of many of the strategies described by Brown and Levinson (1990). These strategies and examples of them found in the textbooks are listed below.

3.3.1. The bald-on-record strategy

The bald-on-record strategy seems to be most frequently used in the analyzed textbooks. Brown and Levinson (1990:94) 'treat the bald-on-record strategy as speaking in conformity with Grice's Maxims'. Paul Grice ([1968] 1991:308) distinguished four categories of maxims of conversation, the first being the category of Quantity encompassing such maxims as: 'make your contribution as informative as is required (for the current purpose of the exchange)' and 'do not make your contribution more informative than is required'; the second – the category of Quality including two maxims: 'do not say what you believe to be false' and 'do not say that for which you lack adequate evidence'; the third – the category of Relation with only one maxim: 'be relevant'; the fourth – the category of Manner embracing the supermaxim 'be perspicuous' and maxims such as: 'avoid obscurity of expression', 'avoid ambiguity', 'be brief (avoid unnecessary prolixity)', and 'be orderly'. The use of the bald-on-record strategy may be exemplified by the following fragments:

> Znak [. . .] pojawiający się w procesie porozumienia językowego między ludźmi ma znaczenie konkretne [*A sign occurring in the process of verbal communication between people possesses a concrete meaning*] (AF:131); Efektywność komunikacji polega na zgodności zamierzenia subiektywnego nadawcy z rezultatem społeczno-obiektywnym przypisywanym danej, podjętej przez nadawcę czynności [*The effectiveness of communication is based on the agreement between the sender's subjective intent and the socio-objective result ascribed to the sender's activity*] (TZ:39); główne typy klasyfikacji języków to typologia geograficzna, genetyczna i

strukturalna [*the main types of classifications of languages are geographical, genetic, and structural typologies*] (JP:88); W dowolnym punkcie ciągu artykulacyjnego [...] nie ma ostrego przejścia [*In any point of the articulatory string there is no sudden change*] (JB:110); afiksy [...] nie mogą występować samodzielnie [*affixes cannot occur separately*] (TM:87).

Extensive use of the bald-on-record strategy in the analyzed textbooks is not surprising, because it is used, according to Brown and Levinson (1990:95), 'where maximum efficiency is very important' and effective communication seems to be one of the major goals of any textbook.

3.3.2. Positive politeness strategies
The authors of the analyzed textbooks also made use of several positive politeness strategies which are discussed below.

3.3.2.1. INCLUDE BOTH THE SPEAKER AND THE HEARER IN THE ACTIVITY
One of the positive politeness strategies used by the authors of the analyzed textbooks was *Include both S and H in the activity*. This strategy, as Brown and Levinson (1990:127) point out, may be realized 'by using an inclusive "we" form, when S really means "you" or "me"'. The examples might be as follows:

Pamiętajmy, że ... [*Let us remember that ...*] (AF:6); Nie zapominajmy [...], że ... [*Let us not forget that ...*] (AF:10); weźmy pod uwagę ... [*let us take into consideration ...*] (JP:87); rozważmy [let us consider] (TZ:21; JB:278); Wyobraźmy sobie, że ... [*Let us imagine that ...*] (AF:103); spróbujmy [*let us try*] (TZ:19); Wracamy tu do ... [*Here we are coming back to ...*] (TZ:38); zdajemy sobie sprawę, że ... [*we realize that ...*] (AF:33); Twierdzimy, iż ... [*We state that ...*] (AF:14); mamy do czynienia z ... [*we have to do with ...*] (TZ:22; JB:278); Zauważamy [...], że ... [*We notice that ...*] (JB:122); musimy [*we have to*] (AF:26, 22); możemy [*we can*] (AF:16; JB:226; TM:6); Wyróżniamy [*We distinguish*] (TM:53); nazywamy [*we call*] (TM:19); rozumiemy [*we understand*] (JP:78; TM:5); widzimy [*we can see*] (TM:5); zwrócimy uwagę na ... [*we will pay attention to ...*] (TZ:41); rozpoczniemy [*we will begin*] (AF:36; TZ:12); Zobaczymy później, że ... [*Later we will see that ...*] (AF:10); ograniczymy się do ... [*we will limit ourselves to ...*] (AF:12); scharakteryzujemy [*we will characterize*] (JP:77); Usiłowaliśmy [*We have been trying*] (TZ:71);

nasza praca [*our work*] (TM:7); nasze rozważania [*our considerations*] (AF:6).

3.3.2.2. INTENSIFY INTEREST TO THE HEARER
The next positive politeness strategy distinguished by Brown and Levinson (1990:106), i.e. *Intensify interest to H*, could also be found in the analyzed textbooks. This strategy, according to Brown and Levinson (1990:106–107), may be realized by using the 'vivid present' to talk about past events or by trying 'to exaggerate facts, to overstate'. However, it seems justified to state that the strategy in question manifested itself also in some other ways. One of them consisted in illustrating the argument with examples which students may be familiar with. The next way was to present the speaker's personal experiences or to use metaphors. Here are selected examples:

3.3.2.2.1. Use 'vivid present'
W r. 1816 F. Bopp wydaje rozprawę o koniugacji indoeuropejskiej [...] W r. 1818 R. Rask określa [...] stosunki genetyczne między językami północnogermańskimi a [...] łaciną [...] W 1820 W. Humboldt wygłasza słynny odczyt [*In 1816 F. Bopp publishes a dissertation about Indo-European conjugation ... In 1818 R. Rask establishes genetic relationships between North-Germanic languages ... and Latin ... In 1820 W. Humboldt delivers a famous lecture*] (AF:9); Językoznawstwo zaczyna być wówczas dyscypliną autonomiczną [*Then, linguistics begins to be an autonomous discipline*] (TZ:56); W dalszej ewolucji odpowiedniki dźwięków nabierają coraz większego znaczenia [*In the course of evolution the counterparts of sounds gain more and more meaning*] (TM:11).

3.3.2.2.2. Exaggerate facts, overstate
Trud wielu [...] uczonych [...] którzy nierzadko poświęcali całe życie na zbieranie wiadomości o budowie i dziejach języków i w końcu stawali bezradni wobec nawału słów i form gramatycznych [*The labor of many ... scientists who often devoted all their lives to acquiring knowledge about the structure and history of languages and who finally stood helpless facing the multitude of words and grammatical forms*] (AF:10); uczeni [...] podjęli z entuzjazmem badania [*the scientists with enthusiasm took up the research*] (AF:11); gwałtowna „semiologizacja" tych nauk [*rapid 'semiologization' of the sciences*] (AF:30); człowiek określa nazwami wszystko i wszędzie [*man gives names to everything everywhere*] (AF:58);

skonstruowanie negacji [...] było jednym z największych wyna-
lazków [*the construction of negation was one of the greatest
inventions*] (AF:72); Powstała [...] sytuacja paradoksalna [*A
paradoxical situation occurred*] (AF:77); w jaki sposób – z niczego
właściwie – narodziło się owo zdumiewające zjawisko, jakim jest
język [*how – actually out of nothing – the surprising phenomenon of
language was born*] (AF:77); ogromne triumfy święci w lingwistyce
strukturalizm [*structuralism triumphs in linguistics*] (TZ:46); kody
[...], nieskończenie bogatsze w sygnały ... [*the codes infinitely
richer in signals*] (TM:18–19); cały ogrom zmian [*the whole
multitude of changes*] (TM:127–128).

3.3.2.2.3. Give examples
Zdarza się przecież, że ten, do kogośmy się zwrócili, nie usłyszał
naszego głosu [*Sometimes it happens that the person we have spoken
to didn't hear our voice*] (AF:54); Każdy z nas zetknął się w życiu z
dzieckiem, które uczy się mówić [*Each of us has met a child who is
learning to talk*] (AF:58); Informację o [...] deszczu można uzyskać
[...] z komunikatu meteorologicznego, z obserwacji barometru
[*One can get information about rain from the weather forecast, from
observation of a barometer*] (TZ:32); spostrzegamy czerwone
światło. Jest to forma znaku [*we notice a red light. It is a form of
a sign*] (TM:9).

3.3.2.2.4. Present your own experiences
Pewnego [...] dnia stałem w kolejce [*One day I was queuing*]
(AF:65); Kiedy przed kilku laty przebywałem w Budziszynie
[*When I was staying in Budziszyn several years ago*] (AF:65); Od
małej dziewczynki [...] usłyszałem... [*I heard from a little girl ...*]
(AF:71).

3.3.2.2.5. Use metaphors
Te stare systemy [...] współdziałają w obrębie mowy [...]
człowieka, która jest orkiestrą wszystkich rodzajów znaków [*These
old systems cooperate within the speech of man, which is an orchestra
of all kinds of signs*] (TM:26); Sam [...] język, [...] jest skarbnicą
wiedzy o [...] świecie [*Language itself is a repository of knowledge
about the world*] (AF:59); Ujmując rzecz [...] metaforycznie, znak
jest [...] mostem przerzuconym ponad przepaściami wyobrażeń
[*Speaking metaphorically, a sign is a bridge over the gulf of
imaginations*] (AF:61); głosy [...] roztapiały się w powodzi
szczegółowej wiedzy i niewiedzy językoznawczej [*the voices

dissolved in the flood of detailed linguistic knowledge and ignorance]
(AF:74).

3.3.2.3. PRESUPPOSE/RAISE/ASSERT COMMON GROUND

A positive politeness strategy is also to *presuppose/raise/assert common
ground*. One has to do with this strategy, as Brown and Levinson
(1990:118) claim, when the speaker stresses 'the common ground he
shares with H – common concerns, and common attitudes towards
interesting events'. The use of this strategy could be illustrated by the
following fragments:

> Jak widzimy ... [*As we can see* ...] (TM:13); jak widzieliśmy ... [*as
> we could see* ...] (AF:82; TM:63); Widzieliśmy zaś [...], że ... [*we
> could see that* ...](AF:176); jak pamiętamy ... [*as we remember* ...]
> (JB:166); jak pamiętamy z poprzednich uwag ... [*as we remember
> from our previous remarks* ...] (JP:79); Jak wspomniano ... [*As has
> been mentioned* ...] (TZ:20); wspomniano wyżej, że ... [*it was
> mentioned above that* ...] (TZ:17); Jak już wspominaliśmy ... [*As
> we have already mentioned* ...] (JP:96; JB:192); Powiedzieliśmy
> wyżej, że ... [*We stated above that* ...] (AF:101); Powiedzieliśmy
> już, że ... [*We have already stated that* ...] (JB:239); jak już
> założyliśmy [*as we have already assumed*] (JB:113); Umawiamy się
> jednak, że nas będą interesować ... [*We agree however that we will
> be interested in* ...] (AF:51); Znamy wszyscy ten typ języka [*We all
> know this type of language*] (AF:156); W świetle poprzednich
> rozważań ... [*In light of the previous considerations* ...] (TZ:42).

3.3.3. Negative politeness strategies

The analyzed textbooks also contain fragments in which the authors
followed negative politeness strategies which will be presented below.

3.3.3.1. QUESTION, HEDGE

One of the negative politeness strategies noticed by Brown and
Levinson (1990:145) is the *Question, hedge* strategy which consists in
using so called hedges. A hedge, as Brown and Levinson (1990:145)
understand it, is 'a particle, word or phrase that modifies the degree
of membership of a predicate or noun phrase in a set; it says of that
membership that it is *partial*, or true only in certain respects, or that
it is *more* true and complete than perhaps might be expected'. While
discussing the problem of hedges Brown and Levinson (1990:164)
notice that they may be divided in reference to Grice's Maxims.
Following this division it was possible to find in the analyzed

textbooks hedges addressed to the maxims of quality (i.e. quality hedges), and hedges addressed to the maxims of quantity (i.e. quantity hedges). In Brown and Levinson's (1990:164–166) understanding, quality hedges 'suggest that the speaker is not taking full responsibility for the truth of his utterance', and the role of quantity hedges, as Brown and Levinson (1990:166) assume, is to 'give notice that not as much or not as precise information is provided as might be expected'. The fragments quoted below seem to illustrate the use of quality and quantity hedges in the analyzed textbooks.

3.3.3.1.1. Use quality hedges
nie jest to prawdopodobnie [...] zależne od nadawcy [*it probably doesn't depend on the sender*] (JP:85); opisy [...] prawdopodobnie zostaną [...] udoskonalone [*the descriptions will probably be improved*] (TM:68); jest ona [...] najprawdopodobniej powiązana ze ... [*most probably it is connected with* ...] (JP:84); [...] status lingwistyki [...] jest raczej trudny do [...] określenia [*it is rather difficult to establish the status of linguistics*] (TZ:11); Możemy więc przypuszczać że ... [*We can suppose that* ...] (TM:210); nie możemy się zatrzymać przed sformułowaniem przypuszczenia, że ... [*we cannot refrain from formulating a supposition that* ...] (AF:22); Gdybyśmy się nie lękali hipotez, moglibyśmy powiedzieć, że ... [*If we were not afraid of hypotheses, we could say that* ...] (AF:83); Powyższego założenia nie należy jednak traktować jako całkowicie pewnego [*The above assumption cannot be treated as absolutely certain*] (JB:199).

3.3.3.1.2. Use quantity hedges
Wyniki [...] możemy przedstawić w następującym uproszczonym schemacie [*The results may be presented in the following simplified diagram*] (AF:53); Dokonując pewnego uproszczenia [...] można ... [*Making a simplification, one can* ...] (JB:128); Upraszczając nieco sprawę można ... [*Simplifying the problem, one can* ...] (JB:164); W oparciu o ten skrótowy przegląd ... [*Basing on this brief survey* ...] (TZ:16); Mówiąc [...] skrótowo ... [*Briefly speaking* ...] (TZ:40); przedstawiony zostanie bardzo syntetyczny i skrótowy przegląd [*a very synthetic and brief survey will be presented*] (TZ:45); Nie wdając się w subtelności metodologiczne, można krótko stwierdzić, że ... [*Without going into methodological subtleties, one can briefly state that* ...] (JP:82); Omówiwszy pokrótce ... [*Having briefly discussed* ...] (TM:89); te pobieżne [...] spostrzeżenia [*these brief remarks*] (AF:167); Najogólniej rzecz

ujmując ... [*Broadly speaking* ...] (TZ:30); Intuicyjnie mówiąc ... [*Intuitively speaking* ...] (JP:106); kilka wstępnych słów na temat ... [*a couple of introductory words about* ...] (AF:24); nasze rozważania będą miały jedynie charakter wstępny [*our considerations will only be of introductory character*] (JB:157–158); coś, co bardzo nieprecyzyjnie można by nazwać ... [*something that very imprecisely could be called* ...] (AF:92); Zadaniem naszym nie będzie tu jednak szczegółowe przedstawienie budowy akustycznej ... [*Our task however will not be to present in detail the acoustic structure* ...] (JB:149); Nie wdając się jednak w szczegółową dyskusję postaramy się podać tylko pewne intuicyjne wskazówki [*Without going into a detailed discussion we will try to give only intuitive instructions*] (JB:311).

3.3.3.2. IMPERSONALIZE THE SPEAKER AND HEARER

A negative politeness strategy *Impersonalize S and H* is proposed by Brown and Levinson (1990:190) to consist in phrasing 'the FTA as if the agent were other than S, or at least possibly not S or not S alone, and the addressee were other than H, or only inclusive of H. This results in ... avoiding the pronouns "I" and "you"'. Therefore it is assumed that the following impersonalized structures may illustrate the use of the strategy in question:

można [*one can*] (AF:5; TZ:13; JP:77; JB:112; TM:5); trzeba [*it is necessary/one should*] (AF:6; JB:157; TM:11); należy [*it is necessary/ one should*] (AF:12; TZ:23; JP:77; JB:112; TM:83); okazywać się [*turn out to be*] (AF:20; TZ:40; JP:87).

3.3.3.3. BE PESSIMISTIC

Be pessimistic is also a negative politeness strategy and, as Brown and Levinson (1990:173) notice, it 'gives redress to H's negative face by explicitly expressing doubt that the conditions for the appropriateness of S's act obtain', which can be achieved by using the conditional mood. The following fragments seem to be the outcome of the application of this strategy:

Jednym z działów [...] byłoby literaturoznawstwo [*One of the sections could be theory of literature*] (AF:119); o jednej [...] dyscyplinie, która zajmowałby się badaniem języka [...], a która mogłaby się dzielić [...] na ... [*about one discipline that would deal with investigation of the language and could be divided into* ...] (AF:119); najprostszą odpowiedzią [...] byłoby stwierdzenie, że ... [*the easiest answer would be the statement that* ...] (TZ:12);

Znakiem byłaby zatem ... [*So a sign would be* ....] (TZ:34); Wymiar (v) mógłby zawierać takie cechy jak ... [*Dimension (v) could embrace such features as* ...] (JB:155); sylaby byłyby więc ... [*syllables would therefore be* ...] (JB:183); Jedną z konsekwencji byłaby możliwość ... [*One of the consequences would be a possibility of* ...] (JB:210).

3.4. *The effects of Brown and Levinson's strategies*

Finishing the analysis of politeness strategies in the selected textbooks one more remark is necessary. Following a particular strategy of doing an FTA is presented in this paper as a possible means of satisfying the teacher's needs that require interpersonal contacts but are different from the need to teach. Obviously, when the researcher limits himself only to the study of the output of participants in a given linkage, it is impossible to state exactly the character of the need which might have induced the participant to follow a particular strategy of doing an FTA. However, based on the observations made by Brown and Levinson (1990:71–72) it is possible to briefly characterize the way in which certain strategies of doing FTAs influence and shape the interpersonal relationships between the participants in a given linkage. Thanks to the bald-on-record strategy the speaker can, for example, 'get a credit for honesty', 'avoid the danger of being misunderstood', and simply be efficient in his communication (Brown and Levinson 1990:72). The application of positive politeness strategies stresses mutual friend-ship between the speaker and the addressee, and may result in a situation in which the addressee is liable to regard the speaker as a person 'of the same kind', or as a person who simply likes the addressee (Brown and Levinson 1990:72). Finally, the speaker using negative politeness strategies shows 'respect, deference to the addressee', and 'can maintain social distance, and avoid the threat ... of advancing familiarity towards the addressee' (Brown and Levinson 1990:72).

4. Conclusion

This paper shows that the influence of individually perceived human needs on the way people communicate with one another may be viewed from the perspective of human linguistics. Moreover, having reconstituted the ideas of Rittel (1997) and Brown and Levinson (1990) in terms of task hierarchies, it shows that carrying out studies

concerning the strategies of discourse construction and the phenomenon of politeness in human communication is also possible within
human linguistics.

Notes

1. All quotations taken from the sources written in Polish are translated by
   the author.
2. In the documentation of the passages illustrating the use of particular
   strategies the following abbreviations will be used:

   AF   *Językoznawstwo otwarte* by Antoni Furdal (1977)

   TM   *Językoznawstwo* by Tadeusz Milewski (1975)

   JB   the part of *Wstęp do językoznawstwa* written by Jerzy
        Bańczerowski (1982:110–333)

   JP   the part of *Wstęp do językoznawstwa* written by Jerzy
        Pogonowski (1982:76–109, 334–337)

   TZ   the part of *Wstęp do językoznawstwa* written by Tadeusz Zgółka
        (1982:11–76)
3. The analyzed textbooks in linguistics:
4. Bańczerowski, Jerzy, Pogonowski, Jerzy, and Zgółka, Tadeusz (1982),
   Wstęp do językoznawstwa. Poznań: Wydawnictwo Naukowe Uniwersytetu im. Adama Mickiewicza w Poznaniu.
5. Furdal, Antoni (1977), *Językoznawstwo otwarte*. Opole: Opolskie
   Towarzystwo Przyjaciół Nauk.
6. Milewski, Tadeusz [1965] (1975), *Językoznawstwo*. Warsaw: Państwowe Wydawnictwo Naukowe.

References

Brown, Penelope and Levinson, Stephen C. (1978), 'Universals in
   Language Use: Politeness Phenomena', in Esther Goody, *Questions and
   Politeness*. Cambridge: Cambridge University Press, pp. 256–311.
Brown, Penelope and Levinson, Stephen C. (1990), *Politeness: Some
   Universals in Language Use*. Cambridge: Cambridge University Press.
Engler, Barbara (1985), *Personality Theories: An Introduction*. Boston:
   Houghton Mifflin.
Gajewska, Grażyna (1997), *Problemy-dylematy wynikające z teorii potrzeb
   dla teorii i praktyki opieki nad dzieckiem*. Zielona Góra: Wydawnictwo
   Wyższej Szkoły Pedagogicznej.
Grice, Paul [1968] (1991), 'Logic and conversation', in Steven Davis,
   Pragmatics: a Reader. New York and Oxford: Oxford University Press,
   pp. 305–315.
Hilgard, Ernest [1953] (1972), *Wprowadzenie do psychologii*, translated from
   English by Józef Radzicki. Warsaw: Państwowe Wydawnictwo Naukowe.

Jankowski, Kazimierz [1975] (1976), *Od psychiatrii biologicznej do humanistycznej*. Warsaw: Państwowy Instytut Wydawniczy.

Labocha, Janina (1997), 'Dyskurs jako proces przekazywania wiedzy', in Teodozja Rittel and Jan Ożdżyński, *Dyskurs edukacyjny*. Krakow: Oficyna Wydawnicza 'Edukacja', pp. 31–37.

Maslow, Abraham (1959), 'Psychological data and value theory', in Abraham Maslow, *New Knowledge in Human Values*. New York: Harper & Row, pp. 119–136.

Maslow, Abraham [1954] (1964a), 'Teoria hierarchii potrzeb', translated from English by Stanisław Mika, in Janusz Reykowski, *Problemy osobowości i motywacji w psychologii amerykańskiej*. Warsaw: Państwowe Wydawnictwo Naukowe, pp. 135–164.

Maslow, Abraham (1964b), *Religions, Values, and Peak Experiences*. New York: Viking.

Maslow, Abraham (1970), *Motivation and Personality*. New York: Harper & Row.

Maslow, Abraham (1971), *The Farther Reaches of the Human Mind*. New York: Viking.

Murray, Henry, A. (1938), *Explorations in Personality*. New York: Oxford University Press.

Murray, Henry, A. (1951), 'Toward a classification of interactions', in Talcott Parsons and Edward A. Shils, *Toward a General Theory of Action*. Cambridge MA: Harvard University Press, pp. 434–464.

Obuchowski, Kazimierz [1965] (1967), *Psychologia dążeń ludzkich*. Warsaw: Państwowe Wydawnictwo Naukowe.

Obuchowski, Kazimierz (1977), 'Autonomia jednostki a osobowość', in Janusz Reykowski, Olga Owczynnikowa, and Kazimierz Obuchowski, *Studia z psychologii emocji, motywacji i osobowości*. Wroclaw: Zakład Narodowy imienia Ossolińskich, pp. 77–102.

Rittel, Stefan, J. (1997), 'Modelowanie dyskursu edukacyjnego', in Teodozja Rittel and Jan Ożdżyński, *Dyskurs edukacyjny*. Krakow: Oficyna Wydawnicza 'Edukacja', pp. 53–62.

Yngve, Victor, H. (1986), *Linguistics as a Science*. Bloomington and Indianapolis: Indiana University Press.

Yngve, Victor, H. (1996), *From Grammar to Science: New Foundations for General Linguistics*. Amsterdam/Philadelphia: John Benjamins.

PART VI

PRACTICAL APPLICATIONS

Chapter 18

The Question of Translation

Martina Ožbot

1. The relevance of translation to human linguistics

For hard-science linguistics, the central research question can be formulated as 'How do people communicate?' (Yngve 1996:113, 307). Though apparently simple and straightforward, it is in reality extremely broad and complex, and cannot even tentatively be answered before substantial research on various aspects of human communication is undertaken and reliable results are achieved. An important subquestion which should eventually provide a partial answer to the main one is 'How do people communicate cross-culturally?' An obvious answer would be 'By means of translation', which is true. But in order to see what this in fact means, it is first necessary to understand what translation actually is, what elements it involves, and how they are interconnected.

Within human linguistics, the question of translation is indeed an important one for a number of reasons: first, it is a fact that in the rapidly shrinking and, at least from the communicative point of view, ever-more globalized world in which we live the role played by translation is becoming increasingly significant, and it would be difficult to over-emphasize its instrumentality in promoting exchange of ideas, acquisition of knowledge and experience, and cooperation between single individuals and between groups of individuals. It is, of course, on translation that the political, economic, cultural, and scientific collaboration at the international level depends. The intensity of translational activity is nowadays extremely high and, correspondingly, the amount of communication made possible by means of translation is enormous. The importance attributed to translation in today's world is also reflected in academia: there already exist numerous translator and interpreter training schools and university departments, and new ones are continually being founded; in these and in other institutions of learning and research a lot of work is currently being carried out on various theoretical, descriptive and applied[1] aspects of translation. Second, considerations of translation call our attention to and highlight issues of linguistic theory that we might not see equally clearly when studied from the point of view of only one language; for example, questions concerning the use of metaphor in communication, issues of style, problems related to the relationship between the individual's extralinguistic knowledge, and his/her ability to participate successfully in a given communicative event may all be solved more thoroughly if examined also from a translational perspective. Third, the very concept of translation is of special importance in the endeavor to reconstitute linguistics on a standard-science basis. In actual fact, such a reconstitution involves an act of translation, certainly not between different natural languages, but in the sense of switching from the old concepts and terms common in the linguistics of language and reflecting the bias of the grammatical tradition to new ones designed, as much as possible at the current stage of research, to serve as appropriate instruments in discussing issues concerning the reality of human communication. It is not only new terminology that is being created through translation of part of the traditional repertoire, it is also a new conceptual and theoretical structure that is being built as valid insights of the traditional discipline are being translated into the new framework. In other words, in reconstituting linguistics as a hard science both a new target culture (in the form of a new theoretical framework) is being created and a new target language (in the form of a new terminology) is being invented on the basis of a source culture and a source language respectively.

In view of these considerations, this paper represents an attempt to deal with translation as cross-cultural communication from the perspective of hard-science linguistics, trying to reformulate the question of translation by means of 'translating' the traditional discourse into the framework of the new science.

2. Translating: basic characteristics

2.1. Functional considerations

As stated by functional translation theory – developed mainly by

German translation scholars, among whom most notably by Hans J. Vermeer and Katharina Reiß, the authors of the so-called *skopos theory*[2] (German *Skopostheorie*, from the Greek lexeme σκοπος meaning 'target', 'goal'), which has exerted a seminal influence upon a number of individual approaches to the study of various aspects of the phenomenon of translation – the objective of the translating process is to produce a communicatively appropriate text in language B on the basis of a given text in language A. In view of the fact that the concept of 'text' is relatively obscure and hard to define in a scientifically rigorous and empirically reliable manner, let us limit the term as much as possible for the time being and call these two entities the *translatum*[3] and the *original* respectively.[4] The most important general criterion, at least in a prototypical case, on which the translator's decisions in producing the translatum are based is its prospective function, i.e. the purpose it is intended to serve in the target culture, in which it will probably be used by an audience that differs, at least in principle, from the source readership in terms of its typical cultural horizons.

Also in cases when the functions of the original and the translatum are supposed to be identical, rather substantial modifications of the translatum with respect to the original may be necessary if the former is to serve successfully as the basis upon which communication can take place. In view of such modifications, the translating process differs enormously from linear reproduction of the units of the original such as phrases, clauses, or even sentences by means of the target-language material (Snell-Hornby 1996:20ff.). For example, when a text which serves as a business letter in the source culture is expected to preserve the same function in the target culture – in which it could, alternatively, have the purpose of, for instance, 'merely' giving the target readers an idea of how a business letter is typically structured in the source culture – the translatum must, in principle, be written according to the conventions characteristic of target-culture business letters, which can often only be achieved if appropriate modifications in the information structure are made (i.e. rearrangement of information, omission of some and/or introduction of other pieces of information). In a similar way, a magazine article referring to one and the same event or problem concerning a given country or culture is likely to be written according to different textual traditions and will probably offer somewhat different kinds and pieces of information when it is written for a domestic audience and when it is translated with the aim of enabling readers of a different culture to learn of the same extralinguistic reality. If the translator does not pay due attention to the characteristics of the target situation relevant to the production of the translatum, communicative behavior can meet obstacles and, if these are severe enough, it will even fail to take place.

Different presentations of the same reality in translata with respect to their originals are often related to the well-known fact that natural languages vary not only with respect to the patterns in which they arrange the linguistic material in different textual genres but also with respect to the rather different ways in which they structure the extralinguistic reality. Semantic networks – i.e. representations of ways in which extralinguistic reality is organized by linguistic means – are always language-specific and our knowledge of them remains to a considerable extent intuitive, so that at this stage their actual functioning does not appear completely predictable (although it is realistic to assume that further research into the reality of human communication will enable us to arrive at a deeper understanding of the functioning of language-specific semantic networks and of the mechanisms of their activation in concrete communicative situations). What the translatum will actually look like always heavily depends on concrete linguistic elements available in the natural language in which the translatum will be written, and it is, in its turn, the reality to be represented in a concrete communicative situation that plays a fundamental role in determining which of those elements will be activated and which will remain latent. From the point of view of Charles Fillmore's scenes-and-frames semantics, which over the past two decades has been successfully applied to the study of translation from a functional perspective (Vannerem and Snell-Hornby 1986; Snell-Hornby 1986b; Vermeer and Witte 1990; Kußmaul 1994), a frame (i.e. a linguistic unit) of language A may in different contexts correspond to different frames of language B, if the scenes (i.e. extralinguistic representations) triggered by the frame of the original and by the frame of the translatum are to be functionally comparable. This point can be illustrated with the following example taken from the opening scene of Shakespeare's *Romeo and Juliet* in the original and in two translations, one into Italian and one into Slovene:

- Sampson: Gregory, on my word, we'll not carry coals.
  Gregory: No, for then we should be colliers.
  Sampson: I mean, an we be in choler, we'll draw.
  Gregory: Ay, while you live, draw your neck out o' the collar.
  Sampson: I strike quickly, being moved.

Gregory: But thou art not quickly moved to strike.
Sampson: A dog of the house of Montague moves me.
Gregory: To move is to stir, and to be valiant is to stand; therefore, if thou art moved, thou runnest away.
Sampson: A dog of that house shall move me to stand: I will take the wall of any man or maid of Montague's.

- Sansone: Sulla mia parola, Gregorio, non manderemo insulti giù nella strozza.
  Gregorio: Certo, perché saremmo degli strozzini.
  Sansone: Volevo dire che se la collera aumenta tireremo fuori la spada.
  Gregorio: Credo che finché sarai vivo, tirerai fuori il collo dal collare.
  Sansone: Io faccio presto a muovere le mani, quando mi eccito.
  Gregorio: Già, ma non ti ecciti facilmente per muovere le mani.
  Sansone: Basta un cane di casa Montecchi per farmi eccitare.
  Gregorio: Ma eccitarsi significa muoversi, mentre chi ha coraggio resta fermo; se ti muovi troppo finirai per scappare.
  Sansone: Dico che un cane di quella casa mi ecciterà a star fermo. Avrò il lato del muro da qualunque servo, ed anche serva, di casa Montecchi che incontrerò.

- Samson: Gregor, ti povem – žaljivih svinjarij ne bova prenšala.
  Gregor: Seveda ne, saj nisva prenšalca svinjarij.
  Samson: Hočem reči, kar potegnila bova, če nanese.
  Gregor: Potegnila in jo stegnila, brž ko bova utegnila.
  Samson: Hitro mahnem, če me zdraži.
  Gregor: Ampak te zlepa ne zdraži.
  Samson: Zdraži me pes iz Montegove hiše.
  Gregor: Kdor je zdražen, bo poražen; kogar je kaj v hlačah, stoji pri miru.
  Samson: Njihov pes me zdraži, da prav trdo stojim pri miru. Tako da mi bo za vsakega Montegovega, naj bo hlapec ali dekla, zid prav prišel.

To understand the passage it is necessary to grasp the unique interplay between what is stated directly, i.e. at the level of denotation, and what is only implied, i.e. expressed at the level of connotation. The interaction between the two levels hinges principally upon the allusiveness of language-specific wordplay by means of which the author exploits the associative and figurative potential of English to present a particular extralinguistic reality. The words and phrases upon which the wordplay is based, at least to an important extent, are *carry coals, colliers, choler, collar*, all of which are similar from the phonetic point of view, but differ in the semantic potential they have. Apart from these four elements the wordplay is developed further by the use of verbs referring to some kind of real or figurative movement (*to strike, to move, to stir, to run*) or to the absence of it (*to stand*), which are here related to Gregory's and Sampson's planned confrontation with the Montagues' servants who have allegedly insulted them. All these elements are juxtaposed in such a way as to generate wordplay in the given context.

In order to reproduce the interplay between denotation and connotation in the Italian and the Slovene versions quoted above, the two translators could not use lexemes which would be denotatively similar to the original ones; therefore they have had recourse to words and phrases which have different denotations but which are, in the two target contexts at least, connotatively close to the English lexemes. On the basis of the two translata, which necessarily present frames that are different from those of the English text, it is possible to reconstruct a scene which corresponds to the original one: the rivalry between the Montague and the Capulet families, around which the whole play revolves, is announced and the facetious attitude of the two servants toward it is suggested.

In the Italian and the Slovene versions, the wordplay is similar to the original one in that in both cases it is partly based on motion verbs. As to the function of phonetic similarities between different items, it plays an important role especially in the Italian version where two sets of phonetically close elements can be identified (*strozza* 'throat', *strozzini* 'loan sharks, usurers'; *collera* 'anger', *collo* 'neck', *collare* 'collar'); except for *collera*, they also present semantic affinities, since they refer, either directly or indirectly, to the throat or the neck. In the Slovene version, on the other hand, such phonetic similarities have a less significant role in the wordplay, which is, however, in some sense compensated for by a particular importance given to the rhyme (*potegnila*, from *potegniti* 'to draw', *stegnila* from *stegniti* 'to stretch', *utegnila* from *utegniti* 'to manage'; *zdražen* 'irritated', *poražen* 'defeated') as a parallel means of generating wordplay.

It is evident from the example discussed that translating cannot be equated with mere mechanical conversion of source linguistic material into a different linguistic code. Every act of translating in actual fact involves decision-making and choosing between different options. The choices of the translator are, in principle, made on the basis of the reality of the existing source text and with a view to the envisaged target situation. The fundamental question for him/her is how to create a translatum which will be capable of serving the intended target function. In order to solve it successfully, he/she has to possess thorough knowledge of the elements of the linkage[5] within which the translating process takes place and in which he/she as an active participant takes part; among these elements are the other participants, in particular the imagined target audience, as well as the commissioner and possibly someone else like the publisher; the channels, i.e. the original and the translatum *in statu nascendi*; and the props like dictionaries, computers, etc.

Let us at this point examine the characteristics of the translating process from a closer perspective.

2.2. *Translating as a complex task*

Translating can be considered a top-level task performed by a person whose purpose is to mediate between members of linguistically heterogeneous cultures and thus make communication between them possible. Such mediation can have a written or an oral form. In the first case it can be referred to as *translating proper*, whereas in the second it could conventionally be named *interpreting*. It is important to keep the two types of intercultural communication separate, since they differ in important respects, like, for example, the frequent possibility of direct feedback from the addressee in interpreting, which enables the mediator to keep the process of communication under control, whereas in translating backchannelling is not available to the participants in a linkage (Yngve 1996:298–300). The present paper deals exclusively with translating and does not take into account interpreting, which would require separate treatment.

Translating as a complex task consists of various subordinate tasks. Typically, these would include the translator's choice of the text to be translated (or his/her being assigned such a text if the choice is made by the commissioner of the translation, as, for instance, the publisher), the analysis of possible target linkages in which the translatum is expected to serve as a prop or channel and, in particular, the establishment of its prospective function as a prop part or channel part; next, the analysis of the original based upon target linkage considerations; and, finally, the production of draft versions, each of them followed by correction, sometimes carried out on the basis of the translator's own efforts and sometimes after the commissioner and/or some other readers have gone through the draft and commented on it. Concrete realizations of the translating process may vary to an extent with respect to the standard model. For example, an important subordinate task, often observable at various stages of the process of translating, is represented by the translator's consultation of various reference works (e.g. mono- and bilingual dictionaries, encyclopedias, etc.) and other material (for instance, the so-called 'parallel texts',[6] i.e. texts dealing with the same reality and/ or intended to be used for similar purposes as the prospective translatum), which function as instruments that help him/her solve problems encountered in the translating process.

Regardless of what particular subordinate tasks the process of translating consists of and regardless of the order in which they follow each other, it eventually results in the *translatum*, a concrete piece of writing, which, having the potential for functioning as the channel, is supposed to be used by the recipients as a basis upon which a given communication process can take place.[7] What is important is that on the basis of the translatum properties of the extralinguistic reality which must be available to the target recipients if communication is to take place can be reconstructed in accordance with the intended function of the translatum.

Such reconstruction is, necessarily, mediated, for it is only through the translator's interpretation of the original that the translatum can be understood by the target recipients. In principle, every translatum is essentially characterized by the way in which the translator understands the original or by the way in which he/she wants the target audience to understand it. If the target audience is unable to make sense out of a given translatum[8] – for example, because of their insufficient knowledge of the reality to be recovered from it or because of the translatum's inherent deficiencies concerning the presentation of information, or because of both – communication cannot take place. In this respect, communication by means of translata obeys the same rules applicable to communication in general: it is bound to fail if certain properties of the system in which communication takes place cannot be accessed by the participants because they are not present in their domains of control (Yngve 1996:276–277, 294–297).

In some cases such communication failures can be predicted and, possibly, avoided. This is proved, for example, by those translators who appear to be aware of the specific expectations, knowledge, and needs the target readers may have in a given instance of communication, as far as such expectations, knowledge, and needs can be known in advance and *in abstracto*. As can be observed in the passage from Shakespeare presented above, both the Italian and the Slovene translators appear to have taken into consideration the specificities of the target situations in order to give their translata the potential for functioning successfully in the target culture. It has indeed been a central concern of good translators in general to enable the target readers to make sense out of a given translatum in spite of the language- and culture-specific horizons of their knowledge. In order to see on what grounds the decisions of such translators are based, it is necessary to understand the basic principle underlying their activity as intercultural mediators.

2.3. The role of the translator in the translating process

The translator's role in the process of translating is in actual fact quite extraordinary when compared to the role of the other participants in the same process and also when compared to the role different participants have in other kinds of communication processes, for instance, in a casual chat between a group of friends over a cup of coffee, a telephone conversation between a bookshop assistant and a student who makes an inquiry about a book she has ordered ten days ago, or a television address made by a country's president to the citizens, etc. It is difficult to imagine a communication process the success of which would depend to such a crucial extent on one single participant as is the case with the translating process. The reason is that the translating process is a mediated one and that the participants who are in reality supposed to communicate with one another cannot do so in a direct manner. Being usually the only participant to have access both to the source language and culture and to the target language and culture, the translator is in actual fact the one who knows better and is in a position to master the process of communication in which he/she is involved. As a bilingual and bicultural communicator, he/she is not only endowed with power, but is also entrusted with exceptional responsibility. In order to be successful in his/her role as a professional intercultural mediator, the translator has to possess different types of expertise, among which the most important are knowledge of the source and target languages, knowledge of the source and target cultures, knowledge of the reality presented in the original, knowledge of the source-culture and target-culture communication models – which are related to the traditional concepts of text types and text genres – projections concerning target readers, knowledge of the mechanisms of the translating process itself and the ability to deepen his/her insight into it through self-reflection, etc.[9]

Since the basic problem he/she has to face is how to construct the translatum in such a way that it will be functional in the target culture – i.e. that it will serve as a suitable basis upon which the process of communication could take place – it is particularly important that he/she is able to assess the degree of familiarity with the textual world which can be expected from the target audience. In other words, it is up to the translator to try to make sure that commonality of conditional and situational properties, which is indispensable in any process of communication, is established (Yngve 1996:294–296; Ožbot 1999:68). However, given the nature of the translating process, the establishment of commonality of conditional and situational properties may not always be easy to achieve. The principal reasons for this can be summarized as follows:

(1) Translation is by definition cross-cultural communication and, as has already been pointed out, it is *differences between the source and the target cultures* which have to be overcome to a sufficient degree if the translating process is to come off successfully.

(2) Translation is *written communication*. In the majority of cases, this prevents the translator from being able to check whether the communication is actually being successful, i.e. whether his/her translatum is actually being understood by the recipients (Yngve 1996:228–230, 302).

(3) Following from the characteristics of translation as written communication is also the fact that in a large number of cases, the translating process represents an instance of what L. Bloomfield would refer to as '*displaced speech*', i.e. talking about what 'is not immediately present' (Yngve 1996:296–297) in the environment in which the process of communication is taking place. This is true of virtually all literary works (including the play from which the above passage is taken), apart from theatrical pieces or parts of them when they are in actual fact performed and when the reality dealt with in them is physically present on the stage. A great deal of nonliterary texts are also instances of 'displaced speech', with the exception of, for example, instructions which accompany various apparatuses and similar objects when they are bought and which are typically read in settings which also include these apparatuses and objects.

In view of these properties, the translating process often appears to be a rather delicate and precarious enterprise endangered by obstacles of various kinds. It depends in large measure on the translator whether these obstacles are likely to be overcome by a

harmonious interaction between the slice of source culture epito-
mized in the translatum and the target audience.

3. Conclusion

As could be gathered from our discussion, a fundamental property of
the translating process is the fact that it involves *switching between two
different environments*, i.e. the source culture and the target culture.
In a typical instance of the translating process, one could say that the
original and the translatum refer to some common extralinguistic
reality, again, as far as one can speak of the sameness of a reality if it is
perceived by different observers and from different perspectives.

In a similar way, human linguistics attempts to translate concepts
proper to the grammatical tradition into the language of a new
epistemology which therefore reflects a new angle from which the
reality of human communication can be observed. If such a paradigm
shift enables us to get a more 'realistic' insight into that reality, then
the journey that is about to start should certainly prove worthwhile.

Notes

1. For a distinction between the three types of translation-related research
   see Holmes (1988:67–80) and Toury (1995:9–10).
2. For an overview of the basic tenets of the skopos theory written in
   English see Vermeer (1996); a thorough presentation is offered in Reiß
   and Vermeer (1984).
3. I use the term translatum, in as consistent a manner as possible, when I
   have in mind the final material product of the translating process; in the
   linguistics of language this product is usually referred to as a
   translation. 'Translation' in this paper is used as a cover term
   designating the whole variety of activities related to the translating
   process. There is also the term 'target text', largely employed in
   contemporary translation studies, which is problematic inasmuch as it
   perpetuates the old logical-domain bias (Yngve 1996:107–109).
4. As to the problem of the terminology of 'pre-scientific' linguistics see
   Yngve (1996:107–109).
5. 'Linkage' as well as other terms such as 'communicating individual',
   'participant', 'channel', etc. are used in the sense given to them in
   Victor H. Yngve's theory of human communication put forward in
   various papers and articles and fully developed in Yngve (1996). A
   concise overview of the theory is offered in Yngve (2000).
6. The concept of a 'parallel text' has proved very useful in translation
   studies and has been given separate treatment by some authors. See,
   among others, Kvam (1992).

7. The same basic principle holds not only in the case of translation between different languages (interlingual translation), but also when a given text is translated within one and the same language (intralingual translation), and when translation takes place between different sign systems, e.g. verbal and figurative (intersemiotic translation). See Jakobson (1959) for the distinction between the three types of translation.

8. In terms of the logical-domain linguistics, this should read as 'if the translation appears to lack textual coherence ...'.

9. From the viewpoint of functional translation theory, problems concerning the translator's competences, his/her role in the translating process, as well as the status of his/her profession in society have been dealt with by various scholars, most thoroughly perhaps by Hans G. Hönig and Paul Kußmaul, two experts based at Mainz University, Germany. See Hönig (1986, 1990, 1995), Kußmaul (1991, 1995), and Hönig and Kußmaul (1982). See also Ožbot (1997).

References

I

Shakespeare, William (1987 [1947]), *Romeo and Juliet*, ed. Ralph E. C. Houghton. Oxford: Oxford University Press, p. 27.

Shakespeare, William (1982), *Romeo e Giulietta*, tr. Salvatore Quasimodo. Milan: Arnoldo Mondadori, pp. 7–9.

Shakespeare, William (1991), *Romeo in Julija*, tr. Milan Jesih. Ljubljana: Mladinska knjiga, pp. 12–13.

II

Holmes, James S. (1988), *Translated! Papers on Literary Translation and Translation Studies*. Amsterdam: Rodopi.

Hönig, Hans G. (1986), 'Übersetzen zwischen Reflex und Reflexion – ein Modell der übersetzungsrelevanten Textanalyse', in M. Snell-Hornby (ed.), pp. 230–251.

Hönig, Hans G. (1990), 'Sagen, was man nicht weiß – wissen, was man nicht sagt. Überlegungen zur übersetzerischen Intuition', in Reiner Arntz and Gisela Thome (eds), *Übersetzungswissenschaft. Ergebnisse und Perspektiven. Festschrift für Wolfram Wilss zum 65. Geburtstag*. Tübingen: Narr. pp. 152–161.

Hönig, Hans G. (1995), *Konstruktives Übersetzen*. Tübingen: Stauffenburg.

Hönig, Hans G. and Kußmaul, Paul (1982), *Strategie der Übersetzung. Ein Lehr- und Arbeitsbuch*. Tübingen: Narr.

Jakobson, Roman (1959), 'On linguistic aspects of translation', in Reuben A. Brower (ed.), *On Translation*. Cambridge, MA: Harvard University Press, pp. 232–239.

Kußmaul, Paul (1991), 'Creativity in translation processes: Empirical approaches', in Kitty M. van Leuven-Zwart and Ton Naaijkens, *Translation Studies: the State of the Art. Proceedings of the First James S. Holmes Symposium on Translation Studies.* Amsterdam/Atlanta: Rodopi, pp. 91–101.

Kußmaul, Paul (1994), 'Semantic models and translating'. *Target* 6 (1), 1–13.

Kußmaul, Paul (1995), *Training the Translator.* Amsterdam/Philadelphia: John Benjamins.

Kvam, Sigmund (1992), 'Zur Rolle von Paralleltexten bei der Translation – Am Beispiel deutsch-norwegischer Übersetzungsfälle'. *TEXTconTEXT* 7, 193–217.

Ožbot, Martina (1997), *Ustreznost sporočila v slovenskem prevodu 'Zgodovine italijanske književnosti' A. Momigliana. (Magistrska naloga.)* Ljubljana: Univerza v Ljubljani, Filozofska fakulteta, Oddelek za romanske jezike in književnosti.

Ožbot, Martina (1999), *Prevajalske strategije in vprašanje koherence ob slovenskem prevodu Machiavellijevih 'zgodovinskopolitičnih spisov'. (Doktorska disertacija.)* Ljubljana: Univerza v Ljubljani, Filozofska fakulteta, Oddelek za romanske jezike in književnosti.

Reiß, Katharina and Vermeer, Hans J. (1984), *Grundlegung einer allgemeinen Translationstheorie.* Tübingen: Niemeyer.

Snell-Hornby, Mary (ed.) (1986a), *Übersetzungswissenschaft – eine Neuorientierung.* Tübingen: Francke.

Snell-Hornby, Mary (1986b), 'Übersetzen, Sprache, Kultur', in M. Snell-Hornby (1986a), pp. 9–29.

Snell-Hornby, Mary (1996), *Translation und Text.* Vienna: WUV-Universitätsverlag.

Toury, Gideon (1995), *Descriptive Translation Studies and Beyond.* Amsterdam/Philadelphia: John Benjamins.

Vannerem, Mia and Snell-Hornby, Mary (1986), 'Die Szene hinter dem Text: "scenes-and-frames semantics" in der Übersetzung', in M. Snell-Hornby (1986a), pp. 184–205.

Vermeer, Hans J. (1996), *A skopos theory of translation.* Heidelberg: TEXTconTEXT-Verlag.

Vermeer, Hans J. and Witte, Heidrun H. (1990), *Mögen Sie Zistrosen? Scenes & frames & channels im translatorischen Handeln.* Heidelberg: Julius Groos.

Yngve, Victor H. (1996), *From Grammar to Science: New Foundations for General Linguistics.* Amsterdam/Philadelphia: John Benjamins.

Yngve, Victor H. (2000), 'The depth hypothesis and the new hard-science linguistics', in Irena Kovačič *et al.* (eds), *Linguistics and Language Studies: Exploring Language from Different Perspectives.* Ljubljana: Filozofska fakulteta Univerze v Ljubljani, pp. 191–202.

Chapter 19

Communicating Scientific Experiments in Journal Articles

W. John Hutchins

1. Introduction

It has been common practice to describe texts and their structures independently of authors and readers, as if they have 'meaning' in themselves. In such a perspective it would seem legitimate to describe the communicative function of texts as something existing without communicating individuals. The practice has been common among linguists investigating discourse to describe the interpretation of texts as a process with universal validity, as a process that all readers do, with greater or less success.

In human linguistics, however, the focus is on people and their structure, not on texts and their presumed structure. The question then arises as to how to reconstitute in human linguistics the valid linguistic insights already won but expressed in terms of a linguistics focused on text. We will investigate here what scientists do linguistically during the conduct and reporting of their scientific research.

2. Basic features of the scientific article

The motivation for conducting a scientific investigation or experiment is frequently the desire of a scientist to resolve a problem or anomaly in what is currently known about a particular set of facts, or in what is commonly regarded as an explanation or hypothesis for particular phenomena, events, effects, or processes. In order to resolve the problem or anomaly, the scientist will typically formulate a new hypothesis about the 'state of affairs' and will undertake tests of the hypothesis. These tests will provide evidence for or against the hypothesis, which may consequently alter the perception or understanding of the phenomenon in question.

Typically, scientific explorations are concerned (a) with the investigation of a particular problematic area and proposals for resolving difficulties, (b) with the examination of alternative hypotheses regarding some problem of interpretation, or (c) with the development of methods for experimentation. There are thus three different types of scientific article: (a) Problem-Solution, (b) Hypothesis-Testing, and (c) Methodological. In each type there is typically an introductory section describing the current 'state of affairs', the area of problem or deficiency which is the 'topic' of the article, and then statements about what is to be tested (practically or theoretically).

In the Problem-Solution paper (a), the author will describe the current situation and the problem he[1] is tackling, and then the methods he will use. In the Hypothesis-Testing paper (b), the author will state the 'problematic' area and describe the various proposals that have been suggested, and then examine each for their advantages and disadvantages. In the Methodological paper (c), the author will state the deficiencies of current methods and propose a 'new' method, which he will then demonstrate by tests as an improvement (or substitution) for other methods.

There will follow in each type of article a section of tests, results, and evaluations (or judgments), and a statement of the solution, hypothesis, or method the results indicate (although this section may be implied only). Finally, there will usually (but not invariably) be the author's observations about what his findings may mean for other areas of the science (often labeled as 'Implications'), and what further investigations might be undertaken ('Further Work'). Schematically, the typical Problem-Solution type – the type discussed in this paper – has the following overall structure:

Situation: description of common knowledge about field X; statement of current hypothesis
Problem: anomaly in some area of X; drawbacks of current hypothesis
Hypothesis(es): statement of proposed solutions, new hypotheses
Tests (Basis for evaluations): experiments/testing of hypotheses
Evaluation: results of tests/experiments; proof of new hypothesis
Solution: adoption of one hypothesis
Implications: what the 'solution' may mean for other areas of X
Further Work: how the 'solution' could be developed in the future

In practice, authors provide scientific articles with more simple section headings. We find typically an 'Introduction', embracing the first three sections ('Situation', 'Problem', 'Hypothesis') and including a statement of the overall 'topic' of the paper; it will be followed by 'Experiments and Results', covering the three sections 'Tests', 'Evaluation', 'Solution', and a final 'Conclusions' (with sections of 'Implications' and 'Further Work').

3. The scientist as author

In the Situation section, the author triggers in the reader (or brings to the foreground of his attention) a particular 'domain of reference' (area of knowledge). This is achieved by referring to phenomena (real or mental) by means of anaphoric and deictic expressions, i.e. to things presupposed by the author to be already known by the reader. Referring can also be indirect by citing previous publications – which may or may not be known to the reader, but which he can consult. The domain is described or alluded to by referring to particular relevant parts of the domain – those parts sufficient to trigger the whole of the reader's area of knowledge. As Yngve describes it, mention of a train brings into the field of interest also known features of 'trains' such as engines, wheels, drivers (engineers), etc. The effect of this section is therefore to change the reader's initial state (precontext) where there is no focus on the subject area to a state (postcontext) where the reader is attending to a particular domain of reference.

In the Problem section, the author alerts the reader to anomalies or problems in this domain ('state of affairs'). The problem may be one already familiar to the reader or it may be 'new' in some sense – perhaps not completely new, in that the reader may have had a feeling of unease, disquiet, or dissatisfaction about some aspect, but could not formulate where. The author's description of the 'problem' may itself refer to other aspects of the domain which the author assumes the reader has some previous knowledge of, but primarily the intention is to inform the reader that a problem exists that requires solution. In the reader there is thus set up an expectation that the author will offer some solution.

In the Hypothesis section, the author suggests one or more ways in which the problem may be solved. These may include 'solutions' already familiar to the reader, or which he may infer from what he knows already, or which the author may demonstrate can be derived (logically) from what is already known. Some 'solutions' may, on the other hand, be completely new to the reader, and the author will be aware that he has to do some persuasion. The most effective means of persuasion are to describe some experiments or tests.

In the Tests section, the author brings to the foreground other areas of knowledge, namely those concerning methods of testing, evaluating, proving the truth or falsity of a particular event (or rather the author's explanation for the phenomenon). Again the type of test proposed may be already known to the reader, at least in essence, and the author may perhaps assume familiarity with tests employed in other (previously undertaken) experiments. Tests can be of many kinds, not just physical experiments but also mental arguments (*Gedankenexperimente*). Referring to such already known (or presumed known) tests may also be explicit by citing previous publications or by quoting from them.

In the Evaluation section, the author provides his opinion on the success or failure of the tests undertaken. The background for such assessments will be generally assumed to be part of the knowledge of any reader concerning the conduct of research in the particular area of science. Evaluations may range from simple assertions that the tests were successful (e.g. that they showed the results and values expected) to more extensive discussions pointing to further tests (which may be described), and perhaps referring to previous experiments by the author or other scientists (by citation.)

In the Solutions section the author informs the reader of the solution, based on evaluations of the tests. Its effectiveness (persuasiveness) depends on the reader's satisfaction with the author's evidence and argument. Here, the author will refer back to preceding parts of the text (which can now be assumed to be known), and only rarely to external domains not previously mentioned. (If there are such references then this may represent a weakness in the author's presentation.)

In the Implications section, the author will probably again refer to the initial domain of reference (the Situation), since his aim is probably to point out what other parts of this domain could be affected by his solution. He may refer to other problematic areas (known or unknown to the reader) which could also be solved by the proposal he has made. Alternatively, he may point out that his solution produces further (new) anomalies in the 'state of affairs', which in turn demand resolution.

Finally in a Further Work section (which is not always present, or it may occur instead of an Implications section), the author will suggest how the proposed Solution may be improved or how it may be applied in other areas of the subject field. Again, the author will refer implicitly or explicitly to the Situation and to other of its problematic aspects, some of which may not have been known to the reader before reading the article.

For each of the sections (paragraphs) there are overt linguistic signals for the functions and relationships of segments within the total text. These signals should be regarded within a human linguistics as arousing conditions or triggering procedures that cause appropriate changes in the reader's plex.

The signals have long been studied by discourse analysts, and their findings are of obvious relevance, but they need to be placed in the context of human linguistics. While discourse analysts would interpret linguistic elements (lexical items, anaphors, etc.) as signs of particular textual relationships or functions, in the present context we would understand them as triggering particular conditions and networks (plexes) for the knowledge and awareness of individual writers and readers. In this framework, texts are interpreted not as entities in themselves, i.e. as objects that 'contain' messages, but as epiphenomena of authors communicating to readers.

4. Text understanding: scientist as reader

In order to interpret a text the reader must bring with him (i.e. have already present in his plex of properties) the same or a similar realm of common knowledge about the state of affairs as the author presupposes his readers will have when they start to read his text. He must also, of course, know the same language. What this means in human linguistics terms is the subject of intensive research. And he must have familiarity with the ways in which knowledge and information is spoken and written about by others, i.e. an ability to recognize general patterns (such as those outlined in sections 2 and 3).

A crucial contact-point for the reader of a scientific article is the introductory section (or paragraph) – the 'base section' – where the author reviews the research (the current state of knowledge), points out lacuna, inconsistencies, and anomalies, and then states as clearly as possible what he has discovered or concluded from the work being reported. In this section (typically labeled 'Introduction'), it is quite common for the author to state explicitly what he considers to be its 'topic' as a whole, what he contends it to be 'about'.

Successful understanding of a scientific text presupposes also that the reader knows the scientific field. He must know (have learned or experienced) most, if not all, of those aspects, features, objects, concepts, events, etc. that the author writes about as presupposed elements (i.e. the elements of the initial sections where the author invokes background knowledge). He ought also to know as much as possible about any other items of special knowledge that the author assumes his readers will already know. Of course, not all readers will have all this knowledge – indeed, perhaps very few, particularly in the leading edges of science – and many readers may have to refer to other scientific articles (some by the same author) on the same subject in order to learn more and understand more. This is one of the reasons why authors refer to the writings of others. On the other hand, there may well be some readers for whom not only will the author's presupposed knowledge be fully familiar but even some (or much) of what the author believes or assumes to be new. This may be because the experiment and the ideas are not as original as he may have supposed. More likely, however, it will be new information because he is writing not for the experts who know most of it already, but for others who do not. In any case, even for the experts there may be something that is new; in particular, some of the results and some of the conclusions. Since it is obvious that readers of a scientific article come from many different backgrounds and many different levels and spheres of knowledge, the relevance of a particular article to their own information needs will be highly variable.

In this respect, the reader will clearly make his own judgment of what the text is 'about'. It will quite possibly differ in some (perhaps many) respects from what the author states its 'topic' to be. The reader may well identify various elements of the text as 'topics'; they are likely to include subjects of particular interest to the reader at the time when he is reading it, e.g. in the case of a scientific article, it might be a particular method of chemical analysis – for such a reader the article may be mainly 'about' this method. It follows also that 'topics' can change over time; what may interest the reader on one occasion may be of no interest to him on a later occasion. And vice versa, what may have seemed irrelevant (or not understood, and therefore not given topic status) when first read may later become of greater interest on later reading. The individual reader's state of knowledge (his plex of conditional properties) change over time – from experience, from learning, and from reading.

In general, we may say that from the perspective of human linguistics, the reader's task combines an attempt to 'reconstruct' the associative knowledge network that the writer has constituted and an attempt to integrate this network (or part of it) into his own associative knowledge network. The nature of this network is of course unknown. It may or may not be similar to the kinds of networks conceived by linguists and researchers in artificial intelligence, i.e. 'semantic networks' of hierarchical (hyponymic, etc.) relationships among the senses (meanings) of lexical items, where 'meanings' are defined in terms of 'primitive' ('atomic') sense elements and logical relations. It may also be that 'reconstruction' of networks operates by processes activated by various strategies at different levels: linguistic, cognitive, emotional, inferential, etc. (as described by Van Dijk and Kintsch 1983.)

The difference will be, of course, that the networks are conceived not as interconnected atoms of meaning in the logical domain but as interconnected nodes of plex structures of people, dispositions, intentions, and conditions with the potentialities of producing texts and of understanding texts.

5. Tasks and subtasks

Within the human linguistics framework we may describe the activities of authors and readers as sets of tasks and subtasks, sequential, parallel, and overlapping. We may also describe the particular activities of the scientist-author as a specific set of tasks and subtasks within his general activity as a scientist, as a researcher, as a human being, etc.

The primary task of the scientist-author is to communicate the outcomes of his investigations (mental and physical) to his fellow scientists or to the general public. As we have described above, there are different types of scientific papers depending on the nature of the investigation or the way in which the author chooses to present his findings. In the Problem-Solution type of paper, the author has two basic subtasks: to determine the nature of the 'problem' and to describe a 'solution'. Setting up the 'problem' may itself involve various subtasks: describing the 'state of affairs', citing previous relevant work, highlighting anomalies and difficulties, etc. Likewise, the 'solution' subtask involves other lower-order subtasks: stating a hypothesis, describing the tests and their results, determining whether they constitute solutions or not, and so forth. Some of these subtasks may be common to other writing tasks, e.g. the citation of previous work; others may be specific to this type of scientific paper, e.g. the evaluation of possible solutions to scientific problems.

The activities of the scientist-reader are also divisible into tasks and subtasks. Some are common to all readers: understanding deictic and anaphoric referring, qualification, and modification; some are common to readers of the subject: the specific vocabulary of the field, the manner of discussion and argument in the subject, etc.; others are specific to texts of this type, e.g. the structure of 'problem-solution' scientific texts; and other tasks are specific to this particular text: i.e. understanding the specific background information presumed by this particular author, following his arguments, and integrating the new knowledge into the reader's own previous knowledge.

Both authors and readers are also operating within a wider context. In this case, as scientists their overall task is to understand scientifically some part of reality or the natural world. Writing and reading are subtasks within this framework. From his reading of scientific papers, the scientist may be stimulated to try new methods, investigate new areas, gain greater understanding, formulate new ideas and hypotheses, etc. The completing of one task (or subtask) may lead to starting another task (or subtask) before the end of another, or may lead to abandoning a task begun in favor of another one. For example, reading about the methods used by another scientist may inspire him to begin a new investigation even before he has finished the text that he is reading.

6. Linguistic activity of scientists as experimenters

Before he is an author, the scientist is an experimenter, and in this role (which he probably sees as his principal role) he carries out linguistic activity in addition to those described already. When considering whether to undertake a particular experiment or test a particular hypothesis, he will be not just interested in finding information in general in his field of study, he will want to find specific information relevant to what he intends to do. For this purpose he may undertake a search through the literature of his subject using the indexes and abstracts available (as we describe below). Having found articles appearing to be relevant, he will read them with the specific intention of augmenting his knowledge (the plex area related to his focus) so that he is fully up to date with what other scientists have been doing. These other authors will be candidates for the set of bibliographic references he will be making when he writes up his experiment.

The next stage of linguistic activity is likely to be some discussion with colleagues (or, in the case of a student, with his professor or supervisor), either directly or at a distance (by telephone, by email, by letter, etc.). Such discussions will be exploratory, seeking information about aims, methods and, probably, about the prospects of achieving significant results.

Before doing any experiments, it may be necessary to obtain funds, and for this the scientist may well have to submit an application. Typically, fund applications involve descriptions of what is known already in a specific field, what experiments are to be undertaken, and what the expected results may reveal. Evidently, some of the content of grant applications parallels the content of the final scientific article – indeed, as we know, scientists sometimes have the impression that in order to obtain a grant, they have to do all the experiments first! The writing of project proposals and grant applications is clearly another area worthy of separate investigation.

When doing experiments, he will interact linguistically with a number of people, not just colleagues, but also technicians, administrators, secretarial and cleaning staff. Experimental activity is fraught with frustrations, mistakes, and failures. These 'diversions' will give rise to much linguistic activity, but very little (probably none) of it will be alluded to in the final writing up. The experiments will be idealized, spoken and written about as if they proceeded perfectly. This is the centuries-old scientific tradition.

Before starting to write, the scientist will inevitably (it is presumed) reflect upon the validity of his results, and whether they demonstrate what he intends them to demonstrate. There will at least be an internal monologue, and quite possibly further dialog with colleagues. Finally, he will formulate (plan) his article, setting out the background, the hypotheses, the tests, the results, and the conclusions somewhat (in broad outline) as described above. The process will involve a further stage of idealization, since he will want to adhere as much as appropriate to the standards and norms of his peers. An illustration of how complex this activity can be, particularly when there is more than one author (which is now quite frequent in science), is provided by Knorr-Cetina (1981). Idealization means that the precise processes of experimentation are not described, false starts and faulty experiments are omitted, as well as disputes and criticisms within the laboratory. What are also left out are the financial, commercial, and academic motivations of the experimenter(s) and the real reasons for undertaking the experiment. In the case examined by Knorr-Cetina, for example, the new technique which is the major finding of the paper was developed in response to difficulties with existing techniques; most of the time in the laboratory was spent on making sure the method worked. But none of this is reported in the paper. Instead, the paper seeks to provide a relevant contextual framework to justify the new technique, and these are not technical justifications but 'scientific' ones, describing it in the context of what is known about the current methods and their disadvantages. According to Knorr-Cetina, it is such 'recontextualization' in a conventional framework that is the aim of the introductory sections of the paper. Furthermore, this introductory context may well be the last part to be written – as Knorr-Cetina observed, the first sections to be written are the 'results' and the 'conclusions' (what the scientists regarded as the 'core' content of the paper); only later do the authors set down the background and the justifications for doing the work described.

The desire on the part of scientists for their work to be accepted into the scientific consensus encourages them to minimize their criticism (even implicit) of their fellow scientists and of their methods and results. In the case of the Knorr-Cetina example, the authors refrained even from making assertions about the implicit but clear and distinct advantages of the proposed method over existing methods.

7. Indexing and abstracting

Between the author and reader there are commonly also other acting individuals who facilitate the processes of scientific communication. These are the editors of journals, the referees of articles, the publishers, the subscription agents, the workers in the mailing services, the staff in the institutions receiving the journals, etc. In particular, however, there are the individuals who index and abstract articles, who provide the secondary written (printed) texts which scientists (as seekers of information) consult in order to locate articles that may interest them (as readers). These individuals are often helped by authors who provide summaries of their articles, but the processes of indexing and abstracting are separate activities where individuals also pass from initial states (of ignorance) to final states (of some knowledge). They may or may not be familiar with the specific problem area, but their aim is to describe what it is, and (in the case of abstracts) what the author has discovered and what he proposes as an explanation.

There is a familiar distinction made between indicative abstracts and informative abstracts. In indicative abstracts, the abstractor aims to compose a summary (topic paragraph) describing the focal points of the content of the original article in general. Unfortunately, many readers are not satisfied with only statements about the overall topics of articles, they want to know precise pieces of information, e.g.

whether a particular chemical was used in an experiment, whether a particular method was adopted, whether a particular effect was observed, etc. This is the function of the informative abstract, to serve as a useful pointer for information embedded in the article outside the introduction and not indicated as topics by the author himself. The distinction between indicative and informative is not rigid or absolute: abstracts commonly combine both functions; as with texts, the abstractor (as author) takes into account the expected needs and background of the reader (or user) of the abstract.

Abstracting (or summarizing) would appear to be primarily a function of generalization, guided by text features and clues commonly understood by all readers, but directed to the particular end of communicating the essential core. Generalization itself must be considered a basic operation for all communicating individuals, basic to all learning, apprehension, and comprehension, involving (it may be presumed) awareness of similarities and convergences among different sets of (internal) conditions and procedures in the plexes of individuals.

In indicative abstracts, what is summarized is generally only the overall topic of the article, i.e. the subject area and the specific problem being discussed. This may be regarded as a generalization based on the known elements (mainly in the base sections) and ignoring most of the new information.

Indexing carries indicativeness another stage further. It reduces topic statements to sets of individual independent words or phrases (index terms), which together are intended to cover the content. In effect, index terms are hooks (points of contact) between texts and their potential readers. The task of indexing for a wide range of potential readers is difficult for reasons already given: each reader comes to an article with a different plex of knowledge and understanding. Each will formulate his own idea of what the text is about. All that the indexer can do is to select index terms that capture the topic and perhaps part of the presupposed knowledge of the article for some ideal reader (scientist). In this way, the indexer seeks to provide readers with a common starting point. The author has made presumptions about what readers should already know; the indexer can use these to provide a bridge from a reader's presumed state of knowledge to the author's text.

Fortunately, as we saw above, most authors of scientific articles state in the introductory (base) sections of their papers precisely what they consider its topic to be. These statements can be readily located by both indexers and readers. Since the indexer may presume that this topic statement is what the reader would look for when determining whether the article is of interest, the indexer can select it as the basis for producing a standardized set of index words and phrases.

In the indexing (and abstracting) process we have a communicating individual (usually not himself a scientist in the particular subject domain), who functions as a reader of a text (when analyzing, understanding, or evaluating a scientific article) and simultaneously – apparently – as an author of (a set of) index terms or an abstract. In this authoring function it is possible to envisage the index terms as constituting a 'language' analogous to a natural language (of original texts), which indexers use to refer in ways similar to those when using natural language (cf. Hutchins 1975).

Index entries (and abstracts) are also texts which are read by scientists. As when reading texts, the index user comes with a particular background of knowledge about the field. He formulates his search topic in terms of this background, and when he finds an entry containing these terms he understands it in the light of his own knowledge. What he then expects is that the text (scientific article) to which the index entry refers will in fact be relevant to the topic he is looking for. We should not be surprised that the process can lead to failure, since the background knowledge of the reader (as index user) is unlikely to be close to that of the indexer and that of the original author. In fact, what is surprising is that the process is often successful. It succeeds because authors of scientific articles make reasonably clear what they assume as base knowledge and what they consider their topics to be; indexers learn to interpret the topics of articles and to express them in terms (i.e. index terms) that they expect index users to formulate searches in; and readers (and index users) learn how to express what they are seeking in terms which they expect authors and indexers to use. Just as authors anticipate in their texts the questions that readers are likely to ask, so indexers anticipate in their texts (index entries) the searches that index users are likely to make.

8. Texts in collections

Indexing and abstracting relate texts to each other by virtue of common index terms (topics). Apart from author-reader linkages there are what we may refer to loosely as text-text associations. Scientific texts are not written in a vacuum, but have relations to other preceding texts. The most obvious of these associations have already been mentioned: the citations made by authors to other scientists, the publication of articles in journals devoted to the same topic, the collection of texts in libraries and databases, and the juxtaposition of bibliographic entries for articles and books in indexes and catalogues. But there are other associations hidden or implicit in the author's establishment of his base of presupposed knowledge. This is the knowledge that previous scientists have established from previous investigations in the particular scientific field. What is expressed by anaphora, by deixis, and other linguistic cues are indirect references to this familiar background. Since much of this background has been communicated in other texts, these references are also indirect references to 'associative networks' set up by authors of other texts – and it is these associations from text to text which constitute the idea of 'public knowledge'. It has been common practice to describe texts and their structures independently of authors and readers, as if they have meaning in themselves. The practice is particularly tempting in the case of scientific communication whenever there is reference to the scientific literature as constituting 'public knowledge' (Ziman 1968).

However, we must not forget that these are indirect relationships, which should be regarded as occurrences within a higher order of linkages embracing the scientific community, i.e. as group participants and as collections of texts as props. References to other texts from a text are made by communicating individuals even if the results are recorded visibly as written forms. The links are activated only when they are triggered by the internal procedures of individual readers (scientists, indexers, etc.)

The situation is obscured by the fact that databases of texts (particularly electronic databases) record relations between texts which do not appear to originate from activities of communicating individuals. Index entries can be, and are now almost invariably, derived automatically from occurrences of words (sequences of symbols) in corpora of texts. It seems that only the computer program which does the indexing is the work of a person; its application to texts is automatic. Collections of interconnected and indexed texts are now essential for all scientific work. The fact that the embedded text relationships do not exist in the mind of any particular scientist – indeed, they are unknown until a search of the literature is undertaken – does not mean that these relationships constitute 'objective knowledge' existing independently of any originators.

It is true that written documents seem often to have an existence beyond the life of their creators, e.g. when texts are interpreted in ways contrary to the intention of authors. But the important point is that interpretation has to take place. Popper defines the 'objective knowledge' contained in a book (true or false, useful or useless) as 'its possibility or potentiality of being understood, its dispositional character of being understood or interpreted, or misunderstood or misinterpreted ... And this potentiality or disposition may exist without ever being actualized or realized' (Popper 1972: 116).

The discovery by Swanson (1990) through a search of medical literature that a certain drug might help to cure a certain disease was an act of interpretation, an act of true scientific research, *viz.* the finding of plausible hypotheses for further investigation, and the investigating of properties of large and complex sets of biomedical data. It was Swanson who recognized the significance and relevance of the connections, not the inert data and documents themselves. Relationships between texts (whether produced automatically or by indexers, etc.) become significant, 'meaningful', or relevant only when readers (e.g. scientists) make judgments – just as the effectiveness of an information retrieval system is assessed by its success in retrieving documents that users consider to be relevant to their requests. Texts and text relationships are interpreted by individual readers on the basis of their own conditions and states of knowledge at the particular time when they are read.

Note

1. Here following the convention of using the masculine pronoun to refer to individuals of either gender.

References

Hutchins, W. J. (1975), *Languages of Indexing and Classification: A Linguistic Study of Structures and Functions.* Stevenage, UK: Peter Peregrinus.

Knorr-Cetina, K. D. (1981), *The Manufacture of Knowledge: An Essay on the Constructivist and Contextual Nature of Science.* Oxford: Pergamon.

Popper, K. R. (1972), *Objective Knowledge: An Evolutionary Approach.* Oxford: Clarendon Press.

Swanson, D. R. (1990), 'Medical literature as a potential source of new knowledge'. *Bulletin of the Medical Library Association*, 78, 29–37.

Van Dijk, T. A. and Kintsch, W. (1983), *Strategies of Discourse Comprehension.* New York: Academic Press.

Yngve, V. H. (1996), *From Grammar to Science: New Foundations for General Linguistics.* Amsterdam/Philadelphia: John Benjamins.

Ziman, J. M. (1968). *Public Knowledge: An Essay Concerning the Social Dimension of Science.* Cambridge: Cambridge University Press.

PART VII

DISCIPLINARY CONSIDERATIONS

Chapter 20

The Riches of the New World

Victor H. Yngve and Zdzisław Wąsik

Why are so many of us working so hard to move linguistics into modern standard science? It is the lure of the vast riches for linguistics to be found there. We have an obligation to develop these riches for the good of the discipline. Here is a brief inventory of some of the advantages of such a move illustrated in the papers collected in this volume and some of the additional advantages that can be foreseen in such a move.

1. To achieve secure knowledge

Modern standard science as it has developed over the last four centuries since Galileo and his contemporaries is the best method known for achieving a secure understanding of the natural world. Linguistics can share in these riches and achieve secure knowledge if it studies part of the natural world and embraces modern standard science. But language as understood in received linguistic theory is not part of the natural world, so a proper scientific linguistics cannot study language as it has usually been conceived. But there is no doubt that people are part of the natural world and understanding people inevitably involves understanding how they communicate. Furthermore, the question of how people communicate can be shown to encompass all of the important questions asked by linguists. So the true task of a scientific linguistics must be to achieve a scientific understanding of how people communicate. That is the main reason why we have been working so hard to move linguistics into modern standard science – to achieve secure knowledge. But there are other riches waiting for us there.

2. To achieve agreement

Current linguistics is populated by many incompatible brands of grammar differing in their criteria and assumptions. Since their relative merits are a matter of opinion, arguments between them are inconclusive. We are left with a linguistics with no established agreed-on body of theory, and worse, a linguistics that offers no hope of ever coming to agreement on matters of theory because there is no agreement on the criteria to be applied. In the face of this some linguists have given up and advocate an ecumenical attitude, an open-minded tolerance of, as it were, different faiths.

But the truth about nature is not a matter of freedom of opinion or about faith. Some of the riches available in science are that there are uniform standard criteria for deciding what to believe about the natural world and uniform standard assumptions on which the various hard sciences have been built. Experience has shown that accepting only these criteria and assumptions leads in the end to agreement and to knowledge about each part of the world that fits with and is supported by what is already known across a wide range of disciplines. In this way a vast self-consistent web of knowledge about nature is created. New foundations are now available for a hard-science linguistics built on these same standard assumptions and honoring only the same standard criteria as all the other hard sciences. This opens the way for linguists to share in these riches and to achieve agreement in their discipline where only idiosyncratic opinions once ruled.

3. To relate individuals and groups

People do not just communicate alone, they communicate with others. Linguistics must therefore be concerned with both individual phenomena and group or community phenomena. But linguistics has up to now offered only one order of theory, grammar, and it has never been completely clear whether grammar relates to the individual or to the community or to neither. Human (hard-science) linguistics offers instead two orders of theory, one focused on the individual and one on the group, and it provides a theory of the relation of the individual to the group and of the group, to the individuals that make it up. And at the same time it treats the relation of small groups to larger groups and to the community as a whole and the community to the smaller groups and individuals that make it up. These riches are completely beyond the reach of grammatical theories.

4. To unify all of linguistics

Our linguistic curiosity has many facets. They are focused not only on the individual and on the community, but on linguistic variation and historical change, on learning and developmental processes, and on social and cultural issues. Hard-science linguistics offers a way to unify all these related but previously rather disparate and only loosely connected branches of linguistic inquiry. Grammatical theory has proved unable to serve that function very well. In addition, current linguistic theory is fragmented into often incompatible theories of phonology, morphology, syntax, semantics, pragmatics, and others. Hard-science linguistics offers a way to unify our knowledge in all these areas.

5. To answer perplexing questions

In current linguistics a number of nagging questions arise, such as: What is language? What is a sentence? What is a word? What is meaning? How can we handle anaphora and deixis? How can we handle connotations, metaphor, and figurative language? How does rhetoric fit in? How can the total context of situation be taken into account? How does pragmatics fit in? How can we understand pidgins and creoles? How can we understand 'code switching'? How do children learn to speak? How can we understand linguistic change? What is the role of gestures and bodily movement? What is the relation of writing to speech? Some of these questions are artefacts of traditional theory that simply disappear in hard-science linguistics. The rest can be approached straightforwardly in hard-science linguistics if they can be formulated as genuine scientific questions.

6. To integrate linguistics into science

Although linguistics has been defined in its textbooks as a science, the scientific study of language, linguists often affirm correctly that linguistics is autonomous. It has few or no close ties to the rest of science. This has set linguistics apart from the other sciences and in fact has placed it outside of science. On the other hand, hard-science linguistics is explicitly integrated with the physics of sound, the biology of hearing and speaking including ecological and evolutionary considerations, and with physiology and psychology. In this way, hard-science linguistics is not autonomous, it is an integral part of science.

7. To connect the individual and social sciences

The natural sciences from physics through chemistry to biology fit together in a complexly interconnected whole and unify our knowledge of the natural world. But there has been a gap between these and the social and psychological sciences, which are often correctly considered soft sciences. Many have seen that the rightful place of linguistics among the sciences is to fill this gap and stand between and connect the individual and social sciences. However, traditional linguistics cannot properly fulfil this role because of its autonomous and inappropriate logical-domain grammatical theory. But a human (hard-science) linguistics can properly fulfil this role by virtue of its scientific elucidation of the relation of individuals to groups, which is basically communicative. This allows linguistics finally to fulfil its long dreamed-of destiny of standing between and connecting the individual sciences and the social sciences, thus completing the hierarchy of the sciences that reaches from the social and cultural sciences all the way down to biology, chemistry, and physics.

8. To support related disciplines

Since communicating is the glue that holds social groups together and is the means of handing on knowledge from generation to generation, a scientific understanding of how people communicate is necessary as a foundation for sociology, social psychology, and anthropology, and for the study of learning and development. Hard-science linguistics is designed to supply the needed support. It may also aid these disciplines in their own efforts to move completely into the hard sciences. How people communicate is also centrally involved in the subject matter of neurology and communicative disorders. Hard-science linguistics is well-suited to supporting these sciences whereas our current theories have come up short.

9. To support applied linguistics

Since it is people who learn, human (hard-science) linguistics is well suited to providing scientific support for first-language and second-language teaching. It can support the teaching of composition, rhetoric, and scientific and technical writing and literary studies. It can also support studies of ethnic and standard languages and issues of translating and interpreting, topics that are becoming more important in a shrinking world. And since it supports writing, it can support our efforts to deal competently with our vast heritage of recorded literature in every field.

10. To explore and obtain new knowledge

There are undoubtedly many important questions in linguistics that have not yet been asked or even thought of. Science is open and congenial to asking new questions about the world and undertaking new investigations at the frontiers of research. On the other hand, the ancient semiotic-grammatical tradition that we have been following has come down to us through normative grammar, philosophy, and our common Western culture. Dating to Aristotle and the Stoics of 300 to 150 BC, it has changed little in its essence in the last two millennia. Based in ancient philosophy rather than modern science, it still remains relatively closed and stifling of efforts to explore intellectual forefronts and reach for new secure knowledge. It cannot support the needs of current linguistics.

★ ★ ★

To realize the advantages outlined above, linguistics must leave this tradition of over two millennia and fully embrace the 400-year tradition of modern standard science. So we are faced with moving from an ancient tradition to a modern one, from one culture as it were to another, a prospect not unfamiliar to linguists who have some familiarity with exotic languages and cultures. This is an exciting prospect. It involves exploring a new land, a whole new world for linguistics still largely unexplored.

Chapter 21

Coping with Cultural Differences

Victor H. Yngve and Zdzisław Wąsik

The culture of modern standard science is quite different from the culture of language and grammar. Reconstucting linguistics as a standard science involves leaving grammar altogether. This is a much greater move than simply adopting a different brand of grammar. So the explorer needs to remain alert and expect the unexpected.

To help the reader understand some of the conceptual issues involved in such a move and to avoid possible confusions, we outline here a few of the major differences between (a) the modern hard-science tradition and (b) the ancient semiotic-grammatical tradition.

1. Physical rather than mental objects of study

The hard sciences propose physical-domain theories of the real world whereas the semiotic-grammatical tradition proposes logical-domain theories of theories.

The hard sciences study physical objects of the real world that are given in advance of the questions the scientists ask and the investigations they carry out. They remain in place in the real world when the investigators leave. Here we have the physical-domain disciplines of physics, chemistry, biology, and various other related sciences, and now hard-science linguistics. The real-world objects of study in hard-science linguistics are the people, individually and collectively, who communicate, the sound waves of speech and other communicative energy flow, and the parts of the physical surroundings relevant to how they communicate.

On the other hand, the semiotic-grammatical tradition studies logical-domain objects in an imaginary world created by the assumptions of the investigators. They disappear when the investigators leave. Examples include language, signs, words, meanings, and the many other objects introduced into linguistics by assumption. Ferdinand de Saussure noticed this difference between linguistics and the other sciences when he pointed out that

> Other sciences work with objects that are given in advance and that can then be considered from different viewpoints; but not linguistics ... Far from it being the object that antedates the viewpoint, it would seem that it is the viewpoint that creates the object. [1916:23, 1959:8]

Leonard Bloomfield then created and explicitly introduced by means of his famous fundamental assumption of linguistics just the objects not given in advance that he needed on which to build the grammatical linguistics he was striving for (1933:78).

So the possible source of confusion to guard against here is that hard-science linguistics offers physical-domain theories of people and how they communicate whereas the tradition offers the conceptual structure of grammar based on a logical-domain fabric of assumptions.

2. Starts with things rather than words

In physical-domain research, the thing to be investigated comes first, that is, the real-world object or objects that are given in advance, then there follows a scientific investigation of the object or objects which may lead to a proposed explanation of the observed phenomena and in the end maybe a word is proposed for it. Typical questions are 'How far away is the moon?', a question in astronomy,' Why does ice float?', a question in physics, 'Why does iron rust?', a question in chemistry, 'What causes malaria?', a question in bio-medicine, and 'How do people communicate?', the leading question in hard-science linguistics. So it's: thing to be investigated, scientific investigation, proposed explanation, maybe a word for it.

On the other hand, in the logical domain the word comes first, which is not a real-world object, then some intuitive reasoning about it, then an explication, which is a favorite method in philosophy, and maybe a definition, often the goal of a philosophical investigation. Typical questions are 'What is truth, love, etc.?', as asked by Plato and the ancients, 'What is meaning?', asked in a logical-domain semantics, 'What is a word, a noun?', asked in the traditional logical-domain linguistics of language, 'What is language?', a question that linguists studying language would like to find a good answer to, 'What is communication?', a logical-domain question often inappropriately asked by linguists seeking real-world relevance for their discipline.

So in the logical domain it's: word, then intuitive reasoning, then proposed explication, and maybe a definition. This is just the reverse of how a physical-domain investigation is carried out. Instead of asking the logical-domain question 'What is communication?', the appropriate real-world question to ask is 'How do people communicate?'. That starts with real-world people and communicative energy flow. It requires moving linguistics into the physical domain and making it a (human) hard science.

3. Testable theories rather than untestable theories

Hard-science theories of the real world are testable against the real world through observations of the real world and experiments on the real world. In contrast, logical-domain theories are untestable. This is a major difference between the hard sciences and philosophy. Insisting on the testability of theories is responsible for the remarkable advances in our understanding of the natural world through physics, chemistry, biology, and related sciences. It sets the hard sciences apart from the soft sciences, which try to be scientific in some respects but also accept untestable assumptions and theories that render them unscientific. Likewise it sets the hard sciences apart from the mass of folk theory handed down in the common culture, which inevitably includes ancient and modern nonscientific influences that render its claims unscientific. Insisting that theories be testable also sets the hard sciences apart from speculation, intuition, guesswork, assertions of superior insight, and claims of knowing the revealed truth. These are idiosyncratic and lead to special appeals and modes of argumentation irrelevant to finding out the truth about nature. Contrary to what some people have believed, grammatical theories are in fact untestable. They include unsubstantiated assumptions and they rely on philosophical methods such as explication, abstraction, and intuition.

4. Standard criteria rather than no standard criteria

The hard sciences have developed standard criteria for what to accept. The standard criterion for accepting theories in the hard sciences is that their predictions pass tests against real-world observational and experimental evidence. The standard criterion for accepting observational and experimental evidence is that it be replicated, preferably independently by other investigators. In practice each scientist makes up his own mind as to what to accept and is free to challenge any theory or to reinvestigate any reported observational or experimental findings. But since everyone is playing by the same rules and honors the same standard criteria, there is an inevitable movement toward agreement. That's how new knowledge is accepted in the sciences. Although nearly everyone comes to agree by this process, it's clearly not simply a matter of voting. It's more like judging an election. Once the ballots have been counted and the counting process validated, the decision is accepted.

On the other hand, in the logical domain there are no agreed standard criteria for accepting theories. Statements are sometimes made simply on the authority of the author, and if pressed, the author cannot provide a good reason for believing them. Various criteria from a long list are often appealed to, depending on the choice of the particular author. Some of the many criteria suggested or invoked include simplicity, symmetry, analogy, intuition, superior insight, tradition, authority, loyalty to a teacher, following a party line, perceived popularity, mainline or conventional wisdom, geographic or ethnic bias, fear of reprisals, personal profit, and various others. None of these disparate criteria is universally accepted, nor how it should be applied in practice. One author's conception of simplicity or symmetry may differ from another author's conceptions and one author's intuitions may be different from those of another author. In each case there is no agreed-upon way to settle the inevitable differences of opinion, which depend on each author's differing criteria, and there is no clear way to choose among them and reach agreement on the issues.

5. Limited standard assumptions rather than unlimited free assumptions

The hard sciences accept only four assumptions, which have become standard: (1) that there is a real world out there to be investigated, (2) that it is coherent so we have a chance of finding out something about it, (3) that from true premises we can reason to true conclusions, and (4) that observed effects flow from immediate causes. All other proposed assumptions are either converted to hypotheses and put to the test or they are abandoned.

Philosophy and the semiotic-grammatical tradition, on the other hand, allow unlimited assumptions. Some of them are: that the sound waves of someone speaking are not simply unstructured sound energy flow, they are structured utterances, that utterances are segmented into speech sounds, that there are meanings, that utterances 'carry' meanings, that words are real things, that words 'have' meanings, that language is a real thing, that people 'have' language, that people 'use' language, that language is a relation between sound and meaning, that it is part of a sign relation between word, thought, and thing, and that language is governed by grammar and lexicon. (The reader should realize here that when I talk about grammar, I am talking about it as a theory of language in the realm of linguistics, not practical grammar involved in correcting and editing one's writing, which is quite useful.)

All of these assumptions are either false or they are scientifically unsupported. How can we have a linguistics without at least some of these familiar, even ubiquitous assumptions? The beginning of an answer is found in this book, where a number of pioneers have tried their hands at building a human linguistics focused on people as part of the real natural world and how they communicate rather than on words, meanings, and utterances in the unreal illusory world of language and signs. One should hasten to add that this book can only be the beginning. There is much to learn, much to do, and many exciting opportunities for adventuresome linguists.

6. Summary of differences and potential areas of confusion

We can summarize the differences between hard-science linguistics and the traditional linguistics of language as follows: hard-science linguistics offers a direct approach to the study of how people communicate whereas the linguistics of language can, at best, offer only an indirect approach through grammar. Hard-science linguistics is scientific, operates in the physical domain, and studies real-world objects whereas the linguistics of language is philosophical, operates in the logical domain, and studies nonreal assumed objects. Hard-science linguistics is part of science and uses scientific evidence whereas the linguistics of language is autonomous and accepts nonscientific evidence. Hard-science linguistics adheres to the standard criteria and accepts only the standard assumptions of all science whereas the linguistics of language does not hesitate to use nonstandard criteria and it accepts uncontrolled assumptions. And hard-science linguistics is dynamic and is pragmatic from top to bottom whereas the linguistics of language is static and basically representational.

References

Bloomfield, Leonard (1933), *Language*. New York: Holt. [Reprint: Chicago: University of Chicago Press, 1984.]

Saussure, Ferdinand de (1916), *Cours de linguistique générale publié par Charles Bally et Albert Sechehaye avec la collaboration d'Albert Riedlinger* (5th edn 1955). Lausanne: Payot.

Saussure, Ferdinand de (1959). *Course in General Linguistics*, translated by Wade Baskin. New York: The Philosophical Library. [Reprint: New York: McGraw-Hill, 1966.]

Chapter 22

The Conduct of Hard-Science Research

Victor H. Yngve

The hard sciences study the real physical world and operate with standard criteria and assumptions (Yngve 1996 Chap. 8). Hard-science linguistics seeks to understand how people communicate. Although there is no single universally valid method for conducting hard-science research in general or hard-science linguistics in particular, here is one suggested step-by-step procedure to try:

(1) Identify the phenomena you are interested in studying and try to formulate a succinct research question in the way that is most natural for you on the basis of your background.

(2) Identify the people and other parts of the real physical world involved in the phenomena identified above. What is the physical reality behind the phenomena you are interested in?

(3) If the phenomena and the research question have been stated in terms of language or grammar or some other nonphysical abstractions, as may often be the case, restate them in terms of real people and parts of their physical environment. What are they doing? What is really going on here?

(4) Set up appropriate systems such as communicating individuals, linkages, participants, role parts, channels, etc. as objects of theory to represent the people and other physical objects you have identified. Set them up in the way you think may be most convenient for delimiting in theory the real-world objects behind your research question.

(5) Develop (guess, invent) appropriate testable theory in the form of plex structures of these systems. These may be informed guesses on the basis of other known related results.

(6) Predict (derive, calculate) observable consequences from the theory.

(7) Look for the predicted real-world consequences by appropriate observation or experiment.

(8) If careful observations or experiments do not agree with the predictions of theory, try refining the observations or experiments or their interpretation to ensure their soundness. If they appear to be sound, go back to an earlier step and try to develop improved theory and predictions.

(9) If there still are difficulties, go back to step 1 and identify a simpler research question or one less contaminated by preconceptions from the semiotic-grammatical tradition.

Carrying out only a few steps may make an important contribution. Different steps may be carried out by different people at different times. There can be a division of labor, as between theory and observation or experiment. Some of the best scientists, however, have advanced both theory and observation or experiment.

(1) Identify the phenomena you are interested in studying and try to formulate a succinct research question in the way that is most natural for you on the basis of your background.

It is very easy to ask a question that is too difficult or so broad that it cannot be answered at all in a short time. The overarching question in hard-science linguistics is 'How do people communicate?'. This question is obviously too broad to be answered within the scope of a short paper. The question of how to reformulate the depth hypothesis in hard-science linguistics is also too broad. It deals with how a person's limited temporary memory might cause problems in speaking, how people might tag things as awkward, how awkwardness might influence what a person does or does not say, how a child learns to speak, whether the child also learns awkwardness from others, how the speaking of individuals may influence changes in the linkage properties of the group, and how these may change over time. Each of these parts is also probably too big a job for a short paper. Each would seem to require that a large part of linguistics be reconstituted first.

The thing we should try to do is to find small questions that we may be able to answer. The game of tag example in the 1996 book was an attempt to find phenomena that could be studied in a small scope and could be used in developing research methods.

The phenomena of turn-taking in conversation is another example that I have examined at some length. But it happens that turn-taking phenomena interact with other phenomena associated with the execution of and completion of speaking tasks and subtasks and expectations of their completion. Considerations of topic and its changes are also factors in turn-taking. Referential phenomena are also important. Each of these areas may offer opportunities to find small research topics to work on.

We expect that if we try to answer a small question we will see that it interacts with other questions. No one can do it all. It's a situation that requires cooperation and collaboration. An important feature of hard-science linguistics is that as each of these smaller questions is answered, the answers will fit together with answers to other small questions found by others and our view of the whole will become clearer. Lacking answers to these other questions, the only thing to do is to characterize the interacting phenomena as clearly as we can prior to their definitive treatment, perhaps by others. If we do this, we will also be providing hints to those others studying those questions.

(2) Identify the people and other parts of the real physical world involved in the phenomena identified above. What is the physical reality behind the phenomena you are interested in?

This is the first step in moving to the physical domain. It is a step crucial to successful work in hard-science linguistics: identify what parts of the real world are involved. Where is the real source of the phenomena? What people are involved? What groups of people? What other parts of the real world? At this stage rule nothing out. Be complete. Be sure to include everything in the real world that might potentially be relevant. One can judge the degree of relevance of any particular part and limit the scope of investigation later.

If you are dealing with face-to-face interaction, identify all the small or large groups involved. Don't forget the larger including groups or communities providing context for parts of the interaction. Don't forget third parties in the vicinity whose perceived presence may affect politeness or other aspects of what is said or how it is said. If multilingual or contact phenomena are at issue, or what has been called 'code switching', or translation or interpretation phenomena, do not forget to include the relevant groups and communities that provide an important part of the context, including the translators and interpreters.

If you are concerned with what have been seen as semantic associations, connotations, or figurative language, think about it carefully and be sure to include any special groups, small or large, that might be relevant for your investigation of the phenomena.

Similarly, if you are concerned with stereotypes based on nationality, ethnicity, religion, occupation, status, sex, or life style, consider what groups might be involved in forming such associations and in passing them on to others.

Don't forget the physical environment and any significant objects. If you are dealing with written records, be sure to include those who wrote them, those who would presumably read them, and the groups and communities in which the written records played a role. If historical considerations are involved, be sure to include the historically known groups and individuals behind your data, and if relevant, the individuals and groups that figure in the preservation of your data.

(3) If the phenomena and the research question have been stated in terms of language or grammar or some other nonphysical abstractions, as may often be the case, restate them in terms of real people and parts of their physical environment. What are they doing? What is really going on here?

Note that questions are always understood within a context. The most usual context for questions in linguistics has been the semiotic-grammatical tradition. So it is likely that the research question at this point has been stated in terms of language or grammar or linguistically structured texts or discourse or relations between sound and meaning in conformity with this tradition. As we know, the question would then involve untestable logical-domain assumptions that are not scientifically justified.

We need to move from seeing the phenomena in logical-domain terms to seeing them in testable physical-domain terms. We need to move from theories of theories to theories of real-world objects. We need to move from questions about logical-domain objects like words, sentences, grammars, languages, and such, to questions about physical-domain objects like people and the other real-world objects that may be relevant.

In previous steps we have already identified those parts of the real world that are involved in the phenomena we are interested in. In this crucial step in moving to a hard-science linguistics we restate our question in terms of physical realities: the people that are interacting and the relevant physical environment. We need to ask: What are they doing? How are they changing? What is going on?

And we need to ask this question without leaning on grammatical or other logical-domain concepts or terms. This of course rules out asking about internal grammars, about using language, about speaking or understanding sentences, about parsing, about conveying meaning, about doing things with words, or about intuitions of well-formedness or grammaticality. So one will need to be cautious and careful, especially if one is a trained linguist.

(4) Set up appropriate systems such as communicating individuals, linkages, participants, role parts, channels, etc. as objects of theory to represent the people and other physical objects you have identified. Set them up in the way you think may be most convenient for delimiting in theory the real-world objects behind your research question.

Having asked a proper physical-domain question we now undertake our first theoretical act: defining for purposes of theory the systems that we wish to treat. This is a creative act requiring insight into the phenomena and designed to set the arbitrary but carefully chosen limits of our proposed specific domain of theory so as best to encompass in theory the phenomena of the real world we are concerned with. We expect that in analyzing these systems in terms of their properties and changes in properties and how the systems interact with each other we will find a satisfactory testable answer for our question.

Remember that setting up systems involves arbitrary choices. You have complete freedom to define systems to suit your particular research topic so as to include those things that are relevant and you wish to treat and exclude those things that are not relevant or that you are not specifically treating at this time. If a system that you are not treating nevertheless has an important effect that should not be ignored, you can take it into account through inputs and outputs across the system boundaries.

Do not neglect interacting systems since a number of phenomena have their explanation in these terms. Examples include not only multi-party conversations with direct coupling of the dinner-table type, but also linkage hierarchies in a community, 'code switching', contact phenomena, translation, politeness factors, and a number of other social and historical phenomena.

There may not be one best way of setting up systems for your research topic; some ways might be more convenient for treating certain aspects of the question, other ways for other aspects. But they are all related as different representations of parts of the same real world. Delimiting convenient systems for treating a question can in itself make a valuable contribution.

For guidance see Chapters 7 and 9 of the 1996 book for

background, Chapters 10 and 14 for basic theory, and Chapters 15–18 for suggested and illustrative configurations and interrelations of systems useful for various purposes.

(5) Develop (guess, invent) appropriate testable theory in the form of plex structures of these systems. These may be informed guesses on the basis of other known related results.

A large part of the 1996 book is about properties of systems, procedures, plex structures, task hierarchies, and the ever-present influence of context as represented in the domain of control. Only a few hints can be offered here about how one might proceed.

Task hierarchies can sometimes be seen as related to discourse analysis and studies of cohesion and coherence. One must, of course, keep in mind the vast difference between the structure of text or discourse and the structure of people carrying out communicative behavior. What appears to be cohesion in text is often the result of lower-level tasks in the same task hierarchy. Thus research in discourse analysis can sometimes provide initial suggestions as to what kinds of task structures to postulate.

Task hierarchies may to some extent resemble syntactic phrase structure and this can provide initial suggestions as to what kinds of structures to postulate. One must, of course, keep in mind the vast difference between the structure of language and the structure of people carrying out communicative behavior.

A major difference is that syntax, like much of the linguistics of language, is usually an exercise in ignoring the effects of context external to the immediate structure being considered whereas task hierarchies are always embedded in a larger context of conditional properties, the effects of which can easily be formalized.

Another major difference is that tasks can almost always be seen as pragmatic in that the execution of tasks changes conditional properties that then may figure at some later time in selecting which among several other tasks will be executed.

The execution of tasks is thus conditioned by the conditional properties. The currently active conditional properties are visualized as making up the domain of control.

Another major difference is that people often do more than one largely unrelated thing at a time. Thus there may be several loosely interacting parallel task hierarchies executing at the same time. For example, a person may at the same time be asking a question, showing respect to the person being asked, trying to impress a third person, displaying ethnic solidarity, and changing the subject away from something potentially embarrassing. The five task hierarchies could first be treated independently and the interactions between them handled later in simultaneously active conditional properties that select among alternative procedures or tasks.

When working out task hierarchies, remember that they are postulated properties of systems representing some aspects of individual people or groups. A valuable source of insight is to work out parallel task hierarchies at the individual and participant levels and related parallel task hierarchies at the role-part and linkage levels. It may well be the case that several parallel task hierarchies at the participant level are related to different role parts in different linkages that are thus coupled in the individual through the dinner-table type of direct coupling.

(6) Predict (derive, calculate) observable consequences from the theory.

Remember that much of our initial analysis will be of particular people and particular interactions. By analyzing in terms of properties (which are set up to express generalizations) and in moving to types (see section 15.4 in the 1996 book) we are enabled to generalize and the generalizations can be tested against observations of other particular people and particular interactions.

One can take advantage of the fact that tasks are pragmatic in that they make changes in the conditional properties in all the relevant plexes. It is often possible to test for the values of conditional properties. For example, we can tell whether someone has the property of being asked a question by observing whether the person attempts to answer or deal with it in some other way. There are many other examples in the book. You should be able to find others especially suited to your own research.

(7) Look for the predicted real-world consequences by appropriate observation or experiment.

We often know, of course, from personal experience, that the predicted phenomena do in fact occur. This can be a great initial help. But we must exercise extreme care. There are pitfalls concerned with the insecurity of intuition, the possibility of bias from a not disinterested observer, the effect of normative preconceptions, the influence of expectations from irrelevant grammatical theory, and the ease with which the unexpected will escape notice.

Observation by videotape has a lot to recommend it, but care needs to be taken that interfering effects of the observer or camera are minimized. One advantage of studying videotaped interactions is that one often sees new phenomena that one had not previously anticipated, and this can lead to new analyzes, new tests, and new validated hard-science knowledge. Videotape is much to be preferred over audio tape. Since we are studying people, we should record people and what they do rather than simply the sound of their voices, and then, worse, transcribing it in a normalized orthography or preconceived system of transcription. Those who have used videotape have found that it opens a whole new world. In either case, proper permission needs to be secured from the people being recorded.

Of course in the case of historical studies, written records are often about the only thing we have, and they are the only evidence that grammatical theory has provided formalisms for treating. But the human linguistics theoretical structure can actually accommodate and formalize in terms of properties much more information about the people we are studying than can be accommodated in grammar. Often such additional information will be available and relevant, for example historical records of movements of peoples and archaeological information about the conditions of life and culture of the people we are studying.

(8) If careful observations or experiments do not agree with the predictions of theory, try refining the observations or experiments or their interpretation to ensure their soundness. If they appear to be sound, go back to an earlier step and try to develop improved theory and predictions.

For example, in my early CLS 6 study of turn-taking (Yngve 1970), I wanted to study the simple property of a person having the turn in conversation and then not having the turn, and what kind of procedures were involved in changing this property. I expected from grammatical preconceptions of isolated sentences that one party would speak for a while, then perhaps give some kind of turn-change signal, and then the other person would speak for a while. Not being initially aware of any overt turn-change signal, I wondered what it was that did serve to change the turn property. You can see here the early hard-science influence in thinking in terms of people and their turn properties in a nascent state theory still mixed with the older language-like idea that one should look for some sort of discourse-like signals.

Videotape studies revealed that the phenomena were much more complex than implied by this oversimplified preconceived theory.

First, it was not true that one person held the turn for a while and then the other person held the turn. People were often observed to speak out of turn in what I called signals in the backchannel and others came to call 'backchannel utterances' or 'backchannels' under the older influence of thinking in terms of utterances and their properties rather than simply in terms of physical energy flow. And because of the strength of the tradition of studying language or discourse the main hard-science and human-linguistic point of this paper is still to this day not generally understood.

Second, no overt turn-change signal could be found. Instead, turn-change phenomena seemed to be complexly concerned with prosodic structure and other discourse characteristics that were not immediately obvious. It only later became clear to me that the goal should not be to understand how people 'use language' to communicate but simply to understand how people communicate. This led to an analysis in terms of properties, procedures, task hierarchies, and physical energy flow rather than 'signals' or 'utterances' or other language-related or discourse-related concepts.

(9) If there still are difficulties, go back to step 1 and identify a simpler research question or one less contaminated by preconceptions from the semiotic-grammatical tradition.

It may be that you can move ahead by going back and reformulating your question, redefining your systems, and revising the plex structures you have postulated. Although you may have to start at the beginning more than once before finding an appropriate topic, you will find that the research on any small topic is relatively simple and straightforward.

And your results, if validated scientifically, will be perfected and secured in their permanence by being related to and embedded in the validated work of others representing other aspects of the same physical reality. Hard-science linguistic theory is properly cumulative in the scientific sense. No one has to do everything alone. Each small piece will make an important contribution.

Remember that without the advantage of modern hard-science foundations it took over 2300 years of logical-domain speculation from Plato, Aristotle, and the Stoics up to modern times to develop the body of scientifically unjustified and unjustifiable semiotic-grammatical theory we find today in modern linguistics. Because of the continuing strength of that long tradition, it is only now after two centuries of striving that this scientifically flawed tradition is being replaced in linguistics by the overwhelmingly successful methods, criteria, and assumptions developed as standard in the hard sciences over the last four centuries. The long-sought key is to study people, not language, and not people through language. It's as simple as that.

Note

1. This is a lightly edited version of a paper that was distributed as 'Hard-Science Linguistics Memorandum no. 2', January 31, 2000 and subsequently discussed at the 27th LACUS Forum, Houston, Texas, July 25–29, 2000 and at the 33rd meeting of Societas Linguistica Europaea (SLE) at Poznań, Poland, August 31–September 2, 2000, and published in the workshop proceedings (Yngve 2000).

References

Yngve, Victor H. (1970), 'On getting a word in edgewise', in M. A. Campbell *et al.*, *Papers from the Sixth Regional Meeting, Chicago Linguistic Society*. Chicago: Chicago Linguistic Society, pp. 567–578.

Yngve, Victor H. (1996), *From Grammar to Science: New Foundations for General Linguistics*. Amsterdam/Philadelphia: John Benjamins.

Yngve, Victor H. (2000), 'The conduct of hard-science research', in V. H. Yngve and Z. Wąsik, *Exploring the Domain of Human-Centered Linguistics from a Hard-Science Perspective*. Poznań: The School of English, Adam Mickiewicz University.

Chapter 23

To be a Scientist

Victor H. Yngve

One of the things that attracted me to linguistics 35 years ago was the realization that it dealt with a large area of natural phenomena not yet well understood that could be approached scientifically. It was a frontier with the challenge of the unknown. Linguists advertised their discipline as a science, and it did seem reasonable that there could be a linguistic science, for there were complex phenomena that could be observed, and the observations could be replicated. It reminded me of the complex phenomena in cosmic-ray physics that I had been working on, but it seemed more important and more interesting.

Then as I got into the discipline and started doing research, it came over me that linguistics had serious problems in regard to its scientific status. One of the first things I noticed was that much of the writing in linguistics was polemical. This was in stark contrast with the well-mannered writing that I had become accustomed to in physics. Furthermore, it developed that there were many different theories and points of view in linguistics, and the criteria for choosing among them were not clear. At first I thought it was simply because the discipline was not yet very highly developed, for physics, too, had been polemical in earlier centuries. The thing to do was to try to develop linguistics further as a science. So when I put forth a scientific hypothesis about the relation of phrase structure to temporary memory, I expected that linguists working on different languages would test it on the languages they studied, and some did and found that the hypothesis held. But the most vociferous reaction in this country was a polemical attack as if the hypothesis were a competing political ideology or religion. Some people were obviously not playing by the same rules that I had learned through my apprenticeship in science.

Believing that this was a temporary aberration in the discipline, I circulated a letter to some colleagues to see if I could get agreement on how to play the game – on what constituted good scientific practice. The letter contained a hundred-odd points elaborating on the conduct of scientific research as I understood it and on the ways in which some of the work appearing in the linguistics literature fell far short of even the minimum standards of scientific acceptability. The letter was responded to with apparent agreement by the linguists to whom I sent it. There may be some here who received it and responded.

I don't know what effect it may have had on the recipients, but this exercise helped me to be explicit about what I saw as serious problems in the discipline. It has helped to guide the conduct of my research, and it has served as a background for reading the history of linguistics and the history of science. I have also used these points in class from time to time, a few at the end of each period, and they have been taken up eagerly by the students, for they are brief and invite discussion and elaboration.

I have recently become convinced that the problem is not a temporary aberration, it is a growing cancer. Much that has occurred in linguistics in the last several decades has pulled the discipline in a direction opposite from science. A knowledge of what science is, and what it is to be a scientist, cannot, or can no longer, be taken for granted as part of the normal equipment of a trained linguist. So with the anticipated publication of my book *Linguistics as a Science* in November, it is appropriate that I also lay out in more detail what it is to be a scientist.

How does one learn to be a scientist? The answer is to study science under scientists. I would certainly encourage students contemplating a career in linguistics to take all the science they can get, for science is a way of life that is best learned by osmosis during an apprenticeship. It is a tradition that has been developed through trial and error by scientists over the last 400 years or so. One learns about these things best by doing, and by studying under good teachers what others have done. Lacking such opportunities, one should read in the original the works of scientists, especially under the guidance of knowledgeable scientists. I would particularly recommend starting with the works of Galileo, which are quite readable in the English translations of Stillman Drake, and under the guidance of his essays on Galileo. These are particularly helpful, for linguistics today faces some of the same sorts of problems with philosophy, folk theory, authority, and entrenched opinion that physics faced in Galileo's time. Galileo wrote for a general audience, and he wrote clearly.

What I am publishing here may be of some help, especially if you get a chance to discuss the points with true scientists. You can look on these points as notes for an ethnographic report on the culture of science by someone who also has some acquaintance with the current linguistic culture and has tried to bring out some of the important contrasts. It is a report based on my education and socialization in science through three degrees in physics and while studying under some of the most illustrious physicists of their day.

Next a few words on the relation of philosophy to science. There is a literature on the philosophy of science that looks deceptively like a prescription for doing science. That is not its purpose, however; its purpose is to investigate philosophical questions in epistemology and the theory of knowledge, not to teach science, and you will likely be misled. Different philosophers differ on what they think scientists are doing, and their writings are largely ignored by scientists, who take full responsibility for their own disciplines. At best these philosophers serve as critics, but one would not learn to play the violin from a music critic, no matter how insightful his comments might be.

Linguistics owes much to philosophy, for it was born of philosophy. But if linguistics is to be a science it must cut its ties to philosophy as the other sciences have done. This is rendered particularly difficult for linguistics because its basic theory has developed out of the ancient Stoic dialectic or theory of knowledge. As a result, linguistics is still very much dominated by philosophical concerns, which are detrimental to its development as a science. Chomsky's works, for example, are much more in the realm of philosophy than of science, as has been pointed out more than once in the literature. One can not expect to learn much about science from them; their influence has been to pull the discipline toward philosophy and away from science.

The biggest problem that a scientific linguistics has with philosophy, and the greatest danger that philosophy poses to the development of a scientific linguistics, is that philosophy is not science. The criteria of truth in philosophy are not the criteria of truth in science. The criteria of truth in science have been known and agreed upon by scientists for centuries: they are ultimately observations by the senses, for science studies phenomena in the physical domain. Philosophy, on the other hand, deals with the logical or metatheoretical domain where the criteria of truth have always been and still are controversial. Consider, for example, the continuing controversy over empiricism versus rationalism. So first, a would-be scientific linguist would do well to stay within science and not stray into philosophy for instruction in how to be a scientist. Learn your science from scientists, not from philosophers.

Second, and this would go without saying in science but becomes important for us in contrast to familiar patterns in linguistics: work in the physical domain like other scientists rather than in the logical domain like philosophers. This means in the case of linguistics that we should study people, sound waves, and other linguistically relevant physical objects, rather than the convenient fictions of language, and we should seek a scientific understanding of how people communicate, rather than a scientific understanding of language, which, as I have shown elsewhere, is impossible.

After 20 years I have had to make only a few changes in the following list of points. They have held up well, being a matter of tradition and checkable against scientists willing to serve as informants. I should add that probably no scientist is such a paragon that he always lives up to all the ideals presented here, but if he is a good scientist, he tries his best to do just that.

A. What is science?

A1. Origin of science

Science probably has its origin in curiosity about the environment, a trait that man seems to share with many other species of animals.

A2. Adaptive mechanism

The ability of an organism to ascertain regularities in the environment and to predict events on the basis of the regularities is an adaptive mechanism and has survival value. It is not difficult to think of clear examples where a knowledge of the environment obtained through curiosity would save a person's life.

A3. Control of environment

Knowledge of the environment and an ability to predict has made it more and more possible to control the environment. The possibility of controlling the environment has provided an additional motive for pursuing knowledge. Application of knowledge to problems of controlling the environment is not, however, included in science as I am using the term.

A4. Search for knowledge

Science is concerned with a search for knowledge – to know the unknown – to discover new regularities in the environment that can be relied upon as a basis for prediction.

A5. Sophisticated common sense

It has been said that science is only sophisticated common sense. I take it that by common sense is meant the ability that most people have of predicting events in their everyday lives on the basis of ascertained regularities in the environment, and of acting in a rational way on the basis of the predictions. Science, however, is concerned more with understanding the regularities in the environment than on taking rational action, and in this it differs from technology, which uses the knowledge obtained by science and applies it to practical ends.

A6. Regularities

Science places an emphasis on a systematic explanation of similarities and underlying unity as a solid basis for predictions. In this it differs from the arts, where emphasis is more often placed on the unique differences that constitute aesthetic qualities, and where it is often said that artistic interest lies in unpredictable deviations from the commonplace or from the norm.

A7. Science and the humanities

It is sometimes alleged that science and the humanities are incompatible. This is not true for linguistics, however, which is in the humanities on the basis of its subject matter and in the sciences on the basis of its methods.

A8. Classification of science

The partitioning of science into separate disciplines is for convenience and division of effort only. As science advances, some of the most interesting research takes place at the borders between separate disciplines as conceived in terms of an older classification.

A9. Universality

There is no place for parochialism in science. Specialization and division of labor are, of course, useful. But the various parts of science are interconnected and no area of science should try to cut itself off from the rest.

A10. Linguistics as part of science

If linguistics is science, it is not isolated and autonomous, but part of science. The conception here is that there is only one science, and the various parts of it are interconnected and relevant to various different phenomena. It is important to emphasize this unity and inter-connectedness because there are many well-established results in science that bear on linguistic phenomena in important ways.

A11. One science

There is and can only be one science. There cannot be competing sciences built on different principles. Thus if linguistics is part of science, there can only be one linguistics, a scientific linguistics. This in not to say that there couldn't be competing tentative scientific theories concerned with the same observations.

A12. A program

Science is not an *ism*. It is a program. It is a program aimed at trying to get as close to the truth about nature as possible. This search requires that one keep an open mind, for one doesn't know ahead of time where the truth may be found. *Isms* imply prior commitments which can only get in the way of doing good science. For the last 150 to 200 years linguists have been scientists to some extent. This modern era in the history of linguistics can be read as a struggle between the science of the future and the *isms* of the past. The abandoning of prescriptivism is but one example

A13. Regularity in nature

The scientist believes, or accepts as a reasonable working hypothesis, that nature is regular and capable of being investigated, that there are regular phenomena for us to observe, describe, and to understand. But our theories and hypotheses will always be tentative. One could enter here into a philosophical discussion as to whether this regularity is or is not imposed upon nature by its observers. Nevertheless, the ability to predict what will happen tomorrow is based on observed regularities from the past and the belief that these regularities will continue into the future.

A14. Role of belief

The role of belief in science is a minor one. A scientist tries to operate with very few beliefs or articles of faith in the realm of science. He does, of course, believe many things in science, but his basis for believing them is not ultimate belief or faith. He knows that knowledge obtained through science is tentative. In any context certain things are accepted (believed) but in appropriate contexts they can be challenged.

A15. Revelation

There is no place in science for revelation or revealed truth. Belief and revelation belong in the realm of religion, and are outside of science.

A16. Rejection of the supernatural

Science rejects the occult and the supernatural because no convincing scientific evidence has been provided for accepting them. Magic, superstition, and the mystical are rejected as means for ascertaining or expressing regularities in the environment and predicting events.

A17. Cults

There is no place in science for fervor, sectarianism, discipleship, orthodoxy, conversion, proselytizing, or propaganda. Different points of view confront each other in objective discussion.

B. A scientist's choice of direction

B1. Goals not absolute

The validity of a scientist's goals and the intrinsic interest of a line of work or results are not absolute, but relative to a frame of reference.

Often this frame of reference is some current theoretical question, or some current incompletely understood set of observations.

B2. Divergent goals

There is the possibility of valid but apparently conflicting goals in a line of scientific research. Any effort expended in arguing about which goal is better or 'right' would be wasted, for it is often the case that the knowledge obtained while pursuing one goal turns out to be very relevant to another. A scientist should be free to choose his own goals.

B3. Not a fad

The validity of a scientist's goals and the interest of a line of work or results is not a matter of fad or vogue. It is true that many of the results in science take place at what may be called a forefront. When certain results become available, certain other work is the natural next step. Therefore there tends to be a natural accumulation of workers in specific areas on the forefront, but if they are scientists or aspiring scientists, they are not there because it is a current fad, but because they feel they can learn more in an area that is rapidly opening up.

B4. Don't fence me in

A scientist refuses to be fenced in by a narrow definition of a discipline. If the pursuit of scientific knowledge takes him outside of his area of competence, he will try to interest other scientists in taking up the pursuit, or he may prepare himself in the new area, and go after it himself.

B5. Pursuit of truth

A scientist shows a willingness to pursue truth wherever it might lead, and his pursuit is relentless.

B6. A questioning mind

The scientist is always asking questions and trying to answer them. He actively looks for questions to ask. Perhaps the most tragic event in the lives of some children is when their natural curiosity is squelched.

B7. *Meaningless questions*

The scientist refuses to ask meaningless questions, and feels that it is important to examine the questions he is asking to see if they are meaningful or not. A meaningless question is one that might seem reasonable at first, but on adequate examination it would turn out to be incapable in principle of being answered. Often the fact that a question is meaningless is quite obscure, and sometimes considerable scientific progress results from recognizing that a question on which much effort has been spent is in fact meaningless, and thus incapable in principle of resolution. The question of how people use language to communicate, which I was asking in 1969, seemed reasonable, but on closer examination it has turned out to be meaningless.

B8. *Clarification*

When it is discovered that a question, posed in all seriousness, is actually meaningless, an attempt is made to revise and restate it and to put it into a meaningful form. A revised and meaningful question is 'How do people communicate?'.

C. The methods of science

C1. *Democracy*

Scientific truth is not arrived at by vote or consensus. Democracy has its place in public life and in the management of scientific institutions and universities, but scientific truth is arrived at by scientific means, not by voting. It is true that observations and theories get accepted or rejected by the scientific community, but there is a higher tribunal, so to speak, than the vote or consensus of scientists. The history of science is full of cases where the respected majority of scientists was wrong, and the scorned minority right.

C2. *Authority*

Knowledge is not accepted on ultimate authority. Again there is a higher tribunal. It is true that much of what we know we individually accept on authority, but in science there is always the possibility of appeal at any point to the ultimate test against observational evidence, which is open to anyone. Scientists are suspicious of pronouncements put forth with an air of authority.

C3. Observation

Science is grounded in observation, and all scientific knowledge must submit to tests based on careful observation.

C4. Analysis

Scientific progress and understanding is based on the use of reason. All scientific knowledge comes about through observational evidence and reasoning from that evidence.

C5. Balance

There is a delicate interplay between observation and theory. A proper understanding of this interplay, and an appreciation of its importance, is required of every scientist, so that a proper balance may be maintained between the two.

C6. Gambling

In the conduct of scientific research, the hunches of the investigators play an important role. Since science is pursuit of the unknown, the scientist cannot know completely, ahead of time, what he will find out. Thus research must, by its very nature, be a gamble. Some research efforts are relatively sure fire, whereas others are long shots. Successful scientists are those that have the best hunches, often based on a well-developed intuition of what there might be to find out. A scientific hunch is an educated guess. The role of luck may be as important as it is in other forms of gambling. A scientist is not to be derided if he loses a gamble in research.

D. Observation

D1. Pure observation

Some observations are the result of general exploration, as when a botanist arrives on a new island, or a linguist comes upon a new language. However, all observation is based on theories at a lower level, which influence the way in which the sense impressions of the observer are organized into observations.

D2. Collection of data

An important activity in science is the collection of data, as when a botanist collects specimens, or the linguist collects texts and notebooks full of informant responses.

D3. Classification

Data collected are often given a preliminary classification on the basis of lower level theories, or on the basis of other convenient criteria that suggest themselves. This classification is of course tentative and for convenience in handling the data.

D4. Experimental method

Here is where observation makes contact with theory. The predictions of theories are compared systematically with observations. This systematic comparison is called experimentation.

E. Techniques of experimentation

E1. Experiments suggested by theory

A theory that properly accounts for some observations will predict the possible results of other observations. Experiments are then performed to see if the predictions of the theory are confirmed. Thus the theory is put to the test of observation.

E2. Nature of data

Data taken as a result of observations are always correct, except for instrumental malfunction and simple mistakes in reading. The problem comes in knowing which of the conditions under which the observations were taken are relevant for their interpretation. It is hoped that some of the conditions are relevant and the data are significant. But the data, whether they are significant or not, are correct for the given conditions.

E3. Honesty

Data are not to be disregarded in favor of some theory. A theory predicts what one expects to find if the theory is correct, but it cannot be used for deciding whether the data are appropriate or whether they are correct, for data thus tampered with or fudged cannot be trusted to shed light on the validity of the theory.

E4. Meticulous care

Great care is taken in collecting data to eliminate mistakes, instrumental errors, and other interfering influences.

E5. Personal bias

The scientist tries to remove all personal biases, since they may warp his judgment and get in the way of determining the scientific truth. Precautions are often taken to eliminate unintended personal bias through such means as double blind experiments.

E6. Detachment

And the scientist habitually stands in the background so as to remain objective and remove himself and his prejudices as much as possible from the research.

E7. Reproducibility

The scientist is most confident in his data when he can reproduce his observations at will. Thus he will repeat experiments to assure himself that the data can be trusted.

E8. Control of variables

An effort is made in doing experiments to eliminate all the variables except the ones under observation. This is often very difficult and sometimes involves considerable auxiliary experimentation or the use of statistical techniques in order to discover what all the extraneous variables are or how to keep them constant or eliminate their effect on the results.

E9. Sources of error

When data are reported, they are always accompanied by a careful examination and assessing of the possible sources of error. The experimenter is in the best position to know to what extent the data can be trusted, and it is up to him to report a realistic and honest assessing of the potential errors. In this he tries to be cautious, for he knows that he may be overly optimistic in assessing the accuracy of the data. He knows he may have overlooked errors due to his ignorance of additional variables not brought under control.

E10. Game

Many scientists even talk as if they were playing a game with Nature, trying to wrest her secrets from her, while Nature tries her best to conceal her secrets and to delude the scientist with counterfeits. In other words, the scientist should regard his discoveries with suspicion as possible delusions.

E11. Comparison with theory

When an experiment has been completed, the resulting data are analyzed and carefully compared with the predictions of theory. In this way light is shed on the validity of the theory in question. All discrepancies must ultimately be accounted for in terms of experimental error or uncontrolled variables, or on the basis of inadequate theory or inappropriate application of the theory.

F. Theory

F1. Stem from observation

Theories are suggested ultimately by observations, since it is their purpose to express regularities in the environment and to predict events on this basis.

F2. Hunch

Theories often start out on the basis of a hunch or guess concerning what may lie behind certain observations.

F3. From inadequacies

Theories are often suggested by older theories and their particular inadequacies in handling certain experimental results. Sometimes these experimental results were not at hand when the older theories were developed.

F4. Inference

The processes of inference and induction in working out the first steps of a theory are very sketchy and approximate. The scientist here works intuitively. He may use rough analogies.

F5. Theory building

As the theory takes shape, decisions are made as to how to generalize from other theories and from observations. It is not necessary that a theory have an *a priori* or principled basis that can be defended as independently valid, and it is a mistake to search for one. The validity of a theory is tested in other ways.

F6. Simplicity

There is nothing mystical or *a priori* about simplicity. The need for simplicity in science stems from the need of man to be able to predict reliably as large a range of phenomena as possible with his limited mental capabilities. Some phenomena are complex and require a complex theory for their explanation. Practically never are we in a position to compare two theories that deal equally with observation, and differ only in simplicity, and when theories differ in respects other than simplicity, these other respects are nearly always the controlling factors in acceptance or rejection.

F7. Limits of the theory

It is often expedient to push a theory to the very limit and beyond in order to find that limit. In so doing, a theory may be pushed into territory that it does not economically handle. Later theories may push back and regain some of the ground.

F8. Taxonomy

A proper theory separates phenomena that are different and puts together phenomena that are the same. In this sense all theories are taxonomic. A taxonomy may also be predictive if it contains open positions that it predicts will be filled.

F9. *Experimental method*

When a theory is ready, it is in the form of a hypothesis which can be checked by means of observation and experiment. A theory which cannot be compared with observation cannot be tested and cannot be proved wrong. It cannot become part of science and should at best be considered as speculation. Perhaps new methods will make a test of the theory possible in the future.

G. Techniques of theory development

G1. *Deduction and prediction*

In order to test a theory against observation, it is necessary to draw predictions from it. This is done by a process of reasoning, often formal or mathematical in nature. The utility of formalism in theory is for ease in drawing predictions, not for comparison with any *a priori* principles.

G2. *Details of prediction*

When predictions are drawn from a theory, it is important to know in detail how each specific prediction of the theory is related to the structure of the theory as a whole. In this way it will become clear for each prediction what the consequences of its not being borne out would have for the theory.

G3. *Check against observation*

The specific predictions of a theory can then be compared with a large body of observations if these are available. This is the first careful check of the theory.

G4. *Experiments*

A theory generally predicts the results of certain observations which have not yet been made, and in this sense a theory suggests experiments. The results of such experiments can be used to shed light on the correctness of the theory. If two credible theories predict different outcomes for a particular experiment, this experiment assumes the role of a crucial experiment, and is often interpreted as favoring one theory over the other, although neither may turn out to be correct in the end.

G5. Evidence

Often the evidence of experiment is only indirect. Sometimes the evidence bears on a point that is predicted by nearly all theories in the field. Sometimes the line of reasoning from the evidence to the theory requires additional experimental links that have not yet been closed.

G6. Substantiation and rejection

Favorable experimental evidence for a theory only tends to substantiate the theory, but unfavorable evidence can cause a theory to be rejected in whole or in part. Sometimes the theory can be kept but amended.

G7. Tentativeness of theories

No theory is ever established as the ultimate truth. Theories, by their nature, are all tentative. For this reason the scientist is a professional fence-sitter. It has often happened in science that the most strongly held theories have toppled.

G8. Non-uniqueness

It is possible to have more than one valid theory of the same phenomena. An outstanding example of this in physics is thermo-dynamics and statistical mechanics. A wide range of phenomena is accounted for by both, and each accounts for the phenomena differently from the other. But the theories do not contradict each other: there are certain reduction relations between them.

H. Role of mathematics in science

H1. Mathematics as a tool

The major role of mathematics in science is as a tool or language in which theories can be stated and in which deductions from them can be drawn to be compared with observation. Under mathematics in this sense we must include logic and formal reasoning of all kinds. Informal reasoning is also commonly used at many places in theory building and in comparisons with experiments.

H2. Appropriateness

When deductions are made from a theory for comparison with experiment, the appropriateness of the mathematics and logic used must be examined. If the theory predicts correctly, the appropriateness of the calculations used in this instance tends to be substantiated along with the theory.

H3. Pseudomathematics

A competent scientist does not pepper his manuscripts with mathematical notations that serve no good purpose in computation or exposition. Mathematical notation is not to be used as window dressing.

H4. Innovations in mathematics

Often the needs of a particular scientific theory can only be met by the invention of new methods in mathematics. These new methods may lack the rigor of the more carefully worked out areas of mathematics, but work perfectly well in the particular scientific application. They are often cleaned up later by mathematicians and made more general and more rigoros. Sometimes whole branches of mathematics have their origins in the needs of a particular scientific theory.

H5. New applications

It is sometimes the case that a branch of mathematics investigated for its own sake is later applied in science in a way that could not have been foreseen at the time of its development. It offers a mode of reasoning appropriate to the new subject matter.

H6. Role of statistics

Most of our basic theories are not statistical in nature. Often, however, the difficulties of observation, either inherent or due to unknown interfering effects, prevent an exact comparison of theory with experiment. In such cases statistics are often used to average over the interfering phenomena. We give up the possibility of exact prediction of all details and gain an ability to predict averages, which often can be compared directly with observation.

H7. *Role of* a priori

While the role of *a priori* is very substantial in mathematics and logic, it has no direct application in science. A scientific theory, or any of its parts, is not required to have any *a priori* truth or justification. Its truth can only be investigated by means of comparison with observations and experiments which would tend to confirm or to disconfirm the theory as a whole or in part.

H8. *Pure mathematics*

Although much of scientific theory is couched in mathematical terms, mathematics itself is outside of science, as we have been using the term. Mathematics and logic are based on the *a priori* and on arbitrary but interesting definitions. They are in the logical domain and thus are not subject to comparison with experiment or observation.

H9. *An inappropriate model for linguistics*

A linguistics conceived on the model of mathematics or logic, and therefore not subject to comparison with experiment or observation, would not be part of science. It would not have contact with reality, and any relationship to linguistic phenomena would be speculative at best, for it could not be tested.

I. Scientific knowledge and the community of scientists

I1. *A cooperative venture*

Science advances by means of an accumulation of knowledge as a community or cooperative venture of scientists.

12. Scholarship

A scientist requires knowledge of prior work. This he may obtain through scholarship. There is a very important role of education in science. The tradition is thus handed on and continually reexamined.

13. Reproducible experimental results

Science involves the building of a tradition that includes a body of accepted reproducible experimental results. These results accumulate by accretion, and have to be accounted for by theory. They must be reproducible so that if they are ever brought into question, they can be checked. They are in fact brought into question and checked whenever any doubts arise. Of course some observations can, unfortunately, never be checked because the occasion is lost in history. If this is the case, the best we can do is to try to assess the amount of confidence we can have in the observations and in any conclusions based on them.

14. Accepted but tentative theory

Science involves the building of a body of accepted but tentative theory. Since theories can never be completely validated, they must always be tentative. However, a tentative theory can be accepted as the basis for building additional theory and as a basis for suggesting experiments.

15. Progress

Progress in science requires attempting to reconcile conflicting evidence and conflicting theories, often by improvements in theory and in experiment.

16. Limitations of theory

In science it is imperative that there be full knowledge of and discussion of the limitations of current theory. Such discussion should not be construed as attacks on the theory or its inventor. It is appropriately initiated by the inventor himself.

I7. Discrepancies

When discrepancies are discovered between different theories, between different observations, or between theories and observations, the way may be opened up to achieve new insights. Such discrepancies are to be viewed as opportunities and not an occasion for polemics.

I8. Presentation

In presenting the results of a scientific investigation, facts and theories should speak for themselves. No argument for them should be brought forward that is irrelevant to the way in which they have been arrived at or could be judged.

I9. Advocacy

The scientist is a searcher for knowledge, not an advocate of a position, like a lawyer before a judge or a jury. In science it is presumed that all scientists are on the same side, that is, the side of trying to find out the truth about the phenomena in question, whereas in law the presumption is that there are adversaries, each with a personal stake in a different outcome. This point of view is foreign to science.

I10. Polemics

Polemics and prowess in argument and disputation do not settle questions in science or prove a view to be right or wrong. Scientific truth is arrived at not by argument, but by reasoning from the evidence.

I11. Character assassination

There is no room in science for character assassination. A scientist, in his publications and private utterances, keeps his eye on the subject matter and the cooperative venture of arriving at scientific truth.

I12. Means to an end

The burden of building and maintaining this body of knowledge falls mainly on publication by scientists and accumulation of publications in libraries. The importance of libraries in storing the information and arranging for easy and convenient access to it cannot be overemphasized.

J. Publication

J1. Purpose of publication

The purpose of publication is to add to the available knowledge in such a way that other scientists can make use of it.

J2. Open publication

It is important for the advancement of science that results be published in an open manner so that they are available to all other scientists. The burying of important results in manuscript form, or leaving them as rough notes or as tentative reports to sponsors, acts to impede the unrestricted flow of scientific information. Likewise, the restricting of results to employees of one company or citizens of one country is to be deplored. The cooperative effort necessary for scientific progress cannot flourish if unnatural barriers to information flow are erected.

J3. Prompt publication

It is important, when a piece of scientific research is finished, that it be reported promptly. Delays in the publication of important results impede scientific progress and tend to foster duplication of effort.

J4. Complete publication

When a piece of research is published, it should be published in complete enough form so that the work can be repeated and verified by others.

J5. Responsible publication

It is important that the scientist refrain from publishing prematurely, carelessly, or repetitiously. Sloppy scientific publication wastes the valuable time of the more competent workers by competing for their attention against more worthwhile activities, and by introducing misinformation into the literature that could impede our future understanding.

J6. Honest publication

It is important that standards of honesty, truthfulness, and accuracy in publication be of the very highest. A piece of work is of no use if it is suspected that it has been put forth with less than complete honesty, truthfulness, and accuracy, for other scientists would hesitate to use the results until they had verified them themselves.

J7. Sources of errors

It is important that a publication include a careful reporting of all discrepancies, doubts, and sources of error remaining after all due care has been taken. The scientist who did the research is in the best position to assess the sources of error and it is incumbent upon him to report them clearly and honestly.

J8. Fair publication

Authors would do well to give credence to the possibility of conflicting theories or experimental results. They should present a fair discussion of the pros and the cons.

J9. Credits

All publications should contain careful and honest citation of prior work so that due credit is given to other investigators.

J10. References

For the benefit of future students and researchers, bibliographic references should be given for important citations. It should be possible for a person who becomes interested in the work to follow back through the references and uncover all the important prior work on this point. The references should ultimately lead back to initial or basic papers.

J11. Who to cite

Citations and references should be chosen on the basis of their relevance to the subject matter for readers of the work at hand, not on the basis of personal considerations of the author. Citations are not to be used as impressive window dressing, as symbols of solidarity with a group, as salutes of allegiance to a leader or a movement, or as patronage for one's friends; and the exclusion of relevant citations should not be used as ammunition in a war between opposing camps.

J12. Advertising

The purpose of publication is not for advertising a particular theory, a particular group or school, or any other entity.

J13. Personal aggrandizement

The purpose of publication is not to build personal reputations.

J14. Built-in conflicts

There is the possibility of conflicts within the individual scientist because his personal advancement often depends strongly upon the research that he has done and therefore upon his publications. Thus each scientist tends to find himself in a position where personal considerations might conflict with the requirements of science and scholarship. The scientist resolves these conflicts in favor of science.

K. Terminology

K1. Careful use of terms

It is important that terminology be used carefully for the purposes of communication, and to carry accepted meanings.

K2. Change in terminology

Terminology should not be changed needlessly. This can only introduce confusion. The development of agreed-upon terminology is part of the community effort in science.

K3. *Banners, badges, or trademarks*

Words should not be used as banners, badges, or trademarks to indicate allegiance to a particular point of view or school, or for empire building. Neither should unfavorable allusions be added to words to make them into weapons to hurl against other scientists. Such use of words removes the author from the cooperative endeavor of science, and puts him into a position of advocacy of special interests.

K4. *Narrow definitions*

A scientist will not insist that his narrow and egocentric area of interest be used to define the scope of a broad field such as linguistics, and then use this definition as a club in argument, claiming that his adversaries are not linguists. Such usage again removes the author from the community of science.

L. Personal characteristics

The scientist therefore cultivates the following personal virtues, among others:

L1. *Inquiring mind*

A scientist will cultivate an inquiring mind and will actively seek out new sources of data and new questions to ask.

L2. *Competence*

A scientist will try to develop his competence as an investigator, and not be satisfied with mediocrity in his own performance as a scientist.

L3. *Pride of craftsmanship*

The scientist takes pride in craftsmanship – in doing the best job that he is capable of. He does not go to the extreme, however, of worrying unduly and protractedly over minor and petty details that are clearly not relevant to the scientific and scholarly quality of his work.

L4. Scholarship

The scientist maintains contact with the intellectual tradition in his field. He makes it his business to know what has been done. He is careful to achieve a thorough understanding of the prior work and to assess it on its merits. He distrusts secondary sources.

L5. Open-mindedness

The scientist tries to maintain an open mind, and is ever ready to entertain new ideas and new theories. He is tolerant of new approaches, and realizes that a diversity of backgrounds among scientists in a given discipline can be the source of great strength.

L6. Colleagueship

The scientist is a good colleague of other scientists. He considers them to be his teammates, playing in a game with the only adversary being Nature and her secrets.

L7. Intellectual honesty

A scientist develops intellectual honesty and personal integrity. These he makes habits not only in his scientific work, but also in his personal life, believing that there can be no compromise in these matters.

L8. Perseverance

A scientist will cultivate an ability to push an idea that shows promise as far as necessary, even in the face of great discouragement, but he maintains an ability to know how far to push an idea and when to drop it. This takes finesse because good ideas should be pushed to completion and bad ideas should be dropped as soon as possible. Often it is not known at the outset whether an idea is good or bad.

L9. Modesty

The scientist is fully aware that his work may turn out to be wrong in spite of his best efforts. He therefore puts it forth with all due modesty.

L10. Arrogance

Arrogance is out of place in a scientist, since it tends to commit him emotionally to the position he is currently holding, and makes it more difficult for him to change as progress is made. Excessive arrogance may lead to the personal domination of other scientists with a resulting constricting and inhibiting effect.

L11. The right to be wrong

A scientist does not cling stubbornly to an idea that proves to be wrong, and he grants to other scientists the right to have been wrong. He knows that science can only advance by means of change and improvement in theory and observation. What is right on the basis of current evidence may turn out to be wrong when additional evidence is in. Some of the world's greatest scientists have been wrong and it does not detract from their stature.

Finally, this last point is perhaps central to why there can be no *isms* in science.

L12. Personal responsibility

A scientist assumes personal responsibility for the work that he chooses to do and for the decisions as to what theories he will tentatively accept and what methods he will use. In these matters he does not bow to external authority or to scientifically irrelevant considerations, as his personal scientific integrity is at stake. And, as we have seen in earlier points, he applies scientific criteria in deciding what to believe. This idea of personal responsibility and the application of scientific criteria of truth is the reason that science, in the long run, converges on agreement as to the best current tentative understanding of nature.

Note

1. This paper is the Presidential Address presented at the annual LACUS meeting in the summer of 1986 and published in the proceedings: *The Thirteenth LACUS Forum 1986,* ed. Ilah Fleming. Lake Bluff, IL: LACUS, 1987, pp. 3–15.

Contributors

There is now a web page at
http://humanlinguistics.utoledo.edu/
To join the email list inquire of "Douglas W. Coleman"
< douglas.coleman@utoledo.edu >

Mojca Schlamberger Brezar
University of Ljubljana
Send mail to: Mojca Schlamberger Brezar
            Filozofska fakulteta, Oddelek za prevajalstvo
            Aškerčeva 2
            1001 Ljubljana
            Slovenia
email: mojca.brezar1@guest.arnes.si

Lara Burazer
University of Ljubljana
Send mail to: Lara Burazer
            Filozofska fakulteta, Oddelek za prevajalstvo
            Aškerčeva 2
            1000 Ljubljana
            Slovenia
email: lara.burazer@guest.arnes.si

Anna Cisło
University of Wrocław
Send mail to: Anna Cisło
            ul. Parkowa 48/15
            51-616 Wrocław
            Poland
email: acislo@uni.wroc.pl

Douglas W. Coleman
University of Toledo
Send mail to: Douglas W. Coleman
            Department of English
            University of Toledo
            Toledo, OH 43606-3390
            USA
email: Douglas.Coleman@utoledo.edu

Piotr Czajka
University of Wrocław
Send mail to: Piotr Czajka
            ul. Parkowa 48/15
            51-616 Wrocław
            Poland
email: czajkapiotr@yahoo.com

Douglas N. Honorof
Haskins Laboratories
Send mail to: Douglas N. Honorof
            Haskins Laboratories
            270 Crown Street
            New Haven, CT 06511-6695
            USA
email: honorof@haskins.yale.edu

W. John Hutchins
University of East Anglia, Norwich (Retired)
Send mail to: W. John Hutchins
            89 Christchurch Road
            Norwich NR2 3NG
            England.
email: WJHutchins@compuserve.com

Laura L. Koenig
Long Island University, Brooklyn Campus
and Haskins Laboratories
Send mail to: Laura L. Koenig
            Long Island University, Brooklyn Campus
            One University Plaza
            Brooklyn, NY 11233
            USA
email: koenig@haskins.yale.edu

Janusz Malak
Opole University
Send mail to: Janusz Malak
            Uniwersytet Opolski
            Instytut Filologii Angielskiej
            45-040 Opole
            Pl. Kopernika 11
            Poland
email: magoret@poczta.onet.pl

Carl Mills
University of Cincinnati
May 5, 1942 – August 23, 2003

Martina Ožbot
University of Ljubljana
Send mail to: Martina Ožbot
              Filozofska fakulteta, Oddelek za romanske jezike in
              književnosti
              Aškerčeva 2
              1000 Ljubljana
              Slovenia
email: Martina.Ozbot@guest.arnes.si

Bernard Paul Sypniewski
Rowan University – Camden Campus
Send mail to: Bernard Paul Sypniewski
              Rowan University – Camden Campus
              Broadway and Cooper Street
              Camden, NJ 08102
              USA
email: syp@eticomm.net

Elżbieta Wąsik
Adam Mickiewicz University in Poznań
Send mail to: Elżbieta Wąsik
              ul. Mylna 21/7
              60-856 Poznań
              Poland
e-mail: elawasik@amu.edu.pl

Zdzisław Wąsik
Adam Mickiewicz University in Poznań,
Philological School of Higher Education in Wrocław
and Nicolaus Copernicus University in Toruń
Send mail to: Zdzisław Wąsik
              ul. Mylna 21/7
              60-856 Poznań
              Poland
e-mail: wasik@ifa.amu.edu.pl *or*
              z.wasik@wsf.edu.pl *or*
              wasik@cc.uni.torun.pl

Victor H. Yngve
The University of Chicago
Send mail to: Victor H. Yngve
             28 Crest Drive Dune Acres
             Chesterton IN 46304
             USA
email: v-yngve@uchicago.edu

Index

Manley, Geoffrey A. 91
Manuel, S. Y. 54, 55
Maslow, Abraham 269
Matthies, M. L. 51, 73, 76
Mattingly, I. G. 71, 73, 78
Mayday
  example 225–239
memory
  echoic 94, 99
  for interpreted speech 101
  for uninterpreted sound 100
  rote 99
Milewski, Tadeusz 269
Miller, George
  span of immediate memory 5
Miyawaki, K. 58
model building
  Labov's 202–203
monitoring
  learning to speak 101
  tasks 151–152
Morais, J. 74
Morse, Philip M. 107 n.5
Munhall, K. G. 72, 102
Murray, Henry 269
Murray, Joel 90

Nadler, R. D. 76
Nearey, T. M. 50
needs in Educational
  discourse 269–287
negotiating
  analyses 142–173
Neisser, Ulrich 94, 99
Nie, H.-Y. 74
Nielsen, K. M. 232
Nittrouer, S. 58

O'Malley, G. D. 105 n.2
Obuchowski, Kazimierz 269
Ohala, J. J. 79
Ohde, R. N. 58
Okalidou, A. 56
Olsen, J. F. 107 n.8
Ottoson, D. 107 n.7
Ožbot, Martina 300

participants
  definition 31

perception
  ecological approach 69–71
performatives
  betting 174–187
  reconstituting 129–141, 174–187
Perkell, J. S. 51, 73, 76
Perkins, Jeanne 105
Perrier, P. 50
Peterson, G. E. 50
phonetics, phonology
  hard-science 87–110
phonetics-phonology
  reconstituting 49–109
phonology
  theories reviewed 74–75
Pick, A. D. 69
Pillarization
  of society 217–218
Plank, Pieter H. van der 215
plex
  definition 23
plex structures
  definition 32
  domain of control 32
  task hierarchies 32
Pogonowski, Jerzy 269
politeness
  tasks 150–151
Polka, L. 58
Popper, K. R.
  public knowledge 317
Pouplier, M. 75
Powers, David 105
procedures
  dynamic causal laws 30
  expectation 96–99
  introduced 22–23
  parallel subtasks 96–99
properties
  communicating individual 19
  dynamic causal laws 30
  how structured 32
  linkage 19
  procedures 30
properties of systems
  changes of 21–22
  evidence for 21–22
props
  definition 31